Word, Sound and Music in Radio Drama

Word and Music Studies

Series Editors

Walter Bernhart
Michael Halliwell
Lawrence Kramer
Steven Paul Scher†
Werner Wolf

VOLUME 21

The book series WORD AND MUSIC STUDIES (WMS) is the central organ of the International Association for Word and Music Studies (WMA), an association founded in 1997 to promote transdisciplinary scholarly inquiry devoted to the relations between literature/verbal texts/language and music. WMA aims to provide an international forum for musicologists and literary scholars with an interest in intermediality studies and in crossing cultural as well as disciplinary boundaries.

WORD AND MUSIC STUDIES publishes, generally on an annual to biannual basis, themeoriented volumes, documenting and critically assessing the scope, theory, methodology, and the disciplinary and institutional dimensions and prospects of the field on an international scale: conference proceedings, collections of scholarly essays, and, occasionally, monographs on pertinent individual topics.

The titles published in this series are listed at *brill.com/wms*

Word, Sound and Music in Radio Drama

Edited by

Pim Verhulst and Jarmila Mildorf

BRILL

LEIDEN | BOSTON

Cover illustration: Photograph of a rehearsal of CBS Radio's The Mercury Theatre on the Air (1938), printed in many US newspapers following the broadcast of "The War of the Worlds". Subjects include Orson Welles, with arms upraised; Bernard Herrmann, conducting the CBS Radio orchestra; actor Ray Collins at the CBS microphone; Richard Wilson (white shirt) beside him; William Alland to Wilson's left; and Arthur Anderson. Acme Telephoto, Public domain, via Wikimedia Commons.

The Library of Congress Cataloging-in-Publication Data

Names: Verhulst, Pim, editor. | Mildorf, Jarmila, editor.
Title: Word, sound and music in radio drama / edited by Pim Verhulst and
    Jarmila Mildorf.
Description: Leiden ; Boston : Brill, 2024. | Series: Word and music
    studies, 1566-0958 ; volume 21 | Includes index.
Identifiers: LCCN 2023032264 (print) | LCCN 2023032265 (ebook) |
    ISBN 9789004549593 (hardback) | ISBN 9789004549609 (ebook)
Subjects: LCSH: Radio plays–History and criticism. | Radio and music. |
    Narration (Rhetoric)
Classification: LCC PN1991.65 .W67 2024 (print) | LCC PN1991.65 (ebook) |
    DDC 809.2/22–dc23/eng/20230804
LC record available at https://lccn.loc.gov/2023032264
LC ebook record available at https://lccn.loc.gov/2023032265

Typeface for the Latin, Greek, and Cyrillic scripts: "Brill". See and download: brill.com/brill-typeface.

ISSN 1566-0958
ISBN 978-90-04-54959-3 (hardback)
ISBN 978-90-04-54960-9 (e-book)
DOI 10.1163/9789004549609

Copyright 2024 by Koninklijke Brill NV, Leiden, The Netherlands.
Koninklijke Brill NV incorporates the imprints Brill, Brill Nijhoff, Brill Schöningh, Brill Fink, Brill mentis, Brill Wageningen Academic, Vandenhoeck & Ruprecht, Böhlau and V&R unipress.
All rights reserved. No part of this publication may be reproduced, translated, stored in a retrieval system, or transmitted in any form or by any means, electronic, mechanical, photocopying, recording or otherwise, without prior written permission from the publisher. Requests for re-use and/or translations must be addressed to Koninklijke Brill NV via brill.com or copyright.com.

This book is printed on acid-free paper and produced in a sustainable manner.

Contents

List of Illustrations VII
List of Tables IX
Notes on Contributors X

Word, Sound and Music in Radio Drama: An Introduction 1
  Jarmila Mildorf

PART 1
Historical, National and Institutional Contexts

1   From Acoustic Scenery to Sonic Dramaturgy: Music in Radio-Specific Drama of Weimar Republic Germany 19
      John Gabriel

2   Transmedial Perspectives on Music and Sound in Early French Radio Plays from the 1930s: the Tangible Legacy of *Le Douzième coup de minuit* 45
      Emilie Capulet

3   Music in Radio Drama in the Netherlands: A Short History in Four Acts 76
      Philomeen Lelieveldt

4   Not Just Words, Not Just Music: Some Remarks about the Development of a Radio Art and Radio Drama in Italy 102
      Angela Ida De Benedictis

5   Composing the Radio: Musical Collaborations and Border Crossings in Drama and Features at the Australian Public Service Broadcaster 130
      Virginia M. Madsen

PART 2
Case Studies of Radio Drama

6   Experiments in 'Symphonic Drama' on the US Radio (1937–1938) 167
      Tim Carter

7 The *Radiokapellmeister* at Work in Danish National Radio: Oscar Wilde's *Salome* as Radio Drama with Symphonic Orchestra (1930)   191
    Michael Fjeldsøe

8 Our Language Beats against Its Limitations: Music, Musicality and Musicalisation in Norman Corwin's *They Fly through the Air with the Greatest of Ease* (1939)   212
    Troy Cummings

9 Themes, Backgrounds, Bridges and Curtains: A New Musical Language for American Radio Dramas, 1930–1950   233
    Peter Graff

10 Referenced Music in Radio Drama: Jef Geeraerts' *Concerto* (1970) and Samuel Vriezen's *Schade* (2017)   257
    Siebe Bluijs

11 Functions of Music in the 1992 German Radio Play Adaptation of J.R.R. Tolkien's *The Lord of the Rings*   275
    Jarmila Mildorf

12 *The Spy* (BBC Radio 4, 2012): Creating Historical Ambiance through Music in British Radio Drama   293
    Leslie McMurtry

13 Musical 'Speech Score' as Soundscape: Elfriede Jelinek's *Die Schutzbefohlenen* (2014) on the Radio   310
    Caroline A. Kita

14 Scoring the Unseen: Composing 'Film Music' for Radio Drama   326
    Alan E. Williams

    Index   347

Illustrations

Figures

3.1 Fragment of the 'Ouverture' for *Paul Vlaanderen* by Koos van de Griend, Stichting Omroep Muziek, with the kind permission   83
4.1 'Stereophonic dramaturgy' in Bruno Maderna's *Don Perlimplin*   123
4.2 Bruno Maderna, *Don Perlimplin*, autograph. Archive of the Studio di Fonologia Musicale di Milano della RAI, with kind permission   125
4.3 Bruno Maderna, 'Progetto di Montaggio' sketched for *Ages*. Bruno Maderna Collection, Paul Sacher Foundation, with kind permission   126
7.1 Emil Reesen, *Salome*, No. 1, mm. 6–10. Danish Radio Music Archives and the Danish Royal Library, with kind permission   200
7.2 Emil Reesen, *Salome*, No. 3, mm. 1–4. Danish Radio Music Archives and the Danish Royal Library, with kind permission   201
8.1 The Crash of Bomber No. 6. Laszlo Matulay, with kind permission   225
9.1 Ralph Sandor [Alexander Semmler], "Transition No. 1" from *Incidental Music Book II* (1944)   247
9.2 Louis Katzman and Milton Rettenberg, "Furioso" from *Bridges Moods Interludes* (1943)   249
11.1 Excerpt from motif 58 in *Der Herr der Ringe*. Forschungsinstitut Brenner-Archiv, Legacy Peter Zwetkoff, Shelfmark 230-008-007-001-025   284
11.2 Excerpt from motif 68 in *Der Herr der Ringe*. Forschungsinstitut Brenner-Archiv, Legacy Peter Zwetkoff, Shelfmark 230-008-004-003-005   285
11.3 Excerpt from motif 7a/b in *Der Herr der Ringe*. Forschungsinstitut Brenner-Archiv, Legacy Peter Zwetkoff, Shelfmark 230-008-006-001-248   287
12.1 Functions of music in *The Spy*   300
14.1 Part of 'La Habana', the original lead sheet with the *Kraken Wakes* theme   342

Examples

9.1 Jesse Crawford, "Voice Background No. 1", from *Jesse Crawford's Radio Dramatic Series* (1940)   242
9.2 Muriel Pollock, "Rustic Revel" (mm. 9–24), from *Muriel Pollock's Musical Moods Book 2* (1943)   242
9.3 John Gart, "Expectation", from *Serial Moods* (1946)   243
9.4 Charles Paul, "Home Sweet Home to Bustle", from *Charles Paul's Radio Transitions* (1942)   245

9.5   Charles Paul, "Climactic Moment to Hockey Game", from *Charles Paul's Radio Transitions* (1942)   246
9.6   Charles Paul, "Sucker for Xmas No. 3", from *Charles Paul's Radio Transitions* (1942)   246
9.7   Charles Paul, "Heavy Tension (Background) to Chord", from *Charles Paul's Radio Transitions* (1942)   248
9.8   Harry Salter, "Mysterioso Creepy", from *Airway Incidentals* (1942)   248
9.9   Roy Shield, "Dramatic Transition No. 48", from *Roy Shield's Musical Transitions for Radio: Folio II* (1946)   250
9.10 Edward Truman, "Interlude for Effect", from *Broadcast Mood Music* (1943)   250
9.11 Charles Paul, "Closing in on Suspects to Motion", from *Charles Paul's Radio Transitions* (1942)   250
9.12 John Gart, "Money Curtain", from *Serial Moods* (1946)   252
9.13 Burt Buhrman, "Curtain No. 4", from *Interludes and Curtains* (1942)   252
9.14 Lew White, "Curtain Music No. 11", from *Lew White's Dramatic and Novelty Folio* (1939)   253

Tables

4.1 List of the radio dramas and electronic works by Berio and Maderna produced at the Studio di Fonologia (RAI) from 1954 to 1975   117
6.1 Overview of the Federal Theatre Project's thirteen *Experiments in Symphonic Drama*   177
7.1 Correspondences of music, characters and action in Emil Reesen's music for Oscar Wilde's *Salome*   204
10.1 The composition of the radio play *Schade* by Samuel Vriezen   266
14.1 Music cues agreed with writer Val McDermid prior to composition   334

Notes on Contributors

Siebe Bluijs
(s.v.bluijs@tilburguniversity.edu) is an Assistant Professor at the Tilburg Center of the Learning Sciences (Tilburg University, the Netherlands). He holds a PhD in Dutch Literature from Ghent University (Belgium). His research interests concern literature education and the relations between media and meaning making in literary works. In his PhD project he analysed the form and functioning of the postwar literary radio play in the Low Countries, focusing on innovations in narrative and semiotic composition. His current research focuses on the relevance of 'digital literature' (e.g., computer-generated poetry, literary smartphone applications and narratives in virtual reality) for the development of digital literacies. Additionally, Bluijs has a background in graphic design, with a specialisation in book design and typography.

Emilie Capulet
(e.capulet@trinitylaban.ac.uk) is an international award-winning concert pianist, musicologist and lecturer. As well as a Master of Music in Performance from the Guildhall School of Music and Drama, her interest in the arts as a whole has earned her an MA on Shakespeare and a PhD on musical aesthetic in modernist literature. She has published on many aspects of music history and contemporary music performance practices, as well as on music in healthcare. Her research is at the interface of historical enquiry, musicology, performance and intermedial/transmedial cultural studies and has been funded by the Arts and Humanities Research Council and the Arts Council UK. Her research on the French composer Henri Tomasi (1901–1971) in particular has led her to an investigation into how early radiophonic techniques contributed to shaping early musical radiophonic compositions and broadcasting, as well as cinema and film scores. Emilie is a Fellow of the Higher Education Academy, and she has lectured at the University of Surrey and the London College of Music, University of West London, where she was Head of Classical Performance. She is currently Programme Leader for the undergraduate music degree at Trinity Laban Conservatoire of Music and Dance.

Tim Carter
(cartert@email.unc.edu) is the author of books on opera and musical theatre ranging from the late sixteenth century through Mozart to Rodgers and Hammerstein. He has held fellowships at the Harvard Center for Italian Renaissance Studies in Florence, the Newberry Library in Chicago, and at the National Humanities Center. In 2013 he was awarded by the American

Musicological Society both the Claude Palisca Prize and the H. Colin Slim Prize for his work, respectively, on Kurt Weill and on Claudio Monteverdi. He is an honorary member of the American Musicological Society, the Royal Musical Association (UK), and the Society for Seventeenth-Century Music. He is David G. Frey Distinguished Professor Emeritus of Music at the University of North Carolina at Chapel Hill.

Troy Cummings
(troyacummings@gmail.com) holds a Master's of Musicology from the University of Missouri-Kansas City Conservatory of Music. His 2013 thesis, 'Mood-Stuff and Metaphoric Utterance: Norman Corwin's Radio Art', is a pilot study in musicology and radio art. He contributed the chapter, 'Media Primer: Norman Corwin's Radio Juvenilia', to the 2017 Kraszna-Krausz Best Moving Image Book Award winner, *Anatomy of Sound: Norman Corwin and Media Authorship*, edited by Jacob Smith and Neil Verma.

Angela Ida De Benedictis
(aidadebenedictis@gmail.com) studied musicology and musical philology at the University of Pavia (Cremona). In 2001, she graduated in musicology with a thesis on the radio play and radiophonic art. In 2005–2007, she received a Postdoctoral Fellowship from the Alexander von Humboldt Foundation for a research project on music and technology in Berlin. After teaching at various universities (Padua, Salerno, Pavia), she joined the scientific board of the Paul Sacher Foundation (Basel) in 2014 as musicologist and curator for music manuscripts, where at present she is responsible for about thirty collections, among them those of Berio, Berberian, Boulez, Grisey, Lachenmann, and Maderna. She is Scientific Director of the Centro Studi Luciano Berio and member of the Scientific Committee of the Nono Foundation in Venice. Her main research interests are electronic music, music and media technology, the study of creative processes, new musical theatre, authorship and radio studies. Her main publications include *Utopia, Tradition, Innovation: Bruno Maderna's Cosmos* (2022); *La musica alla radio 1924–1954* (2015), *Imagination at Play: The Prix Italia and Radiophonic Experimentation* (2012), *Radiodramma e arte radiofonica* (2004).

Michael Fjeldsøe
(fjeldsoe@hum.ku.dk): his research has focused on art music and applied music in the nineteenth and twentieth centuries, especially in Central and Eastern Europe and Denmark. Research questions are concerned with relations of music and politics, music and society, music and nationalism; in short, how music impacts society. Since his PhD (1999) on the reception of modernist art music in Denmark (1920–1940), a major interest has been Danish musical culture in

the nineteenth and twentieth centuries. A much wider perspective on musical culture, including genres of applied music such as theatre music, political music, music for revues, cabarets and education, and the role of progressive music in society, was applied in his DPhil *Kulturradikalismens musik* (2013). A continuous main topic is Danish music and music history, regarded as the history of musical culture, with Carl Nielsen and other composers represented in a number of studies and scholarly critical editions of musical works. Currently, he is head of a collective research project which will provide a new monograph on Carl Nielsen as a European composer (forthcoming).

John Gabriel
(john.gabriel@unimelb.edu.au) is a Lecturer in Musicology at the University of Melbourne. His research focuses on, but is by no means limited to, German and Czech speaking Central Europe from the fin de siècle to the early Cold War. He is currently completing a monograph on the music theatre of the New Objectivity in Weimar Republic Germany, with recent and forthcoming publications on representations of China in German opera, the Communist propaganda music of Hanns Eisler, and the relationship of the New Objectivity to the 'middlebrow'. Before coming to Melbourne, he held academic appointments at the University of Hong Kong and the Peabody Conservatory at Johns Hopkins University.

Peter Graff
(peteralangraff@gmail.com) is a Visiting Assistant Professor at Denison University (Granville, OH) and holds a PhD in musicology from Case Western Reserve University (Cleveland, OH). His research primarily examines music in American popular culture, particularly in film, theatre and radio. Peter served as a contributing editor for *The Grove Music Guide to American Film Music*, and his articles in *Film History* and *Notes: Quarterly Journal of the Music Library Association* trace film scoring models and exhibition practices from the silent era to today.

Caroline A. Kita
(ckita@wustl.edu) is Associate Professor of German and Comparative Literature at Washington University in St. Louis. Her research examines German and Austrian literature and culture in the nineteenth and twentieth centuries, with a special focus on German Jewish culture, music and the German language radio drama (*Hörspiel*). She is the author of *Jewish Difference and the Arts: Composing Compassion in Music and Biblical Theater* (Indiana University Press, 2019) and the co-editor of *The Arts of Democratization: Styling Political Sensibilities in Postwar West Germany* (University of Michigan Press, 2021).

NOTES ON CONTRIBUTORS   XIII

Philomeen Lelieveldt
(phillelie@live.nl) is a musicologist and was Assistant Professor at the Department of Media and Culture Studies, Faculty of Humanities, Utrecht University, in the Netherlands. Her research and teaching activities cover art and media policies, music radio programming and artists' careers. In 2017–2018, she worked as a research fellow at Sound and Vision, Institute for Media Culture in Hilversum to prepare a chapter on the dynamics between the music world and radio broadcasting in the Netherlands for *Hundred Years of Radio in the Netherlands 1919–2019*, edited by H. Wijfjes (Boom, 2019).

Virginia M. Madsen
(virginia.madsen@mq.edu.au) is a Senior Lecturer and Director of the Centre for Media History at Macquarie University, Sydney. She has written extensively on sound and radio culture and history in all aspects. She was formerly a producer with the ABC in Australia, and also a founding member of its renowned audio arts programme, The Listening Room. Currently, she has two major projects underway: she leads the ARC funded Discovery project 'Cultural Conversations: A History of ABC Radio National', a history of the Australian public broadcaster's culture and ideas network. She is also writing an account of the 'documentary imagination' in radio from the 1920s to the present. This project is both international and transnational in scope.

Leslie McMurtry
(leslie.mcmurtry@gmail.com) is Lecturer in Radio Studies at the University of Salford. She has written on radio drama for *The Journal of Radio and Audio Media*, *Palgrave Communications* and *The Journal of Popular Culture*, and contributed to collections such as *The Routledge Companion to Radio and Podcast Studies* (2022) and *The Oxford Handbook of Radio Studies* (forthcoming). In 2017, she was the Artist in Residence at the Badlands National Park. Her first book, *Revolution in the Echo Chamber: Audio Drama's Past, Present, and Future* (Intellect, 2019), is a historical and critical analysis of audio drama in the US and the UK.

Jarmila Mildorf
(jarmila.mildorf@uni-paderborn.de) teaches English language and literature at the University of Paderborn (Germany). Her research interests are audionarratology, socionarratology and conversational storytelling, autobiography, oral history, dialogue, literature and medicine/the medical humanities. She is the author of *Storying Domestic Violence: Constructions and Stereotypes of Abuse in the Discourse of General Practitioners* (University of Nebraska Press, 2007) and *Life Storying in Oral History: Fictional Contamination and Literary Complexity*

(De Gruyter 2023), and co-editor of fifteen essay collections and special issues/themed journal sections, among them: *Audionarratology: Interfaces of Sound and Narrative* (with Till Kinzel; De Gruyter 2016), *Narrating Sounds* (with Till Kinzel; thematic forum published in *Partial Answers* 15.1, 2017), *Dialogue across Media* (with Bronwen Thomas; John Benjamins 2017), *Aural World-Making: Audionarratological Approaches to Sound and Narrative* (thematic section published in *CounterText* 5.3, 2019), *Radio Art and Music: Culture, Aesthetics, Politics* (with Pim Verhulst; Lexington Books 2020), *Audionarratology: Lessons from Radio Drama* (with Lars Bernaerts; Ohio State University Press 2021) and *Narrative and Mental Health: Reimagining Theory and Practice* (with Elisabeth Punzi and Christoph Singer; Oxford University Press, 2023).

Pim Verhulst
(pim.verhulst@uantwerpen.be) is a postdoctoral researcher at the University of Oxford and a teaching assistant at the University of Antwerp. His research combines genetic criticism, intermediality and audionarratology to study the work of (late) modernist and postwar authors from the British Isles. His articles have been published in *Variants, Genetic Joyce Studies, The Harold Pinter Review, Samuel Beckett Today/Aujourd'hui* and the *Journal of Beckett Studies*, of which he is an editorial board member. He has published book chapters in *Beckett and BBC Radio* (Palgrave 2017), *Beckett and Modernism* (Palgrave 2018, co-edited), *Pop Beckett* (Ibidem 2019), *Beckett and Technology* (Edinburgh UP 2021), *Beckett and Media* (Manchester UP 2022) and *Audionarratology: Lessons from Radio Drama* (Ohio State UP 2021). His recent co-edited collections include *Radio Art and Music* (Lexington 2020), *Tuning in to the Neo-Avant-Garde* (Manchester UP 2021) and *Beckett's Afterlives* (Manchester UP 2023). His monograph *The Making of Samuel Beckett's Radio Plays* is forthcoming with Bloomsbury.

Alan E. Williams
(A.E.Williams@salford.ac.uk) is a composer and writer on contemporary music and culture. He studied at the Universities of Edinburgh and Manchester and at the Liszt Academy, Budapest. His music has been performed by world leading ensembles such as the BBC Philharmonic, the BBC Singers, the Philharmonia, and Psappha, and has been broadcast on BBC Radio 3, BBC Radio 4, MDR (Germany), NEC (Brazil) and Bartók Rádió (Hungary). He is Professor of Collaborative Composition at the University of Salford. His Recent opera with Ian McMillan, *The Arsonists*, was featured widely on UK TV, including ITV News, BBC News Channel, and Sky News.

Word, Sound and Music in Radio Drama: An Introduction

Jarmila Mildorf

As an art form for the ear, music belongs to radio just as naturally as do words, voices, sounds and, to a lesser degree, silences. Numerous studies have therefore focused on music and its various functions in radio art or on radio more generally (see Baade and Deaville 2016; Barnard 1989; Chase and Fisher 2013; Cohen 2015; Coley 2022; Fairchild 2012; Grant and Stone-Davies 2013; Michelsen et al. 2018; Mildorf and Verhulst 2020; Rumpf 2007; Stoller 2018; Toudoire-Surlapierre and Lécroart 2015). Far fewer studies have taken into view the role that music plays in radio drama specifically (see, however, De Benedictis 2004; Hobl-Friedrich 1991; Cacchione 2020; Mildorf 2020; Smith 2022; Verhulst 2021), which in itself is an art form that was long neglected but has received a little more scholarly attention again during the last couple of decades (see, among others, Arteel et al. 2021; Bernaerts and Mildorf 2021; Chignell 2019; Crook 1999, 2020; Ellett 2019; Hand 2014; Hand and Traynor 2011; Huwiler 2005; Heuser 2013; Klotz 2022; Mohn 2019; Rea 2020; Rinke 2017; Verma 2012). And yet, as radio dramatist David Pownall (2010) writes: "Sound theatre is a performance art of special purity, cousin to music. It happens in the receptive mind with no help from flashier aids of entertainment" (8). One may of course object that words, voices, music, sounds and silences in radio drama also become 'flashy' or engaging and lead to dramatic involvement on the part of audiences, especially if one considers that listeners – as Pownall also alludes to – are not distracted by visual input and thus arguably experience the aural storyworld in a more intimate way. However, even in the all-acoustic medium that radio constitutes, the different sonic elements vie for listeners' attention. One can technically *hear* speaking voices, sounds and noises as well as music all at the same time, but it will be hard to *listen to* all of them attentively and to parse them equally in our brains. This limitation of one's attention clearly poses a challenge to radio drama producers, and it inevitably has an impact on how and to what extent music can be employed in the art form.

It therefore does not come as a surprise that music rarely continues for long when dialogue begins, or if it does, usually recedes into the background by being lowered in volume. Unlike in film, where music may accompany a lengthy stretch of a (wordless) visual scene, to have music play for longer in radio drama is more problematic because one needs to be told – whether directly or by implicit suggestion – what to imagine while the music is playing or to be given a reason or motivation for this extended use of music. So, while many functions that music fulfils in radio drama are comparable to similar functions it has in film and other audiovisual media, they are never entirely co-extensive. In this connection, it is also interesting to consider the shift from radio plays that are word-centred, usually narrative in nature and based on literary or theatrical traditions, to those that move in the direction of independent sound pieces, which came to be subsumed under the term "Ars Acustica" (Krug 2008: 125).

Definitions of radio drama vary across time and countries, as is also manifest in the different chapters compiled in this book. Furthermore, the boundaries between radio drama and other radio genres such as the feature can be blurred. To illustrate the problem of definitions, let me juxtapose some viewpoints. Douglas Cleverdon (1969), for example, defines the radio play as "a dramatic work deriving from the tradition of the theatre, but conceived in terms of radio", while a feature is "any constructed programme" derived from "the apparatus of radio" (17). This definition strikes one as limiting given the fact that some early radio plays by Bertolt Brecht, Walter Benjamin and others were already produced specifically for radio and with radiophonic conditions in mind (see Rösch 2022). Accordingly, later theorists who were more informed by media studies perspectives foregrounded the independence of radio drama as an art form rather than its being a derivative from theatre or literature (see Huwiler 2004). More recently, Peter Klotz has emphasised both the production and reception side of radio drama and has pointed out how radio drama elements can be used in features to make them engaging for the audience (2022: 215). In this introduction, I will focus on typologies related to the presence of music.

Sound theoretician José Iges Lebrancón (1997), for instance, distinguishes between narrative-textual and musical genres in radio art, the latter of which entail such electroacoustic subgenres as radio operas, sound collages and soundscapes (Sánchez Cardona 2020: 23). Needless to say, radio drama can and did cross the boundaries of such neat categories. The *Neues Hörspiel* (New Radio Play) in Germany, for example, was influenced by the emergence of new sound technologies such as stereophony, which allowed radio plays to explore the sonic-musical space between two poles (Krug 2008: 94–95). Likewise, radio drama producers used the Dramatic Control Panel and later the mixing board in analogy to a musical instrument or an orchestra, 'composing' and 'conducting' their works as one would a symphony (see Lakoff 2020). Indeed, much of the new music and sound experiments of the second half of the twentieth century turned sounds and noises into quasi-musical compositions. Such experiments – also including music for radio plays – were undertaken at the BBC Radiophonic workshop in Great Britain (Eichenberger 2021), the Studio di

Fonologia della RAI di Milano in Italy (De Benedictis 2020) and the Elektronisches Studio of the Westdeutscher Rundfunk (WDR) in Germany (Morawska-Büngeler 1988), to name only a few.

So, one can see how, throughout the history of radio play production, music became increasingly important in two interrelated ways: first, it gained in significance for the aesthetics of such sound tapestries as were required and made possible by new radio technologies; second, radio drama producers themselves used music as a *metaphor* to discuss their own work and practices (see also Crook 2021, and Gabriel in this volume). The analogy between music and radio drama that Pownall alludes to was already keenly felt, for example, by Rudolf Arnheim (1936: 34), who championed the use of musical vocabulary to describe the sonic-vocal qualities and expressivity of speech production in radio drama, among other aspects. It is not least for these actual and metaphorical uses of music that it deserves to be taken into view in its own right when discussing radio drama. At the same time, it cannot feasibly be discussed separately from other sonic-semiotic channels as it constantly interacts with them (see below).

1 Music and Narrative in Radio Drama

Since radio drama can be considered a narrative-mimetic genre like theatrical drama or film, discussions of music in this art form must also touch upon the more general debate concerning narrativity and music, if ever so briefly. A recent collection of essays by scholars in the fields of musicology, cultural studies and narratology brings together the various (conflicting) viewpoints on the question whether music can narrate (Grábocz 2021). Generally, one can distinguish between those scholars who claim that music has narrativity because it shares some fundamental features with narrative, such as movement in time and space, orderly structuration and especially sequentiality, and those who reject this claim by pointing to music's lack of referentiality and thus its impossibility to tell about anything in the past tense, for example (Abbate 1991: 52), or relate to a storyworld with characters, times, places, etc. (Heldt 2013: 55; for an overview of different positions, see also Mildorf 2017).

Some musicologists have drawn upon narratological conceptual frameworks including, among others, *story* and *discourse* (Micznik 2001), Vladimir Propp's plot functions (Tarasti 1979) or Mieke Bal's (1997) version of focalisation (Meelberg 2006) in their discussions of music. However, since the musical sign system is different from language in that it can refer to something only by way of analogy instead of 'arbitrary stipulation', as Beate Kutschke (2005: 196–197) points out, any claim to musical 'narrativity' ultimately rests on a metaphorical usage of this term. This metaphorical usage has been criticised, for example, by Jean-Jacques Nattiez (1990: 257). In a later article (2011), however, he concedes that one might consider music a "proto-narrative" because of the many features it shares with language: rhythm, intonation, a kind of syntax or structure, passing in time, an emotional or affective appeal (see also Bailes and Till 2014; Walsh 2011).

A third group of scholars argues that music is non-narrative in a strict or narrow sense of the term but may fulfil narrative functions in combination with other sign systems, especially language, and be narrativised in the reception process (see, for example, Heldt 2013; Trautsch 2015; Wolf 2002, 2015, 2017, 2021). Still, the medial conditions of radio drama need to be borne in mind. For instance, the story/discourse dichotomy used in narratology, which relates to *what* is told on the one hand and *how* it is told on the other, is further complicated in media that go beyond the verbal aspect. Elke Huwiler (2005: 86) therefore adds a third category for radio drama, that of "Darstellung" (presentation), which encompasses the specific radiophonic means and channels used in the medium. One could argue that music, as part of a radio play's sonic means of presentation, cuts across story and discourse. It may stand in for or characterise story existents such as characters, times and settings while also contributing to different ways of conveying the narrative, e.g., by creating focalisation (see Bluijs in this volume), by helping to structure scenes and sequences, by suggesting a certain mood, etc. Listeners, in turn, are encouraged and expected to attribute such narrative functions to music.

2   Functions of Music in Radio Drama

Several contributions in this volume offer typologies for the various functions that music can assume in radio plays. For example, Peter Graff discusses music's role in establishing themes, background, bridges or curtains, emphasising the analogy to theatre. In my own contribution, I draw a comparison with film music and additionally refer to Angela Ida De Benedictis's (2004) typology of eight functions of music in radio drama: opening and closing; separation or transition between scenes; background; commentary, amplification or counterpoint; intradiegetic music; presentation of characters; distinction between levels of action and narration; characterisation of the presented epoch, place, etc. Alan E. Williams, who himself scores music for radio drama, allows us an insight into practical considerations from commissioning to production. As he points out, the main difference between radio and film music is that in productions for the wireless a "collaborative ethos prevails" while film composers usually do their job after the film has been shot. I do not wish to anticipate too much of these various typologies or discussions here and refer any readers interested in them to the subsequent chapters. Instead, I would like to focus on some general questions that are important when considering music in radio drama.

Mechtild Hobl-Friedrich (1991: 33) distinguishes between three basic ways in which music can be related to radio drama: *music in radio plays* ("Musik im Hörspiel") refers to instances of music whose function it is to structure (as pauses or bridges, etc.), to support or underscore what happens in the radio play. *Radio play music* ("Hörspielmusik"), by contrast, is used by Hobl-Friedrich to designate any kind of music that is specifically composed, arranged or put together for a particular radio play and that can therefore not be used for other radio plays. The third category, *music as radio play* ("Musik als Hörspiel") is used for all those sound experiments mentioned above where sounds and music together constitute a radio play composition in its own right and become increasingly independent of the spoken word. Radio works by Mauricio Kagel or Heiner Goebbels come to mind here. Whether this distinction, especially the one between the first two categories, is tenable is open to debate. One could argue that any music that was specifically selected or composed and put to use in a radio play – whether it is original or canned – becomes radio play music because it fulfils very specific and presumably idiosyncratic functions in that production. It also seems unlikely that radio play producers will use the same kind of music for exactly the same purposes across various radio plays, as some chapters in this volume confirm. In fact, it is safe to assume that music in radio drama is polysemous to the extent that it will most certainly 'mean' different things in different radio plays.

The reason for this is that music, even though one may momentarily single it out for analytical purposes, is closely woven into the texture of the radio play as a whole and unfolds its potential in combination with the other sonic-semiotic channels, as I pointed out above and as becomes manifest in this volume's case studies. It is certainly useful to differentiate between original music specifically composed for a particular radio play and already existing music that is then (re)combined in specific ways. Still, what emerges in both cases is a rather unique sound piece with its own inherent word-music-sound relationships. This is also why it is so difficult to talk about functions of music in radio drama in the abstract. One can clearly identify certain basic functions as outlined in the typologies mentioned above, but it is exceedingly problematic to try and map specific musical features or qualities onto particular, recurring functions across radio plays. A dark instrumental timbre may signify a mysterious atmosphere in one radio play and characterise someone as a trustworthy fatherly figure in another. Quick musical movements may express jocundity and liveliness in one instance and underline someone's nervous disposition in another. More importantly, while such interpretations are suggested by the surrounding verbal-dialogical scene, this does not guarantee that listeners will arrive at the same interpretations of the music presented at any moment. Radio drama – and the music it employs – can thus be considered an "open work" in Umberto Eco's (1989) sense. It gives room to intended as well as unintended meanings which emerge in listeners' engagement with a radio play.

Coming back to the various roles that music can perform in radio drama, it is interesting to note that the critical vocabulary used to analyse these functions seems to require metaphors. Williams (in this volume), for example, argues that, apart from representing or being an action in the radio play, music may also assume a commenting function – just like the chorus in Greek tragedy. That music may 'comment' on the action presented in radio drama is identified and discussed in examples by several other contributors, which is noteworthy as it counters the assumption mentioned above that music technically cannot refer to anything in particular and therefore cannot narrate. However, despite instrumental music's lack of referentiality, it may become narrativised in connection with other semiotic channels such as words or sounds. The case studies seem to suggest that the metaphorical conception of music as a 'commentator' or 'narrator' is sometimes needed to describe what is going on in radio plays and may therefore serve as a heuristic tool despite its metaphoricity.

Another metaphorical set of terms – this time borrowed from linguistics – is the distinction between *syntactic* and *semantic* functions of music (Huwiler 2005: 61). These terms acknowledge the fact that music is sometimes used for structuring the sonic architecture of a radio play, e.g., as a means of separating or linking scenes, for opening and closing the radio play, and sometimes for supporting its content and meaning as when it characterises a moment or a place, conveys a mood, signifies different time levels, and so on. As I show in my own case study in this book, however, these functions are not always discrete and easily distinguishable. Again, one needs to look at the individual instance to decide what exactly music accomplishes there.

The same difficulties arise with the terms *diegetic* (or *intradiegetic*) and *non-diegetic* (or *extradiegetic*). The terms are used in narratology to differentiate between elements that are part of the actual storyworld or outside of it respectively. While the application of these terms is certainly desirable from an audionarratological perspective (see Mildorf and Kinzel 2016; Bernaerts and Mildorf 2021) and may help us differentiate between instances where music occurs as part of the narrated world and those where it does not, the boundaries between those two modalities are not always clear-cut. In fact, it is not uncommon for music to be used story-externally and then blend into music that is played inside the storyworld, or the other way around. One could call this a kind of musical metalepsis. Rather than bemoan such fuzziness, one must ask: what effects do such transgressions create? What do they signify? Here, too, one may arrive at a myriad of answers – depending on the radio play in question – not the least of them being that radio drama simply wants to make things interesting for listeners and to capture their attention.

So, while it is difficult, if not impossible, to map certain musical qualities, movements or figures onto specific functions or the other way around, one can identify the analytical categories that may be useful when describing and analysing features of music in radio drama. As Karl Ladler (2001: 40) points out, one can start by distinguishing between instrumental and vocal music, and between music played by traditional instruments or electronically created music. Prosodic features of music include pitch, volume, timbre, changes in velocity and pauses. Furthermore, one has to consider aspects of harmony, tone colour, tensions between the tone colours of different instruments or groups of instruments. In vocal music, the same categories apply. What Ladler does not mention, but what is equally important when analysing music in radio drama, is general musical structures, which also require musicological vocabulary: for example, repetitions and reprises, variations, movements, themes, counterpoints, etc. The question of genre – whether the music used is classical or modern, popular or jazz and so on – is obviously also relevant as each category comes with its own set of associations for listeners. In fact, the predominant usage of a certain musical genre may even determine a whole radio-dramatic subgenre, as is the case with pop radio drama (see Rinke 2017).

As far as the relationship between music and its surrounding sonic and verbal contexts is concerned, a number of things need to be considered, as Ladler (2001: 41) further demonstrates. Drawing on Hobl-Friedrich (1991: 75–81) and others, he argues that, in relation to the spoken word or dialogue in radio drama, music can occur simultaneously or without text. If it occurs simultaneously, it is either subordinated to the text or co-equal to it – although this is rare or unusual given the concerns for acoustic clarity I mentioned above. Music can function as incidental music, i.e., occur in a given scene, which corresponds to the narratological category of "intradiegetic music". It may also illustrate or further characterise the text and thus serve a host of different functions ranging from anticipation, commentary, irony, contrast, counterpoint, variation and alienation. Music may offer recognisable leitmotifs or ciphers, the latter of which is defined by Hobl-Friedrich (1991: 77) as a musical theme or phrase that communicates a text's more hidden messages. One also needs to consider where music is used in a radio play, when it begins and when it ends, as well as whether and, if so, how it structures the radio play's plot. Music may be used to represent some other sound or stand in for an element that one wishes to leave non-verbalised, e.g., states of mind, emotions or moods. Finally, Ladler (2001: 42) also points to the symbolic implications or qualitative ascriptions that some instruments were assigned, for example during Romanticism. Thus, shawms and flutes are typically associated with the pastoral tradition, while the oboe was considered 'virginal', the clarinet 'sensual' and so on. Trumpets can signal a mighty ruler and horns hunters. Again, all these connections must be analysed in the context of each individual radio play, as their meanings may also shift or be inverted.

What this brief overview already indicates is that the analysis of music in radio drama requires an attentive ear and ideally a minimum of musical knowledge on the part of listeners and scholars. This is why the present volume brings together contributors working in musicology, literary and cultural studies, radio drama history and practice. The first section addresses various historical, national and institutional contexts in which radio drama and radio music emerged, looking specifically at German, American, British, Dutch, Italian and Australian radio. The contributions indicate many similarities and differences in these countries concerning the development of radio drama music out of classical and popular musical formats. They also illustrate how developments in electronic music production and radio drama crossfertilised one another. Moreover, what becomes apparent from these contributions is that institutions such as radio stations and electronic music or art workshops played an immense role in also propelling the development of radio drama.

The second section attends to the relationship among music, language, sound and narrativity in case studies drawn from a number of different national radio drama traditions, including the UK, USA, France, Flanders and the Netherlands, Germany and Denmark. The chapters are arranged in a more or less chronological order to show with concrete examples some of the developments that the historically oriented chapters already delineated. The contributions to this second section not only attest to the creativity of radio producers and sound musicians over time and in diverse contexts but illustrate the many different functions that music can fulfil in radio plays. For the sake of accessibility, a short chapter outline is provided in the remainder of this introduction.

3 Chapter Outline

John Gabriel opens the volume with his contribution on innovative radio experiments in Weimar Republic Germany (1919–1933). He shows how early musical radio genres such as radio-specific opera ("Funkoper") and the fully musical radio play ("musikalisches Hörspiel") influenced later production formats, e.g., the "Hörfolge", a montage-like series of scenes of an epic dimension, and sound film. He also discusses how, in the early days of radio drama, music offered a conceptual framework for radio practitioners to think and write about their own practices.

Emilie Capulet discusses French radiophonic music during the 1930s, which was largely composed for radio drama. By focussing on one important piece from that time, *Le Douzième coup de minuit*, Capulet shows how radiophonic techniques offered a creative impulse for theatrical and musical performance and in a sense anticipated Pierre Schaeffer's radiophonic experiments in acousmatic music.

Philomeen Lelieveldt's chapter provides an overview of live music production for radio drama in the Netherlands between 1924 and 2020, acknowledging not only the conceptual influence of high art forms such as literature, theatre and opera but also light music stage formats such as (silent) cinema, vaudeville and revue. Lelieveldt's survey illustrates the collaboration among authors, radio drama directors, composers, musicians and technicians and their creative use of new technologies for radio drama.

Angela Ida De Benedictis retraces the development of radio drama in Italy after the Second World War by focussing specifically on how music composed for radio impacted on the genre. She also points to the interrelated developments of radio drama and radio opera and to the role that institutions such as the Studio di Fonologia della RAI di Milano played in making innovative approaches to electronic music possible – for radio more generally, but also for radio drama production.

Virginia Madsen concentrates on the Australian broadcasting company ABC and its audio-visionary creativity, especially from the 1930s onwards and after the Second World War. Her survey demonstrates the 'border crossing' that took place in radio's forms and genres, which brought writers, sound or performance artists and musician-composers together to work on new creations. These were at the intersection of music, musicality, sound arts, new compositional experiments and hybrid instances of writing for radio, all of which became a feature of a significant strand in Australian radio creativity from the mid 1970s to the early 2000s.

Tim Carter describes the US Federal Theatre Project, which was established in 1935 as part of President Roosevelt's 'New Deal'. It also created a Radio Division, whose broadcasts included two series of "symphonic dramas" in 1937–1938. Carter discusses the role of music in these series in more detail, highlighting the fact that playwrights were hired to provide "original dramatisation" for existing classical orchestral works. As a result of this initiative, Carter argues, radio fostered various vernacular modernisms in what he calls "a peculiarly American context".

Michael Fjeldsøe's contribution opens the second section. His case study is a live broadcast of Oscar Wilde's play *Salome* aired on Danish National Radio in 1930. It was presented as a radio drama with symphonic music composed and conducted by Emil Reesen (1887–1964). By analysing the score as well as the speech parts, Fjeldsøe unravels the various methods and procedures involved in the adaptation process. He also uses this example to foreground the significance of the "Radiokapellmeister" (radio orchestra conductor) as a key figure in early radio history, at a time when almost all music was broadcast live.

Troy Cummings applies the terms "music, musicality and musicalisation" to Norman Corwin's (1910–2011) *They Fly through the Air with the Greatest of Ease* (1938). These terms denote instrumental and vocal music in radio drama, the 'musical' quality of any sound presented in a radio play, and the way in which words and sounds become music or musical through semantic processes. In extending the notion of what can be understood and analysed as 'music' in radio plays, Cummings demonstrates the potential complexity of radio drama compositions and their multiple musical layers.

Peter Graff identifies what he considers the "four primary functions" of music in radio drama: themes, backgrounds, bridges and curtains. He traces their formal lineage to earlier film and theatre traditions but also shows how the new medium of radio necessitated a distinct musical language. Surveying radio music anthologies and broadcasting manuals from the 1930s and 1940s, Graff demonstrates how composers ultimately overcame these unique challenges. He thus also offers glimpses into early American radio drama.

Siebe Bluijs presents one Flemish and one Dutch case study, Jef Geeraerts's *Concerto* (1970) and Samuel Vriezen's *Schade* (2017), which both show how radio drama music can become a site for implicitly conveying political-ideological issues of the time period in which the radio plays are broadcast. His audionarratological analysis also reveals the ways in which intradiegetic music can either be played or alluded to by characters or narrators and how it dovetails with the semiotic system of language to give access to characters' inner states.

In my own contribution, I undertake a close audionarratological analysis of music in the German radio play adaptation of J.R.R. Tolkien's *The Lord of the Rings* from 1992, one of the longest and first digital radio productions on German radio. I show how the music, which was expressly composed for the radio play by Peter Zwetkoff, functions not simply as a background to the unfolding story but actively participates in the construction of plot, suspense, characters, settings, moods and overall narrative coherence.

Leslie McMurtry focuses on music's role in creating a sense of immersion. As her case study – *The Spy*, a BBC Classic Serial from 2012 based on the 1821 novel by James Fenimore Cooper – illustrates, it does not matter whether the music accurately corresponds to a historical period as long as it is evocative enough to create historical ambiance. McMurtry demonstrates how such usage of quasi-historical or historicising music fits within the production paradigm of current BBC radio practice and economically as well as effectively helps immerse listeners in an 'authentic' historical storyworld.

Caroline A. Kita considers Austrian writer Elfriede Jelinek's experimental prose texts, which the author herself referred to as "Sprachpartituren" (speech scores). Kita examines the adaptation of these texts for radio, using as her case study *Die Schutzbefohlenen* (*Charges*) from 2014. She illustrates how music, alongside a polyphonic dialogue between characters and chorus, is used in this contemporary German-language radio drama to articulate cultural critique.

Alan E. Williams recounts his first-hand experience as a composer of the process of commissioning, negotiating and composing an orchestral score for radio drama. His example is BBC Radio 4's adaptation of John Wyndham's novel *The Kraken Wakes*, which was first broadcast in May 2016. Drawing on film music theory, Williams explores the different types of representation used in music for audio drama and shows with his personal example how these representations led to a hybridised artistic product between live event, radio drama and film score.

Taken together, the contributions to this volume offer a rich picture of highlights in music production for radio drama across countries and throughout the history of the medium from its beginnings to the present. They show how both radio drama and music are bound up with the times in which they emerged and how they were influenced by and in turn also left their mark on other art forms and media. We hope that radio historians, scholars of radio drama, literature and cultural studies, media studies experts and anyone else interested in radio drama can learn from the cultural-historical enquiries as well as the various case studies presented here.

References

Abbate, Carolyn (1991). *Unsung Voices: Opera and Musical Narrative in the Nineteenth Century*. Princeton: Princeton University Press.

Arnheim, Rudolf (1936). *Radio*. Margaret Ludwig, Herbert Read, transl. London: Faber and Faber.
Arteel, Inge, Lars Bernaerts, Siebe Bluijs, Pim Verhulst, eds. (2021). *Tuning in to the Neo-Avant-Garde: Experimental Radio Plays in the Postwar Period*. Manchester: Manchester University Press.
Baade, Christina L., James Deaville, eds. (2016). *Music and the Broadcast Experience: Performance, Production, and Audiences*. Oxford: Oxford University Press.
Bailes, Sara Jane, Nicholas Till, eds. (2014). *Beckett and Musicality*. London: Routledge.
Bal, Mieke (1997). *Narratology: Introduction to the Theory of Narrative*. 2nd ed. Toronto: University of Toronto Press.
Barnard, Stephen (1989). *On the Radio: Music Radio in Britain*. London: Open University Press.
Bernaerts, Lars, Jarmila Mildorf, eds. (2021). *Audionarratology: Lessons from Radio Drama*. Columbus, OH: Ohio State University Press.
Cacchione, Olivia (2020). "Voicing the Other World: Music and the Victorian Occult in Mid-Century American Radio Drama". Jarmila Mildorf, Pim Verhulst, eds. *Radio Art and Music: Culture: Aesthetics, Politics*. Lanham: Lexington Books, 169–184.
Chase, Gilbert, Sterling Fisher, eds. (2013). *Music in Radio Broadcasting: NBC-Columbia University Broadcasting Series*. Literary Licensing.
Chignell, Hugh (2019). *British Radio Drama, 1945–63*. London: Bloomsbury.
Cleverdon, Douglas (1969). *The Growth of Milk Wood: With the Textual Variants of Under Milk Wood by Dylan Thomas*. New York: New Directions.
Cohen, Andrea (2015). *Les compositeurs et l'art radiophonique*. Paris: Éditions L'Harmattan.
Coley, Sam (2022). *Music Documentaries for Radio*. London/New Nork, NY: Routledge.
Crisell, Andrew (1994). *Understanding Radio*. 2nd ed. London: Routledge.
Crook, Tim (1999). *Radio Drama: Theory and Practice*. London: Routledge.
Crook, Tim (2020). *Audio Drama Modernism: The Missing Link between Descriptive Phonograph Sketches and Microphone Plays on the Radio*. London: Palgrave Macmillan.
Crook, Tim (2021). "The Audio Dramatist's Critical Vocabulary in Great Britain". Lars Bernaerts, Jarmila Mildorf, eds. *Audionarratology: Lessons from Radio Drama*. Columbus, OH: Ohio State University Press, 17–40.
De Benedictis, Angela Ida (2004). *Radiodramma e arte radiofonica: storia e funzioni della musica per radio in Italia*. Torino: EDT.
De Benedictis, Angela Ida (2020). "Between Art and Promotion: The Prix Italia, Its Historical Context and Aims in the First Fifty Years 1949–1998". Jarmila Mildorf, Pim Verhulst, eds. *Radio Art and Music: Culture, Aesthetics, Politics*. Lanham: Lexington Books, 85–97.
Eco, Umberto (1989). *The Open Work*. Anna Cancogni, transl. David Robey, ed. Harvard, MA: Harvard University Press.

Eichenberger, Tatiana (2021). "Radiophonisc Art and Electroacoustic Music: An Aesthetic Controversy during the Establishment of the BBC Radiophonic Workshop and the Radiophonic Poem *Private Dreams and Public Nightmares*". Inge Arteel, Lars Bernaerts, Siebe Bluijs, Pim Verhulst, eds. *Tuning in to the Neo-Avant-Garde: Experimental Radio Plays in the Postwar Period*. Manchester: Manchester University Press, 46–66.

Ellett, Ryan (2017). *Radio Drama and Comedy Writers, 1928–1962*. Jefferson, NC: McFarland.

Fairchild, Charles (2012). *Music, Radio and the Public Sphere: The Aesthetics of Democarcy*. Basingstoke: Palgrave Macmillan.

Grabócz, Márta, ed. (2021). *Narratologie musicale: topiques, théories et stratégies analytiques*. Paris: Hermann.

Grant, Morag Josephine, Férdia J. Stone-Davis, eds. (2013). *The Soundtrack of Conflict: The Role of Music in Radio Broadcasting in Wartime and in Conflict Situations*. Hildesheim: Georg Olms Verlag.

Hand, Richard J., Mary Traynor (2011). *The Radio Drama Handbook*. London: Continuum.

Hand, Richard J. (2014). *Listen in Terror: British Horror Radio from the Advent of Broadcasting to the Digital Age*. Manchester: Manchester University Press.

Heldt, Guido (2013). *Music and Levels of Narration in Film: Steps across the Border*. Bristol: Intellect.

Heuser, Harry (2013). *Immaterial Culture: Literature, Drama and the American Radio Play, 1929–1954*. Bern: Peter Lang.

Hobl-Friedrich, Mechtild (1991). *Die dramaturgische Funktion der Musik im Hörspiel: Grundlagen, Analysen*. Erlangen: University of Erlangen.

Huwiler, Elke (2004). "Klangwelten in der Literaturwissenschaft: Zum Phänomen des Hörspiels und dessen Integration als Forschungsgegenstand". Elke Huwiler, Nicole Wachter, eds. *Integrationen des Widerläufigen: Ein Streifzug durch geistes- und kulturwissenschaftliche Forschungsfelder*. Münster: LIT Verlag, 47–57.

Huwiler, Elke (2005). *Erzähl-Ströme im Hörspiel: Zur Narratologie der elektroakustischen Kunst*. Paderborn: Mentis.

Iges Lebrancón, José. (1997). *Arte Radiofónico: Un arte sonoro para el espacio electrónico de la radiodifusión*. Universidad Complutense de Madrid, Departamento de ciencias de la Información.

Klotz, Peter (2022). *Hörspiel und Hörbuch: Literatur als Performance*. Berlin: Erich Schmidt Verlag.

Krug, Hans-Jürgen (2008). *Kleine Geschichte des Hörspiels*. 2nd ed. Konstanz: UVK.

Kutschke, Beate (2015). "Semiotische Grundlegung musikalischer Narration". Frédéric Döhl, Daniel Martin Feige, eds. *Musik und Narration: Philosophische und musikästhetische Perspektiven*. Bielefeld: Transcript, 193–225.

Ladler, Karl (2001). *Hörspielforschung: Schnittpunkt zwischen Literatur, Medien und Ästhetik*. Wiesbaden: Deutscher Universitätsverlag.

Lakoff, Jeremy (2020). "Maestro, If You Please: The Radio Producer as Musician". Jarmila Mildorf, Pim Verhulst, eds. *Radio Art and Music: Culture, Aesthetics, Politics*. Lanham: Lexington Books, 33–48.

Meelberg, Vincent (2006). *New Sounds, New Stories: Narrativity in Contemporary Music*. Leiden: Leiden University Press.

Michelsen, Morten, Mads Krogh, Steen Kaargaard Nielsen, Iben Have, eds. (2018). *Music Radio: Building Communities, Mediating Genres*. London: Bloomsbury.

Micznik, Vera (2001). "Music and Narrative Revisited: Degrees of Narrativity in Beethoven and Mahler". *Journal of the Royal Musical Association* 126/2: 193–249.

Mildorf, Jarmila (2017). "Musik". Matías Martínez, ed. *Handbuch Erzählen*. Stuttgart: Metzler, 87–91.

Mildorf, Jarmila (2020). "Music and Politics in the BBC Radio Adaptation of Alan Bennett's *The Madness of George III*". Jarmila Mildorf, Pim Verhulst, eds. *Radio Art and Music: Culture, Aesthetics, Politics*. Lanham: Lexington Books, 205–215.

Mildorf, Jarmila, Till Kinzel, eds. (2016). *Audionarratology: Interfaces of Sound and Narrative*. Berlin: De Gruyter.

Mildorf, Jarmila, Pim Verhulst, eds. (2020). *Radio Art and Music: Culture, Aesthetics, Politics*. Lanham: Lexington Books.

Mohn, Matthias (2019). *Die Inszenierung von Furcht und Schrecken im Hörspiel: Eine interdisziplinäre Untersuchung der Grundlagen, Mittel und Techniken der Angsterregung in der elektroakustischen Kunst*. Münster: Waxmann.

Morawska-Büngeler, Marietta (1988). *Schwingende Elektronen: Eine Dokumentation über das Studio für Elektronische Musik des Westdeutschen Rundfunks Köln 1951–1986*. Köln-Rodenkirchen: Tonger.

Nattiez, Jean-Jacques (1990). "Can One Speak of Narrativity in Music?" *Journal of the Royal Musical Association* 115/2: 240–257.

Nattiez, Jean-Jacques (2011 online). "La Narrativisation de la musique". *Cahiers de Narratologie* 21. DOI: 10.4000/narratologie.6467 [27/02/2022]

Pownall, David (2010). *Sound Theatre*. London: Oberon Books.

Rea, Lauren (2020). *Argentine Serialised Radio Drama in the Infamous Decade, 1930–1943: Transmitting Nationhood*. London: Taylor and Francis.

Rinke, Günter (2017). *Das Pop-Hörspiel: Definition – Funktion – Typologie*. Bielefeld: Transcript.

Rösch, Eva (2022). *Die Restitution des Epischen unter den Bedingungen der Medienkonkurrenz: Das epische Hörspiel bei Walter Benjamin, Bertolt Brecht und Max Frisch*. Heidelberg: Universitätsverlag Winter.

Rumpf, Wolfgang (2007). *Music in the Air: AFN, BFBS, Ö3, Radio Luxemburg und die Radiokultur in Deutschland*. Berlin: LIT Verlag.

Sánchez Cardona, Luz María (2020). "The Making of a Nomenclature: José Iges on Radiophonic Art". Jarmila Mildorf, Pim Verhulst, eds. *Radio Art and Music: Culture, Aesthetics, Politics.* Lanham: Lexington Books, 9–31.

Smith, Kenneth (2022). "Music in Radio Drama: The Curious Case of the Acousmatic Detective". *Journal of the Royal Musical Association* 147/1: 105–134.

Stoller, Toni (2018). *Classical Music Radio in the United Kingdom, 1945–1995.* Basel: Springer.

Tarasti, Eero (1979). *A Semiotic Approach to the Aesthetics of Myth in Music, Especially that of Wagner, Sibelius and Stravinsky.* The Hague: Mouton.

Toudoire-Surlapierre, Frédérique, Pascal Lécroart (2015). *Marges de l'opéra: Musique de scene, musique de film, musique radiophonique 1920–1950.* Paris: Vrin.

Trautsch, Asmus (2015). "Orpheus, Till Eulenspiegel, Major Tom: Über die Möglichkeit musikalischer Narrative". Frédéric Döhl, Daniel Martin Feige, eds. *Musik und Narration: Philosophische und musikästhetische Perspektiven.* Bielefeld: Transcript, 85–109.

Verhulst, Pim (2021). "Music, Voice and (De)Narrativization in Samuel Beckett's Radio Play *Cascando*". Lars Bernaerts, Jarmila Mildorf, eds. *Audionarratology: Lessons from Radio Drama.* Columbus, OH: Ohio State University Press, 196–214.

Verma, Neil (2012). *Theater of the Mind: Imagination, Aesthetics, and American Radio Drama.* Chicago: University of Chicago Press.

Walsh, Richard (2011). "The Common Basis of Narrative and Music". *Storyworlds* 3: 49–72.

Wolf, Werner (2002). "Das Problem der Narrativität in Literatur, Musik und bildender Kunst". Vera Nünning, Ansgar Nünning, eds. *Erzähltheorie transgenerisch, intermedial, interdisziplinär.* Trier: WVT, 23–104.

Wolf, Werner (2015). "Literature and Music: Theory". Gabriele Rippl, ed. *Handbook of Intermediality: Literature – Image – Sound – Music.* Berlin: De Gruyter, 459–474.

Wolf, Werner (2017). "IV.1.6 Erzählen in der Musik". Martin Huber, Wolf Schmid, eds. *Grundthemen der Literaturwissenschaft: Erzählen.* Berlin: De Gruyter, 499–513.

Wolf, Werner (2021). "Narrativité et musique instrumentale. Une approche narratologique et prototypique d'un problème délicat". Márta Grabócz, ed. *Narratologie musicale: topiques, théories et stratégies analytiques.* Paris: Hermann, 121–142.

PART 1

Historical, National and Institutional Contexts

CHAPTER 1

From Acoustic Scenery to Sonic Dramaturgy: Music in Radio-Specific Drama of Weimar Republic Germany

John Gabriel

Abstract

Weimar Republic Germany (1919–1933) witnessed the development of experimental dramatic forms created specifically for the radio, celebrated for their technical and dramaturgical innovation, including the *Hörfolge*, which montaged pre-recorded sounds, narration, and dramatic scenes in a non-linear narrative, and the *Tonfilm*, in which sound was recorded on the film used for audiovisual sound film, but without images. I argue that these dramatic forms also emerged out of the practice and discourse of music in earlier, more conventional genres such as radio-specific opera (*Funkoper*) and the fully musical radio play (musikalisches *Hörspiel*). First, I examine the discourse surrounding early radio plays and the way music shaped ideas about creating drama specifically for the radio. Second, I analyze Walter Goehr's *Malpopita* (1931), Walter Gronostay's *Mord* (1929) and *Glocken* (1930s) and Eugen Kurt Fischer's *Trommel, Trommel, Gong* (1932) as examples of early radio play productions.

The 1923 debut of public radio in Weimar Republic Germany opened tantalising new opportunities for theatre, both spoken and musical. As a mass medium, radio promised to expand audiences from a handful of elites with the means and inclination to regularly attend the theatre to the entire populace. In theory, anyone could tune in; in practice, radio remained the domain of the middle to upper-middle classes (cf. Ross 2011: 28). Radio broadcasting also posed new challenges. Among them, it laid bare the degree to which works written for the stage relied on scenery, stage action and other visual elements to convey essential information. For such works, a new, purely acoustic approach to 'staging' needed to be developed. This realisation inspired others to advocate for the creation of an entirely new form of radio-specific, purely acoustic theatre.

In the early years of German radio, stations initially compensated for the lack of a visual element by adding naturalistic sound effects throughout works: characters entering and leaving scenes were accompanied by the sounds of opening and closing doors; characters in motion were indicated with footsteps; scenes set on ships had continuous background sounds of splashing waves. The term for this practice, *akustische Kulisse* (acoustic scenery), reflected its function as a substitute for the visual elements of stage productions. Pervasive use of acoustic scenery quickly fell out of favour as it became clear that listeners did not need constant sonic reinforcemen. If it was clear from the spoken text that a character was walking, the sound of footsteps was superfluous; the sound of splashing water at the start of a scene alone was enough to indicate the location without continuing it throughout. Too much acoustic scenery distracted listeners from the text, exhausted their ears and constrained their imaginations.

Responses to this realisation can be roughly divided into three broad trends. In the first, acoustic scenery was reduced to only those moments necessary for listeners' comprehension, but it remained scenery: naturalistic reproduction of sounds that supplemented the text and did not challenge the text's status as primary conveyer of meaning. In the second, all sound effects (and sometimes all music) were stripped from the production and only the text was read. When broadcasting works were originally written for the stage, certain key information about the dramatic events was lost, but this was considered preferable to supposedly corrupting the text with narration, sound effects, etc. New radio-specific works in this format sought to convey all necessary information via the text alone. The most common labels for this approach were *Wortspiel* (word play), *Worthörspiel* (word radio play), or *literarisches Hörspiel* (literary radio play). In the final approach, sound effects and music were elevated to equal partners with the text, each carefully conceived as independent carriers of information that, in combination, provided a complete aural representation of the dramatic action. I call this approach 'sonic dramaturgy'.

Speculative discourse about sonic dramaturgy and isolated works that attempted to realise it go back to the first years of German radio, but it was only in the years 1928 and 1929 that sustained practical experimentation began.[1] There are many reasons for this delayed start. Technology had, in the

---

1 Christiane Timper (1990: 17–18) chronicles a number of such works from the early years of radio in Germany, but as Solveig Ottmann notes, Hans Flesch, then Intendant at the Frankfurt station and soon to become Intendant at the Berlin station, claimed in 1928 that "he had not yet heard a radio work 'that did not turn out to be a disguised stage play that had eliminated its optical element'" (Flesch qtd. in Ottmann 2013: 346).

words of one critic, only just reached the point of "basic tolerability" (Hernried 1930: 39).² Additional factors included larger budgets, as the number of radio subscribers increased, and changes in personnel. In the early years of radio, stations' theatre departments were dominated by established figures from spoken stage theatre who were gradually replaced by new personnel with more practical radio experience and a desire to explore the unique possibilities radio offered.

When sustained experimentation began, it took three main forms. The first preserved the model of the spoken stage play, but gave music and sound effects a greater role. The second was as sonic montage, generally constructed of a series of short scenes that might include dramatic sketches, musical numbers and reportage (actual or imitation reporting from outside the studio, like sports broadcasts, political debates, or 'roaming microphones' visiting zoos, factories, train stations, etc.). These scenes could be performed live or played from recordings. While scholars have explored the influence of silent film on this approach, the important role of music and music theatre has been largely overlooked. The third was radio-specific music theatre, which built on the integration of music and text in stage genres like opera as a prototype for sonic dramaturgy.³ In modern scholarship, radio music theatre has been treated as a purely musical phenomenon that developed in parallel to approaches based in sonic montage. Intersections between the two, as well as the important role of text and sound effect in radio-specific music theatre, have equally been under-examined.⁴ Additionally, the history of radio-specific music theatre in Weimar Germany usually cuts off in 1930 or early 1931, as works that were specifically labeled *music* theatre (or related labels, like radio opera) fell off.⁵ The enduring influence of radio-specific music theatre on the sonic dramaturgy of radio works not explicitly labeled 'musical' has also been under-appreciated.

In this chapter, I argue that music played a significant role in the development of sonic dramaturgy in radio-specific works throughout the Weimar Republic. My argument has two parts. First, I demonstrate the role that music played in conceptualising the new function of text, sound effect and music, as well as in their combination on a micro-level. Then, I examine the role of

---

2   All translations are my own.
3   This approach was especially championed by Hans Flesch and Ernst Schoen at the Frankfurt and later Berlin stations. For a focussed examination of their work and biographies, see Ottmann (2013).
4   Timper, for example, excludes the sonic montage experiments of Fritz Walter Bischoff and the Breslau station (cf. 1990: 44).
5   Ludwig Stoffels, for example, argues that "the musical radio play must be considered a central radio-specific genre" but does not pursue its legacy after 1930–1931 (1997b: 939).

music theatre in the more sustained practical experimentation with sonic dramaturgy in the second half of the Weimar Republic and its impact on the development of large-scale works with sonic dramaturgy. I show how both the experience of adapting stage music theatre to radio and of creating radio-specific music theatre impacted approaches to sonic dramaturgy not only in specifically musical works, but also in montage works and those more closely modelled on spoken theatre.

1 Music as Metaphor

On the most basic level, advocates of sonic dramaturgy drew on music as a metaphor for their ambitions of a purely sonic artwork. One of the earliest and most vocal of such advocates, critic Hans Siebert von Heister, claimed in 1926 that "pure radio art is absolute, like music" (qtd. in Stoffels 1997b: 943). Such analogies remained current through the end of the Weimar period. Critic Rudolf Arnheim argued in his 1933 book *Rundfunk als Hörkunst* (*Radio: An Art of Sound*) that "as a purely acoustic art, [radio] is much more closely related and connected to music than to other acoustic arts (sound film, theater)" (22f.).

Two specific musical metaphors are revealing. The first is the symphony as a reference for a non-narrative, abstract collection of sounds that was considered meaningful and achieved the status of an artwork.[6] Von Heister, for example, described "the new radio play" as a "symphony of sounds [*Klangsymphonie*]" (qtd. in Schneider 1984: 17). Creators of radio works also designated their works 'symphonies' to lend credibility to new and unfamiliar formal structures. The most influential example of this was Fritz Walter Bischoff's *Hallo! Hier Welle Erdball!* (*Hello! Station Planet Earth Calling!*), produced at the Breslau station in 1928. The work is usually labeled a *Hörfolge*, or acoustic scenic montage: individual scenes, or *Hörbilder*, take the listener on a world tour by dropping in on fictional radio broadcasts from around the globe, including a soccer match, news reports, a dispatch from a jungle expedition and music. Bischoff, however, initially labelled the work a *Hörspielsinfonie*, or radio play-symphony.

Bischoff's use of the word symphony had multiple references. As was widely discussed at the time, it linked his sonic montage to Walter Ruttmann's 1927 film *Berlin: Die Sinfonie der Großstadt* (*Berlin: Symphony of a Great City*), a montage of documentary footage of urban life and technology in the city of

---

6 This way of understanding the artistic treatment of sound effects continues into postwar scholarship on Weimar German radio (cf. Würffel 1978: 14).

Berlin. But as critic Herbert Urban observed, both Bischoff's and Ruttmann's uses of the word symphony also drew on associations with the musical genre. Exploring the appropriateness of the metaphor, Urban first notes that the *Hörspiel* (radio play or radio work) component of *Hörspielsinfonie* was not entirely accurate. "*Hör-Film-Symphony*" or acoustic film symphony would be more appropriate, due to the work's montage form and debt to film. Urban considers the reference to the symphony, however, to be apt. The term, he explains, refers to "something a priori musical, traditional", and specifically to "something cohesive" (1928: 490). Such a claim to formal unity defended against criticism that montage-based works consisted of randomly thrown-together sounds, or, in Ruttmann's case, images. Urban, however, does not push the symphony metaphor any further than to claim that both Ruttmann's film and Bischoff's *Hör-Film-Symphony* evince formal unity, provided in the former by "the red thread of the progression of a work day", and in the latter by its "topicality [*Aktualität*]" (ibid.). The musical means by which symphonies are generally considered to form coherent wholes, like motivic development or harmonic schemes, are not mentioned.

Second, opera's integration of music and text, and of sonic and visual dramaturgy, made it an attractive metaphor for the combination of music, text and sound effect on radio. The most obvious example of this was the anachronistic adoption of the term *Gesamtkunstwerk* in radio discourse. *Gesamtkunstwerk* refers to a specifically Wagnerian approach to opera, but the only aspect of it that was really taken up in radio discourse was a vague sense of the integration of all the elements of stage opera: music, text and staging. Carl Hagemann, for example, argued:

> The pure radio work [...] will likely make use of all acoustically effective means, from primitive noises, to all possibilities of musical expression, to the enlivened word in spoken or sung passages. The pure radio work will, to all appearances, be an acoustic *Gesamtkunstwerk*. (1928b: 231)

Similarly, Bischoff described his experiments with sonic dramaturgy as "continuations of the idea of the radio work as the creation of an acoustic *Gesamtkunstwerk*" (Wittenbrink 1997b: 1174), and von Heister claimed that "a radio work should be pure radio art, in which sound effect, music, and words work together and form a *Gesamtkunstwerk* like the opera" (qtd. in Stoffels 1997b: 943). Regardless of whether all opera constituted a *Gesamtkunstwerk*, the role of music in opera led some in the early years of radio to believe that stage opera would require little adaptation for radio broadcast. Composer and radio critic Kurt Weill, for example, argued in 1925 that

> [adapting stage spoken theatre for radio] creates so many difficulties, but also so many new possibilities, that certainly sooner or later a new genre of acoustic theatre will develop. The opera, however, is capable of continuing to broadcast existing works from the operatic literature. It can make use of the panacea of music, which is able to portray and paint all the outer and inner events of the plot, the dramatic and the emotional.
> (1925/2000b: 275)

The naivety of Weill's initial claim was quickly proven by the experience of broadcasting stage opera. While operatic music often provides the "inner" or "emotional" insight as Weill describes, listeners soon realised that it does not consistently provide the kinds of "outer" or "dramatic" information that Weill himself notes are lost when stage spoken theatre is broadcast, like "stage decoration, gestures, and costumes, [...] the entire involvement of the eye". Indeed, two years later, Weill (1927/2000b: 347) described Wagner's *Der Ring des Nibelungen* (*The Ring of the Nibelung*, 1876) as poorly suited to the radio precisely because, as a *Gesamtkunstwerk,* the visual elements of the work played an essential role that was lost in radio broadcast.

Opera broadcasting in Germany took two forms: live broadcasts from opera houses and live broadcasts from radio studios.[7] The latter allowed stations more leeway to adapt operas for radio, but in both cases a variety of strategies emerged to compensate for the lost visual information, with no single solution finding universal acceptance. A major question was whether to use narration to compensate for radio's lack of visual information. While this was also an issue when broadcasting spoken theatre, opera's musical content posed an additional challenge. Most stations were loath to modify an opera's musical score beyond cuts for length.[8] As Renate Schumacher notes, "the aesthetic quality" of opera was thought to "lie primarily in the audible", as opposed to

---

7 Broadcast from recordings was initially not possible for technical reasons. The first opera to be played from recording on German radio was *La Bohème* (1896) on 1 March 1929. After the technology was developed, it remained controversial. Radio's liveness was considered by many to be one of its defining features, and playing from records as a cost-cutting measure was criticised for putting musicians out of work. See Stoffels (1997a: 714–716).

8 It was quickly determined that it was more difficult for radio listeners of both spoken and music theatre to maintain concentration than audiences at a staged performance. In radio discourse, this was largely attributed to the audio-only nature of the medium, which required the ear to do all the work instead of dividing the work over the ear and the eye. For opera and music theatre, 90 minutes was generally agreed to be the maximum a listener could maintain focus (cf. Ettinger 1931: 110).

spoken theatre, where it lay "in the visible" (1997: 1198). Adding narration to opera was thus especially tricky.

In its bluntest form, narration in broadcasts of spoken theatre involved a voice reading a play's stage directions (cf. Wittenbrink 1997a: 1041–1044). Such interruptions would occur wherever the stage directions appeared, including mid-scene. Opera made such a technique impossible, as the music regulated the pace. Interjecting such narration required disrupting the score, either pausing the music or adding narration as voice-over. Substantial reconfiguration to allow narration to play a greater role, as in the *Opernquerschnitt*, a genre we will return to below, was controversial, and narration was therefore usually only inserted where breaks in the music already occurred, primarily between acts. This points to music's two key contributions to the development of sonic dramaturgy. First, music's regulation of the pace of opera became a model for the coordination of the elements of sonic dramaturgy. Second, the strategies developed to add narration to opera created new formal models for radio works with sonic dramaturgy.

2   Music as Acoustic Regulator

In 1929, composer Walter Gronostay penned the text and the music to the *musikalische Hörspiel*, or musical radio play, *Mord (Murder)*. This work tells the story of a factory director who discovers his wife in bed with another man, kills them both, and then goes on the run from the police. With the exception of an extended imitation of a radio news report at the end, the work is scored musically throughout. Text is either sung or its spoken rhythm is exactly indicated. No sound effects are used, but certain key noises, like the revving up of a car's motor, are imitated in the orchestra or by the chorus. *Mord* was one of the first commissions of the Berlin station in its brief effort to support the development of sonic dramaturgy by calling for specifically *musical* radio-specific theatre. The rationale for such a musical campaign was captured by Gronostay in an article introducing the work, in which he claimed that his initial motivation had not been to compose a specifically *musical* work, but rather that he turned to music "as an acoustic regulator" (1929: 1429).

Music's ability to serve as an acoustic regulator was made possible by a new understanding of the other sonic elements of radio works – sound effects and the sounds of language – as musical. Looking back on the development of sonic dramaturgy, Arnheim described "the rediscovery of the musical sounds within noise and language" as the first step in the process of the "combining of music, noise, and language into a unified sonic material" (1933/1979: 22).

After such a rediscovery, "music recommends itself to [radio] as a wonderful aide to work out the pure formal characteristics of its building materials [i.e., the unified sonic material]" (ibid.: 23). On the one hand, music was a way of understanding the new role of sound effects and the sounds of language as independent carriers of meaning. On the other hand, thinking of sound effects and the sounds of language as musical opened new ways of conceiving, notating, rehearsing and performing them.

Let us consider the reconceptualisation of sound effects first. In the commonplace and over-determined dichotomy of noise as meaningless and music as meaningful, sound effects had previously fallen into the category of noise. They were considered incapable of carrying independent meaning and thus relegated to reinforcing meaning created by the text. Advocates of sonic dramaturgy sought to elevate sound effects to the category of meaningful. Critic and author Rudolf Leonhard, for example, argued in 1928:

> Sound effects [...] must [...] not be accompaniment, nor generically applied stock sounds [*Akzidenz*], but also not explanatory. Rather [they must be] the expression itself. [...] They must not be scenery, they should not stand on the sidelines, but rather in the center of the action. (161f.)

Typical of such advocates, Leonhard drew on music. In his schema, music was the "most organised and greatest example" of a sound effect. His emphasis on music's organisation here is notable, and he writes that all sound effects should aim to achieve music's level of organisation. This idea also informed experimental sound-effect devices that sought to achieve the same nuanced and precise production of sound effects that musical instruments did for music.[9] For example, Hamburg radio producer Hans Bodenstedt reported in 1927 on his station's efforts to develop a sound machine "that makes it possible to bring forth the most complicated sounds as if from an organ with registers at every needed volume" (qtd. in Stoffels 1997b: 943). Discussing this machine, scholar

---

9 The reconceptualisation of sound effects as music bears certain similarities to avant-garde music of this period, especially Italian Futurism and the work of Luigi Russolo. The invention of a sound effect organ furthers this similarity, as Russolo spent some time in the late 1920s living in Paris and working on a sound organ for use accompanying silent film (cf. Davies 2017: 256). Although the general ideas of Italian Futurism and descriptions of Russolo's noise music were well-circulated, it is unclear what, if any, exposure German sound technicians or others involved in sonic dramaturgy had to specific Futurist manifestos, works, or noise makers. It is therefore difficult to speak of any specific influence of Italian Futurism on German radio. There is, however, evidence that German radio sonic dramaturgy directly influenced Futurist approaches to radio (cf. Berghaus 2007: 109).

Ludwig Stoffels notes that its purpose was the "rhythmicisation and musicalisation of sound effects" (ibid.). Meaningfulness was thus linked to control and precision, qualities that music was thought to exemplify.

Another regularly recurring idea was that "naturalistic" sound effects could be supplemented or even replaced by "stylised" sound effects produced on musical instruments. Critic Robert Weege, for example, argued that "the music of radio works" should be "stylised sound effects, divested of their actual sounds and recreated as musical [*tönend*] and rhythmic sonic-structures [*Tongebilde*]" (qtd. in Timper 1990: 31). Meanwhile, Carl Hagemann, Intendant of the Berlin station, wrote that "one should use naturalistic sound effects in radio works as little as possible", but that stylisation "elevated sound effects into the sphere of artistic expression" (1928a: 309). We can see how the musicalisation of sound effects provided a framework for their combination and manipulation in one of the earliest radio works with sonic dramaturgy, *Bellinzona*, written by theatre director Rolf Gunold in 1924.[10] Gunold sought to sonically portray a recent real-life train crash "without connecting dialogue" (Braun 1968: 43). Instead, he based the work primarily around sound effects and music that imitated the sounds of trains. In line with trends we have already seen, the work was often described as a "symphony" (ibid.). In his review of the work, Kurt Weill emphasised the specific musical techniques employed by Gunold. This included "six different pedal points taken from acoustic recordings of speeding trains that follow each other or overlap like musical motives", "words, calls and 'gestures' [that] grow from a friendly allegro over an anxious foreboding andante to a raging prestissimo", and "the terribly shrill dissonances of the collision" (1925/2000a: 280). As we will see, musical terminology for qualities like tempo and dynamics were widely adopted to discuss other sonic phenomena on radio.

Sonic dramaturgy also required a new sonic understanding of text, involving both the sounds produced when speaking and the sonic qualities of the voice itself.[11] Arnheim went so far as to argue that "in works for radio, the sound of the word is more important [...] than the meaning of the word" (1933/1979: 20). This new focus on language as sound was also shared by advocates of text-only radio works, who believed that greater attention to the sonic qualities of language and voice would help obviate the need for sound effects and music.

---

10   Theresia Wittenbrink notes that von Heister, an early advocate of sonic dramaturgy, called *Bellinzona* "a 'trailblazer' of the radio play that was not recognised and supported early enough" (1997b: 1163).

11   Also at play here was radio's connection to the development of sound poetry. For example, Kurt Schwitters adapted and performed his "Sonate in Urlauten" (originally written 1923) for the Stuttgart station in 1932.

Hermann Kesser, for example, argued: "The best acoustic scenery is not made by noises, but rather by the voice, by the characteristic voice, the distinguishable voice, the modulatory, vibrating voice. [...] In radio, we need voices that can create an atmosphere" (1931/1984: 189). Music played an important role in this new understanding of the voice for advocates of both word-only and sonic dramaturgy. Kesser, to name one, attributed Alfred Braun's status as "one of the best radio speakers in the German language-zone" to his background in music. This lent Braun a diverse range of advantages, from a better ability to manage tempo and pacing to "a powerful, musically-disciplined and highly-nuanced breath control" (ibid.: 190). Musical practice also became a model for directing speech on radio. Arnheim claimed that there was "no proper terminology" for speech direction and lamented that "it is only vaguely known" among directors of spoken radio plays "how one can work with musical terms" for qualities like the tempo, volume and phrasing of speech (1933/1979: 24).

Such musical approaches to the voice impacted the way authors shaped their texts. Arnheim advocated a musical model for the assignment of voices to roles and the order of scenes with attention to both timbre and range. For timbre, he proposed thinking of voices as resembling the sounds of instruments: "the long-windedness [and] powerfulness of the deep brass [...] twanging, inhibition, [and] thinness of the woodwinds" (ibid.: 26). Authors could make use of the associations vocal timbres carry to inform listeners about a character's personality or motivations. The other component of voice was range, "like in music, [...] soprano, alto, tenor, bass" (ibid.: 30). Arnheim argued that one of the primary structural goals in the form of a radio work should be contrast and variation, and that this variation is achieved at three levels: first in the assignment of voice types to characters, second by building each scene around contrasting voice types, and finally in the ordering of scenes so that different combinations of voice types come to the fore. Arnheim also cautioned that pairing similar voices together was difficult, but could work when "for example two basses [...] are fiercely fighting each other" (ibid.: 30f.). Meanwhile, Carl Hagemann noted that such contrasts among voices could also help make clear when characters enter and leave a scene. He further extended this newly-musical understanding of language and the voice to blur the line between speech and singing with a more flexible division between speech and song, and also with "spoken-singing [*Sprechgesang*] (or even singing) with instrumental accompaniment [...] during emotionally heightened outbursts – during dramaturgically important moments in the dialogue – at the high points of the scenic progression" (1928b: 231).

In addition to the musicalisation of sound effects and speech, sonic dramaturgy also necessitated an expanded role for music in radio works. The original role of music in acoustic scenery, as described by Alfred Braun, one of its leading proponents at the Berlin station, was "for the clarification of the interior and exterior situation of a scene, for the characterisation of a particular setting [and] for the underscoring of dialogue" (1929/1984: 182). Advocates of sonic dramaturgy, however, were interested in exploring ways that music could be used to provide greater structural unity and additional levels of meaning. One early example of this, which seems not to have caught on, was developed by Bischoff, the Intendant at the Breslau station. In a 1926 radio adaptation of Georg Büchner's *Woyzeck* (1836–1837, unfinished), he and director Viktor Heinz Fuchs replaced acoustic scenery with "symbolic sound illustration" provided by a solo clarinet (Wittenbrink 1997a: 1088). A more influential early contribution was Kurt Weill's music to a 1926 radio adaptation of Christian Dietrich Grabbe's 1822 play *Herzog Theodor von Gothland*. In the words of a critic identified only as Dr. C. St.: "Kurt Weill's music blazes a new path [...]. It avoids programmatic underscoring, like leitmotivic characterisation, and concerns itself only with elements of the overarching plot." (1926: 2580) Weill's music met the plot "on the magical level of meaningful content and thus achieves a synthesis that will be of enduring importance for playwriting and composition" (ibid.). One example of how Weill achieved this was a textless chorus whose music provided a kind of detached observation and commentary on the action, like "the chorus of an ancient tragedy" (ibid.). Meanwhile, emotional impact was heightened with strategic mixing of speech and music. For example, switching from singing back to speech "in the beautiful song, whose verse the castaway woman speaks while the saxophone takes over the melody" brought the work "to a harrowing highpoint" (ibid.). Weill's approach bears many similarities to the kinds of innovations he and other composers associated with the New Objectivity in music were pursuing in their music theatre for the stage, where he also sought to give music a more independent role and a more critical, detached relationship to the plot.[12] We will return to this below.

After sound effect and voice had been musicalised and the role of music had been expanded, musical notation provided a means of planning and realising their combination. Specifically musical works like *Mord*, discussed above, or Bertolt Brecht, Kurt Weill and Paul Hindemith's frequently discussed example *Der Lindberghflug* (*The Flight Across the Ocean*, 1929), made use of actual musical notation with imitations of sound effects composed into the musical parts. In Paul Hindemith and Robert Seitz's *Sabinchen* (*Little Sabine*, 1930), traditional sound effects were notated in the score in a manner reminiscent

---

12   On New Objectivity and stage opera in the Weimar Republic, see Cook (1988: 27–39) and Grosch (1999: 101–180).

of percussion parts. In less thoroughly musical works, musical notation also provided a model for how to coordinate all the sonic elements of a work. In an article introducing his work *Ballade von der Stadt* (*Ballad of the City*, 1928), author Theodor Csokor described the necessity of developing a "sonic score [*Geräuschpartitur*]" to accompany his script "line by line" (1928/1984: 156f.) This terminology was also picked up by critic Alfred John, who described the scripts for the experimental scenic montages of the Breslau station like *Hallo! Hier Welle Erdball!* as "radio play scores [*Hörspielpartituren*]" (1929: 3).

Musical notation could also help in the planning of sonic montages for radio. Noises could be transcribed into musical notation or a close approximation thereof, which was then cut and pasted to mock-up the final product. This process was essential in complex sonic montages, including perhaps the most complex sonic montage produced in Weimar Republic Germany: Walter Ruttmann's *Weekend* from 1930. *Weekend* was a sonic sibling to Ruttmann's film *Berlin: Die Sinfonie einer Großstadt*. This time, Ruttmann used sound film to record sounds, but not images, from around Berlin. He then cut and reordered segments of the film to create a loose narrative of a weekend in Berlin, from the end of work on Friday to the start of the workday on Monday with an excursion to a lake in between. As he planned out the work, Ruttmann transcribed the recorded sounds onto a music staff (albeit with only three lines), which enabled him to capture key elements like shape, gesture and rhythm (cf. Goergen 1989: 130f.).

The use of notation was not just a practical means of organising sonic events, but also a physical representation of the musical way of thinking thought necessary to create a coherent sonic dramaturgy. While there were a handful of composers, like Walter Gronostay, who were successful sole-creators of radio works with sonic dramaturgy, the more revealing examples are sole-creators from other domains, like Ruttmann and Bischoff. Writing about the creation of *Weekend*, for example, while Ruttmann claimed that his primary guide in the process was "simple instinct", he also admitted that his process in assembling the work followed "similar rules to those of music" (Eisner 1930/1989: 130f.) Meanwhile, a film critic identified only as Christophor described sound in the work playing an unfamiliar "dual role": "the sounds come from *reality*, but have also been processed *musically*" (1930/1989: 132). The need for such a musical sensibility also spurred a new valorisation of collaboration between writers, composers and sound technicians/directors. Critic Jochen Klepper, for example, wrote that "the writer of a radio word play [*Worthörspiel*] should come from poetry, [and] the author of the sound radio play [*Geräuschhörspiel*] from music" (1931–1932/1984: 193). Klepper justified this distinction by noting that the latter "must be able to work as easily with the rolling of a diesel train, the rattling of machines, the roaring of the wind and the chirping of birds as the conductor of an orchestra is [able to work] with his different instrumental voices" (ibid.). Von Heister, meanwhile, described the "creator" of works with sonic dramaturgy as "simultaneously a poet of musical tones [*Ton*] and words" (qtd. in Schneider 1984: 17). Nevertheless, such collaboration still required a heightened musical sensibility from each participant. According to Arnheim, "the author, who only writes plot and text and leaves it to the director to translate this piece of literature into the language of sound [...], is useless" (1933/1979: 123). Indeed, this is the process described by Csokor above. His radio scripts included detailed "technical notes" of the sounds or music required, which he then relied on composers and sound technicians to translate into a sound score (1928/1984: 156f.).

Musical understandings further influenced the assembly of sonic dramaturgy in how formal coherence was created across a radio work. Drawing from music, there were two primary ways to do this. The first involved the consistent use and development of recognisable motives (via concepts like motivic work, developing variation or Wagnerian *leitmotifs*). The second involved the use of specific music-dramatic forms. While we have seen how musical forms like the symphony or *Gesamtkunstwerk* were used as vague metaphors, we will return to the way specific music dramatic forms were adopted below. Before that, let us consider how a musical conception of motivic unity was translated to sonic dramaturgy.

At least as early as 1925, von Heister introduced the idea that sonic dramaturgy should be built around "a unifying theme, a persistent auditory motif that tied the work together" (qtd. in Jelavich 2006: 84). At the end of the Weimar period, Arnheim developed this idea at length: "A *Hörspiel* should have a sonically graspable basic motive." (1933/1979: 28f.) This basic or "sonic motive" should "strongly follow the content" of the work and manifest across all its sonic elements: speech patterns, sound effects and music (ibid.). Arnheim relates this practice to that of the Wagnerian *leitmotif* (as with *Gesamtkunstwerk*, this term was widely and loosely used) (ibid.: 100). As an example, Arnheim uses a radio play on the story of the Golem with a "hollow, groping" sonic motive (ibid.: 29f.). This motive "does not simply involve the sound of the Golem's voice or the Golem's style, but rather much more generally translates the character of the Golem into sound" (ibid.) In another example, a sound effect is established to have a certain meaning. Arnheim cites an unnamed play in which a ticking clock is the sole sound effect at a character's mother's house. This sound then assumes the meaning of a feeling of comfort and security the character feels there. Once this meaning is established, it can then be recalled, like a reminiscence motive, throughout the work (cf. ibid.: 67)

Furthering the musical model, Arnheim also calls for a contrasting secondary motive or motives to highlight the conflict that drives the drama (cf. ibid.: 30).

3 Operatic Adaptation and Music-Theatrical Form

Returning to our discussion of narration above, let us turn to how efforts to adapt stage opera to radio, specifically by creating spaces for narration, shaped the discourse and practice of sonic dramaturgy. In both spoken theatre and opera, critics were divided over whether narration was an unacceptable intrusion into the existing work, a regrettable necessity or a completely acceptable (even positive) feature of the new medium. For instance, radio executive and advocate of an explicitly musical approach to sonic dramaturgy Ernst Schoen (see 1934) believed narration to be a viable option for opera broadcasts, but musicologist and critic Ludwig Misch complained that it brought the opera "into the realm of the epic, the oratorio" (1931a: 378). This, in turn, led Misch to consider the possibility that "the oratorio – in the history of its development known to be the twin of the opera free from the stage – may prove itself to be the form most appropriate to the presentation of a plot set to music on the radio" (ibid.).

Misch was hardly the first to suggest that the oratorio was well-suited to radio's audio-only format. One of the earliest arguments for the oratorio as a radio-appropriate genre came from Wilhelm Heinitz in 1924. After dismissing "spoken drama, spoken theatre, opera, and operetta" as unfit for radio, he boasted: "In Hamburg, the radio has recently conquered a new realm (of music), namely, the oratorio. We believe that the strengths of the radio on the musical-artistic side lie here." (373f.) Heinitz derived this argument from a vocal defence of narration. For him, strategies that subsumed information traditionally conveyed visually, like setting or stage action, into dialogue or monologue were insufficient. He argued that "we do not trust [a speaker] when he admits to standing before us as an actor", but that "we [do] trust him, when he stands before us as a narrator" (ibid.: 373).

Advocacy for the oratorio bloomed in the late 1920s alongside the first sustained wave of experimentation in sonic dramaturgy and radio-specific music theatre. Critic Richard Stein, for example, criticised the call for new radio-specific genres as reinventing the wheel. Playing on the fact that the most commonly used German word for radio play, *Hörspiel*, did not include the term "radio [*Radio-* or *Funk-*]" but instead the term "acoustic [*Hör-*]", he claimed: "An acoustic(/radio) play [*Hörspiel*] has already existed for centuries, that is, the *oratorio*. [...] If one really wants to create a musical play specifically for radio, one must in all cases begin with the secular oratorio." (1928: 567) Indeed, as radio stations began commissioning radio-specific music theatre in the late 1920s, a number of composers turned to the oratorio and related genres, like the cantata. For example, Bertolt Brecht, Kurt Weill and Paul Hindemith's *Der Lindberghflug* was alternately labeled a *Lehrstück*, radio cantata and even "sport oratorio [*Sport-Oratorium*]" (Steinhard 1929: 216). Hanns Eisler and Ernst Toch composed radio cantatas – *Tempo der Zeit* (*Tempo of Time*) and *H2O*, respectively – and Erwin Schulhoff dubbed his radio-specific work *H.M.S. Royal Oak* a "jazz oratorio".

Another genre thought to be closely related to the oratorio that attracted similar interest as a model for radio-specific works was the revue. Rudolf Arnheim, for example, described an unnamed *Funkrevue* (radio revue) by Karl Schnog and Walter Gronostay as having an "abstract oratorio style" (1932/1984: 117). By this, he meant the way the work featured both traditional (i.e., human/animate) characters as well as choruses representing larger institutions (like a record company). Radio's audio-only nature freed listeners of seeing or even needing to imagine physical singers or their characters; acousmatic voices could be accepted as representing abstract referents. The lack of a visual element in radio thus opened up new possibilities of theatrical representation.

A key similarity between the oratorio and the revue in radio discourse was their perceived epic character, a quality they shared with the *Hörfolge* (acoustic scenic montage) and related radio genres. While genre labels like the distinction between the *Hörspiel* and the *Hörfolge* could be subjective, in a 1932 article Klepper noted one rough distinction that could be drawn between them: "The *Hörspiel* is the form that is closer to drama. It has a through-going plot, conveyed by main characters. [...] The *Hörfolge* has a more epic character." (193f.) In his 1930 monograph *Das Hörspiel*, Hermann Pongs emphasised a related similarity between the oratorio and *Hörfolge*: "The goal of radio oratorios [*Funkoratorien*] is the formation of collective ideas in thematic scenes and *Hörfolgen*" (36; see also Warschauer 1930: 88–90). This emphasis on collective, as opposed to individual, expression and appeal was widespread in the discourse on the New Objectivity in music and literature, and played a key role in growing interest in the oratorio as a stage genre. As a mass medium, radio also appealed to advocates of this new collectivism.[13]

---

13 These ideas were widespread in the discourse. For some examples related to works discussed here, see Preussner (1929) on Hindemith; Strobel (1928) and Mersmann, Schultze-Ritter, Strobel, Windsperger (1928) on Stravinsky. For a counterargument against collectivism in music and opera, see Abendroth (1931).

The label *Hörfolge* emphasised the montage-like *Folge*, or series, of individual scenes or musical numbers. When scenes imitated (or made use of actual) news reportage or consisted of musical numbers, the form appeared particularly epic and oratorio-like. This is especially relevant for the sonic dramaturgy of the radio-specific works that were produced by Fritz Walter Bischoff and his collaborators at the Breslau station. Many of these collaborations were built around or prominently included reportage and musical numbers, and they were alternately labelled both radio-revues (*Funkrevue*) and *Hörfolgen*.[14] The radio-revue *Song*, for example, brought together songs with texts by leading writers set to a jazzy popular-music idiom by leading composers.[15] Meanwhile, Pongs described Bischoff and composer Edmund Nick's collaboration *Leben in dieser Zeit* (*Life in This Time*), a piece its creators dubbed a "*Hörfolge* with music", as a typical example of a "radio-oratorio [*Funkoratorium*]" (1930: 36).

In *Hörfolgen* and related genres, the lines between epic and dramatic and between oratorio and opera could be blurred when individual scenes portrayed events dramatically within the larger epic form. An important precursor to such blended forms arose in the adaptation of stage opera for radio broadcast. Beyond the addition of narration to stage opera that Misch complained about above, entirely new dramatic forms emerged in which radio producers attempted to cut operas' lengths, convey the visual elements of the work acoustically and preserve the integrity of the musical score. One such form was the *Opernquerschnitt*, literally an opera cross section, that used new spoken text to create a coherent narrative out of highlights from an opera. A common approach was to rearrange the work as an individual character recalling the events of the opera after the fact. An early example of this was produced at the Breslau station in 1924 (before Bischoff's arrival) by reframing Bizet's *Carmen* as *Josés letzter Traum* (*José's Final Dream*). A similar approach blended operas with the original texts on which they were based, so that musical numbers were linked by the accompanying passages in the original story. This approach was less common as it was only possible when the original text lent itself to such treatment, as was the case with Albert Lortzing's opera *Undine*, based

---

14 For example, the critic Silesius designates "Bei mir – Grammofon!", "Hochzeitsreise auf Wellen" and a third unnamed work as all being both revues and "musical *Hörfolgen*" (1929: 529). Meanwhile, as Theresia Wittenbrink notes, "most of the Breslau station's newly commissioned works of the 1929/30 season were supposed to further develop the form of the radio-revue [*Funkrevue*], for which Bischoff had delivered an example with *Song*" (1997b: 1174).

15 In addition to contributions from Bischoff (as author) and Nick (as composer), *Song* featured (among others) texts by Bertolt Brecht, Erich Kästner and Kurt Tucholsky, and music by Paul Hindemith, Kurt Weill and Richard Enders.

on the fairy tale of the same name by Friedrich de la Motte Fouqué. In such treatments, the narrator was perceived less as an intrusion into the opera than as a storyteller naturally part of the artwork. Notably, this approach was the brainchild of Oswald Kühn, who described it as a move to an "epic form of radio-opera" (qtd. in Stoffels 1997b: 902).

While the influence of the oratorio and of hybrid epic-dramatic approaches is most clearly demonstrated in radio-specific *music* theatre, it was also felt in radio-specific works with sonic dramaturgy that were more directly modelled on spoken theatre. In his review of one such work, *Tanz von Cölbigk* (*Dance from Cölbigk*, 1926), Weill praised the way that text and sound were woven together in the sonic dramaturgy: "An artistic form emerges that is near to a spoken oratorio" because music "follows the formal organisation of the whole", as opposed to "follow[ing] some naturalistic attempt at representation" (1927/2000a: 337). *Tanz von Cölbigk* made use of two levels of narration, one – a female voice – providing overarching narration related to the broad sweep of the plot, and the other – a male voice – providing the more specific details of individual moments and scenes, while the scenes themselves presented events dramatically. Weill comments that "the writer has managed to elevate an epic story-telling to a certain dramatic tension", but that "the mistakes that are particularly noticeable in a radio broadcast and that mark the work as not yet a truly radio-specific work lie primarily in the fact that the epic element is overemphasised" (ibid.). He proposed the 1918 music theatre piece *L'Histoire du soldat* (*The Soldier's Tale*), by composer Igor Stravinsky and author Charles-Ferdinand Ramuz, as a model for "the kind of new dramatic form to which an alternation between the narrator and the dramatic characters can lead" (ibid.). Echoing arguments we encountered earlier about the need for collaboration in the creation of sonic dramaturgy, Weill further suggested that *Tanz von Cölbigk*'s author "Gerhart Hermann must work together with a musician in the continuation of his efforts" (ibid.). Such a development of this spoken oratorio format "can certainly point the way to a new kind of radio play [...] that is adapted to the sensory perception of the ear to make dramatic events clear without giving up the aesthetic advantages of the theatre" (ibid.: 338), that is, to sonic dramaturgy.

4   *Malpopita*: The First Radio-Specific Opera

While the oratorio and oratorio-like adaptations of stage opera provided one set of models for radio-specific works, another stream in the development of sonic dramaturgy sought to develop forms that were more recognisably operatic with a predominantly dramatic, as opposed to epic, structure. Although several works had been billed as *Funkopern*, or radio-specific operas, the first such work to which the label stuck was *Malpopita* from 1930 with music by Walter Goehr and libretto by M. Friedrich Mendelssohn and Robert Seitz. Drawing on many of the trends that informed the contemporary stage opera genre of *Zeitoper*, or topical opera, *Malpopita* told the story of a factory worker who takes work on a ship sailing to the South Pacific, looking for adventure. The ship crashes on the eponymous tropical island, where he briefly enjoys an idyllic life until one of the other sailors discovers oil. Industry comes to the island, and the worker finds himself back at the factory.

Malpopita's reception was sharply divided over ideas about opera and radio-specificity. For some, Goehr, Mendelssohn and Seitz had created a work that preserved the essential qualities of opera while also being completely adapted to the specifics of radio. For others, *Malpopita*'s creators had sacrificed defining features of opera in their pursuit of radio-specificity, resulting in a work that might be an effective *Hörspiel*, but not an opera. This debate focussed on two specific features: narration and the role of music. Ultimately, neither *Malpopita* nor subsequent *Funkopern* could reconcile competing expectations about these features. Although the genre fizzled out in the Weimar period, the reception of these *Funkopern* reveals the confluence of approaches to sonic dramaturgy in radio-specific music theatre and other radio-specific theatre in the final years of the Weimar period.

There was no narration in *Malpopita*. The work was carefully constructed so that all necessary information was either clear from the dialogue or from the music. For some critics, this 'solved' one of the great challenges of adapting stage opera for radio, and they praised the work for preserving a dramatic (as opposed to epic) approach. Ludwig Misch, for example, prefaced his review with a definition. Radio opera "may neither be aided by the explanatory word, as the 'Opernquerschnitt' does as a substitute [for the visual], nor by the narrating word, which serves the epic genre of the oratorio" (1931b). From this perspective, Misch found *Malpopita* "a thoroughly successful attempt to convey a 'plot' solely through the ear" (ibid.). In order to achieve this dramatic structure, Misch was willing to accept other features of the work, such as a relatively simple dialogue and action-driven plot (as opposed to one full emotional reflection by characters), and music that was "primarily illustration" of setting and action (ibid.).

Misch's assessment was shared by a critic identified only as Henschel, who echoed the belief that radio's lack of a visual element required a straightforward plot, and praised *Malpopita* for nevertheless stimulating the listener's imagination. Henschel (n.d.) focussed on the effective use of sonic dramaturgy in the work. Information about the setting was carefully embedded in characters' dialogue, for example while music alternated between stylised sound effects and elevated musical accompaniment. Here, Henschel credited Goehr for diverging from certain expectations of stage opera in order to make the work more radio-appropriate, including replacing recitative with spoken text and arias with musical numbers closer to popular song (cf. ibid.). Operatic singing was felt, by some, to be unsuited to radio. Arnheim, for example, complained that the fullness and volume of opera singing made the voice sound distorted and the text difficult to understand. Instead, he called on opera singers "to learn a more intimate, less massive, more microphone-appropriate way of singing from their frivolous colleagues, the gramophone singers" (1933/1979: 51; see also Leonhard 1928/1984: 161). Henschel (n.d.) does not note that this was also related to current practice in modern stage opera, with composers like Weill drawing on popular music in this way as well.

This points to the broader role of music in *Malpopita*. As mentioned earlier, in order to avoid narration, the music provided stylised sound effects and other 'descriptive' passages to inform listeners about the scenes. Generally, the music was in the style of the New Objectivity (see above). As Christopher Hailey (1994) has shown, this style was well-suited to radio and was popular with many composers writing for radio, including Hindemith and Weill. In addition to its creative engagement with jazz and popular music (styles on which many other radio composers, like Bischoff's collaborator Edmund Nick, drew heavily), the New Objectivity in music eschewed the kind of emotional or subconscious expression and lyricism that had characterised much nineteenth and pre-WWI twentieth-century opera. Some critics, however, felt these musical characteristics took *Malpopita* too far away from essential qualities of opera. As critic Lothar Band wrote: "*Malpopita*, this most recent attempt to discover the new land of the radio opera, remains completely in the realm of the *Hörspiel*. [It] is fundamentally only an extension of [...] earlier musical expansions [of the radio play]" (1931b: 148). Band was especially critical of the radio-appropriate New Objectivity elements in the music, particularly the lack of lyricism and the replacement of traditional arias sung with full voice for popular music-inspired songs. Another critic, identified only as W.H. Bol., similarly complained that the use of spoken text with musical accompaniment as opposed to recitative "makes clear the spoken radio play as an overemphasised starting point" (1931). Other critics focussed on how Goehr's music fulfilled the dual role of stylised sound effect and musical accompaniment, the former of which they deemed inappropriate for opera.

Ultimately, Band suggested that radio-specific opera may not be possible. Instead, he advocated turning to the oratorio as a model for radio-specific music theatre and abandoning the label (and ambition) of radio *opera* (cf. 1931b: 148). That is, in order to preserve key elements of what Band and his colleagues deemed essential to opera and to music theatre generally – like lyricism and music free of stylised sound effect – they were willing to accept narration or other epic elements reminiscent of the oratorio. Band's approach evinces a conservative view of opera, either unaware of the latest trends in stage opera or implicitly rejecting them, but so does Misch's insistence that opera should not contain epic elements. Many stage operas of the time also explored epic/dramatic blends. In addition to the well-known collaborations of Weill and Brecht, one particularly influential example was Stravinsky's 1927 "opera-oratorio" *Oedipus Rex*. Notably, Weill claimed that this work's "oratorio-like form" also "makes [it] particularly well suited to the radio" (1928/2000: 3177).[16] Such blending would become even more prominent in later radio-specific works.

5   After *Malpopita*

By the end of 1931, much of the enthusiasm that had greeted the idea of the first radio-specific opera when *Malpopita* premiered had evaporated. Band noted in December of that year that "one speaks but rarely of 'radio-specific' opera", even though broadcasts of stage opera continued unabated (1931a: 409f.). Erwin Schoen, who commissioned a number of the oratorio-like works mentioned above (like Schulhoff's *H.M.S. Royal Oak*), lamented in September 1932: "While in the last few years the radio play as a specific theatrical genre has made undeniable progress, there has been no such advancement in the operatic literature. There is still no radio opera" (Ottmann 2013: 214). Although interest in works explicitly labelled as radio-specific music theatre or opera had fizzled out by 1931, the impact of such works on the development of sonic dramaturgy endured.

Composers like Gronostay and Goehr continued to contribute to new radio works in which music and sound played ever greater roles. Goehr, for example, provided music for a *"Hörspiel* with music" with a text by Seitz titled *Die Carry Moore G.m.b.H.* (*Carry Moore Ltd.*) that one critic described as a "modern operetta" (Stoffels 1997b: 923). Another of his projects was the music for *Die verhexte Stunde* (*The Bewitched Hour*), a *Hörfolge* from 1932. The text of this work was assembled by Ernst Bringolf, combining original material with excerpts from

---

16   On the broader interest in oratorios at the time and their impact on modern stage opera, see Epstein (1928).

Edgar Allan Poe, Gustav Meyrink and Guy de Maupassant. Christiane Timper (cf. 1990: 41) has suggested that *Die verhexte Stunde* may have been modelled on the *Opernquerschnitte* discussed above. The plot loosely describes a series of spooky, horrific events around the world unleashed by a mysterious demonic force. Music and creatively deployed sound fill much of the work. Goehr's music combines elements of his Weill-esque style from *Malpopita* with Schoenbergian atonality (he had studied with Schoenberg) and sound effects generated by musical instruments. For example, sound effects and musical stylisations of them imitate the beeping of wireless telegraph transmissions, followed by text imitating news reports which seem to emerge out of and translate the supposed Morse code. Other text involves naturalistic portrayals of characters responding to horrors with whispers, gasps, screams, etc. Throughout, both kinds of text are overlaid in a manner reminiscent of the oratorio-like voice leading in spoken works described by Arnheim and Weill.

Gronostay also remained closely involved in the development of sonic dramaturgy in radio works, writing music for them and directing sound effects and vocal performance. Reviewing an unidentified radio play in 1932, Rudolf Arnheim described Gronostay's contribution in ways that anticipate Arnheim's own description of music as a model for "voice-leading" and directing spoken text: "It was very revealing how Gronostay the musician as a dialogue-director set the voices against each other as purely characteristic sounds; how he used the sound of groaning, moaning, and sighing as acoustic sign language; how he overlaid the voices in sections" (1932/1984: 112). Another work for which Gronostay attracted praise was *Glocken (Bells)* from 1930. This *Hörfolge* did not have a unified plot, but instead consisted of a series of scenes that all had diegetic bell sounds in the background. The sounds of bells, provided by Gronostay, permeated the entire work, and scenes seemed to emerge out of and retreat back into the peals. Critic Felix Stiemer praised the use of sound, writing:

> The sound of the bell, which creates a massive space for itself, surrounded virtually the entire broadcast. Its individual scenes did not separate themselves from each other, but instead appeared at a rapid pace in the background of this sounding space. [...] Here one can no longer speak of underscoring the events, as the sound has itself become the dramatic event that speaks more clearly and directly to the listener than words ever could. (1930: 65)

This thorough use of sound represented a refreshing new direction in *Hörfolgen*, which Stiemer complained had "begun to stagnate" in their "picture book [*bilderbogenartige*] schema": "One could think of this *Hörfolge* being realised in the usual way as an acoustic film, in which the direction only generates transitions and interweaving – here, however, a new *Hörspiel* has appeared that is coherently built on acoustic events." (ibid.) Achieving such effects required not just technological advances (in recording, fading, etc.), but also new creative approaches to sound and music.

How Gronostay achieved the bell effect in *Glocken*, for example, is unclear in the preserved sources, but descriptions suggest novel uses of recording technology and/or compositional technique. Stiemer comments that it was "very noteworthy that [the bell effect] was not achieved with complex new technology, but with the simplest, long familiar technical means" (ibid.). As Ralph Kogelheide (see 2017) has documented, Gronostay was involved in a project recording actual sounds, including church bells on gramophone for use on radio and in stage theatre productions.[17] These recorded sounds may have been used in *Glocken*, and if so, they may have been somehow manipulated during playback. Alternatively, Gronostay may have composed music that imitated the sounds of bells and manipulated the sound compositionally.

The reception of *Glocken* tantalisingly hints at early experimentation in sound manipulation that (like Ruttmann's *Weekend*) anticipates later developments in electronic and tape music. Another such work that achieved similar effects via live musical performance was *Trommel, Trommel, Gong* (*Drum, Drum, Gong*, 1932), conceived and directed by Eugen Kurt Fischer. In an article on music in radio works from late in the Weimar period, Fischer called for a new kind of "simple and quiet melody [emerging] from the agitated vibrato of the gong" (qtd. in Timper 1990: 26). After an opening gong sound, students and performers from the Mary Wigman School in Dresden began improvising on percussion instruments and recorders, inspired by rhythms and sounds of the gong's vibrato and likely working with some predetermined rhythmic and melodic cells.[18] The work is non-narrative, "combining scenic [portions] with songs and politically-critical spoken texts" (Fischer n.d.: 21). These texts consisted of a man speaking to both the masses (a speaking choir) and his own inner voice (a single female voice for contrast) about "how far the individual should or should not subordinate himself to the masses" (Timper 1990: 43). The group improvisation of music neatly mirrored this dilemma in the text,

---

17   Gronostay also composed and recorded original music that could be used as generic background (pastoral music for rural settings, etc.), but Kogelheide (cf. 2017: 136) affirms that the bell sounds are real recordings, not instrumental imitations.

18   Fischer claimed there was no score because they could not afford a composer (cf. n.d.: 21). However, the recording of the work evinces certain well-defined motives which were likely worked out in advance.

with performers having to balance individual improvisation with the need to create a coherent ensemble product.

6 Conclusion

In this chapter, I have explored the development of sonic dramaturgy in the radio drama of Weimar Republic Germany, arguing that music and music theatre played an important and heretofore underappreciated role in the development of radio-specific theatre in this period. Music served as a model for the new role of sound effect and language in sonic dramaturgy and for their combination in new radio-specific works. Meanwhile, the adaptation of stage music theatre for radio provided formal models. While radio-specific music theatre has tended to be analysed separately from forms modelled on spoken theatre or from montage forms modelled, in part, on film, I have shown that music was a formative influence on all of these genres. Furthermore, the legacy of radio-specific music theatre continued in these other genres even after radio stations largely ceased actively pursuing radio-specific music theatre.

References

Abendroth, Walther (1931). "Musik und Politik in unserer Zeit". *Allgemeine Musik Zeitung* 58/19–20: 365–367.

Arnheim, Rudolf (1932/1984). "Der Rundfunk sucht seine Form". *Die Weltbühne* 10. (Reprint: Schneider, Irmela, ed. *Radio-Kultur in der Weimarer Republik: Eine Dokumentation*. Tübingen: Gunter Narr Verlag. 113–119).

Arnheim, Rudolf (1933/1979). *Rundfunk als Hörkunst*. Munich: Carl Hanser Verlag.

Band, Lothar (1931a). "Neue Formen – neuer Inhalt. Ein Rückblick auf das Programm des Jahres 1931. Musik". *Funk* 52: 409–410.

Band, Lothar (1931b). "Ziele und Wege der Funkoper. Ein Nachwort zur Berliner Uraufführung von *Malpopita*". *Funk* 19: 148.

Berghaus, Günter (2007). "F.T. Marinetti's Concept of a Theatre Enhanced by Audio-Visual Media". *Forum Modernes Theater* 22/2: 105–116.

Bol, W.H. (1931). "Funkoper under Kleiber. *Malpopita* von Walter Goehr". *Berliner Tageblatt*, 30 April.

Braun, Alfred (1929/1984). "Hörspiel". Hans Bredow, ed. *Hans Bredow: Aus meinem Archiv: Probleme des Rundfunks*. Hamburg. (Reprint: Schneider, Irmela, ed. *Radio-Kultur in der Weimarer Republik: Eine Dokumentation*. Tübingen: Gunter Narr Verlag. 179–183).

Braun, Alfred (1968). *Achtung, Achtung, Hier ist Berlin! Aus der Geschichte des Deutschen Rundfunks in Berlin 1923–1932*. Berlin: Haude & Spenersche.

Christophor (1930/1989). "Hinter den Kulissen des Rundfunks". *Die Welt am Montag* [Berlin] 23, 10 June. (Reprint: Goergen, Jeanpaul, ed. *Walter Ruttmann: Eine Dokumentation*. Berlin: Freunde der Deutschen Kinemathek. 132).

Cook, Susan (1988). *Opera for a New Republic: The* Zeitopern *of Krenek, Weill, and Hindemith*. Ann Arbor, MI: UMI Research Press.

Csokor, Theodor (1928/1984). "Mein Hörspiel *Ballade von der Stadt*". *Funk* 6. (Reprint: Schneider, Irmela, ed. *Radio-Kultur in der Weimarer Republik: Eine Dokumentation*. Tübingen: Gunter Narr Verlag. 156–157).

Davies, James Rhys (2017). "Luigi Russolo's Imagination of Sound & Music". PhD Thesis. Royal Holloway Univ. of London. Unpublished.

Eisner, Lotte H. (1930/1989). "Ruttmanns photographisches Hörspiel". *Film-Kurrier* 133, 1 March. (Reprint: Goergen, Jeanpaul, ed. *Walter Ruttmann: Eine Dokumentation*. Berlin: Freunde der Deutschen Kinemathek. 130–131).

Epstein, Peter (1928). "Opera-Oratorio. Zur Gegenwartslage der Oper". *Die Musik* 20/12: 866–872.

Ettinger, Max (1931). "Opernfunk – Funkoper!" *Funk* 21: 110.

Fischer, Eugen Kurt (n.d.). "Rundfunk-Erinnerungen". Typescript dated to 1950s. Deutsches Rundfunkarchiv Frankfurt am Main (DRAF). A18/3.

Goergen, Jeanpaul, ed. (1989). *Walter Ruttmann: Eine Dokumentation*. Berlin: Freunde der Deutschen Kinemathek.

Gronostay, Walter (1929). "Über mein Hörspiel *Mord*". *Der deutsche Rundfunk* 7/45: 1429.

Grosch, Nils (1999). *Die Musik der Neuen Sachlichkeit*. Stuttgart: Metzler.

Hagemann, Carl (1928a). "Hörspiel-Probleme". *Rundfunkwesen* 26, 22 June: 308–309.

Hagemann, Carl (1928b). "Die Verwendung der Musik im Hörspiel". *Die Sendung* 20: 231–232.

Hailey, Christopher (1994). "Rethinking Sound: Music and Radio in Weimar Germany". Bryan Gilliam, ed. *Music and Performance During the Weimar Republic*. Cambridge: CUP. 13–36.

Heinitz, Wilhelm (1924). "Rundfunkoper oder Oratorium?" *Funk* 26: 373–374.

Henschel (n.d.). "Zur Uraufführung der Funkoper Malpopita am 29.IV". Clipping in Deutsches Literatur-Archiv Marbach (DLA), H: Seitz, Robert. Dokumentationsstelle. A – Texte. Box 1218. 279–280.

Hernried, Robert (1930). "Geistige Probleme der Rundfunkoper". *Funk* 10: 39.

Jelavich, Peter (2006). *Berlin Alexanderplatz: Radio, Film, and the Death of Weimar Culture*. Berkeley, CA: Univ. of California Press.

John, Alfred (1929). "Funktheater im Breslauer Sender". *Funk* 1: 3.

Kesser, Hermann (1931/1984). "Bemerkungen zum Hör-Drama". *Die Sendung* 29. (Reprint: Schneider, Irmela, ed. *Radio-Kultur in der Weimarer Republik: Eine Dokumentation*. Tübingen: Gunter Narr Verlag. 188–192).

Klepper, Jochen (1931–1932/1984). "Was unterscheidet das Hörspiel vom Drama?" *Volksbühne* [Berlin] 10. (Reprint: Schneider, Irmela, ed. *Radio-Kultur in der Weimarer Republik: Eine Dokumentation*. Tübingen: Gunter Narr Verlag. 193–198).

Kogelheide, Ralph (2017). "Jenseits einer Reihe 'tönender Punkte': Kompositorische Auseinandersetzung mit Schallaufzeichnung, 1900–1930". PhD Thesis. Univ. Hamburg. Unpublished.

Leonhard, Rudolf (1928/1984). "Die Situation des Hörspiels". *Funk* 49. (Reprint: Schneider, Irmela, ed. *Radio-Kultur in der Weimarer Republik: Eine Dokumentation*. Tübingen: Gunter Narr Verlag. 158–163).

Mersmann, Hans, Hans Schultze-Ritter, Heinrich Strobel, Lothar Windsperger (1928). "Strawinsky: *Oedipus Rex*. Zur Frage der Antikenoper". *Melos* 7/4: 180–183.

Misch, Ludwig (1931a). "*Malpopita* – eine Funkoper". *Allgemeine Musik Zeitung* 58/19–20: 378.

Misch, Ludwig (1931b). "*Malpopita*. Ursendung durch die Funkstunde". *Berliner Lokalanzeiger*, 30 April.

Ottmann, Solveig (2013). *Im Anfang war das Experiment: Das Weimarer Radio bei Hans Flesch und Ernst Schoen*. Berlin: Kulturverlag Kadmos.

Pongs, Hermann (1930). *Das Hörspiel*. Stuttgart: Frommanns Verlag.

Preussner, Eberhard (1929). "Gemeinschaftsmusik 1929 in Baden-Baden". *Die Musik* 21/12: 895–903.

Ross, Corey (2011). "Cinema, Radio, and 'Mass Culture' in the Weimar Republic: Between Shared Experience and Social Division". John Alexander Williams, ed. *Weimar Culture Revisited*. New York, NY: Palgrave MacMillan. 23–48.

Schneider, Irmela (1984). "Einleitung". *Radio-Kultur in der Weimarer Republik: Eine Dokumentation*. Tübingen: Gunter Narr Verlag. 13–29.

Schoen, Ernst (1934). "Opernregie im Rundfunk?" *Anbruch* 16/7, September.

Schumacher, Renate (1997). "Radio als Vermittlung von Gegensätzen: ein Resümee". Joachim-Felix Leonhard, ed. *Programmgeschichte des Hörfunks in der Weimarer Republik*. Vol. 2. Munich: Deutscher Taschenbuch Verlag. 1196–1207.

Silesius (1929). "Reformen im schlesischen Funkprogramm". *Die Sendung* 33: 529.

St., Dr. C. (1926). "Die Aufführung des *Herzog Theodor von Gothland*". *Der deutsche Rundfunk* 4/37: 2580.

Stein, Richard H. (1928). "Vier Jahre Berliner Rundfunkmusik". *Die Musik* 20/8: 567.

Steinhard, Erich (1929). "Tonfilme, Liebhaberkunst, Rundfunkmusik in Baden-Baden". *Melos* 9/9: 216.

Stiemer, Felix (1930). "Mahagonny – Glockenstimmen". *Der deutsche Rundfunk* 8/17: 65.

Stoffels, Ludwig (1997a). "Kunst und Technik". Joachim-Felix Leonhard, ed. *Programmgeschichte des Hörfunks in der Weimarer Republik*. Vol. 2. Munich: Deutscher Taschenbuch Verlag. 682–724.

Stoffels, Ludwig (1997b). "Rundfunk als Erneuerer und Förderer". Joachim-Felix Leonhard, ed. *Programmgeschichte des Hörfunks in der Weimarer Republik*. Vol. 2. Munich: Deutscher Taschenbuch Verlag. 847–947.

Strobel, Heinrich (1928). "Opernpublikum". *Melos* 7/3: 111–113.

Timper, Christiane (1990). *Hörspielmusik in der deutschen Rundfunkgeschichte*. Berlin: Wissenschaftsverlag Volker Spiess.

Urban, Herbert (1928). "*Hallo! Hier Welle Erdball*. Ein Hörspielsymphonie in Breslau". *Der deutsche Rundfunk* 6/8: 490.

Warschauer, Frank (1930). "Was geschieht im Rundfunk?" *Melos* 9/2: 88–90.

Weill, Kurt (1925/2000a). "Ein Anfang. Die ersten Funkdramen". *Der deutsche Rundfunk* 3/31: 1945. (Reprint: Weill, Kurt. *Musik und Musikalisches Theater. Gesammelte Schriften*, Stephen Hinton, Jürgen Schebera, eds. Mainz: Schott. 279–281).

Weill, Kurt (1925/2000b). "Rückblick auf die erste Opernsaison im Berliner Rundfunk". *Der deutsche Rundfunk* 3/30, 26 July and 3/32, 9 August. (Reprint: Weill, Kurt. *Musik und Musikalisches Theater. Gesammelte Schriften*, Stephen Hinton, Jürgen Schebera, eds. Mainz: Schott. 274–279).

Weill, Kurt (1927/2000a). "Anmerkung zu einem neuen Sendespielversuch". *Der deutsche Rundfunk* 5/1: 4. (Reprint: Weill, Kurt. *Musik und Musikalisches Theater. Gesammelte Schriften*, Stephen Hinton, Jürgen Schebera, eds. Mainz: Schott. 336–338).

Weill, Kurt (1927/2000b). "Berliner Sendespiele und Übertragungen – Rück- und Vorschau". *Der deutsche Rundfunk* 5/10: 663. (Reprint: Weill, Kurt. "*Rheingold* als Sendespiel". *Musik und Musikalisches Theater. Gesammelte Schriften*, Stephen Hinton, Jürgen Schebera, eds. Mainz: Schott. 347–348).

Weill, Kurt (1928/2000). "Die Schubert-Gedenkwoche". *Der deutsche Rundfunk* 6/47: 3177. (Reprint: Weill, Kurt. "Strawinskys *Oedipus Rex*". *Musik und Musikalisches Theater. Gesammelte Schriften*, Stephen Hinton, Jürgen Schebera, eds. Mainz: Schott. 395).

Wittenbrink, Theresia (1997a). "Rundfunk und literarische Tradition". Joachim-Felix Leonhard, ed. *Programmgeschichte des Hörfunks in der Weimarer Republik*. Vol. 2. Munich: Deutscher Taschenbuch Verlag. 996–1097.

Wittenbrink, Theresia (1997b). "Zeitgenössische Schriftsteller im Rundfunk". Joachim-Felix Leonhard, ed. *Programmgeschichte des Hörfunks in der Weimarer Republik*. Vol. 2. Munich: Deutscher Taschenbuch Verlag. 1098–1195.

Würffel, Stefan Bodo (1978). *Das deutsche Hörspiel*. Stuttgart: Metzler.

CHAPTER 2

Transmedial Perspectives on Music and Sound in Early French Radio Plays from the 1930s: the Tangible Legacy of *Le Douzième coup de minuit*

Emilie Capulet

Abstract

During the 1930s, most French radiophonic music was composed within the context of the radio play. A lack of surviving primary sources has meant that these experimental musical practices have largely gone undocumented and their legacy overlooked. One key work of the period, *Le Douzième coup de minuit*, offers us a lens through which to consider how the medial boundaries between theatrical and musical performance were redefined through radiophonic techniques, and how these, in turn, redefined the scope of radio art more than a decade before Pierre Schaeffer's widely acknowledged radiophonic experiments in acousmatic music.

1   Introduction

On 27 December 1933, just over a decade after the first public radio broadcast from the Eiffel Tower, the listeners of one of the new radio stations of the day, the 'Poste Colonial', heard the premiere of an ambitious new work written specifically for the radio, *Le Douzième coup de minuit*. This work was the result of a collaboration between the avant-garde poet and pioneering playwright Carlos Larronde (1888–1940), the composer Arthur Honegger (1892–1955), the producer and actress Louise Lara (1876–1952) and her husband Édouard Autant (1872–1964), founders of what had become known as the Art et Action theatre group. Honegger and Larronde were very familiar with the methods and aesthetics of this experimental theatre group as they had been members since its earliest days in 1917. *Le Douzième coup* presents an apocalyptic vision of humanity in the hours and minutes leading up to the end of the world, predicted to happen on the twelfth stroke of midnight. In those very last seconds before midnight, the action jumps from the Middle Ages to the present day in spectacular juxtapositions of scenes which pit a Bergsonian conception of subjective time against a measured and objective conception of scientific time. The narrative is framed by the construction of a cathedral, which becomes a symbol of fraternity, eternity and hope as it is brought into sharp contrast with the contemporary tragedies of modern civilisation. Woven into the very fabric of the work, the striking new use of sound and music plays a crucial role in the experience of the listeners, as both the instrumental music combined with the sound effects and the musical handling of the spoken voices connect and underpin the different sections of the narrative. By challenging the traditional demarcation lines between music and words in a musical conception of the spoken voice and a narrative understanding of music and sound, Larronde called this work an 'orchestral poem in two parts and a prologue'[1] (1936: 5), though its radiophonic specificity and its innovative use of voice and text make it stand out from the earlier concert tradition of symphonic poems. As was common practice at the time, the broadcast was of a live studio performance which involved five professional singers, twenty-two actors and chorus members and an unusual seven-piece instrumental ensemble which included a harp, piano duet, organ and a variety of percussion instruments under the baton of the composer and leading radio orchestra conductor of the day, Henri Tomasi (1901–1971).

Le Douzième coup stands out as one of the very few radio plays of the early decades of radio broadcasting to have had a tangible legacy beyond its time and day partly due to the availability of a complete score for the work, including Honegger's instrumental parts and the vocal parts which had been meticulously copied out in 1933 by Lara's niece, Akakia Viala,[2] who had carefully collected them in the Art et Action archives. Unlike most of the other radio plays of the day, which were broadcast only a handful of times at most in what were ephemeral radio performances, *Le Douzième coup* stayed within the radio play repertory until it was recorded in 1944 by the Studio d'Essai, the first official French experimental radiophonic 'laboratory' created by Pierre Schaeffer and Jean Tardieu, and whose 'principal preoccupation' was 'to write an original radio play'[3] (qtd. in Héron 2010: 89). In 1942, Schaeffer, echoing the views of the first generation of influential radio personalities, authors and radio technicians

---

1 "Poème orchestral en deux parties et un prologue".
2 Akakia Viala was a pseudonym for Marie-Antoinette Allévy (1903–1966), actress, producer and librarian of the Institut des hautes études cinématographiques (IDHEC), who archived all of Art et Action's productions.
3 "L'écriture d'un radiodrame original est toujours une des principales préoccupations du Club d'Essai." All translations of the original French quotations provided in the footnotes are mine unless otherwise stated.

such as Gabriel Germinet, Paul Deharme, Carlos Larronde, Paul Dermée and André Cœuroy, had highlighted the need for 'a radiophonic art, a total art, calling for these three sonic currents which are discourse (the discourse of words), the discourse of music and, also, this new thing which is noise'[4] (1942/1990: 102). By recording the work, Schaeffer became intimately familiar with *Le Douzième coup*. He greatly respected Honegger and had openly admired Autant and Lara's musical approach to the voicing of texts in his commentary to his 1942 recording of *Falaise technique et amicale*, a radiophonic work which draws on similar 'symphonic' vocal techniques to those which had been employed in *Le Douzième coup* (Schaeffer 1952). Experimental works such as *Le Douzième coup* opened the door for the "symphonies of noise"[5] (1952/2012: 4) of Pierre Schaeffer and his Club d'Essai de la Radiodiffusion Nationale (RN) in the 1940s and undoubtedly played a role in shaping Schaeffer's theories of acousmatic experience, in turn opening the door to what was to become known as *musique concrète*.[6] This does, however, lead us to challenge the widely held view that the experimental radiophonic practices coming out of Schaeffer's laboratory were the very first attempts at radiophonic art. We might therefore ask to what extent the focus on Schaeffer as radiophonic trailblazer has served to obscure the role and function of new musical practices in radio art in earlier experimental radio works in France, such as *Le Douzième coup*. Whereas the early German

---

4 "un art radiophonique, un art total, qui recourrait à ces trois affluents sonores qui sont le discours (le discours des mots), le discours de la musique, et aussi cette chose nouvelle que sont les bruits".
5 "symphonies de bruits". See Schaeffer's five studies on noise, broadcast as *Concert de bruits* in June 1948.
6 Exploring the aesthetic boundaries between music, sound and noise in artistic production, Schaeffer puts forward a definition of *musique concrète* in his diary of 1948 as "the commitment to compose with materials taken from 'given' experimental sound in order to emphasize our dependence, no longer on preconceived sound abstractions, but on sound fragments that exist in reality and that are considered as discrete and complete sound objects, even if and above all when they do not fit in with the elementary definitions of music theory" (1952/2012: 4). The term 'acousmatic', on the other hand, is used in reference to the concept of *objet sonore* ('sonorous object') which is heard as detached from its source or cause. For Schaeffer, 'there is a sonorous object when I have accomplished, both materially and spiritually, a reduction even more rigorous than acousmatic reduction: not only do I limit myself to the information given to me by the ear, but this information only concerns the sonorous event itself'. ("il y a objet sonore lorsque j'ai accompli, à la fois matériellement et spirituellement, une réduction plus rigoureuse encore que la réduction acousmatique: non seulement je m'en tiens aux renseignements fournis par mon oreille, mais ces renseignements ne concernent plus que l'événement sonore lui-même") (Schaeffer 1966: 94).

experiments with radiophonic *Hörbilder*[7] – made out of live capture and collages of music and everyday sounds, the most famous of which was Walter Ruttmann's *Wochenende* (*Weekend*, 1930)[8] – have been explored and commented on in the literature (see Birdsall 2013), as have the Italian experimental music compositions produced in the wake of works by Ballila Pratella and Luigi Russolo's *The Art of Noises* manifesto of 1913,[9] music in early French radio dramas has been, to all intents and purposes, widely overlooked by critics and scholars.

Schaeffer is widely considered as the founder of postwar French radiophonic music, having stated rather provocatively in February 1944 in his radio programme on "l'art radiophonique" that "there are no names attached to radio, no radiophonic works. There are no archives"[10] (qtd. in Birkenmaier 2009b: 404). Whilst many historians of music and media have discussed the revolutionary nature of Schaeffer's postwar contribution to radiophonic music (see Kane 2014; Paquette 2015; Cohen 2009; Lautour 2017), some tracing it back to early means of sound reproduction and the electroacoustic experiments of the 'bruitistes', the significance and impact of the new musical practices developed within the context of radio plays during the first two decades of the history of French radio have been broadly overlooked, partly because of the unavailability of the scores, and partly because Schaeffer himself did not acknowledge the radio play tradition he had been exposed to in the 1930s. It is only relatively recently that scholars interested in the early history of French radio plays (see Birkenmaier 2009a, 2009b; Chénetier-Alev 2019; Durbec 1996; Duval 1979; Héron 2010; Méadel 1991; Morin 2014; Neulander 2009; Todd 2007) and in the history of music on radio (see Bennet 2015; Cohen 2009) have started mapping the radiophonic landscape of the 1920s and 1930s, highlighting the main landmark broadcasts of the period. However, a study of the music of French radio plays remains elusive, partly for the lack of primary sources and archives. It was not until the first Congrès international de l'art radiophonique in Paris, in 1937, that a call was made for the creation of standardised scores for the music of radiophonic plays and, more importantly, the establishment of a library of these works (cf. Karel and Noceti 1938: 15), but even today there is no centralised catalogue available and the scores for the earlier radio plays remain, at best, unlisted in the archives or, at worst, lost or destroyed. The very nature of

---

7   The term *Hörbilder* literally translates as 'soundscapes' but is often referred to in the English-speaking literature as 'cityscapes'.
8   See also works by Hans Bodenstedt such as *Die Straße* and *Hamburger Hafen*.
9   See Luigi Russolo's 'Risveglio di una città' (Awakening of a city) which was to be played on 'intonarumori', his experimental sound machines.
10 "Il n'y a pas d'archives, de primitifs vers lesquels nous tourner."

live radio broadcasting and the limitations of recording at the time also meant that very few radio plays had been put onto disc before the 1940s.

Music for radio plays in France in the 1920s and 1930s was an ephemeral art form, but one which arguably had a great impact nevertheless on the history of music and radio. As Weiss states, "if the history of mainstream radio is a suppressed field, the history of experimental radio is utterly repressed" (1995: 3), and this is still very much the case as regards the first two decades of French experimental radiophonic plays today. At a time when innovative radiophonic experiments were ephemeral, and when policy, budgetary constraints and the cultural context of radio broadcasting leant more and more towards more popular forms of musical entertainment, the tangible archival elements offered by *Le Douzième coup* and its wider contextualisation within the radiophonic practices of the day will provide us, in this chapter, with a lens through which to consider the ways in which the medial boundaries between theatrical and musical performance were redefined through radiophonic techniques, and how these, in turn, redefined the scope of radio art more than a decade before Schaeffer's widely acknowledged radiophonic experiments.

2 Towards a Radiophonic Music

In his quantitative study of music broadcasting on radio in the 1930s, Christophe Bennet (2010) highlights that no less than 2,185 composers of classical, light and dance music were featured in the 10 months of June that he sampled within the decade on Radio-Paris/Poste national and Radio-L.L.[11] Though many contemporary composers were featured in the programmes, most works broadcast were of live or recorded concert repertoire rather than newly commissioned radiophonic creations. Commenting on this situation in an overview of the new developments in radio broadcasting in his *Panorama de la radio* (1930), the French music critic André Cœuroy had noted the

---

11 At the end of the First World War, France decided to allow private radio stations to develop alongside its national radio network. The first private radio station in France was Radiola (1922–1924), which took on the name Radio-Paris from 1924. It was nationalised in 1933 and its name then changed to Poste national (1933–1940). In the 1930s, it broadcast alongside the other national radio stations, Radio Tour Eiffel (1921–1940), Radio PTT (1923–1940) and the Poste colonial (1931–1938). Many private radio stations were also in operation in the 1920s and 1930s, including Radio-L.L. (1926–1935) which then became Radio-Cité (1935–1940). Other private radio stations in Paris included the Poste parisien (1924–1940) and Radio Vitus (1926–1934). For a discussion of the French network radio landscape, see Cazenave and Ulmann-Mauriat (1995).

unsatisfactory sound quality of live symphonic music broadcasts on radio and the intrinsic unsuitability of existing concert repertoire for radio broadcasting. He deplored in particular the absence of what he defined as "la musique radiogénique" or 'radiogenic music' (175). Quoting his colleague Pierre Descaves, who had described broadcasts of diverse musical styles as all having the same uniform sound characterised by a timbre 'pitiful, disagreeable and ridiculous'[12] (Descaves qtd. in Cœuroy 1930: 176), Cœuroy called for new compositions which would be conceived specifically for live radio broadcasting and developed hand in hand with the technological expertise of the "metteur en ondes" or 'sound director', a sentiment which was echoed seven years later at the 1937 Congrès international de l'art radiophonique, in which 'the musicians demanded a stronger cooperation between the artists and the technicians'[13] (Huth 1937: 258).

Three years earlier, in 1927, to promote the composition of radiophonic music, Radio-Paris had launched a competition, calling for 'orchestral works lasting 6 to 12 minutes, for a maximum of twenty-five musicians and a minimum of three, the genre of music and the types of instruments being left to the discretion of the composer'[14] (qtd. in Antoine 1930b: 7). The work that was awarded the first prize and 5,000 francs was an orchestral piece by Florent Schmitt, which he humorously named *Çançunik* (a play on the expression 'sens unique', a one-way street). Ironically, *Çançunik*, whose radiophonic originality lay in its extensive use of woodwind within the context of a reduced 'radiophonic' chamber orchestra,[15] was not even premiered on radio by Radio-Paris but was first performed in the concert hall of the Concert Poulet on 2 July 1928. This lack of commitment to new radiophonic works on the part of the radio stations, which was compounded by the lack of compositional

---

12   "pathétique, piquante et ridicule".
13   "les musiciens penchèrent pour une coopération plus étroite entre l'artiste et le technicien".
14   "œuvres orchestrales d'une durée de six à douze minutes et pouvant être exécutées par vingt-cinq musiciens au maximum et trois au minimum, toute latitude étant laissée quant à la nature des instruments et au genre de musique".
15   See the review on 22 February 1930: "Il s'agit de deux morceaux pour orchestre réduit, *lied-nocturne* et *scherzo-tarantelle*. Si M. Florent Schmitt a écrit pour un orchestre réduit, c'est justement parce qu'il voyait dans cette réalisation un premier essai de composition musicale radiophonique. Les cordes, toujours en difficulté avec les exigences du micro, ne jouent ici qu'un rôle accessoire." (1930a: 8) 'These are two movements for reduced orchestra, *Lied-Nocturne* and *Scherzo-Tarentelle*. If Mr. Florent Schmitt has written for a reduced orchestra, it is because he considered this orchestration to be a first attempt at radiophonic composition. The strings, always struggling with the demands of the microphone, only play a secondary role.'

training in the creation of music which needed to be adapted to the radiophonic environment,[16] was noted by Jean Antoine, the critic of *L'Intransigeant*, who was scathing of the radio producers of the time who had neglected to feature in their programmes this work written specifically for the radio. He noted that

> those of us who study the conditions in which French radio programmes are made, cannot help but deplore the terrible state of the musical broadcasts. Maurice Bex, André Cœuroy, Paul Dermée, who talk about these issues, have long ago realised that it is ridiculous to ignore the foreign developments. One could cite alongside Hindemith many composers who, beyond our borders, have written works destined not to be played in the concert hall, but in front of microphones and by a specially constituted orchestra for radiophonic broadcast. [...] The story we want to tell you today concerns [...] the very first French work written for broadcast by a great French composer, which has just been played in a premiere in Paris, without anybody realising. The directors of our radio stations have missed their chance because this work, which had an enormous success, was performed by one of the rare Paris orchestras that is not broadcast live on the T.S.F. The Concerts Poulet, as everybody knows, play every week in the hall of the Theatre Sarah-Bernhardt, where nobody has thought of placing any microphones. It is there that Florent Schmitt got his *Çançunik* performed. [...] We are led to think today that the French crisis

---

16 There was certainly no formal conservatoire training available in composing for radio during the first decades of radio broadcasting, and unless a composer had the opportunity for first-hand experience of working in a radio studio and adapting works for radio broadcast, like Henri Tomasi, who became one of the early radio orchestra conductors in Paris in the 1930s and went on to compose many radio play scores, most composers left it to the sound technicians or 'metteurs en onde', conductors and radio musicians to find a way to work around the challenges in broadcasting what was in fact concert repertoire. The conductor Victor Pascal, who arranged and reorchestrated music for his radiophonic ensembles, for instance, was described by Jacques Sem in the context of radio broadcast as being 'one of the best craftsmen of orchestral music' ("un des meilleurs artisans de la musique orchestrale"; qtd. in Bennett 2010: 76). Though Pierre Schaeffer involved many young French composers just out of the Conservatoire in his first practice-based research laboratory in 1942, the Studio d'Essai, replaced in 1946 by the Club d'Essai, and eventually by the Groupe de recherche de musique concrète in 1955, which became part of the Service de la recherche de la radiodiffusion-télévision-française in 1960, it was not until 1968 that an electroacoustic music composition class (the closest that one would get at that time to a radiophonic composition class) was opened at the Conservatoire national supérieur de musique de Paris.

of radiophonic programmes is, first of all, a crisis of culture.[17] (Antoine 1930a: 8)

Most reviewers of the time did not even realise that this was a radiophonic work, though one critic, possibly aware of the new direction this music was taking in terms of orchestration and structure, thought it was a film score (see Dambly 1930: 7). Ten years later, in 1937, there was still a perceived lack of French radiophonic compositions, the critic of *L'Ouest-Éclair* writing that 'very few compositions have been written for the phonograph, a small number have been composed for radio broadcast, but many have been written on the margins of film'[18] (L.B. 1937: 5). What most commentators failed to realise at the time was the significance of the radiophonic musical contributions of French composers to the innumerable radio plays of the period. In the contemporary radiophonic critique of the 1930s, the musical elements of radio plays were often downplayed or simply misunderstood by commentators who were primarily theatre or literary critics and who could be scathing of the music which they found often distracted and detracted from the words. Speaking of the various sound effects and orchestral pieces used in radio plays, the poet and actor Maxime Léry argued that 'when a short story is interesting, well written, worthy of being broadcast, there are no two ways of going about its radiophonic production, it should be read simply and well in front of the microphone [...].

---

17 "tous ceux qui étudient régulièrement les conditions dans lesquelles sont faites les émissions françaises ne cessent de déplorer la tenue lamentable des diffusions musicales. Maurice Bex, André Cœuroy, Paul Dermée, qui traitent ces questions ont depuis longtemps reconnu qu'il était ridicule de nier le mouvement étranger. On pourrait citer avec Hindemith de nombreux compositeurs qui déjà hors de nos frontières composent des œuvres qui sont destinées non point à être jouées en concert, mais bien devant un micro et par un orchestre spécialement constitué en vue des émissions radiophoniques. [...] Mais l'histoire que nous voulons vous raconter aujourd'hui [...] [concerne] la première œuvre française écrite spécialement pour le micro par un grand musicien français et qui vient d'être jouée en première audition, à Paris, sans que personne ait daigné s'en apercevoir. Nos dirigeants radiophoniques jouent de malheur car cette œuvre qui remporta un grand succès fut exécutée par l'un des rares orchestres de Paris dont les concerts ne sont pas retransmis par T.S.F. Les Concerts Poulet, chacun le sait, jouent chaque semaine dans la salle du Théâtre Sarah-Bernhardt où personne encore n'a songé à placer un microphone. C'est là que M. Florent Schmitt a fait exécuter son *Çançunik*. [...] Nous sommes beaucoup à penser aujourd'hui que la crise française des programmes est avant tout une crise de culture."

18 "On a rarement composé des œuvres pour le phonographe, on en a conçu un petit nombre spécialement pour la radiophonie, tandis que maintes participations ont été écrites en marge d'un film."

On the pretext of *creating an atmosphere*, the harmony of the text is destroyed'[19] (qtd. in Méadel 1991: 6).

By the end of 1935, the radio producer, critic and author Paul Dermée, frustrated at the ongoing lack of commitment from radio programmers to commission, feature and regularly re-broadcast innovative radio plays on the airwaves, asked his colleague Gabriel Germinet to draw up a summary of radiophonic theatre in France from its beginnings in 1923 to 1935, in order to create a centralised catalogue of all the new works which had been created during the first decade or so of radio broadcasting. Gabriel Germinet, whose real name was Maurice Vinot, had been the Director of Radio-Paris from 1922 to 1925 and was an early proponent of radio art and one of the pioneers of radio play writing. Germinet included no fewer than 201 works in this "Golden Book of Radiophonic plays" (see Todd 2002).[20] Though many of these works included music in one form or another, what this catalogue reveals is that the drive for new radiophonic works, be they literary and/or musical, was principally coming from authors of literature and theatre, rather than from composers. If anything, apart from a few composers like Milhaud, Tomasi and Schmitt, who were interested in the opportunities that the new medium of radio offered, composers of the time were uneasy about the impact on listeners of the inferior sound quality of the music being broadcast on radio. Part of the issue originated from the limitations of the technology in its early days.

In Chapter 5 of his *Panorama de la radio*, Cœuroy discusses this in some detail, outlining what he thought would make 'good' radio music and raising many issues which explain the low esteem in which radio was held in the collective consciousness of French composers of the time. Cœuroy highlights in particular the lack of acoustics posed by the radio studio. He discusses the absence of depth of sound and how instruments carry differently on the microphone, 'because the violin, playing fortissimo in the higher register, tends to have a timbre similar to that of the flute, and the viola, playing staccato, changes character to imitate a percussion instrument'[21] (1930: 177). He also mentions the problem of ensemble layout and orchestral size in smaller

---

19   "Quand une nouvelle est intéressante, bien écrite, digne enfin d'être diffusée, il n'y a pas deux façons de la mettre en onde, qu'on la lise simplement et bien devant le micro. […] Sous prétexte de *créer l'atmosphère*, on détruit l'harmonie du texte."
20   This was in addition to the 427 entries that were made for the very first radiophonic play competition back in 1924, though only two of these, Gabriel Germinet and Pierre Cusy's *Maremoto* and Paul Camille's *Agonie*, won the competition and were broadcast on radio. For a discussion of *Maremoto*'s broadcast history, see Méadel (1992).
21   "car un violon, en fortissimo dans l'aigu, tend à confondre son timbre avec celui de la flûte, et l'alto, en staccato, abandonne sa personnalité pour imiter un instrument à percussion".

studios (he suggests that a radiophonic orchestra should count no more than thirty-six musicians, compared to a full concert orchestra which usually has over ninety), issues of balance and the delicate and often intrusive positioning of microphones within the orchestras, the issue of how to better capture and boost the lower frequencies of bass instruments through the use of additional double-basses. He was one of the very first to speak about the 'fidelity' of musical sound in the broadcast of woodwind, brass and percussion instruments compared to the distorted timbre of strings, which lost all their richness when captured on the early microphones and were broadcast through unsophisticated radio set speakers or headsets.

But more than highlighting the purely technical and acoustic problems, Cœuroy focuses on the difference between informal radio listening practices and the intensity of the concert hall ambience. He suggests that composers need to also adjust the internal musical elements and structure of radiophonic works to enhance and sustain the listeners' focus because they are no longer kept captive for the duration of the performance within a darkened concert hall, but are potentially easily distracted as they listen in their homes. Musical silences, as well, had such very different implications in broadcasts from silences occurring in the context of a concert hall when gestures were visible. Silence, in radio broadcasting in those early years, was only too easily misunderstood by listeners to be a technical problem. Interestingly, continuous background music (without musical silences) was seen as a way to bridge such radio silence, as the critic of *Le Journal* was to state in 1945:

> Silence is the enemy of radiophonic Art. Any 'holes' in a programme lead to a drop in the attention of the listener [...]. The infinitely short silences which separate the words also create gaps during which words seem to dance without any support, without life. To conciliate these two contradictory demands, music brings its precious aid. The cinema, which also fears silence, relied on a musical accompaniment [...]. How can one conceive a radiophonic work – an art form of a purely acoustic nature – without the quasi constant underpinning of music?[22] (R.C. 1943: 4)

---

22 "Le silence est l'ennemi de l'Art radiophonique. Chaque 'trou' dans le courant d'une émission laisse retomber de plusieurs degrés l'attention de l'auditeur. [...] Les silences infiniment courts qui séparent les mots, creusent eux-même des vides entre lesquels les paroles semblent danser sans support, sans vie. Pour concilier ces deux exigences contradictoires, la musique apporte son précieux concours. [...] Comment concevoir une oeuvre radiophonique – art purement auditif – sans le soutien quasi permanent de la musique."

Such remarks and insights will have changed the way musical silence was employed (or not) by contemporary composers in their works written for the radio and will ultimately have led to a very different understanding of the continuity of sound in contemporary composition on radio, film but also in the concert hall.

3 From Radio Plays to Sound Films

One could argue that the majority of French radiophonic music composed between the two World Wars was done within the context of the radio play. The music critic W.-L. Landowski[23] noted this in an article published in *Le Ménestrel* in July 1939, in which she endeavoured not only to give an overview of the function of music in radio plays over the previous decade but to highlight and promote the quality and innovations of those new compositions underpinning the radio dramas of the time, outlining three types of radio play music: incidental music, sound staging featuring music, and specifically composed soundtracks.

In the first category, which, she argues, pertains to the majority of radio plays broadcast at the time, incidental music took the form of movements chosen from existing and often well-known piano, chamber music, vocal or symphonic repertoire of the eighteenth and nineteenth centuries. These movements were simply played in between the acts of the plays with sometimes only a tenuous connection to the action.[24] In Landowski's second category are the radio plays that feature intradiegetic musical extracts forming part of the 'sound staging' (or "décor sonore" as it was called in French). This often included extracts from songs, jazz bands, distant marching music, dance music, etc. On

---

23 The French music critic W.-L. Landowski was actually Alice-Wanda Landowski (1899–1959), who had taken her father's initials to avoid confusion with Wanda Landowska, the well-known harpischordist, who is not related to her.

24 An example of this can be found in *Le théâtre radiophonique* (1926), where Germinet outlined what he thought would be suitable incidental music for a play based on Noah's Ark, taking a literal approach to the matter by featuring repertoire which had some extra-musical reference to animals, ranging from Haydn's 'Bear' Symphony, Schubert's 'Trout' quintet, Saint-Saëns's *Carnival of the Animals* and Roussel's *The Spider's Feast* (cf. 29–30). Pierre Descaves, a radio journalist and speaker, similarly used a Chopin étude to connect the sections of his radio play *Les Disciples* (1939), writing specifically to '[c]ontinue with the piano to cover the transition' ("Enchaîner avec le piano pour ménager la transition"; 1939: 13) between the acts of the play. The French writer and poet, Géo-Charles, with Claire Goll and Yvan Goll, used extracts from Schubert to punctuate their radiophonic adaption of Schiller's *Die Räuber* in 1938.

the margins of this category are radio plays calling for 'a collection of sound, music, noise, words and voices'[25] (Hubermont 1935: 6), which leading Belgian radiophonic writer Théo Fleischman called "jeux radiophoniques" (roughly to be translated as 'radiophonic entertainments'), usually featuring light subject matter but whose sound effects were already close in their conception to the full-blown soundtracks composed specifically for the medium.[26] To some extent, this found its roots in the music of the 'bruitistes', who celebrated the use of machines and objects to create pieces of music. Finally, in Landowski's third category are those radio plays which use music and sound extensively, to the point that, by the end of the 1930s, radio plays were increasingly described in the press as "radiophonic films" or "sound films" (cf. Etiveaud 1937: 639; Landowski 1939: 194; Mic Mac 1938: 9; R.C. 1943: 4), as they offer an elaborate musical soundtrack similar to those which were developed in the cinema.[27]

The radiophonic works which draw on music to create background continuity were often the result of close collaborations between authors and composers such as Larronde and Honegger (*Le Douzième coup*) or Tomasi (*La Mort du silence*, 1938), Paul Claudel, Darius Milhaud and Honegger (though their collaboration was less focussed on creating radio plays than works for the theatre, operas and oratorios, which were then broadcast on radio), or Julien Maigret and Tomasi (*Tam-Tam*, 1931; *Ajax*, 1934; *Mers du Sud*, 1937). Often, these collaborations led to the composition not only of original musical interludes but also what Paul Deharme called

> dream music, as easy as possible, the music of the old melodrama: this kind of music will 'warn' the listener through tremolos or ritornellos; it will draw a character in short phrases, and his or her return on scene will then be announced by the repetition of that motif. This will make

---

25 "Agencement de sons, de musiques, de bruits, de paroles, de voix diverses."
26 Landowski gives here the example of Théo Fleischman's *Le Soleil de Minuit*: "Pour illustrer ce jeu, M. Théo Fleischman associe les chants d'oiseaux, les hennissements de chevaux, les cris d'animaux au bruit des klaxons, des appareils de T. S. F., des sonneries de téléphone, d'une gare de chemin de fer, et aux battements de la machine à écrire. La musique illustrant cette œuvre n'est pas nouvelle: il s'agit tantôt de la célèbre mélodie Santa Lucia, tantôt de la Chevauchée des Walkyries, quelquefois d'airs de jazz." (1939: 193) 'To illustrate this radiophonic entertainment, M. Théo Fleischman links together bird song, neighing horses, animal cries, car horns, and the sound of distant radios, ringing telephones, train stations and typewriters. The music is not new: from the famous song Santa Lucia to the Ride of Valkyries and at times, some jazz tunes.'
27 Examples cited by Landowski are *Le Scarabée d'or* and *Les Boxeurs*, radio plays by Géo-Charles with music and sound effects by Henri Tomasi (1937), and *Le Douzième coup de minuit* by Larronde and Honegger.

it possible to bend and complicate the action without endangering its clarity; in short, by using expressive phrases music will 'illustrate' the comedy. (1928/2009: 409)

The soundtrack type of music was sometimes extrapolated by the composers and rewritten as pure concert music or symphonic suites, further obscuring the radiophonic origins of the works but at the same time bringing radiophonic practices and compositional devices into the more mainstream concert repertoire. In the notes for the first Congrès international d'art radiophonique, which took place in July 1937, Tomasi deplored the fact that radiophonic music was often overlooked by critics and authors alike and argued that 'more importance should be given in radio theatre to the music which creates the "atmosphere" of a play, connects its episodes *and sometimes, underpins them* [my emphasis]'[28] (1938: 15). An early example of this can be found in the radiophonic play *Tam-Tam*. It was first broadcast on 13 June 1931 to great critical acclaim and described by René Dumesnil as the first ever large-scale radiophonic work. Interestingly, he did not have a word to describe this new genre, terming it a 'lyrical sketch',[29] as he perceived it to be situated somewhere in between opera and radio play in the traditional sense. The reviewer of *Tam-Tam* in the *Mercure de France* stated that

> the words create the atmosphere. The music finishes suggesting everything that the words cannot say. And it is wonderful to see, sorry, to hear, how the alliance of text and music is intimate and complete, and how much the composer, with the means of his art and a sobriety similar to that of the librettist, can impose a clear and defined vision of what he wanted to paint, whilst leaving freedom to the imagination of the listener.[30] (Dumesnil 1933: 459)

Tam-Tam was one of the first works to challenge the way music functions within the genre of a play written for the radio. The music of the symphonic poem demonstrates Tomasi's attention to the challenges that radiophonic music

---

28 "Qu'une grande importance soit accordée dans le radiothéâtre à la musique de scène qui crée le 'climat' d'une pièce, en relie les épisodes et parfois même, les soutient."
29 "un sketch lyrique".
30 "Les mots créent l'atmosphère. La musique achève de suggérer tout ce que les paroles ne peuvent dire. Et c'est merveille de voir, pardon, d'entendre comme l'alliance du texte et de la musique est intime et complète, combien le compositeur a su, par les moyens de son art et avec une sobriété pareille à celle du librettiste, imposer la vision nette et définie de ce qu'il voulait peindre, tout en laissant le champ libre à l'imagination de l'auditeur."

posed in terms of orchestration in an episodic narrative structure which makes use of characteristic foreground and background musical passages alternating between, on the one hand, melodic sections that feature a soloistic musical line, and, on the other hand, repetitive textured background elements more suitable, we surmise, to the accompaniment of a spoken passage within the play. Despite its success as a radio play, its radiophonic score is unfortunately still lost to this day and the work is only available in its orchestral format.[31] This illustrates how the parts of the radio plays of the day often remained in draft manuscript form, the musical scores unpublished and the instrumental and vocal parts often lost. The live performance practices also went largely undocumented. However, such traces of the radiophonic genre persist in its concert adaptation.

4 *Le Douzième coup de minuit*: A Case Study

Le Douzième coup de minuit was broadcast two years after *Tam-Tam*. Tomasi himself, working alongside Honegger, Autant and Lara on the musical elements of this new radio play, was very much implicated in the creative process as he was conducting and rehearsing the work for months before it was broadcast. What was thought truly remarkable at the time about *Le Douzième coup* was the way Larronde, Honegger, Autant and Lara had embraced the technological specificities of the new medium of radio and challenged the French public's listening practices in an innovative exploration of the combination of sound, music, language and voice. At a time when more than half the radio broadcasts of the day were of classical, light or popular music either broadcast live from the studio by in-house musicians, or, increasingly after 1932, of gramophone recordings, and when much radiophonic theatre was similarly taken from live broadcasts from the Paris theatres (see Huth 1937), Larronde's new radio play defied categorisation. Hoping to redefine the scope and nature of radio broadcasting itself, he stated in the preface to this radio play: 'Let us, once and for all, differentiate between the means and the end, between radio considered as a

---

[31] The symphonic poem version of *Tam-Tam* runs for just under 18 minutes and uses a full symphonic orchestra, piano, chorus and solo soprano voice (for the "Chanson des Sables"). Sections also include a tango ("Désillusion") and a foxtrot ("Whisky") adapted from the original radio play score. Apart from the "Chanson des Sables", which includes a sung text, there is no trace of the spoken elements of the original play (itself an adaptation of a novel).

vehicle for the transmission of music and words, or radio taken as an original form of expression, as an autonomous art form.'[32] (1936: v)

From the literary perspective, the work offered a surprising juxtaposition of genres and styles, engaging with the tropes associated with theatre, radio journalism and poetry, whereas from the musical perspective, it brought together oratorio and choral writing, chamber music, church organ music, percussion ensemble and jazz, in a collage of styles reminiscent of early radio's typical potpourri approach to musical programming and which Honegger was to revisit two years later in his stand-alone radiophonic composition, *Radio-Panoramique* (1935). Larronde, Honegger, Autant and Lara had joined the growing number of radio enthusiasts who were particularly critical of those writers and early theoreticians of radio who felt that the new medium was essentially flawed as it lacked an essential visual dimension. For Larronde, who challenged the visually dominated culture of the day by engaging with the aural specificities of radio, it was not about 'compensating for an absence but creating a presence'[33] (ibid.: vi). He had felt compelled to voice his frustration at the lack of engagement of producers and artists with the artistic potential of radio in his 1931 manifesto outlining the future of radio, *L'Art cosmique*, lamenting the fact that '[r]adio never had its Victor Hugo or its Jules Verne. The technology has brought to life a world of wonder which was beyond anything we could have imagined and in front of which we just rehash the same old tunes.'[34] (1931a: 26)

Le Douzième coup was groundbreaking, not only in radio terms but also from the perspective of radiophonic music. It was a far cry from the style and approach of the winners of the first radio play competition in France in 1924 – Gabriel Germinet and Pierre Cusy with their realistic shipwreck, *Maremoto*, or of Paul Camille's intimate confession of a dying man in the monologue, *Agonie*, which was spoken without any sound effects or musical accompaniment. In their 1933 radio play, Larronde, Honegger, Autant and Lara had radically moved away from the realistic and often obvious use of noise and sound effects of the radio plays of the 1920s. The lesson had been learnt from *Maremoto*, which, prefiguring Orson Welles' 1938 radio play *The War of the Worlds*, had been banned from broadcast for causing a panic amongst the listeners who thought they had been hearing the real distress calls of a ship sinking in the Atlantic.

---

32   "Sachons distinguer, une fois pour toutes, entre le moyen et le but, entre la radio considérée comme un véhicule propre à transmettre la musique et les mots, ou comme une forme d'expression originale, comme un art d'autonome."
33   "Il ne s'agit pas de remédier à une absence, mais de créer une présence."
34   "La TSF [télégraphie sans fil] n'a eu ni son Victor Hugo, ni son Jules Verne. La technique a créée un merveilleux qui a dépassé nos imaginations et devant lequel nous rabâchons des rengaines."

Larronde, Honegger, Autant and Lara had extrapolated and applied to radio broadcasting the simultaneist theatre performance practices of the experimental theatre laboratory Art et Liberté (later to become Art et Action), based on theories developed before the First World War by the French poet, critic and dramatist Henri-Martin Barzun (1881–1974). Influenced by Bergson's theories of time and consciousness, and the work in psychology done by Freud on the subconscious, many artists in the early years of the twentieth century were exploring ways of expressing the simultaneity of a multiplicity of views, actions, perceptions and thoughts in a conception of time which was no longer formed of discrete moments neatly ordered in a linear narrative, but subjective time in which the boundaries between past and present overlapped and blurred. Many artists of the day were sounding the workings of our individual conscious and subconscious experiences whilst endeavouring to tap into our collective consciousness to apprehend and improve the human condition. In painting, this was reflected in Cubist works inspired by the multi-dimensional approach, colour modulations, clashing volumes and distorted perspectives of Paul Cézanne's paintings, such as *The Basket of Apples* (1890–1894). The Orphist paintings of the Delaunays were similarly to present multiple viewpoints at once in a style which used the concept of 'mobile perspective'. In literature, Apollinaire and Blaise Cendrars led the way by focussing on bringing together multiple perspectives and elements from different places and times in an implosion of linear time and space (cf. *La Prose du Transsibérien*). Unsurprisingly, the metaphors used to describe these artistic experiments were, more often than not, musical. Bergson himself, in his doctoral thesis *Time and Free Will*, had used music as an analogy for pure duration, i.e., time as we actually experience it (as opposed to the mechanistic time of space, which can be divided into disparate chunks), which "forms both the past and the present states into an organic whole, as happens when we recall the notes of a tune, melting, so to speak, into one another" (Bergson 1913/2001: 100). But it is his 'symphonic' metaphor that was most influential in simultaneist aesthetics. Bergson had compared the complex simultaneous mental processes of the brain to a 'symphony' orchestrating together the various strands of our experiences of life: 'Cerebral activity is to spiritual activity what the movements of the conductor's baton are to the symphony. Just as the symphony is bigger than the sum total of its movements, spiritual life goes beyond the cerebral life.'[35] (1919: 50) But it was not until Autant and Lara's experimental performances

---

35   "L'activité cérébrale est à l'activité mentale ce que les mouvements du bâton du chef d'orchestre sont à la symphonie. La symphonie dépasse de tous côtés les mouvements qui la scandent; la vie de l'esprit déborde de même la vie cérébrale."

that these simultaneist theories found their way into the performance space of live theatre, taking the musical metaphor one step further by developing a musical approach to the spoken word itself in performance. Germinet comments that their *Douzième coup* is an example of a work which 'brings together nearly all the possibilities of vocal simultaneism.' (1937: 3)[36] Only with the advent of radio did their methods find their true potential:

> One could say that simultaneism, as a whole, brings to life the poetics demanded by the microphone. Nothing is more tedious than a broadcast recitation. The art of the ear demands symphonic forms. It is the kingdom of voices. More than any other, it can accommodate sound planes which simultaneism has given poetry [...]. Is not simultaneism that synthetic art which was so often looked for but not found? Lyrical architecture, verbal symphony, theatre of space'.[37] (Larronde qtd. in Corvin 1976: 222f.)

The symphonic effects that Autant and Lara developed were also informed by the notion that our senses were connected through synaesthesia, i.e., that we can hear colours and see music. Synaesthesia was a constant preoccupation of radiophonic writers who felt that they needed to compensate for the absence of actual visual cues by using sound to evoke colours and shading – Germinet himself prefaced his theory of radiophonic plays with a quotation from Wagner as he referred to Tristan's words from *Tristan und Isolde*: "I hear light."[38] (1926: 23) Quoting the film critic Paul Ramain, Germinet argued that 'we have, in fact, in music an example of this power of suggestion by means of the ear. Does not [music] "suggest for many people fast visual images, more or less distinct, and with a constant mobility"?'[39] (1926: 23)

---

36   "réunit presque toutes les possibilités du simultanéisme vocal".
37   "On peut dire que le simultanéisme, dans son ensemble, réalise la poétique exigée par le micro. Rien de plus vite lassant qu'une récitation diffusée. L'art de l'oreille veut des formes symphoniques. C'est le royaume des voix. Mieux qu'aucun autre, il s'accommode des plans sonores dont le simultanéisme a doté la poésie [...]. Est-ce que le simultanéisme ne serait-il pas l'art synthétique, si souvent cherché, jamais trouvé? Architecture lyrique, symphonie verbale, théâtre d'espace."
38   "J'entends la lumière". Germinet significantly quotes this as a statement rather than the original question as it is spoken by Richard Wagner's *Tristan and Isolde*, Act 3, Scene 2: "Wie, hör' ich das Licht?" ('What, do I hear the light?')
39   "Nous avons, d'ailleurs, dans la musique, un exemple de ce pouvoir de suggestion par l'ouïe. Celle-ci 'ne crée-t-elle pas chez beaucoup, des images visuelles plus ou moins rapides, plus ou moins nettes, et une constante mobilité'?"

Autant and Lara had worked on a theory of vowels and colours inspired by René Ghil's theories on "correspondences" (using Baudelaire's term), not only matching vowel sounds to colouristic effects, as Rimbaud had done in his poem *Voyelles*, but also to instrumental timbres: 'A black, organs; E white, harps; I blue, violins; O red, brass; U yellow, flutes'[40] (Ghil qtd. in Corvin 1976: 213). Autant, inspired by Ghil, based his own set of correspondences on Jean-Pierre Rousselot's (1846–1924) scientific approach to phonetics, which attributed specific frequencies to vowels, matching the frequencies of notes to those of the vowels. Finally, he also matched instrumental timbres to the spoken vowels. The frequency of the sound 'A' corresponding, for example, to the colour black and the note A sharp above middle C, played on the French horn, whilst 'O' was blue and corresponded to the B flat below middle C, played on the cello, and the 'I' was red and corresponded to an A sharp two octaves above middle C, played on the flute (cf. Corvin 1976: 215). This approach was similarly used in the performance of *Le Douzième coup*, Autant and Lara having associated voice tones with both vocal and instrumental timbres, thus creating not only a musical but a potentially synaesthetic symphony of voices:

> This laugh, uninterrupted, covers the same scale, descending this time.
> Phonetically, this gives, broadly speaking: o, a, é, i, – i, é, a, o.
> Musically: do, mi, sol, ti – ti, sol, mi, do.
> Then one hears, in unison:
> The laugh of the men on 'o' in the lower register
> of the adolescents on 'a' in a trumpeting register
> of the women on 'é' in a high register
> of the children on 'i' in a piping register.[41] (Larronde 1936: 11)

These theories informed their choices of high and low voices, and the repetitions, patterns and echolalia of the words and phrases in the text, as well as the use of vocal and instrumental shading. Such an 'orchestration' of the voices

---

40   "A noir, les orgues; E blanc, les harpes; I bleu, les violons; O rouge, les cuivres; U jaune, les flûtes."

41   "Ce rire, ininterrompu, parcourt la même gamme, descendante cette fois. Phonétiquement, cela donne, à peu près: o, a, é, i – i, é, a, o.

> Musicalement: do, mi, sol, si – si, sol, mi, do.
> Puis on entend, à l'unisson:
> Les rires graves en 'o' des hommes.
> claironnants, en 'a' des adolescents
> aigus en 'é' des femmes
> flûtés, en 'i' des enfants."

made complete sense within the context of early radio, as one of the major issues encountered in wireless performance was not only in seeking out 'radiogenic' voices, whose timbre carried well on microphone, but in differentiating identities in a dialogue between several characters, as was often the case in a radio play. This is why Deharme had called for a similar technique in 1928, describing the use of "vocal masks" in his *Proposition d'un art radiophonique* (Deharme 1928/2009: 409). Larronde not only divided up and enmeshed the strands of dialogue, but also used variations in rhythm, timbre and pitch to create a polyphony of spoken voices. To support the vocal architecture, each character was furthermore given a specific vocal 'shadowing' by one or more singers, who doubled each character in a technique called *sous-jacente* (i.e., 'underlying' vocal shadowing). The instrumental music itself was woven into the texture as individual instruments and sounds were associated with the different situations. Starting with the spoken voice, *sous-jacente* techniques and some *plain-chant* (i.e., monodic unmeasured chanting) in the opening scenes, the instrumental music gradually becomes more present as we move from the counterpoint of the builder's chorus to the modern-day evocations, brought to life through a moving backdrop of musical pieces.

Le Douzième coup enacts a tongue-in-cheek history of the first decade of radio plays, featuring a fly-on-the-wall stereophonic microphone reminiscent of Walter Ruttmann's 1928 pioneering radio work *Wochenende* (which was well known in France at the time as it had been broadcast on French radio), a parody of the shipwreck scene in Germinet and Cusy's *Maremoto*,[42] and a nod towards the technological flaws of radio itself when the microphone appears to fail at one point,[43] Larronde writing: 'we will have, from the radiophonic perspective, the impression of an interference'[44] (1936: 79). The work also enacts the paradigm shift it announced: from the focus on the spoken voice with musical and sound accompaniment at the beginning towards a fully integrated and musical/vocal soundtrack at the end, prefiguring Schaeffer's radiophonic creations and the future of radio plays.

5   *Le Douzième coup de minuit* in the Press

Le Douzième coup de minuit's potential to change the sonic culture of the day was noted by many of the critics: 'The experiment appears to have disoriented

---

42   Cf. 'The Fishermen', Scene 2, Part 1 (Larronde 1936: 21–23).
43   In the transition between scenes 9 and 10 of Part 2 (Larronde 1936: 79).
44   "On aura, au point de vue radiophonique, l'impression d'une interférence."

the public', wrote the radio journalist and critic Pierre Descaves in the leading French literary journal of the time, *Les Nouvelles littéraires*, on hearing the first broadcast, 'but it did not deceive any of us who follow radiophonic productions as to the value and scope of such an experiment'[45] (1934: [9]). Arnaud, writing in the influential political and literary weekly newspaper, *Marianne*, found that the work was 'extraordinarily original, because this "orchestral poem" presents itself as a symphony of voices, drama with spoken choruses, a radiophonic oratorio'[46] (1934: 5). *Ric Rac's* critic, though complaining of the technical issues inherent in radio broadcasts of the time, which meant that 'certain passages came across in such a confused manner that we lost the thread of the play', conceded that the work 'still allowed us to note the progress made recently'[47] (A.P. 1934: 6). It is the literary critic of *Cyrano* who showed the most enthusiasm and found in *Le Douzième coup* a visionary radiophonic work, stating that

> an art form is being born, if not under our eyes, then to our ears, and who is taking notice? Radio, which could be a marvellous means of intellectual broadcast and artistic elevation, radio which burbles on through the voices of its all too familiar speakers, and which turns away its listeners through boring lecturers, which depresses the mind by its floods of stupidities, radio which overwhelms us with theatrical plays, has despite all this, accomplished a miracle. It has reconciled the poets with the spoken voice, listeners with Orpheus.
>
> This miracle – truth be told – is only just beginning. Very few of the sound producers and heads of stations have understood that a new means of expression should be the answer to the technology and its potential. [...] Mr. Carlos Larronde is a poet. As such, he has completely understood

---

45 "Au théâtre radiophonique français, M Carlos Larronde vient d'apporter une œuvre neuve et forte; pour la première fois, nous venons d'avoir de la 'radiophonie pure'. L'essai a paru désorienter le public: il n'a trompé aucun de ceux qui suivent la production radiophonique actuelle sur la valeur et la portée d'une telle tentative."

46 "Et ce thème singulier a trouvé une expression fort originale, car ce 'poème orchestral' se présente, sous forme d'une symphonie de voix, d'un théâtre avec chœurs parlés, d'un orario [sic] radiophonique."

47 "Il faut reconnaître que plusieurs scènes furent particulièrement réussies, malheureusement, certains passages nous parvinrent d'une façon tellement confuse qu'on perdait un peu le fil. [...] Si l'émission du *Douzième coup de minuit* ne nous a pas apporté le grand chef-d'œuvre du théâtre radiophonique, elle nous a tout de même permis de constater les progrès faits depuis quelque temps."

that the microphone gives him, as well as an immense audience, everything which had up to then been impossible on stage: the mystery, the dreams, the intimate alliance between voice and music, the birth of a verbal polyphony, the free play of lyricism and pure eloquence: a form of poetry which the directors of the Parisian theatres had refused to know anything about.[48] (Quasimodo 1936: 29)

However, many critics voiced misgivings about the general accessibility and impact of *Le Douzième coup*, reflecting the broader controversy around the aims of public radio. Jean Antoine, writing in *L'Intransigeant* four days after the first broadcast, had had a feeling of 'complete satisfaction in how the words, rhythm and sound come together or are strangely juxtaposed, creating a euphoria in the listener',[49] but he was doubtful that listeners would be able to follow and appreciate such experimental work. He cited the familiar dichotomy between traditional theatre and this new form of 'theatre for the blind', as it was then commonly described, such radiophonic experiments being 'more difficult to follow for a listener than for a spectator in a theatre. We wish to be given the chance to learn and we feel that we are led on a bit too quickly'[50] (1933: 7). For these critics, the work was undoubtedly groundbreaking, but unsuitable for

---

48   "Un art est en train de naître, sinon sous nos yeux, du moins à nos oreilles, et qui s'en aperçoit? La radio, qui pourrait être un merveilleux instrument de diffusion intellectuelle et d'élévation artistique, la radio qui balbutie par la voix des speakers trop familiers, qui détourne l'auditeur par l'organe de conférenciers trop ternes, qui décourage l'esprit par les flots de stupidités dont elle nous abreuve, la radio qui nous accable de théâtre, a pourtant accompli un miracle. Elle a réconcilié les poètes avec la voix, le public avec Orphée. Ce miracle – à vrai dire – ne fait que commencer. Rares sont les 'metteurs en ondes' et les chefs de station qui ont compris qu'un mode d'expression nouveau devait répondre à une technique, à des possibilités nouvelles. M. Carlos Larronde est de ceux-là et si je vous parle de lui c'est qu'il vient de réunir en un volume les deux pièces de son Théâtre Invisible, préparées précisément pour la radio. Car M. Carlos Larronde est un poète. Il a très bien compris, comme tel, que le micro mettait à sa disposition, outre un public immense, tout ce qui avait jusqu'alors paru impossible à la scène: le mystère, le rêve, l'alliance intime de la voix à la musique, la naissance d'une polyphonie verbale, le libre jeu du lyrisme et de l'éloquence pure: la poésie, enfin, telle que les directeurs de théâtres bien parisiens refusaient de la connaître."
49   "Lors de l'audition du *Douzième coup de minuit* [...], nous avons retrouvé cette curieuse sensation faite de satisfaction complète parce que texte, rythme et son s'unissent ou se juxtaposent étrangement, créant l'euphorie chez l'auditeur."
50   "Des essais de ce genre sont plus difficiles à suivre pour un auditeur que pour le spectateur d'une salle. Nous réclamons le droit de faire nos classes et nous pensons qu'on a peut-être tendance à nous mener un peu trop vite."

the form of mass entertainment which radio had become. To counter this, Paul Dermée, who had been one of radio's early champions and who had wished for a new radiophonic art form, called, on hearing *Le Douzième coup*, 'for the creation of a *radio-theatre laboratory* open to researchers, and the broadcast, one hour a week, or an experimental radiophonic theatre'[51] featuring 'works that *cannot be played on a stage*'[52] (1937: 69). Responding to the controversy caused by the broadcast of Larronde, Honegger, Lara and Autant's work in the leading cultural newspaper of the time, *Comoedia*, Dermée wrote,

> *can* a leading radio station broadcast *experimental projects*? We have just indeed heard *Le Douzième coup de minuit*, an orchestral poem by M. Carlos Larronde, with music by Arthur Honegger. The work was produced by the Compagnie 'Art et Action', under the direction of Mrs. Lara and Mr. Autant. We know that 'Art et Action' is a theatrical laboratory. However, normally, its experiments are only presented to a few spectators who are already *au fait* with all the audacious research and experiments. And Mr. Carlos Larronde is one of these spectators and collaborators of 'Art et Action'. And yet, here, radio drama – classified as *choreic* – is helping us to make new experiments, and to use the old techniques of 'Art et Action'. It is therefore what we could call an avant-garde production, an adjective which covers everything which is not ordinary, and which Radio-Paris exemplified the other night in *Le Douzième coup de minuit*.
>
> Is it a play? the author answers: 'it is more of a mystery, of which the action starts in a conventional medieval period to continue suddenly in the present day'. [...] The work is not easily accessible to a mass audience. We must admit that some of the more complex sections only came across as a sort of sonorous fog. We need to conclude that *Le Douzième coup de minuit* is not a show for several hundreds of thousands of radio listeners. [...] The oratorio of Larronde, Honegger, Lara and Autant is very rich, not only in its ambition but also in its production and the *means* it uses! There are in this work enough novelties, as much in the writing, as the diction and the movement of the voices, to feed 50 radio dramas! We are very pleased to have personally heard this sensational broadcast and we ask that the Directors of our Radio Stations should encourage the efforts going in this direction. But [...] such experimental theatre should

---

51 "nous demandons la création d'un *laboratoire de radio-théâtre* largement ouvert à tous les chercheurs, et la diffusion une heure par semaine, d'un théâtre de recherches et d'innovations radiophoniques".

52 "des œuvres qui ne pourront être jouées sur une scène".

not be imposed on all the French listeners en masse. We need to create an *experimental radio station*. I propose that it is broadcast from the Tour Eiffel at 206 metres.[53] (1934a: 4)

Descaves, though really interested in Larronde and Lara's vocal experiments, did not understand Honegger's concept of what we could call today a 'soundtrack', which Descaves described as a "commentary" of "supporting music", stating that

> the latest production of Mr. Carlos Larronde has allowed us to make some interesting remarks regarding the 'supporting music', which our radio producers feel is a necessary ornament to their presentations. Without taking anything away from the intrinsic value of the music of Mr. Arthur Honegger, we feel obliged to admit that, though suitably spaced out, this [musical] commentary was perhaps useless. A radiophonic play worthy of the name should support that music be interrupted. If the interweaving of the rhythms of the voices is authentic, it makes its own music. [...]

---

[53] "un grand poste émetteur *peut-il* diffuser des *auditions expérimentales*? Nous venons justement d'entendre *Le Douzième coup de minuit*, poème orchestral de M. Carlos Larronde, avec musique d'Arthur Honegger. L'œuvre fut réalisée par la Compagnie 'Art et Action', sous la direction de Mme. Lara et de M. Autant. On sait que 'Art et Action' est un véritable laboratoire de théâtre. Mais, d'ordinaire, ses essais, qui sont parfois de remarquables réalisations, ne sont présentés qu'à quelques centaines de spectateurs particulièrement au courant de toutes les recherches, et des plus audacieuses. Et M. Carlos Larronde compte parmi les collaborateurs et spectateurs les plus assidues d'"Art et Action'. Or, voici que le théâtre du micro – classé dans le genre *choréique*, – permet de faire de nouvelles expériences, comme d'utiliser des expériences anciennes d'"Art et Action'. C'est donc ce qu'on appelle un spectacle d'avant-garde, épithète qui couvre tout ce qui sort du banal, que Radio-Paris nous a diffusé l'autre soir, sous les espèces du *Douzième coup de minuit*. Une pièce? l'auteur nous répond: 'un mystère plutôt, dont l'action commence dans un moyen âge de convention pour se continuer soudain en pleine vie moderne.' [...] L'œuvre n'est pas aisément accessible au grand public. Avouons, d'ailleurs, que certaines parties trop touffues, trop riches de significations, ne nous apparurent que sous forme d'un brouillard sonore. Aussi devons-nous conclure que *Le Douzième coup de minuit* n'est pas un spectacle pour plusieurs centaines de milliers de sans-filistes. [...] L'oratorio de Larronde, Honegger, Lara et Autant est extrêmement riche, non seulement d'intentions mais de réalisations et surtout de *moyens*! Il y a dans cette œuvre assez de nouveautés, tant dans l'écriture que dans la diction et dans le mouvement des voix pour nourrir cinquante radio-drames! C'est dire que nous sommes heureux personnellement d'avoir entendu cette diffusion sensationelle, et que nous demandons à la Direction de notre Radio-diffusion d'encourager largement tous les efforts qui s'orienteront dans ce sens. Mais [...] le théâtre-hot ne doit pas être imposé à tous les auditeurs français, à la masse. Il va donc falloir créer une *station d'expériences*. Je propose que ce soit la Tour Eiffel sur 206 mètres."

> Indeed music is still necessary in adaptations of literature, but radiophonic theatre should endeavour to liberate itself from it. We hope that Mr. Larronde can make a broadcast of his *Douze coups de minuit* [sic] after having abandoned the musical elements.[54] (1934a: 9)

6   Conclusion: the Transmedial Metamorphosis of the Radio Play

The fact that the text of *Le Douzième coup de minuit*, not the score or performance materials, was eventually published by Larronde in a book titled *Théâtre invisible* highlights the lingering paradox which underpinned the early radio plays of the period: was this work literary or musical, a play with music or an orchestral poem with words? Germinet was later to describe this work's aural ambivalence as the 'artistic decomposition of sound'[55] (qtd. in Todd 1935/2002: 236). Larronde himself focuses on the suggestive qualities of his work in his preface to the first edition of the text in 1936, bringing together words and music under the heading of poetry in a fully integrated conception of radiophonic broadcasting that would transcend established genres. He states that

> we should not consider the listeners as being blind. They are something else. They are 'super-listeners'. Let us give them everything that the ear, the most subtle and internal of senses, can receive of lyricism, of dream or of evocation. Let us make them SEE.[56] (1936: v)

---

54 "la dernière production de M. Carlos Larronde nous a également permis de nous livrer à d'intéressantes constatations en ce qui concerne la 'musique de soutien', dont nos metteurs en onde se croient obligés d'agrémenter leurs présentations. Sans rien retirer à la valeur intrinsèque de la musique de M. Arthur Honegger, nous sommes obligés de convenir que, bien qu'espacé, ce commentaire était peut-être inutile. Une pièce radiophonique digne de ce nom doit supporter que la musique y soit interrompue. Si l'engendrement des voix et des rythmes est authentique, il se crée sa propre musique. C'est dans l'accord de la forme et à sa vitesse propre que la radiophonie doit chercher son suprême accompagnement. Certes, la musique est encore indispensable à toutes les adaptations de la littérature, le théâtre radiophonique pur doit facilement s'en libérer, dans ce domaine. On souhaite que Mr. Carlos Larronde puisse faire une émission de ses *Douze coups de minuit* [sic] en abandonnant la partie musicale."

55 "la décomposition artistique du son".

56 "Non, il ne faut pas considérer les auditeurs comme des aveugles. Ils sont autre chose. Ils sont des 'sur-auditifs'. Sachons leur donner tout ce que l'ouïe, le sens subtil et intérieur par excellence, peut accueillir de lyrisme, de rêve ou d'évocation. Sachons en faire des VOYANTS."

This conception of radiophonic art could be said to have found a catalyst in radiophonic experiments such as *Le Douzième coup* in the early 1930s, a work I would argue is transmedial *par excellence*.

A transmedial work is defined by its condition of medial evolution or metamorphosis: it is a work no longer literary nor, in this case, quite yet musical. It is not a work in which music and text are merely juxtaposed in the multimedial sense, nor is it purely intermedial in its radiophonic essence, inasmuch as neither literature nor music is the dominant medium which governs the principles of the other. It is a work defined by its inherent state of medial flux and therefore impossible to categorise within pre-radio medial frameworks. By confronting head-on established theatrical and musical paradigms, Larronde, Honegger, Autant and Lara articulated in this seminal work an emergent transmedial conception of sonic art at a time when radio remained primarily a vehicle for old forms. As the early radiophonic play visionary Paul Deharme stated: 'Because of its conventional associations, the word "theatre" should be crossed out from the radiophonic vocabulary.'[57] (1930: 22) Radio, in particular, was seen to be a vector of transmedial metamorphosis, leading Jean Tardieu to argue that new 'technical means, as they take over from the fundamental and traditional art forms, are led not only to transmit them and to translate them, but to metamorphose them more or less deeply, more or less quickly'[58] (1957: 180).

The lack of notation and the often improvisatory or ad hoc nature of the musical soundscape performances of the radio plays in the 1920s and 1930s were partly due to the ephemeral conception of the genre by the very people involved in its development. This was compounded by the fact that the musical potential of radio play composition was not really promoted from within the musical community. Another element which contributed to the dearth of archives was that the composers themselves had trouble getting paid a suitable fee when it came to the composition, rehearsal and broadcasting of their radio play music, especially when this concerned the more large-scale compositions (cf. Dermée 1934b: 4; Larronde 1939: 4). The scarcity of archival materials has meant that many of the performance practices have been lost. The innovations and the particular archival status within radio play history of

---

57 "Il faudrait en raison de son contenu conventionnel rayer le mot théâtre du vocabulaire radiophonique."

58 "Les moyens techniques – en particulier la radio – lorsqu'ils prennent la succession des arts fondamentaux et traditionnels, sont amenés non seulement à transmettre ceux-ci et à les traduire, mais encore à les métamorphoser plus ou moins profondément et plus ou moins vite."

Le Douzième coup help us to nuance current approaches to transmediality by directing our attention towards the legacy of the elusive genre of radiophonic plays of the 1930s, elusive precisely because it *is* transmedial and we lack the vocabulary, even today, to apprehend it. The wider implications and the legacy of Larronde, Honegger, Autant and Lara's work in part arise from their synthesis of approaches taken not only from early radiophonic theories and policies, but also derive from the much wider cultural and aesthetic debates arising in the fields of modernist literature and music derived from new insights into human psychology and the workings of memory, the avant-garde theories and practices of the Futurist, Dadaist and Surrealist artists and poets, as well as the changing landscape of experimental theatrical performance practices during the first decades of the twentieth century.

What established Schaeffer's *musique concrète* and acousmatic theories so successfully a decade later, was precisely the fact that he had found an entirely new terminology to apply to the techniques which had evolved out of the radio plays of the 1930s and in particular from Honegger, Larronde, Autant and Lara's collaboration on *Le Douzième coup*. It is undeniable that the first two decades of radio plays drove a real paradigm shift from a traditional text-based and visual performance model to a sound-based, poetic and musical conception of radio theatre in France, opening the way not only to an emerging acousmatic radiophonic model which was to put on the same level words, music and sound, but also to a new acousmatic musical style at the dawn of the invention of the electroacoustic technologies which were to redefine musical composition in the 1950s. Indeed, Paul-Louis Mignon, radio producer and critic who had worked with Jean Tardieu in those early years of the Club d'Essai argued that

> the balance between text and music was our preoccupation. Which is why we brought together, not from a text but from a particular topic or a scenario given to us by a writer, a composer and a sound director. They would elaborate the radiophonic work in a progressive collaboration.[59] (qtd. in Prot 2010)

The underestimated music of the radio plays of the 1930s extended an influence well beyond the domain of radio theatre to touch upon broader discourses on media and listening.

---

59 "L'équilibre du texte et de la musique était notre préoccupation. C'est pourquoi nous avons réuni, non à partir d'un texte, mais d'un sujet ou d'un scénario fourni par un auteur, un compositeur et un metteur en ondes. Ils élaboraient l'œuvre radiophonique dans une collaboration progressive."

Taking his cue from Larronde, Honegger, Autant and Lara, Schaeffer, when setting up a school of radio in 1942, argued against what he described as the 'easy solution which proposes adaptations more or less suitable for theatre or the concert platform'[60] and the 'techniques, also disappointing, of a naturalism or realism which the commonplaces of radio have already done a thousand times'[61] (qtd. in Le Bail and Kaltenecker 2012: 30). It was to Honegger and Schmitt, who had both composed for the radio, that he turned to adjudicate his new radiophonic competition in July 1942. Only this time round, unlike in 1924, many experimental radiophonic works had a radiophonic space in which to be tested, finding a home in Schaeffer and Tardieu's new radiophonic laboratory, which their predecessor, Paul Dermée, had clamoured for in the late 1930s and which he was now a part of. One of the works to come out of this venture, which included spoken voice, noise, music and radiophonic tropes, was 'an immense radiophonic opera' (Schaeffer 1949/1970: 89), *La Coquille à planètes*, written by Schaeffer with music by Claude Arrieu, a composer who was very much familiar with the early techniques and aesthetics of radio art since she had worked as a radiophonic *metteuse en onde* for French national radio between 1936 and 1941. This 'fantasy suite for one voice and twelve monsters'[62] was recorded in 1943 and broadcast as eight 1-hour episodes in 1948. Schaeffer and Arrieu had conceived of the work as a true radiophonic experiment, a 'series of études, without any preconceived subject, without any thought for literary style, written only as a pretext to take apart the radiophonic techniques, at different speeds, from slow-motion to fast-forward, from simple to complex'[63] (Schaeffer qtd. in Brunet 1969: 94). These experiments led Schaeffer to start thinking of sound *per se* as an *objet sonore*, theories of sound that he would develop and put into practice over the next two decades. By leading the way to Schaeffer and Arrieu's revolutionary aesthetics of sound, *Le Douzième coup* marked a veritable paradigm shift in the early 1930s, from vision to sound, from representation to suggestion, from spectatorship to imagination, from externalisation to internalisation, from illusion to reality, and from embodied appearance to disembodied presence in a move towards a purely acousmatic aesthetic experience of music.

---

60 "la solution facile qui consisterait à proposer des adaptations plus ou moins appropriées d'œuvres écrites pour la scène ou le concert".
61 "les procédés, également décevants, d'un naturalisme ou d'un surréalisme avec lesquels les lieux communs de la radio ont déjà été mille fois traités".
62 "suite fantastique pour une voix et douze monstres".
63 "une suite d'études, sans sujet préconçu, sans souci littéraire, à seule fin de donner, dans différentes allures, du ralenti à l'accéléré, du simple au complexe, des occasions de démonter les mécanismes radiophoniques".

References

Antoine, Jean (1930a online). "Simple histoire". *L'Intransigeant*, 22 February: 8. https://gallica.bnf.fr/ark:/12148/bpt6k792841c/f8.item [19/04/2021].

Antoine, Jean (1930b online). "L'Affaire Florent Schmitt". *L'Intransigeant*, 24 February: 7. https://gallica.bnf.fr/ark:/12148/bpt6k792844h/f7.item [19/04/2021].

Antoine, Jean (1933 online). "Notes d'écoute". *L'intransigeant*, 31 December: 7. https://gallica.bnf.fr/ark:/12148/bpt6k7942493/f7.item [19/04/2021].

Arnaud (1934 online). "*Le douzième coup de minuit*". *Marianne*, 24 January: 5. https://gallica.bnf.fr/ark:/12148/bpt6k7642397x/f5.item [19/04/2021].

A.P. (1934 online). "La T.S.F. Théâtre et publicité". *Ric Rac*, 6 January: 6. https://gallica.bnf.fr/ark:/12148/bpt6k5505277o/f8.item [19/04/2021].

Bennet, Christophe (2010). *La musique à la radio dans les années trente*. Paris: L'Harmattan.

Bennet, Christophe (2015). "The Genre of Opera and the Disaffection of French Composers in Favor of the Emerging Genres: The Case of Radio in the Thirties". HAL Archives-Ouvertes. https://halshs.archives-ouvertes.fr/halshs-01146558 [19/04/2021].

Bergson, Henri (1913/2001). *Time and Free Will: An Essay on the Immediate Data of Consciousness*. Frank Lubecki Pogson, transl. New York: Dover.

Bergson, Henri (1919). *L'Energie spirituelle*. Paris: Libraire Félix Alkan.

Birdsall, Carolyn (2013). "Sonic Artefacts: Reality Codes of Urbanity in Early German Radio Documentary". Karin Bijsterveld, ed. *Soundscapes of the Urban Past: Staged Sound as Mediated Cultural Heritage*. Bielefeld: transcript. 129–168.

Birkenmaier, Anke (2009a). "From Surrealism to Popular Art: Paul Deharme's Radio Theory". *Modernism/modernity* 16/2: 357–374.

Birkenmaier, Anke (2009b). "Introduction to Paul Deharme: Proposition for a Radiophonic Art". *Modernism/modernity* 16/2: 403–413.

Brunet, Sophie (1969). *Pierre Schaeffer*. Paris: La Revue Musicale.

Cazenave, Elizabeth, Caroline Ulmann-Mauriat (1995). *Presse, radio et télévision en France de 1631 à nos jours*. Paris: Hachette.

Chénetier-Alev, Marion (2019 online). "Les archives radiophoniques du théâtre. Du théâtre pour les aveugles à un théâtre de sourds?" *Revue Sciences/Lettres* 6: 403–413. http://journals.openedition.org/rsl/1843 [19/04/2021].

Cœuroy, André (1930). *Panorama de la radio*. 6th ed. Paris: Editions Kra.

Cohen, Andréa (2009 online). "Les Compositeurs et l'art radiophonique". *Groupe de Recherches et d'études sur la radio*. January. http://www.grer.fr/article.php?id_article=69 [10/12/2019].

Corvin, Michel (1976). *Le Théâtre de recherche entre les deux guerres – Le laboratoire art et action. Théâtre années vingt*. Lausanne: Éditions L'Âge d'Homme.

Dambly, Paul (1930 online). "Çançunik". *Le Petit Journal*, 19 February: 7. https://gallica.bnf.fr/ark:/12148/bpt6k632065f [19/04/2021].

Deharme, Paul (1928/2009). *Proposition for a Radiophonic Art*. Anke Birkenmaier, transl. *Modernism/modernity* 16/2: 406–413.

Deharme, Paul (1930). *Pour un art radiophonique*. Paris: Le Rouge et le Noir.

Dermée, Paul (1934a online). "Jazz-hot et théâtre experimental". *Comoedia*, 5 January: 4. https://gallica.bnf.fr/ark:/12148/bpt6k76478605/f4.item [19/04/2021].

Dermée, Paul (1934b online). "Cusy et Germinet les Précurseurs". *Comoedia*, 2 February: 4. https://gallica.bnf.fr/ark:/12148/bpt6k76478887/f4.item. [19/04/2021].

Dermée, Paul (1937). "Les Problèmes de l'art radiophonique". *La Revue Musicale*, June-July: 65–70.

Descaves, Pierre (1934 online). "Les 12 coups de minuit". *Les Nouvelles littéraires*, 17 February: [9]. https://gallica.bnf.fr/ark:/12148/bpt6k64521668/f9.item [19/04/2021].

Descaves, Pierre (1939 online). *Les Disciples*. Archival material. https://gallica.bnf.fr/ark:/12148/btv1b105073960 [19/04/2021].

Dumesnil, René (1933 online). "Musique". *Mercure de France* 44/842: 454–460. https://gallica.bnf.fr/ark:/12148/bpt6k202164t/f208.item [19/04/2021].

Durbec, Sylvie (1996). *La voix radiophonique ou le mythe de Schéhérazade*. PhD Thesis. Univ. Lumière Lyon II. Unpublished.

Duval, René (1979). *Histoire de la radio en France*. Paris: Alain Moreau.

Etiveaud, Raymond (1937 online). "Le Théâtre". *La Vie Limousine*, 25 March: 639–640. https://gallica.bnf.fr/ark:/12148/bpt6k65531306/f9.item [19/04/2021].

Germinet, Gabriel (1926). *Théâtre radiophonique – mode nouveau d'expression artistique*. Paris: Chiron.

Germinet, Gabriel (1937 online). "Une chorale dramatique". *Le Front*, 11 February: 3. https://gallica.bnf.fr/ark:/12148/bpt6k5603850i/f3.item [19/04/2021].

Héron, Pierre-Marie (2010). "Fictions hybrides à la radio". *Le Temps des médias* 14: 85–97.

Hubermont, Pierre (1935 online). "Le jeu radiophonique en Belgique". *Les Nouvelles littéraires*, 6 April: 6. https://gallica.bnf.fr/ark:/12148/bpt6k6452225p/f7.item [19/04/ 2021].

Huth, Arno (1937 online). "L'Art du micro". *Le Ménestrel*, 1 October: 257–258. https://gallica.bnf.fr/ark:/12148/bpt6k5618238b/f3.item [19/04/2021].

Kane, Brian (2014). *Sound Unseen: Acousmatic Sound in Theory and Practice*. Oxford: OUP.

Karel, Albert, Jean Noceti (1938 online). "13° Partitions 'Standard'". *Compte rendu des travaux du Premier Congrès International d'Art Radiophonique*. Paris: Bureau International d'Art Radiophonique. https://gallica.bnf.fr/ark:/12148/bpt6k3162296 [19/04/2021].

Landowski, W.-L. (1939 online). "Nouvelle Pièces radiophoniques". *Le Ménestrel*, 14 July: 193–195. https://gallica.bnf.fr/ark:/12148/bpt6k5617018k [19/04/2021].

Larronde, Carlos (1931a). *L'Art cosmique et l'oeuvre musical de Rita Strohl*. Paris: Denoël & Steele.

Larronde, Carlos (1936). *Théâtre invisible. Le douzième coup de minuit – Le chant des sphères*. Paris: Denoël & Steele.

Larronde, Carlos (1939 online). "Notule". *L'Intransigeant*, 18 February: 4. https://gallica.bnf.fr/ark:/12148/bpt6k796117j/f4.item [19/04/2021].

Lautour, Reuben de (2017). "Inaudible Visitors: Theories of Sound Reproduction in the Studio Practice of Pierre Schaeffer". *Organised Sound* 22/2: 161–171.

L.B. (1937 online). "Musiques écrites pour le Microphone". *L'Ouest-Éclair*, 15 October: 5. https://gallica.bnf.fr/ark:/12148/bpt6k6610456/f5.item [19/04/2021].

Le Bail, Karine, Martin Kaltenecker (2012). "Jalons". *Pierre Schaeffer. Les constructions impatientes*. Paris: CNRS Editions. 9–65.

Méadel, Cécile (1991). "Les images sonores. Naissance du théâtre radiophonique". *Techniques et culture*. Éditions de la Maison des sciences de l'homme, no. 16 (July–December): 135–160.

Méadel, Cécile (1992). "Une pièce radiophonique de Pierre Cusy et Gabriel Germinet (1924)". *Réseaux* 10/52: 77–78.

Mic Mac (1938 online). "Entrée par une oreille ... et sortie par l'autre". *Ce soir*, 3 January: 9. https://gallica.bnf.fr/ark:/12148/bpt6k7635201b/f9.item [19/04/2021].

Morin, Emilie (2014). "Beckett's Speaking Machines: Sound, Radiophonics and Acousmatics". *Modernism/modernity* 21/1: 1–24.

Neulander, Joelle (2009). *Programming National Identity: The Culture of Radio In 1930s France*. Baton Rouge, LA: Louisiana State Univ. Press.

Paquette, Morgane (2015 online). "Les débuts de la musique radiophonique. Du Studio d'essai au Service des illustrations de la RTF". *Réseau Canopé*. https://www.reseau-canope.fr/tailleferre/documents/pdf/06_Debuts_Musique_Radiophonique.pdf [19/04/2021].

Prot, Robert (2010 online). "Jean Tardieu et le théâtre à la radio". *Jean Tardieu. Des livres et des voix*. Lyon: ENS Éditions. http://books.openedition.org/enseditions/4810 [19/04/2021].

Quasimodo (1936). "En marge des 'Six Jours'". *Cyrano*, 9 October: 29. https://gallica.bnf.fr/ark:/12148/bpt6k5595774z/f29.item. [19/04/2021].

R.C. (1943). "Théâtre, ou Film radiophonique?" *Le Journal*, 2 September: 4. https://gallica.bnf.fr/ark:/12148/bpt6k7632923d/f4.item [19/04/2021].

Schaeffer, Pierre (1942/1990). *Propos sur* La Coquille. *Notes sur l'expression radiophonique*. Arles: Editions Phonurgia Nova.

Schaeffer, Pierre (1949/1970). *Machines à communiquer 1. Genèse des simulacres*. Paris: Editions du Seuil.

Schaeffer, Pierre (1952). "Archives sonores: Le temps retrouvé". https://www.ina.fr/audio/PHZ03001361/archives-sonores-le-temps-retrouve-audio.html. Institut national de l'audiovisuel [19/04/2021].

Schaeffer, Pierre (1952/2012). *In Search of a Concrete Music*. Christine North, John Dack, transl. Berkeley: Univ. of California Press.

Schaeffer, Pierre (1966). *Traité des objets musicaux*. Paris: Seuil.

Tardieu, Jean (1957). "La radio créatrices d'œuvres lyriques". *Cahiers d'études de radio-télévision* 14: 177–180.

Todd, Christopher (1935/2002). "Gabriel Germinet and the '*Livre d'or du théâtre radiophonique français*' (1923–1935)". *Modern & Contemporary France* 10/2: 225–241.

Todd, Christopher (2007). *Carlos Larronde (1888–1940). Poète des ondes*. Paris: L'Harmattan.

Tomasi, Henri (1938 online). "12° Musique de scène". *Compte rendu des travaux du Premier Congrès International d'Art Radiophonique*. Paris: Bureau International d'Art Radiophonique. https://gallica.bnf.fr/ark:/12148/bpt6k3162296 [19/04/2021].

Weiss, Allen S. (1995). *Fantasmic Radio*. Durham, NC: Duke Univ. Press.

CHAPTER 3

Music in Radio Drama in the Netherlands: A Short History in Four Acts

Philomeen Lelieveldt

Abstract

This chapter gives an overview of almost a hundred years of live music production for radio drama in the Netherlands, beween 1924 and 2020. Not only high art forms such as literature, theatre and opera contributed to the development of radio drama as a multidisciplinary genre, but also light music stage formats such as (silent) cinema, vaudeville and revue. Authors, radio drama directors, composers, musicians and technicians collaborated using the available technical resources to stretch the acoustic and sound dimensions of the radio plays.

1 Prologue: Researching Music in Radio Drama

From the early days of radio, the medium took on the characteristics of many other genres. Radio not only absorbed literary, theatrical and musical formats, but also transformed these formats into radio-specific programmes in which music and sound played a substantial role, such as radio concerts, radio revues, radio operas and radio drama (see Bernaerts 2014; Huwiler 2016; Lelieveldt 2019b). Genre hybridity was inherent to radio drama (see Bernaerts 2017; Huwiler 2016; Krug 2009; Chignell 2019; McMurtry 2019) and resulted in a wide variety of roles for musicians and composers who contributed to this genre. The German and Dutch words for radio drama allow for a certain openness in the different formats that they encompass. Like the German word 'Hörspiel', the Dutch equivalents 'hoorspel' and 'luisterspel' (often abbreviated as 'spel' in radio guides) indicate both the activity of the listener (the act of 'hearing' or 'listening') and the activity of the performer, as in 'role playing' or 'playing' a piece of music. Huwiler elaborates on a third meaning of 'play' – that of 'game playing' – in the experiments with sound, text and other radiophonic means, from *Das neue Hörspiel* in Germany in the 1960s to the live radio drama music projects of Andreas Ammer in the 1990s (see Huwiler 2005, 2016; Mildorf 2021).

I myself have explored the radio drama experiments of poet and radio drama director Ab van Eyk between 1955 and 1992. In collaboration with musicians, composers, actors, writers and sound engineers, he crossed the borders of many disciplines, in both literary radio plays and text-sound art projects. He collaborated with European radio producers, composers and writers who produced *neue Hörspiele* in Germany. New genre formats and radio techniques, which were developed during these experiments, not only found expression in literary radio drama[1] but also in school plays for school radio and documentary radio plays about nonfiction topics, called 'klankbeelden' (sound images) or 'docudrama' (see Lelieveldt 2019b).

In musicological and literary scholarship on radio drama, we tend to focus on the unique artistic quality or literary aspects of the works. However, the most popular plays, which still resonate in public memory, were the entertainment plays or family plays, such as radio detective stories and radio musical comedies. These attracted large audiences in the golden years of radio drama, which for the Netherlands can be dated from the mid-1930s to the early 1960s. In this chapter, I will demonstrate that not only artistic criteria are relevant in the development of radio drama, but also aspects of form and storytelling that were inspired by light music stage formats such as (silent) cinema music, vaudeville and revue. The subgenre labels on the typescripts and musical scores in the Dutch archives show that many radio plays were based on the musical conventions of entertainment culture.[2] Because of the inconsistency in archival sources and historiographies used for this chapter, a 'back-and-forth' approach will be used to switch between a general overview of the development of music in radio drama and a more detailed account of specific plays that represent the introduction of new conventions in the way music was applied.

In the Netherlands between 1924 and 2019 more than twenty broadcasting organisations produced a total of at least 15,000 episodes of radio plays.[3] The

---

[1] Literary plays are specially written for radio or concern adaptations of novels, theatre plays and film scripts.

[2] Genre labels for radio plays with music were: 'muziekspel' (music play), 'musical', 'radio fantasie' (radio fantasy), 'radiofantasie in musicalvorm' (radio fantasy in musical form), 'hoorspel met muziek' (radio play with music), 'hoorspel-reportage' (radio play reportage), 'miniatuur revue' (miniature revue), 'vaudeville in miniatuur' (miniature vaudeville), 'radio comedie met muziek' (radio comedy with music). All translations in this chapter are by Carolyn Muntz, unless otherwise stated.

[3] Circa 13,500 typescripts of the period 1924–2002 are stored in the archives of The Netherlands Institute of Sound and Vision (Nederlands Instituut voor Beeld en Geluid). An unpublished Excel item list (*Plaatsingslijst hoorspelen, NRU/NOS/NOB,* inv.nr. 0302.01) is available

literary scholar Ineke Bulte was the first to explore a part of this immense radio drama heritage. In a ground-breaking dissertation, she analysed the structural and narrative characteristics of 'literary radio dramas' uniquely written for Dutch radio by Dutch authors between 1950 and 1980. She described how the four broadcasting organisations most involved in the genre, the VARA, AVRO, KRO and NCRV (see below) used the radio drama genre to express their religious and political identities. Bulte mentioned that some plays incorporated music, either as gramophone fragments or live music by Dutch composers, but she was not able to further explore their role (see Bulte 1990; Bulte 1984). The musicologist entering this research field is constrained by the fact that although at the time composers, musicians and sound engineers were given credits before and after the broadcasts, for several reasons their names have been lost or downplayed in radio historiographies and composers' biographies.

In the first place, many original recordings, especially of the period until the end of the 1960s, were destroyed, either because of scratches on the records or because of the high cost of early tapes, which resulted in their reuse for new recordings after the first or second broadcast.[4] Secondly, the names of musicians and composers are only rarely mentioned in the available typescripts. Thirdly, many radio guides and newspaper announcements only published the main details of the show (title, author, director, actors). Fourthly, as I will demonstrate below, many radio dramas employed live improvised music, so the broadcast (if preserved) is the only remnant of the musical performance. Lastly, composers themselves refrained from mentioning their radio drama activities in their oeuvre lists (*curricula vitae*), either because they considered these activities as 'applied' music writing or as a way of earning some (extra) money next to their autonomous work (see Lelieveldt 2019b).

However, the availability of digitised audio-visual collections through the Clariah Media Suite and the sheet music collections (www.muziekschatten.nl) of the broadcasting music centre offers new perspectives for music and radio

---

for researchers. Typescripts of circa 1,500 KRO plays are preserved in the KRO Archive in the KDC (Catholic Documentation Center) in Nijmegen.

4   Approximately 30 per cent of the plays have been saved in audio, either as a recording in the audio archives of Beeld en Geluid or by private initiatives such as www.hoorspelen.eu; www.geronimohoorspelen.nl, hoorspelweb.com and the Flemish weblog https://hoorspel.wordpress.com. Spotify also offers Dutch radio drama playlists and on YouTube many plays have been uploaded by anonymous contributors. The Beeld and Geluid collection is made accessible to Dutch academic institutions and schools through the Clariah Media Suite portal.

drama researchers.[5] By combining searches in these catalogues with searches in Delpher, the digitised newspaper and magazine archive of the Koninklijke Bibliotheek (Royal Library), I was able to compile an initial database of 800 plays by 230 composers and musicians who– between 1928 and 2020– wrote or improvised music for different genres of radio drama. This database serves as the starting point for answering the basic questions of this chapter: which composers, musicians and sound engineers in the Netherlands were involved in the live music production of radio drama, and how did their role develop over time?

2 Act 1 (1924–1945): Radio Drama Music Composed by Broadcasting Musicians

In Dutch radio history the broadcast of *Thomasvaer and Pieternel* on 3 January 1924 is generally regarded as the first radio drama (see Bulte 1984; Huwiler 2005; Bernaerts and Bluijs 2019). The author Willem Vogt had won the 1923 competition for radio plays that was commissioned by the NRI (Dutch Radio Industry) of Hanso Idzerda in The Hague. His *Soirée Musicale* of 6 November 1919 is seen as the first radio broadcast in the Netherlands (see Mutsaers 2019). After a period of experimentation by local radio pioneers and entrepreneurs, a membership-based national public broadcasting system was set up in 1924. Five broadcasting societies with different religious or political denominations received licenses to broadcast via one of the two radio channels of Hilversum or Huizen, named after the location of the antennas. The AVRO (neutral), VARA (socialist) and KRO (Catholic) started to produce radio drama in the 1920s and 1930s, whereas the Protestant radio organisations NCRV and VPRO initially kept their distance because theatre practices were considered incompatible with the Protestant principles of modesty and chastity.[6]

---

5 In the Broadcasting Music Centre in Hilversum (www.muziekschatten.nl) about a thousand scores of radio drama compositions have been archived and digitised. Some radio drama scores are preserved in personal archives of composers in the Netherlands Music Institute (www.nederlandsmuziekinstituut.nl) in The Hague. Radio guides of all broadcasting associations are preserved in Beeld en Geluid and are (for the last seventy years) accessible through www.delpher.nl.

6 AVRO (Algemeene Vereeniging Radio Omroep, General Society for Radio Broadcasting); VARA (Vereeniging van Arbeiders Radio Amateurs, Society of Working Men Radio Amateurs); KRO (Katholieke Radio Omroep, Catholic Radio Broadcasting); NCRV (Nederlandse Christelijke Radio Vereeniging, Dutch Christian Radio Society); VPRO (Vrijzinnig Protestantse Radio Vereeniging, Liberal Protestant Radio Society).

The radio play in the Netherlands was initially called 'radio tooneel' (radio theatre) and was rooted in the conventions of literature, theatre and poetry recitation performances ('declamatory art') which were staged by local theatre companies or artists. In 1928 the VARA started a long-running tradition of social realist radio dramas, portraying the isolated individual against a stronger societal force (employer, state, church) (see Bulte 1984). The VARA contracted a radio actors' group, which was led by the declamatory artist and actor Willem van Cappellen, who also developed into a writer of radio drama. In 1928 a short family radio drama, *Familie Mulder,* was written and directed by Willem van Cappellen as part of the children's hour of the VARA. These plays about the family life of father, mother, brother and sister Mulder began with an as yet unidentified opening tune and contained a few songs which were composed, sung and accompanied by Jeanne Bacilek, who also played the mother of the family.[7] The show was so popular that the songs were published for home and school performance (see Bacilek 1930). However, in 1930 the family emigrated to the United States, because the VARA decided to further develop the most popular character of the show, Uncle Keesje (played by Van Cappellen), who had been a regular visitor to the family. The radio drama show *Ome Keesje,* 'for children between 8 and 80 years old', ran from 1930 until 1941 and from 1946 until 1950 (Wijfjes 2012), with new title music composed by Joop de Leur (see De Leur 1947).

In 1928 the first literary VARA play that employed music was produced, *Het Ontslag (The Dismissal)* by the socialist author C. de Dood, which was about a factory worker who was fired because of his alcoholism. Due to a lack of space in the radio studio, the play was produced and broadcast from the attic of the Amsterdam Cinema Royal, where the conductor Hugo de Groot and his cinema orchestra played the illustrative music as well as made the sound effects in one room, while the actors spoke texts in the other and the sound engineer combined the two in the hallway (see Wijfjes 2003).

After sound film arrived in the Netherlands in 1929 and made the cinema orchestra redundant, De Groot and many musicians of the Cinema Royal orchestra were employed by the VARA, where they performed radio concerts and radio drama music as the VARA orchestra or VARA Theatre Orchestra. (Groeneboer 1995). After hearing the 1929 BBC broadcast of *Squirrel's Cage, a Microphone Play (De Eekhoornkooi),* the VARA ordered the typescript and score from the BBC in order to prepare a Dutch adaptation. The text by Tyrone

---

7 Jeanne Bacilek (1901–1984) was an operetta singer who regularly performed in the radio opera company of the station between 1925 and 1930. (Lelieveldt 2019a: 141–143) Later she became a choir conductor.

Guthrie, was translated and adapted by the well-known socialist writer, poet and radio drama writer Martien Beversluis (see Dera 2019), who in an interview referred to that broadcast (13 June 1930) as the first attempt to turn the radio play into a 'work of art' through the integration of text and music (see Van Beek 1935).

The story addresses the boredom and repetitiveness of daily life, symbolised by the squirrel on its treadmill in a cage. The original musical score (piano quartet with trumpet and trombone) by the British composer Owen Mase (1892–1973) was used. A 'minimal music' pattern of three descending notes played by the viola, with long trumpet and trombone notes in 5/4 bars, represented the 'boredom motif' and had to be performed 'in alternation with the scenes and without breaks' (Mase 1929).[8] A gong sound was used for the transition to the next scene, while a siren or shrieking sound reflected the transfer through time and space. *De Eekhoornkooi* was performed by the VARA drama company led by Willem van Cappellen, who also played the main character. Musicians from the VARA orchestra with conductor Hugo de Groot performed the score. In the VARA radio guide, the listener was warned that the music would be boring as it had to express the emotion of boredom. So, it should not come as a surprise that the reviewer of the socialist newspapers *Voorwaarts* and *Het Volk* evaluated the music as effective in the beginning, but boring in the end. The reviewer applauded the artistic character of the entr'acte music and the use of the *Wedding March* by Felix Mendelssohn to tell the story of the wedding of the main character, instead of acting out the scene. Nevertheless, he suggested that in future a collage of well-known musical fragments might please the listeners more ("De Eekhoornkooi" 1930). Until the 1960s, pasting canonical musical fragments into a radio drama, comparable with the musical illustration practice of the early silent movies, would become a dominant – and later also criticised – convention of musical illustration for radio drama (see below).

From the second half of the 1930s, the radio drama production of the VARA increased. Hugo de Groot started to compose original songs and music for radio drama, meanwhile starting a career as a composer of film music. Approximately half of his forty radio drama scores in muziekschatten.nl not only use music to open and end the play, but also contain songs (performed

---

8   For an illustrated explanation about the introduction of the 'boredom motif' by the violas in *De Eekhoornkooi*, see https://www.delpher.nl/nl/tijdschriften/view?coll=dts&identifier=MM NIBG01:005206019:00010 [16/05/2023]. My translation: 'Before the beginning of the play, an overture is played of 45 measures, in 5/4 bars. The violas (6 times solo) start with the following monotony ("De Eekhoornkooi (Zondag)" 1930: 10).

by the actors) that highlight the action or emotions of the characters. A special and popular genre of the VARA was the *Fairy Tales for Grown-ups* series (*Sprookjes voor volwassenen*), which consisted in either translated Andersen or Grimm fairy tales or original tales by Dutch authors, for which not only De Groot but also composer Hans Krieg (1899–1961) wrote substantial musical scores.[9] In these fairy tales the VARA was able to incorporate metaphorical societal critique that otherwise could be censored by the Radio Censor Committee. From the mid-1930s the genre of the 'radio revue', a mixed format of dramatised sketches, political radio cabaret and satirical songs about events in Dutch (political) life, also became very popular. They were broadcast either once a month (VARA) or in the Christmas/New Year period (AVRO and KRO). Not only radio artists but also popular cabaret and entertainment artists were hired to increase the popularity of the broadcasting organisation.[10]

In the 1930s the AVRO also presented a wide variety of plays, from the popular *Boefje* (*Little Rascal*, an adaptation of a children's newspaper feuilleton by the Dutch author M.C. Brusse), to adaptations of (inter)national classical stage plays, novels and detective stories.[11] In 1939 the AVRO radio drama director Kommer Kleijn discovered the *Send for Paul Temple* thriller series of the BBC, written by the British author Francis Durbridge. The play was translated into Dutch and aired from 12 February 1939 on Sunday evenings as a weekly broadcast under the title *Paul Vlaanderen*. For this series new music was composed by the pianist and conductor of the AVRO orchestra, Louis Schmidt (1887–1974), who in the same period became popular with his Kovacs Lajos entertainment orchestra. He wrote a syncopated and dense signature tune, with many chromatic lines and dissonances to create suspense (see Schmidt 1939). After the war,[12] in 1946, the *Paul Vlaanderen* series continued with a new cast of actors as

---

9   Hans Krieg (a refugee from Nazi Germany) composed music to the fairytales *De korenvelden van de vorst* (*Cornfields of the King*) and de *Chinese Fluitspeler* (*Chinese Flute Player*) by E. van Loggem. He contributed to the VARA radio revues (see below) and after the war he composed music for several 'docudramas' (radio features) that reflected on the war (see Pabbruwe 2015).

10 The musicians and composers involved in composing for the VARA revues were Isja Rossican, Cor Lemaire, Hans Krieg and Hugo de Groot.

11 Some of these plays had title or entr'acte music by the conductors of the AVRO radio orchestra, Nico Treep and Louis Schmidt, and by arranger/composer Eddy Noordijk. The composer Dolf Karelsen mainly wrote music for AVRO radio revues and one radio operetta (see Kassies 2018).

12 During the Second World War, the broadcasting organisations were dismantled. From 12 March 1941, Rijksradio Nederlandsche Omroep (RNO), with its Nazi-minded NSB staff, centralised the music production and censored composers and text writers. A new radio drama production department with a group of radio actors was founded and performed

well as newly composed orchestral music.[13] Koos van de Griend (1905–1950), a talented composer of radio drama and film music, came up with a less suspenseful and more festive signature tune as well as closing march for the play, together with some incidental music to guide moments of suspense or relief (see Van de Griend 1946a; 1946b).

FIGURE 3.1   Fragment of the Ouverture for *Paul Vlaanderen* by Koos van de Griend[14]

In its rhythmic pattern and tempo, Van de Griend's signature tune displays some similarities with the second movement of Rimsky-Korsakov's *Scheherazade*, the original tune of the *Paul Temple* series until the *Coronation Scot*

---

historical plays as well as politically and ideologically inspired plays (cf. Bulte 1984: 63; see Van der Logt 2008).

13   Many Jewish staff members did not survive the war (Dolf Karelsen, among others). After the war, many collaborating staff of the radio (among them Louis Schmidt, who had been the head of the light music department of the RNO) were fired or temporarily excluded from their jobs (see Verkijk 1974).

14   See also https://www.muziekschatten.nl/compositie?uri=https://data.muziekschatten.nl/som/386299 [16/05/2023].

by Vivian Ellis replaced it in 1947.[15] The successive series of *Paul Vlaanderen* plays – in the age before television – became so popular that people would stay home for the broadcasts. Several remakes were produced until 2014, always using Van de Griend's signature tune. This tune alone suffices to evoke public memory of the *Paul Vlaanderen* mysteries as the prototypical example of the 'hoorspel' radio genre.[16]

3 Act 2 (1940s and 1950s): Freelance Composers and Sound Engineers Improve Musical Standards in Radio Drama

After the war, starting from 1946, the broadcasting organisations resumed their roles and the Protestant broadcasting organisations NCRV and VPRO, the latter more liberal, also started to produce radio plays. In 1947 the Nederlandse Radio Unie (Dutch Radio Union) was founded to more efficiently provide services and facilities for the broadcasting organisations, such as studios, engineers, actors, musicians, orchestras, sheet music and record libraries. The NRU also coordinated the entries to the Prix Italia (Italia Prize) and other international radio competitions. The central radio drama unit, with thirty-five actors, contributed to a total number of circa 500 productions per year in the golden years of radio drama. Out of a population of 11 million people at the end of the 1950s, an average of 500,000 would listen to radio drama (cf. Bulte 1984: 143).

In the 1940s and 1950s, radio drama music conventions were further developed as a result of artistic deliberations and technical innovations. The majority of the radio plays went without music. If music was used (for the opening, ending or entr'actes), it was from gramophone records, and selected by the director of the play or the sound engineer, not the scriptwriter. In general, radio drama directors tried to use music that reflected the atmosphere of the piece or the emotions of the characters. Random fragments of music were included in a rather clichéd way. For a funeral one would choose Chopin's *Funeral March*, for a wedding Mendelssohn's *Wedding March*. This practice of

---

15   For information on *Paul Temple* adaptations in other European countries, see https://www.geronimohoorspelen.nl/paul-vlaanderen-paul-temple-startpagina/ [16/05/2023].

16   Van de Griend composed music for sixteen literary and documentary radio dramas, of which ten are preserved in his personal archive in the Netherlands Music Institute in The Hague, and the others in muziekschatten.nl. He conducted his first *Paul Vlaanderen* score with the Omroeporkest (see Paap 1950). That recording is lost. A new recording was made in 1958 by the Promenade Orchestra with Hugo de Groot, which is the only radio drama music by Van de Griend in the audio archives.

ripping the classical music art works from their contexts was criticised at the end of the 1940s by radio newspaper critics as well as sound engineers. They pleaded for new expressive ways of composing music for radio drama, comparable to the way film music underlined or commented on the narrative (cf. Lelieveldt 2019b: 56). Whether it was this critique, postwar nationalist sentiments or pressure from the composers' and writers' unions is not yet clear, but what we do know is that from the mid-1940s onwards four broadcasting organisations started to commission more original Dutch radio drama scripts (by organising script competitions for Dutch writers) as well as original music.

The Catholic radio broadcasting organisation KRO collaborated with (Catholic) composers Herman Strategier, Jurriaan Andriessen, Ton de Leeuw, Koos van de Griend, Oscar van Hemel and Else van Epen-de Groot (1919–1994). Daughter of composer and conductor Hugo de Groot, she was one of the most productive and effective names in this genre before she redirected her career towards film music. In the women's magazine *Margriet*, Van Epen's work characterised as melodious and evocative, and radio drama music presented as a genre 'that should not be heard' so one could focus on the story (H. de B. 1948).[17] Van Epen describes her work as creating musical bridges between the spoken word parts of the play and showed confidence in her statement that female composers were better in musical illustration than male composers because women were 'better able to express the subtle nuances' (ibid.).[18] Van Epen's scores were applauded in the newspaper by F. Luisteraar (translated 'Listener', the pseudonym of the authoritative music journalist and musician Wouter Paap) because of her 'intuitive and subtle expression of emotions', whereas the scores of Van de Griend displayed a 'more active and dramatic' character, and often 'wittily expressed the relationship between words and music' (Luisteraar 1948).[19] A closer look at Van Epen's scores demonstrates that her music often was not restricted to marking the opening or ending of a play or the creation of bridges between the scenes but transitioned into the announcement and underlined the scenes.[20]

---

17 Dutch original: "Het klinkt paradoxaal maar deze muziek mag eigenlijk niet gehoord worden."
18 Dutch original: "Zij zijn niet zo sensitief voor kleine nuances."
19 Dutch original: "De muziek van Else van Epen-De Groot is intuïtief en van een dikwijls fijne gevoelsuitbeelding. Koos van de Griend toonde een actiever, dramatischer aard en hij kon tussen woord en toon vaak een geestig verband leggen."
20 Else van Epen-de Groot started her career as Else de Groot and incidentally used pseudonyms, such as Alexander for her comic radio work for the KRO and Derek Laren for some of her film music scores produced for Music de Wolfe, a library music publisher. Between 1946 and 1974, she wrote around fifty radio drama scores of which most have

The application of magnetic tape recorders (in 1949) and of stereophonic audio (from the mid-1960s) in radio drama was of major importance to the next phase in the development of the sonic, acoustic and artistic dimensions of the radio play.[21] The montage of plays became easier, and it paved the way for the integration of electronic music (cf. Lelieveldt 2019b: 56). The introduction of electronic music meant a more intense collaboration between composers and sound engineers. The KRO was the first to broadcast a radio drama with electronic music. *De gravin Catelene* (1952) was an adaptation by the reputable Dutch author A. Roland Holst of the theatre play *The Countess Cathleen* by W.B. Yeats, for which Henk Badings, together with sound engineer Arie Brandon, recorded a 20-minute electronic sound track (cf. Davies 1968: 122).[22] Until 1984, when a national broadcasting Studio for Verbosonic and Electronic Music was opened (see below), radio engineers and composers used makeshift equipment in the radio studios to create electronic musical bridges between radio drama acts. For bigger projects, electronic music tapes from the private electronic music studios of the Technical University of Delft and the Philips Laboratories were used. From the 1970s onwards, to these were added tapes preproduced in the Studio of Sonology of Utrecht University, or in private studios of composers (see Weiland and Tempelaars 1982; Bosma 2017).[23]

---

been preserved in muziekschatten.nl (Van Balkum 2019). Only two original audio recordings of the radio plays with her music have been preserved in Beeld en Geluid: *Le Petit Prince* (Saint-Exupéry, 1948) and music for *The Last Days of Pompeii* by Edward Bulwer-Lytton (1949), which in the 1970s was reused in a series of biblical radio dramas by the AVRO. In 2021 a remake of her 1946 radio musical *Alice in Wonderland* was produced for NPORadio4 by the NTR broadcasting organisation with the Radio Philharmonic Orchestra and Groot Omroep Choir.

21 The first experiments with stereophonic radio concerts in the Netherlands took place in 1946. In 1960 Léon Povel initiated the first stereophonic radio play experiment, with a Dutch translation of the play *Even Schuilen* (*Let's Take Shelter*) to develop ideas for the application of sound effects and acoustics in radiophonic plays (see Knot 2014). Stereophonic radio drama broadcasts started on a more regular basis in 1964, after the recording studios were adapted for stereophonic radio production, and increased after the completion of the FM coverage of radio signals in the Netherlands in 1970 (cf. Lelieveldt 2019a: 154f.).

22 Henk Badings was one of the pioneers of electronic music in the Netherlands, his radiophonic opera *Orestes* having won the 1954 Prix Italia (see Tazelaar 2013). The radio play *Countess Cathleen* was broadcast on 16 December 1952 by the KRO. Although the script was saved, the music and soundtrack have yet to be discovered.

23 The preservation of these tapes is a complicated issue. Many tapes are lost or the equipment to play them is no longer available (see Bosma 2017).

4   Entr'acte: Family Entertainment Plays

Between 1955 and 1967 the radio drama director Léon Povel of the KRO produced three series of the very popular *Sprong in het heelal*, the Dutch adaptation of the plays *Journey into Space* by Charles Chilton, for which new sound effects were 'cut and pasted' by NRU sound effects technicians André du Bois and Ad van de Ven (Van de Ven 1990). After the rocket launches, a high shrieking sound merges into the opening measures of Samuel Barber's *Medea Ballet Suite*, played from scratched recordings of a performance led by Samuel Barber himself.[24] The music is faded in and out during the episodes, and the many sound effects contribute to the excitement and public appeal of this science fiction play. The play and Barber's music still resonate in Dutch public memory because of the repeats in the 1970s, a newly made fourth series called *The Return from Mars* in 2014, as well as audio books of these recordings.[25]

A special type of radio play with original composed music was the VARA production *In Holland staat een huis* (*In Holland There is a House*) about the family Doorsnee ('the average family'). This play was presented in the newspapers as a new format of a serial play in the form of a cabaret. In the radio guide announcements the show was subtitled as a 'radio play with music'. The series ran from 1952 to 1958 and was broadcast as a half hour show every fortnight on Monday evening at 8 o'clock. In total, 91 episodes were produced. A major innovation for the Netherlands was that this play had been recorded with a live audience, in the chamber music hall of the Concertgebouw in Amsterdam. A field trip to the radio studios in the United States inspired the director Wim Ibo to produce a radio comic strip following the lives of a family over the course of many years (cf. Wijfjes 2012: 96). The presence of an audience met some resistance in the broadcasting organisation and among listeners at first. They wondered how an audience could be present in the living room or kitchen of the family. Wouldn't it interfere with the imagination of the listeners? On the contrary, the laughter of the audience became a substantial and essential ingredient in the success of this radio musical comedy, which is, as is generally known in radio drama circles, a difficult genre for radio drama actors because of its timing issues. An omniscient narrator, Wim Ibo, guided the listeners from room to room with a whispering voice, and also made the sound effects ("Sommige mensen" 1956).

---

24   It was performed by the New Symphony Orchestra of London, see https://www.hoorspelen.eu/Hoorspelen/Plus/Spronginhetheelal.htm [24/04/2022].
25   Rubinstein Publishing B.V. is the publisher of these and other iconic Dutch radio drama series.

In this show the concert hall audience members were not only watching and laughing but had to play an active musical part as well. Together with the actors they participated in the community singing of the main theme of the show, the well-known children's song *In Holland staat een huis*. This opening song allowed for the introduction of the main characters, who would throw in a few words during the song as a summary of the topic, themes or emotions of their characters, thus preparing the audience for what was to come.[26]

Familie Doorsnee became immensely popular because it combined everyday subject matters with light humour, and it incorporated many topics that were moral dilemmas– whether or not to emigrate (the topic of overpopulation) or to quit smoking– or were considered taboo, such as sex and relationships (cf. Wijfjes 2012: 201f.; Righart 1995: 87–94). The author Annie M.G. Schmidt (1911–1995) not only had a reputation as an experienced text writer for cabaret, but also as the writer of the non-conformist *Jip and Janneke* children's books and light verse (see Van der Zijl 2002). The music for the songs was composed by Cor Lemaire, a very experienced and long-time radio musician, who also accompanied the actors on the piano, together with the guitarist Jan Blok. Schmidt (1954) praised him as 'the man of a 1000 melodies'[27]. Some songs, such as "Wil joe hef a kup of tie" (phonetic Dutch for 'Will you have a cup of tea'), became top hits on Dutch public radio (see Wijfjes 2012).[28] When television became increasingly popular, this format of 'radio play with music', including the creative team and producers of *Familie Doorsnee,* was transferred to television broadcasting, resulting in the popular television musical comedy *Pension Hommeles* (*Guest house Much a-do*) that ran from 1957–1959 and came to be known as the first original Dutch television sitcom (cf. Wijfjes 2003: 40).[29]

5 Act 3 (1960–1980): Composers, Writers and the Ideal of the Integration of Music and Words

The 1960s saw the rise of popular music and teenage culture. A third radio channel for popular music was launched in 1965, drawing in young audiences,

---

26 An example of this opening is available on YouTube, see https://www.youtube.com/watch?v=U1dakdtCaiE [24/04/2022].

27 "De man van de duizend melodietjes."

28 Philips company made records of the songs in the shows, see https://www.youtube.com/watch?v=1-UPBg4FGhM [24/04/2022].

29 On the radio the KRO took over the tradition of regular broadcasts in the musical comedy format until approximately 1964, with plays by the authors Jan de Cler, Emile Lopez and Alexander Pola, and music by Else van Epen-De Groot, Jan Stoeckart and Jan de Cler.

and television drama gradually took over the role of entertainment from radio plays. The AVRO continued to broadcast popular radio drama and radio detective stories, such as remakes of the 1950s detective series *Mijn naam is Cox,* an adaptation of the German novel series *Gestatten, meine Name ist Cox (Hello, my name is Cox)* by Rolf and Alexandra Becker. Its signature tune "Jack the Dancer" was composed by Dolf van der Linden, the conductor of the Metropole Orchestra, which was a regular contributor to orchestral radio drama scores. During the 1960s and 1970s, in the more conventional radio drama stories, a richer variety of musical genres was represented– mainly from records– reflecting the dynamic musical landscape of the 1960s. Rock music, schlager music, jazz and folk music, Jewish music, gipsy and even Hawaiian music became part of the sound palette of radio dramas.

In this period, the literary and music departments of the NCRV and KRO introduced innovations into Dutch original radio drama programming in an explicit attempt to achieve an independent and artistic radio genre. To this end they started building international networks for the exchange of expertise and collaboration on radiophonic drama with (inter)national authors and avant-garde composers. A pioneering role was played by Ab van Eyk, a poet, radio announcer and declamatory artist as well as a fervent music lover, who developed into a versatile radio drama director for the NCRV. Between 1955 and 1959 he wrote and produced four 'akousticons', radiophonic poems with electronically manipulated sounds produced by composers Meindert Boekel, Henk Badings and the sound engineer Theo van Woerkom.

In 1961 he started a poetry programme based on improvisations of spoken poetry and musical instruments. The jazz canto genre became very popular in the Netherlands after Jack Kerouac had performed in the Concertgebouw of Amsterdam in January 1960, and the VARA Jazz Week had presented a show *Een schreeuw als een roos (A Cry Like a Rose)*, with avant-garde Dutch poets accompanied by jazz musicians Herman Schoonderwalt, Ruud Jacobs and Cees See.[30] Van Eyk asked them, along with some classical musicians, to improvise during the recitation of poems in the radio show *Vers in het gehoor (Fresh to the Ear)*[31] (cf. Lelieveldt 2019b: 62). These *Vers in het gehoor* musicians with the NCRV Radio Choir also became regular contributors to radiophonic NCRV

---

30   Jazz canto performances also became a very popular (amateur) musical practice in schools and universities.

31   Musical improvisation is a common musical practice for organists in historically informed performances and contemporary music. Regular contributors were Maarten Kooij (organist/conductor), Marijke Ferguson (artistic leader of Studio Laren for historical performances) and Tera de Marez Oyens, who was an advocate for improvisation in contemporary music, and organised improvisation workshops for (amateur) musicians.

radio dramas, docudramas and school plays. On 21 May 1964 the first 'radiophonic' radio drama *Dooddoener in de Lift* (*Platitude in the Lift*) was broadcast. It was presented in the radio guide as the first radio play that used new narrative structures and new radio techniques, such as stereophony and innovative montage techniques, to generate new and alienating sound effects to express the 'loss of communication' of the main characters. (Van Eyk 1964) The music for choir and trumpet was composed by classical music composer Tera de Marez Oyens, and the jazz ensemble of Herman Schoonderwalt improvised in between the acts (cf. Lelieveldt 2019b: 63).

Musical improvisation became an increasingly applied concept in radio drama recording, for example in *Het water* (*The Water*) by Yvonne Keuls, where the composers and musicians Joep Straesser and Jos Kunst improvised by using the improvisation schemes of Jan Vriend. In *De Brandstichter* (*The Arsonist*) by author Coen Poort, percussionist Wim Koopman improvised with cellist Max Werner. In the activist docudrama against pollution, *Die vogels schuiven wel een eindje op* (*Those Birds Will Make Way*), recorded live on a ferry crossing the Waddenzee, the jazz ensemble of Tonny Eyk improvised jazz music, and the audience members were invited to participate in creating sound effects by slapping on tables or clapping their hands.

Ab van Eyk became a crucial link in an international network of radio producers, writers and composers who were interested in experimental radio drama and sound art. He presented the oeuvre of poets from the *Konkrete Poezie* (Concrete Poetry) and Sound Poetry movement in his radio programmes. From the mid-1960s on the NCRV collaborated with Radio Bremen, WDR, BRT, Austrian and Swedish Radio. Between 1966 and 1970 a number of multilingual documentary plays called *Over de Grens* (*Over the Border*) were produced, with the *Vers in het gehoor* musicians as well as Flemish and German authors, to express ideals about communication and the power of language or regional dialects, and to emphasise the ability of listeners 'to listen across borders' (Lelieveldt 2019b: 65). Van Eyk disliked the Dutch genre label 'klankbeeld' (sound image) for these types of plays and introduced new labels such as 'sonographies' (narratives about the history of municipalities/cities and their inhabitants, illustrated with period music) and 'docugraphies' (documentaries from the mid-1980s about famous composers or historical figures, accompanied by electronically manipulated sounds) (cf. Lelieveldt 2019b: 75).

After a 1967 international workshop in Breukelen to further the international collaboration of radio producers, writers and composers, Van Eyk introduced the new genre of 'verbosonica' and 'verbosonic radio play' to the Dutch radio public:

Phonetics and music have found each other in the human voice, which besides speaking also screams, sighs and laughs. Language itself has become material for a composition, and the sound of language has become autonomous, just like colour and form. Words and texts sound simultaneously, no longer one after the other, but in and through each other.[32] (ibid.: 66)

The idea of verbosonica was that text was treated 'musically' and music 'textually'. Three different concepts were applied by writers and/or composers: the concept of 'polyphony', by overlaying texts or placing them in close succession; the 'sonorisation' of the text, which meant that vowels were lengthened and given a certain pitch or that consonants would be used as rhythmic patterns; while a third technique was to record a text on tape and afterwards manipulate the spoken word (see Bulte 1984). These plays were set down in a score so they could be performed, making it possible to better express sounds and emotions that could not be noted down or recorded in an ordinary, syntactic and phonetic way.

In the verbosonic radio play *Pente sjawoe kost*, created for Pentecost 1970 by composer Tera de Marez Oyens and writer Gerrit Pleiter, all three techniques were applied. It was a huge experiment, using actors and sung as well as spoken choral parts in seven languages to express the Babylonic speech crisis in Jerusalem. Because of its dense polyphonic structure, the subversive texts of tourists looking for drug store articles such as "sanitary napkins" and saying "verdammt" (damned), as well as the musical references to Frank Zappa's *Mothers of Invention* ("Our Bizarre Relationship") and Melanie Safka's "Beautiful People" at Woodstock 1969, escaped the attention of the Protestant board members of the NCRV, and the play was entered for the Prix Italia (Lelieveldt 2019b: 71). The broadcasts of these experimental radio plays usually took place after 11:00 p.m., which appears to have been an international radio convention (cf. Bernaerts and Bluijs 2019: 13).

In 1970 a workshop for writers and composers was organised in collaboration with Klaus Schöning (Westdeutscher Rundfunk, WDR), the producer

---

32   Original text: "Fonetiek en muziek hebben elkaar gevonden op basis van de menselijke stem, die behalve spreken ook schreeuwen, zuchten, lachen. De taal zelf is materiaal voor een compositie geworden, en de taalklank autonoom, zoals kleur en vorm. Woorden en teksten klinken gelijktijdig, niet meer na elkaar, maar onder elkaar, door elkaar." After the Breukelen workshop, the Swedish participants started the Text – Sound festivals of Fylkingen in Stockholm (see Hultberg 2016).

who was responsible for the development of *Das neue Hörspiel* in Germany (see Schöning 1964). This resulted in a special verbosonic project *da du der bist* by Tera de Marez Oyens and the German author Franz Mon, based on Mon's eponymous poem. The author rehearsed the spoken parts of the play with the actors, while the composer rehearsed the sung parts with the singers. The piece was recorded in Hilversum and electronically post-processed by Tera de Marez Oyens into a radiophonic piece. Like *Pente Sjawoe Kost*, the play was published as a musical score titled *Bist du Bist* (see Marez Oyens and Mon 1972), which allowed this type of radio drama to be reprised on a concert stage in performances by professional and amateur choirs. The collaboration between writers and composers was fundamental to these radio projects and resulted in the 'co-authorship' of writers and composers on these scores (cf. Lelieveldt 2019b: 73).

These radiophonic and verbosonic radio drama projects were expensive and time-consuming, which is the reason why they were concentrated in the anniversary years of the NCRV, when extra budgets were available. The 50th anniversary of the network was celebrated by inviting the Argentinian/German composer Mauricio Kagel, well known for his multidisciplinary and innovative radio projects in Germany, to lead a workshop on 'new radiophonic formats' with a group of young Dutch actors and composers. It resulted in the verbosonic radio play *Jaargangen, of zo hoor je het ook nog eens van een ander (Volumes, or Now You Hear it from Someone Else)* a 'satirical' collage of sung and spoken fragments from historical NCRV radio guides and the 'NCRV-hymn' (see Kagel et al. 1975).

After 1974, the experimental radio drama productions came to an end because of a lack of funding due to the recession following the 1973 oil crisis. Van Eyk had also noticed that many sound artists started to repeat 'the same old tricks' and decided to go in a new artistic direction, with new historical and biblical radio drama series, together with the author Gerrit Pleiter. For the musicians and composers who had participated in earlier NCRV projects, new opportunities for autonomous professional musical employment presented themselves in the music world because of the development of a new subsidy system for jazz, ensemble music and composers (cf. Lelieveldt 2019b: 76).

While the NCRV tapered off its experiments at the interface of music and words, the KRO began setting up such projects within their music department. From the beginning of the 1970s, the music producer Frans van Rossum actively participated in the international network of avant-garde music and radio. Van Rossum had already collaborated with the Holland Festival for broadcasts of music by such (inter)national avant-garde composers as Stockhausen, John

Cage, Berio and Kagel when in 1973 he initiated the radio series *Komponist en radio* (*Composer and Radio*) to further explore the radiophonic and musical dimensions of the medium. An international group of composers was granted four hours of airtime to 'play with' the radio. Some experimented with interactive and alternative ways of storytelling, others also incorporated verbosonic elements in these productions. Although specifically made for the KRO, these plays were not confined to the airwaves. Different staged versions preceded or followed the radio performance.

One example is the radio drama project *Votre Faust: fantaisie variable dans le style d'un opéra* (*Your Faust: A Variable Fantasy in the Style of an Opera*) by the Belgian avant-garde composer Henri Pousseur (1929–2009) and the French author Michel Butor, broadcast on 11 December 1973. Between 1961 and 1968 they had created an interactive opera with the same title, labeling it a "spectacle mobile" ('mobile spectacle') because every performance could have a different form, described as a 'formal indeterminacy, in which pre-composed elements can be re-arranged depending on the choice by the conductor, performer(s) and/or the audience' (Bregegere 2015: 8; see also "Butor" 1973). Although aleatoric principles to 'organise' the form and structure of pieces were regularly applied in the oeuvre of such avant-garde composers as John Cage, it was still innovative to apply this concept to an opera as well as to its radio drama version. The opera premiered as a stage production in 1969 in Milan (Italy) and was adapted for the Dutch radio broadcast by Jan Starink, then the head of the literary department of the KRO. Live from KRO studio 2, Pousseur's Ensemble Musique Nouvelles from Brussels performed the music, and the NRU radio actors performed the spoken parts, joined by a cast of opera singers (see Snel 1974). At specific moments, the audience and listeners were invited to intervene in the development of the story about the composer Henri, who complains that he spends more time talking about contemporary music than composing new works, until he receives a commission to write an opera about Faust. It consisted almost entirely of quotations from canonical European authors of other Faust stories, which inspired Pousseur to incorporate an eclectic musical mix with many references to the canon of contemporary and twelve-tone music (see Bregegere 2015).

In May 1974, Frans van Rossum invited composer Luciano Berio to work with the NRU radio drama actors for three weeks to produce the radiophonic play *A-Ronne*, a tape piece for three male and two female voices. Celebrating the 50th anniversary of the *Surrealist Manifesto*, the piece is a collage of texts by the Italian experimental poet Edoardo Sanguineti, canonical texts from other European writers, biblical texts and Dutch folk songs. Berio described the work as a "documentary on a poem by Edoardo Sanguineti" (qtd. in Horvath

2009: 73). The actors, who in the preceding one and a half years had prepared for this project in weekly singing classes, had to sing, improvise, talk, shout and use all registers of their voices (see Karsenbarg and Veerman 1989). The broadcast on 2 July consisted of an electronically manipulated soundtrack by Berio of the montage of the recorded fragments.[33] This version was also performed live during the 1974 Holland Festival and later used by the Netherlands Dance Theatre (NDT) for the ballet *Caterpillar* (1975) by choreographer Louis Falco (1943–1993). As for *Bist du Bist* by De Marez Oyens and Franz Mon, Berio afterwards produced a musical score to make future performances on the concert stage possible.

When on 28 December 1975 a fourth public radio channel for classical music was launched, the KRO decided to move the KRO radio drama broadcasts to this new platform of dedicated listeners. Mauricio Kagel, who had collaborated with the NCRV in the 1970s, and whose *Ein Aufnahmezustand* (*State of Recording*) and other radio works were broadcast by the KRO in 1974, was invited to produce a new radio play. *Die Umkehrung Amerikas* (*The Reversal of America*), about the repression of the native people of South America by white people, was produced in collaboration with Klaus Schöning of the WDR and Dutch musicians, choir and actors. They spoke and sung text fragments in German, inspired by Gregorian chant, commenting on the gruesome acts of the Spanish conquerors. The treatment of the text fragments of the native people deserves a special mention because the actors had to say the words backwards, which was extremely difficult. Subsequently, the tapes of these recordings were also played backwards, resulting in a very strange-sounding but still comprehensible text, expressing the alienation and enforced second language of the Indian peoples (cf. Bulte 1984: 37). This play was awarded the Prix Italia in 1977.[34]

Ab van Eyk and sound engineer Cor van Doesburg of the NCRV, who had realised many experimental radio drama projects, had been lobbying for quite some years before a studio for radiophonic music and text-sound production

---

33   The KRO recording is saved as BERIO_PROJEKT-AEN5648493G.wav in the Institute for Sound and Vision in Hilversum [24/04/2022].

34   The first broadcast was on 12 April 1977 and was repeated on 27 September 1977. Although artistically challenging radio drama productions usually received considerable press attention before the broadcasts, most plays did not get a press review afterwards. This project was not reviewed until 1991, when it was played during a Kagel concert, where it made a deep impression on the audience (see Voermans 1991). An English language review of the play and sound clips can be found here: https://www.seattlestar.net/2014/01/the-ghastly-impermanence-guided-by-voices-a-new-listeners-guide-to-audio-drama-part-6/ [24/04/2022].

was opened in 1984. This Broadcasting Centre for Electronic and Verbosonic music (SVEM) was equipped with brand new synthesisers, such as the Fairlight CMI IIx, which opened endless possibilities to sample, duplicate and manipulate recorded sounds.[35] Paradoxically, this studio was only incidentally used for radio drama, such as the 'docugraphies' about Monteverdi, Schütz and Bach by Ab van Eyk. After his retirement from the NCRV, Van Eyk created a few new plays for the KRO, such as *Nadir and Zenith*, 'an improvisation for voice and piano with synthesiser',[36] based on a script by the poet Sybren Polet, and composed and performed by Louis Andriessen and Greetje Bijma. The 1992 Prix Italia for this piece was the crown on Van Eyk's long-time efforts to create a unison of words and music (cf. Lelieveldt 2019b: 76).

6 Act 4: Radio Drama in a New Guise, Music in Old Garments

From the mid-1980s onwards, the airtime for radio plays was gradually reduced due to the competition of commercial radio broadcasting and budget cuts in public radio, which led to a more 'rationalised' production. Since television had largely taken over the function of dramatic storytelling, the audience for radio drama decreased. This resulted in a substantial reduction of originally composed music for radio drama. It became a 'project-based' radio genre, funded only through special initiatives like the 'radio drama week' (hoorspelweek), a collaboration of the Flemish and Dutch broadcasting organisations. In many of the plays, music and texts were still combined, but now in more conventional ways, as title and entr'acte music, played from CDs. The radio actors' unit was terminated in 1985, so these new plays were generally produced by freelance staff and actors (cf. Tijdhoff 1991: 50).

In 2000 the timeslots for radio drama were shortened to 15 minutes daily at lunchtime and a repeat at midnight, to adjust to the changed listening habits of radio listeners. This format forced radio drama directors Peter te Nuyl en Krijn ter Braak to be very creative in their adaptation of the seven-volume novel *Het Bureau (The Bureau)* by J.J. Voskuil. The story is about the daily doings of Mr Beerta at the office of the Meertens Institute for Research on Language and Culture. In the 475 episodes that comprised the series, Peter te Nuyl incorporated original music recordings of the main character's favourite artists, as well

---

35 Pictures of the studio can be found at http://mijnmuziek.hcdeboer.nl/music5a_E.htm [24/04/2022].
36 Dutch original: "een improvisatie voor stem en piano met synthesizer".

as 'historical' sounds, in order to create a sound image of his thirty-year career spanning from 1957 to 1987.[37]

Peter te Nuyl used the same principle of combining text, historical sounds, music and silence in the 2017 radio drama *Geen noot is onschuldig* (*No Note is Innocent*, AVROTROS), based on a biography of the cellist and conductor Frieda Belinfante (see Boumans 2015). In the radio adaptation of this book, her musical instrument, the violoncello, is given a male voice to enable an omniscient narrator to tell the story of Belinfante's life in Amsterdam before WWII, her escape to Switzerland and her life as conductor in California after the war. The cello parts are integrated as supporting music, sometimes replacing the narrative. The classical music during the episodes was performed live, and original sounds and voices from the radio archives were also incorporated to stress the historic relevance of this radio piece.[38]

The radio detective stories format was given new life in projects by the Rosa Ensemble. Florian de Backere and Floris van Bergeijk, together with the ensemble, created three series of *De Deense detective* (*The Danish Detective*) (2017–2020, VPRO). Initially intended to innovate the format of classical music concerts, the audience in the concert hall witnessed the production of the radio drama, with the musicians not only playing the music but also acting and producing the sound effects. The performance was recorded, broadcast and made available as a podcast.[39] Although the detective genre format and this way of completely performing a play live hark back to a genre that began in the 1930s, the narrative as well as the cinematographic sound techniques used to manipulate the music, sound effects and voices connect it to the 2020s. The same principle of performing radio drama live on stage and broadcasting the recording afterwards was applied to *Date – a Tinder Opera*, a radio play written

---

37 The series ran between 2002 and 2006. More information about the music can be found here: https://keepswinging.blogspot.com/2009/12/vreemd-is-het-wel-muziek-bij-een.html [24/04/2022].

38 As of 2020 there is only one time slot available on Dutch public linear radio, a 'radio drama half hour', called *De Verhalen* (*The Stories*), on Sunday morning from 1:30 to 2:00 a.m. on NPO Radio 1. Here, repeats of plays or the *Scripts off Screen* productions (KRO/NCRV) are broadcast, allowing film script scenarios which never came into production to be reworked into a radio play or podcast format (see https://www.scriptsoffscreen.nl/ [24/04/2022]).

39 The 2017 and 2019 series are available at https://www.vpro.nl/programmas/de-deense-detective.html [24/04/2022].

by Bert Kommerij with music by the composers' collective Monoták that was broadcast by the Concertzender.[40]

7 Conclusion

We have seen that in almost a century of Dutch radio drama different approaches to music have co-existed, during which contemporary stage music formats also influenced radio drama music-making practices. In the founding years of the genre, broadcasting organisations used the creativity of composers and musicians 'who happened to be around' in the music departments of radio stations as conductors or performing musicians. After the war, freelance composers were more often contracted to compose music for radio drama, as the ambitions to improve the artistic standards of radio drama increased. They contributed to original Dutch literary drama as well as many imported radio plays from abroad. The act of composing for this type of outlet never became a real profession. The total number of commissions for composers was limited, and it did not pay very well because the radio play was usually broadcast only once or twice. Radio drama composing thus mainly provided a laboratory or playing ground for composers who later became active in film and television, or for the concert stage.

On Dutch radio in the 1960s and 1970s the room for experiments with radio drama largely depended on the creativity and ambitions of individual radio drama directors, as well as on their talent to negotiate financial room and airtime for artistic collaborations. Still, figures such as Van Eyk and Van Rossum initiated and participated in international artistic and radio producer networks, and it would be worthwhile to further explore these collaborations as well as the circulation of plays by the neo avant-garde in literature and music. Through the production of musical scores some of these plays became available for live music or theatre performance, but the fact that their origin was in radiophonic broadcasts often seems to have been forgotten. The developments after 2000 show that radio drama producers have succeeded in finding new outlets for their work, within or outside the radio studios. Podcast platforms provide new opportunities for exploring and recreating the old epic plays as well as presenting productions by new generations of radio drama producers. Given the limited scope of this chapter, it was only possible to point to the

---

40   See https://www.concertzender.nl/programma/inventions-for-radio-62/ [24/04/2022]. Broadcast 28 January 2015.

fact that many plays were adaptations of classical novels or plays from abroad, and that, in return, some Dutch plays were distributed to other European broadcasters. It would be interesting to find out more about the adaptation processes, not only of the texts, but also of the music. It would also be fascinating to further explore the narratological and musicological conventions of individual plays, as some chapters in this collection do.

References

Bacilek, Jeanne (1930). *Radiovriendjes, een- en tweestemmige kinderliedjes*. Amsterdam: G. Alsbach & Co. Bibliotheek Nederlands Muziek Instituut, Haags Gemeentearchief, https://hdl.handle.net/21.12124/D48E36A92F39428CAD274F7B043B7432 [09/05/2023].

Bernaerts, Lars (2014). "Verhalen voor het oor: traditie en opleving van het hoorspel". *Ons Erfdeel*, 57/4: 104–111.

Bernaerts, Lars (2017). "Hybride en Multimodaal, nieuwe genretheorie en het literaire hoorspel vandaag". Reindert Dhondt, David Martens, eds. *Cahier voor Literatuurwetenschap* 9. Ghent: Academia Press. 113–125.

Bernaerts, Lars, Siebe Bluijs (2019). "De vergeten luisterhoek van de literatuur. Hoorspel en literatuur in Nederland en Vlaanderen". Lars Bernaerts, Siebe Bluijs, eds. *Luisterrijk der letteren. Hoorspel en literatuur in Nederland en Vlaanderen*. Ghent: Academia Press. 3–32.

Bosma, Hannah (2017). "Canonisation and Documentation of Interdisciplinary Electroacoustic Music, Exemplified by Three Cases from the Netherlands: Dick Raaijmakers, Michel Waisvisz and Huba de Graaff". *Organised Sound* 22/2: 228–237.

Boumans, Toni (2015). *Een schitterend vergeten leven. De eeuw van Frieda Belinfante*. Amsterdam: Balans.

Bregegere, Andre Rene (2015 online). *L'Harmonie révée: An Analysis of Henri Pousseur's 'Votre Faust' and 'Les litanies d'Icare'*. New York, NY: CUNY Academic Works. https://academicworks.cuny.edu/gc_etds/531 [09/06/2021].

Bulte, Ineke (1984). *Het Nederlandse Hoorspel, aspecten van de bepaling van een tekstsoort*. Utrecht: H&S.

Bulte, Ineke (1990). "'Je kunt nu eenmaal geen christelijk hoorspel schrijven als je geen belijdend christen bent.' Levensbeschouwelijke aspecten van et Nederlandse hoorspel 1960–1970". *Jaarboek Mediageschiedenis* 2. Amsterdam: Stichting beheer IISG/Stichting Mediageschiedenis. 217–239.

"Butor wil publiek laten meespelen in zijn opera-parodie" (1973). *Het Parool*, 21 November: 19.

Chignell, Hugh (2019). *British Radio Drama 1945–63*. New York and London: Bloomsbury.

Davies, Hugh (1968). *Repertoire International des Musiques Electroacoustiques / International Electronic Music Catalogue*. Cambridge, MA: MIT Press.

"De Eekhoornkooi" (1930). *De zeefkring. Voorwaarts, sociaal-democratisch dagblad*, Tweede Blad, 16 June 1930.

"De Eekhoornkooi (Zondag)" (1930 online). *De radiogids*, 5/1: 10. https://www.delpher.nl/nl/tijdschriften/view?coll=dts&identifier=MMNIBG01:005206019:00010 [16/05/2023].

De Leur, Joop (1947 online). *Ome Keesjes radio-tune, "Ome Keesje zingt"*. Amsterdam: Les Editions Internationales Basart. http://data.muziekschatten.nl/som/452047 [09/06/2021].

Dera, Jeroen (2019). "Actueel-collectieve hoorspelen in het interbellum: de casus Martien Beversluis". Lars Bernaerts, Siebe Bluijs, eds. *Luisterrijk der letteren. Hoorspel en literatuur in Nederland en Vlaanderen*. Ghent: Academia Press. 91–110.

Groeneboer, Joost (1995). "Hugo de Groot (1897–1986)". *Jaarboek voor Mediageschiedenis* 6. Amsterdam: Stichting beheer IISG/Stichting Mediageschiedenis. 144–165.

H. de B. (1948 online). "'Muziek die niet gehoord mag worden', Else van Epen-de Groot". *Margriet* 37: 5. http://resolver.kb.nl/resolve?urn=MMPM02:000444037:00001 [09/06/2021].

Horvath, Nina (2009). "The 'Theatre of the Ear': Analyzing Berio's Musical Documentary *A–Ronne*". *Musicological Explorations* 10: 73–103.

Hultberg, Teddy (2016). "Fylkingen's Text-Sound festivals 1968–1974". Tania Ørum, Jesper Olsson, eds. *A Cultural History of the Avant-Garde in the Nordic Countries 1950–1975*. Leiden and Boston: Brill/Rodopi. 456–463.

Huwiler, Elke (2005). "80 Jahre Hörspiel. Die Entwicklung des Genres zu einer eigenständigen Kunstform". *Neophilologus* 89/1: 89–114.

Huwiler, Elke (2016). "A Narratology of Audio Art: Telling Stories by Sound". Jarmila Mildorf, Till Kinzel, eds. *Audionarratology: Interfaces of Sound and Narrative*. Berlin: De Gruyter. 99–116.

Kagel, Mauricio (1977). *Die Umkehrung Amerikas, Episches Hörspiel*, Westdeutscher Rundfunk, Köln. Hilversum: Katholieke Radio Omroep.

Kagel, Mauricio, et al. (1975). *Jaargangen, of zo hoor je het ook nog eens van een ander, een radiofonisch experiment*. NCRV, Hilversum. Beeld en Geluid: JAARGANGEN_-AEN5545603B.wav; JAARGANGEN_-AEN554672IW.wav.

Karsenbarg, Hans, Hans Veerman (1989). Interview in *De Radio Vereniging*, VPRO, 28 November 1989. Beeld en Geluid: DE_RADIOVEREN-AEN556583FR.

Kassies, Jan Jaap (2018 online). "Dolf Karelsen (1905–1944)". https://www.muziekschatten.nl/page/30538/dolf-karelsen-1905-1944 [09/06/2021].

Knot, Hans (2014 online). "Even Schuilen, het eerste stereofonische hoorspel". *Soundscapes.info, Journal on Media Culture* 17. https://www.icce.rug.nl/~soundscapes/VOLUME17/Even_schuilen.shtml [09/06/2021].

Krug, Hans-Jürgen (2009). "Musik im Hörspiel". Hans-Jürgen Krug and Holger Schramm, eds. *Handbuch Musik und Medien*. Wiesbaden: Springer Fachmedien. 117–147.

Lelieveldt, Philomeen (2019a). "Kwaliteit en Verscheidenheid, 100 jaar klassieke muziek op de radio". Huub Wijfjes, ed. *De radio. Een cultuurgeschiedenis*. Amsterdam: Boom Uitgevers. 137–172.

Lelieveldt, Philomeen (2019b). "Een huwelijk van taal en muziek. Het artistieke netwerk rondom Van Eyks experimentele hoorspelen bij de NCRV (1955–1992)". Lars Bernaerts, Siebe Bluijs, eds. *Luisterrijk der letteren. Hoorspel en literatuur in Nederland en Vlaanderen*. Ghent: Academia Press. 53–90.

Luisteraar, F. (1948). "Alle muziek is geen hoorspelmuziek". *De Volkskrant*, 13 February: 3.

Marez Oyens, Tera de, Franz Mon (1972). *Bist du Bist. Für Sopran, Alt, Tenor, Bas. 1.Teil*, Amsterdam: Donemus.

Marez Oyens, Tera de, Gerrit Pleiter (1970). *Pente Sjawoe Kost, verbosonische compositie voor gemengd koor en 7 spreekstemmen*. Amsterdam: Donemus.

Mase, Owen (1929 online). *De Eekhoornkooi – hoorspel met muziek*. http://data.muziekschatten.nl/som/372955 [09/06/2021].

McMurtry, Leslie Grace (2019). *Revolution in the Echo Chamber: Audio Drama's Past, Present and Future*. Bristol and Chicago, IL: Intellect.

Mildorf, Jarmila (2021). "'Ja, ja, so schön klingt das Schreckliche': An Audionarratological Analysis of Andreas Ammer and FM Einheit's *Lost & Found: Das Paradies*". Inge Arteel, Lars Bernaerts, Siebe Bluijs, Pim Verhulst, eds. *Tuning in to the Neo-Avant-Garde: Experimental Radio Plays in the Postwar Period*. Manchester: Manchester Univ. Press. 128–149.

Mutsaers, Lutgard (2019). "De grootste gemene deler: Van populaire radiomuziek naar popmuziekradio". Huub Wijfjes, ed. *De Radio. Een cultuurgeschiedenis*. Amsterdam: Boom Uitgevers. 173–212.

Paap, Wouter (1950). "Koos van de Griend". *Mens en Melodie* 5: 233.

Pabbruwe, Aagje (2015). "Hans Krieg, voorvechter behoud Joods erfgoed, Carine Alders, Eleonore Pameijer". Carine Alders, Eleonore Pameijer, eds. *Vervolgde componisten in Nederland. Verboden muziek in de Tweede Wereldoorlog*. Amsterdam: Amsterdam Univ. Press. 156–163.

Righart, Hans (1995/2006). *De eindeloze jaren zestig, geschiedenis van een generatieconflict*. Amsterdam: Amsterdam Univ. Press.

Schmidt, A.M.G. (1954). "Cor Lemaire, de man van de 1000 melodietjes". *Het Parool*, 20 December: 9.

Schmidt, Louis (1939 online). *Spreek met Vlaanderen*. http://data.muziekschatten.nl/som/332631 [09/06/2021].

Schöning, Klaus, ed. (1969). *Neues Hörspiel: Texte, Partituren*. Frankfurt am Main: Suhrkamp.

Snel, Arend (1974). "Componist en radio: 'Votre Faust van Henri Pousseur'". *Mens en Melodie* 24: 45–47.

"Sommige mensen voelen zich gekwetst door de Familie Doorsnee" (1956). *Leeuwarder Courant*, 22 February: 5.

Tazelaar, Kees (2013). *On the Threshold of Beauty: On the Origins of Dutch Electronic Music, 1925–1965*. Rotterdam: Nai010 Uitgevers.

Tijdhof, Leander (1991). "Hoorspel op de Nederlandse radio 1980–1990, artisticiteit en beleid". MA Thesis. Theater-, Film- en Televisiewetenschap, Utrecht Univ. Unpublished.

Van Balkum, Eric (2019 online). "100 jaar Else van Epen-de Groot: componiste met een opdracht". https://www.muziekschatten.nl/page/77542/100-jaar-else-van-epen-de-groot-componiste-met-een-opdracht [09/06/2021].

Van Beek, W. (1935). "Radio en Samenleving, Eenige peilende Interviews, Gesprek met Martien Beversluis. Het verband tussen literatuur en radio". *Het Vaderland*, ochtendblad, 17 November: 4.

Van de Griend, Koos (1946a online). *Paul Vlaanderen, openings- en slotmarsch*. http://data.muziekschatten.nl/som/386299 [09/06/2021].

Van de Griend, Koos (1946b online). *Tusschenspelen bij* A Case for Paul Temple. http://data.muziekschatten.nl/som/334352 [09/06/2021].

Van der Logt, Ad (2008). *Het theater van de nieuwe orde. Een onderzoek naar het drama van Nederlandse nationaalsocialisten*. Amsterdam: Aksant.

Van der Zijl, Annejet (2002). *Anna, het leven van A.M.G. Schmidt*. Amsterdam: Nijgh & Van Ditmar.

Van de Ven, Ad (1990). Harry Vossen in conversation with Ad van de Ven. Beeld en Geluid: ORAL_HISTORY_-AEN5 578302N, ORAL_HISTORY_-AEN5578302O.

Van Eyk, Ab (1964). "De dooddoener in de lift", NCRV-*gids*, May: 17.

Van Eyk, Ab (1969), *Meerjarenplan Verbosonie*, NCRV, afdeling Gesproken Woord, 1969.

Verkijk, Dick (1974). *Radio Hilversum 1940–1945. De omroep in de oorlog*. Amsterdam: Uitgeverij de Arbeiderspers.

Voermans, Erik (1991). "Kagel project, hoorspelen van Mauricio Kagel". *Het Parool*, 15 January.

Weiland, Frits, C. Tempelaars (1982). *Elektronische muziek*. Utrecht/Antwerpen: Bohn, Scheltema & Holkema.

Wijfjes, Huub (2003). "Geluid als kunst: de uitvinding van de Nederlandse hoorspeltraditie". *Tijdschrift voor Mediageschiedenis* 2: 34–42.

Wijfjes, Huub (2009). VARA. *Biografie van een omroep*. Amsterdam: Boom.

Wijfjes, Huub (2012). "Veelkleurige radiogemeenschappen, 1930–1960". Andreas Fickers, Bert Hogenkamp, Sonja de Leeuw, Huub Wijfjes, eds. *Een eeuw van Beeld en Geluid. Cultuurgeschiedenis van radio en televisie in Nederland*. Hilversum: Nederlands Instituut voor Beeld en Geluid. 58–103.

CHAPTER 4

Not Just Words, Not Just Music: Some Remarks about the Development of a Radio Art and Radio Drama in Italy

Angela Ida De Benedictis

> The radio is an instrument – a means.
> And each new instrument (like each new means)
> gives origin to a new form –
> whether in art, in perception or whatever.
> (Alberto Savinio, 1949)[1]

∴

Abstract

This essay is dedicated to the analysis, in historical retrospect, of the development of specific radio art in Italy and to a parallel reflection on the function that music had in the evolution of new aural forms. As in other nations, the birth of the radio service in Italy gradually led to the experimentation with new forms of expression. Because of its equipment and technical potential, the medium was immediately understood as an instrument itself that implied a new way of thinking about music. However, in Italy, the path towards the acceptance of an autonomous sound art was long and complex, as is illustrated here by tracing the history of the new radio genres, going from the beginning of the debate on a 'specific radio art' (ca. 1930) to the analysis of some radio works produced in the fifties-sixties by composers such as Berio and Maderna.

---

1 The Italian musician and writer Alberto Savinio was the brother of the most notorious artist Giorgio de Chirico. The comment is reproduced in Savinio (1989: 977).

Although in the late 1940s – at the time of Savinio's statement – radio broadcasting had been operating in Italy for more than twenty years, there had been until then only the faintest signs of potential 'new forms' of art.[2] One of the main spheres for experimentation in radio broadcasting was actually the particular genre which goes under the name of *radiodramma* or *dramma radiofonico*, a new art form which had its heyday in Italy between the mid-fifties and the seventies.

As a 'genre' associated with a particular country and its technology (i.e., its technological apparatus), right from the outset the Italian *radiodramma* (from now on radio drama) displayed features which set it apart from the German *Hörspiel*, the British *radio play* or the French *théâtre radiophoné*.[3] To avoid ambiguity, we can say that 'radio drama' is generally taken to mean a form of acoustic expression made up of words, music, special sound effects, natural sounds, noises and silence. But at least in Italy, the matter becomes more complicated if we think that the semantic field for the term is very broad and at times confused. Still today, in fact, it is used as a sort of overarching category to refer to such different genres as 'drama broadcast on the radio' (reductions and adaptations of preexisting works), as a genuine 'radio play' (in the sense of an original script for radio) and as 'radio opera' (meaning musical works composed for the radio). As is happens with productions defined in the English radio context as 'drama', 'feature' or 'radio play', these definitions – often abstract in terms of a clear demarcation of style – actually correspond to a "distinction without a difference" (Drakakis 1981: 8).[4]

One can form a better idea of the anomaly in this vague use of the term 'radio drama' in Italy by drawing a comparison with the German context, where the first theoretical elucidations on radiophonic genres were formulated soon after the birth of radio broadcasting. With reference to the use of music in radio plays, as early as 1923 a distinction was made between *Geräuschkulisse* and *akustischer Kulisse* (background noise or sound effects and acoustic backdrop). Within a year, additional and detailed theoretical distinctions were introduced between *Schauspiel* (an existing play broadcast on the radio), *Sendespiel* (an adaptation of an existing play for radio), *Hörspiel* (an

---

2 The following text builds on research conducted at the RAI archives and other institutions since 1999 and which, in some ways, is still ongoing. The main findings are contained in De Benedictis (2004); see also De Benedictis (2012) and (2018).
3 Only genre macro categories are used here, in the knowledge that different nuances and nomenclauture can be found (since the beginnings of radio history) in each country.
4 In the 'feature', a term peculiar to English radio, we find the characteristics of drama, documentary and live reporting mixed in such a peculiar way as to make it difficult to distinguish fiction from reality. See also Glandien (2000: 168f., 172) and De Benedictis (2004: 49).

original play created for radio) and *Funkoper* (a musical work composed for the radio). To these categories have been added the *Hörfolgen*,[5] which is broadcast live, and the *O-Ton-Hörspiel*, while in the sixties a clear distinction was made between *traditionelles* and *neues Hörspiel*.[6] These theoretical differences are a consequence of the specific history of the medium, which has been unique and exclusive for all the broadcasting companies in Europe and beyond. Therefore, a short historical introduction to the Italian radio context is necessary to clarify the peculiarities of an environment which has mirrored the major artistic, cultural and intellectual developments of the twentieth century. In addition, this historical premise will make more understandable the role that music had to play in the definition of new artistic genres related to a new medium.

1 A New Medium in Search of Specific Art Forms

The first radio station was founded in Italy in August 1924,[7] significantly later than other European broadcasters. Its first name was URI (Unione Radiofonica Italiana). It changed in December 1927 to EIAR (Ente Italiano Audizioni Radiofoniche), only to be renamed once again in October 1944, when it took on the definitive acronym RAI (Radio Audizioni Italia).[8] Perhaps more than in other countries, its creation was strongly linked with politics: the inaugural broadcast of Italian radio began with the fascist anthem, *Giovinezza*, which remained the signature tune marking the beginning and end of daily broadcasting through to the end of the regime in 1943.[9] However, unlike the situation in Germany, where the radio was a genuine instrument of power duly 'cultivated' and promoted by the regime, Benito Mussolini (a former journalist devoted to newspapers) struggled to recognise the importance of the new medium. Considered as little more than a plaything, Italian radio in the twenties and thirties was characterised by an amateur and unsystematic approach, which came nowhere near to exploiting its true potential. Between the various areas of programming, notably the cultural one was mainly in the hands of

---

5   See, in particular, Brech (2000: 221). Being among the first *Hörfolgen*, *Leben in diesen Zeiten* (*Life in These Times*) by Erich Kästner and Edmund Nick (1929) should also be mentioned.
6   See, among others, Schöning (1969, 1974, 1982, 2021), Vowinckel (1995: 199–261), Ohmer and Kiefer (2013).
7   The regular broadcasts began only a few months later, on 6 October.
8   From 1 January 1954, with the official inauguration of television broadcasting, the same acronym came to mean Radiotelevisione Italiana, still used today.
9   The fascist hymn *Giovinezza* (music by Giuseppe Blanc, words by Nino Oxilia) can be heard at https://www.youtube.com/watch?v=fvibhFoyaao [01/04/2022].

people who were improvising their vocation from day to day. Thus, it is hardly surprising that in Italy – unlike Britain, Germany or France – up until the second half of the thirties practically no music or experimental broadcasting were devised in terms of the medium's specific characteristics. Both in drama and in the musical field the concept of 'experimentation' for radio simply did not exist – whereas in Berlin the likes of Kurt Weill, Paul Hindemith and Max Butting had been given the opportunity to work within radio environments in search of a specific radio music since the second half of the 1920s.

This difference in approach, moreover, reflects the difference in the diffusion and popularity of the new medium in the various European countries: Italian radio was bringing up the rear around 1930 not only in terms of programming, but also for the number of users, with only 200,000 subscribers as against some 4 million in Germany and a similar number in Britain. This surely makes it easier to appreciate why it was such an uphill struggle for radio in Italy to achieve an autonomous idiom of its own. Theoretical debate on the possibility that the radio could give rise to a specific artistic idiom only got under way in the first half of the thirties, once again considerably later compared to countries such as Germany, France or England. The foremost musicians of the period did not show much interest in the matter, and the only people to respond actively were some *enfants terribles* of the time, namely the Futurists.

For artists like Filippo Tommaso Marinetti, the question 'can there be an art form on the radio?' had to have a positive answer, but only on condition that there was a 'modern content for a modern medium'. It was Marinetti (with his fellow Pino Masnata) who was responsible in 1933 for one of the most visionary Futurist manifestos of the period, entitled "'La Radia': Il teatro futurista radiofonico".[10] For all its self-glorifying and provocative rhetoric, the authors did come up with a definition that may still be valid today for the expressive potential of the radio when they claimed among other things: "Freedom from any point of contact with literary and artistic tradition. [...] A new Art [without time or space] that begins where theatre, film and narration leave off" (Marinetti and Masnata 2009: 294).[11] Marinetti followed up these visionary words with some concrete examples collected in the audio work *5 sintesi radiofoniche* (*5 Radio Syntheses*), created in the same year. These short audio compositions

---

10   First edition in *Gazzetta del Popolo*, 22 September 1933; then in Marinetti (1941: 55–57). Republished in De Benedictis (2004: 211–214). English translation in Marinetti and Masnata (2009: 293–295).

11   The passage in square brackets has been adjusted based on the original in Italian: "libertà [...] un'arte nuova senza tempo né spazio che comincia dove cessano il teatro, il cinematografo e la narrazione" (De Benedictis 2004: 212). All translations from Italian are my own unless otherwise stated.

have eloquent titles: "Un paesaggio udito" ("A heard landscape"), "Dramma di distanze" ("Drama of distances"), "Battaglia di ritmi" ("Battle of rhythms", "I silenzi parlano tra loro" ("Silences Speak among Themselves"), "La costruzione di un silenzio" ("Building a silence").[12] In all of them, the truly radical ideas of simultaneity (a typically Futurist ideal) and of the "construction of an imaginary space" prevail (Luisetti 2012: 283). For their time, these *Sintesi* – abstract and unconventional in their approach to technology and in their "minimalistic aesthetic based on alternating sounds, noises, and silence" (ibid.) – were decidedly surprising. The second one, "Dramma di distanze", could be taken for instance as an example of 'radio zapping' *ante litteram*. It is composed of the following seven fragments (11 seconds each, all taken from gramophone recordings) that merge seamlessly: (1) "a military march in Rome"; (2) "a tango being danced in Santos"; (3) "Japanese religious music being played in Tokyo"; (4) "a lively rustic dance in the Varese countryside"; (5) "a boxing match in New York"; (6) "street noise in Milan"; (7) "a Neapolitan love song sung in the Copacabana Hotel in Rio de Janeiro".[13] Nevertheless, these first Futurist experiments produced no developments or follow-ups and tended to be viewed as little more than passing divertissements.

For the rest of the thirties and up to the declaration of war in 1939, Italian radio remained anchored to its exclusive function as a broadcasting channel. Throughout these years, experimentation in radio was essentially restricted to intellectuals as a subject of theoretical debates involving writers and musicians. For example, a survey conducted in 1937 by the magazine *La Rassegna Musicale*, bearing the title "La radio e la musica", featured composers such as Alfredo Casella, Luigi Dallapiccola, Gian Francesco Malipiero, Goffredo Petrassi and Ildebrando Pizzetti, along with the conductor Gianandrea Gavazzeni. All of them, without exception, made it clear that they did *not* believe in an art form which was specific to radio (or created specifically for it), and declared themselves skeptical, with greater or lesser vehemence, as to the creative potential of the new medium.

War and the restrictions imposed by the regime put paid to any sort of reflection concerning an art form which, in reality, was still at an embryonic stage and had not yet had the opportunity to develop or to prove itself. In the immediate postwar years, too, the theoretical debates and experimental issues at stake failed to make any significant impact, either with the powers that were

---

12   The 5 *sintesi radiofoniche* (1933) are released on *Musica Futurista 1*, CD Cramps Records (MM001), 2010.
13   For more in-depth information, see Luisetti (2012); titles of the 11 fragments as translated on p. 288.

in broadcasting or in musical and artistic circles. This prevailing disinterest is the background for the "death sentence" without appeal delivered by one of the most Italian music critics, Massimo Mila, who in 1952 traced a veritable epitaph addressed to any kind of artistic radio experimentation:

> When the radio was in its infancy, approximately a quarter of a century ago, we were almost all dupes to an illusion: that this technical invention could open up extraordinary and unsuspected perspectives for musical creativity. [...]
>
> It was firmly believed that the radio would create a whole repertory of its own [...], and people were already fantasising about unheard-of sound effects produced by strange applications of the new mechanical medium. [...]
>
> These were mere dreams, a generous illusion, which today has meekly bowed out before the crushing evidence of reality. (89)

Undoubtedly Mila never imagined that, just as he was pronouncing these defeatist words, the "reality" was beginning to be revolutionised by a new generation of composers and artists who also benefited from technical innovations that were advancing (if not revolutionising) the equipment and the instrumentation of radio studios. Among the latter we should at least mention the tape recorder (which came into widespread use in Italian radio around 1948). This 'instrument' opened up new expressive frontiers specifically for radio art, both through the new malleability and variety in which the sound material could be edited, as well as for the level of interaction it made possible between words, music, sounds, noises, etc. The possibility to record every conceivable acoustic type of material on magnetic tape, and then modifying it in subsequent phases of elaboration and editing, enabled the construction of complex sound events that would be impossible to achieve in normal concert halls or on the stage of a theatre. Even more, it made it possible to create a musical link or a sound continuity (i.e., new forms of sonic narration) between instruments, spoken voices, sung voices and sounds generated electronically. As composer Luciano Berio wrote to his colleague Luigi Dallapiccola when illustrating the work conducted on tape in a radio studio on Joyce's *Ulysses*: "The voice becomes music, the music becomes word. It's wonderful! (qtd. in Nicolodi 1975: 93)"[14] The allusion here to the textual level – i.e., the words – is even more relevant considering that the ideal of a 'pure' radio art – of an

---

14   Letter of 22 December 1957; original (in Italian) kept at the Luigi Dallapiccola Collection of the Bonsanti Archive (Gabinetto Vieusseux) in Florence.

acoustic art rather than a musical one – was achieved in Italy *also* through the experience of radio drama.

2   Staging the Invisible: New Expressive Interactions of Word and Music

The aforementioned key distinction between acoustic or musical art deserves a brief historical excursus that takes its cue from the remark that, in Italy, the evolution of a radio art did not derive primarily from experiments conducted exclusively in the musical field. Rather, it seems to be directly related to the attempt to expand and develop, within dramatic or prose productions, the so-called '*musica di scena*' ('incidental music') that includes noises and sound effects to compensate for the listeners' lack of sight. The importance of music for the various functions of stage curtain, imaginary visual frame and connection between the individual parts of the action became clear from the earliest dramatic radio works.[15] The indispensable presence of music as a sound environment intended to replace or supplant the cognitive information provided by a visible scene was already evident to Mario Vugliano, the author of the first radio drama ever realised in Italy, *Venerdì 13* (*Friday the 13th*), broadcast on 18 January 1927.[16] Only a year before inaugurating the Italian 'theatre on the air', Vugliano himself wrote in the pages of *Radio Orario* (the official magazine of Italian radio) that "music, like Symbols for stage art, remains the primary vehicle for the sensations of invisible radio art. Every sound [or] noise must tend to create illusion and suggestion for the hearing" (Vugliano 1926: 4).[17]

In the following decade two different interpretative positions on the purposes and functions of music's presence in radio drama emerged in Italy. In the first one, represented by Rudolf Arnheim's theories, music and sound effects were considered as a sort of stylistic trademark of the director, seen as the only one responsible for the simplicity or complexity of the soundtrack chosen for a

---

15   For more details see De Benedictis (2004: 9–28, 61–150). Similar characteristics are found in early English radio drama; see, among others, Drakakis (1981).

16   The radio drama was broadcast by station URI 1MI. The echo of this event lasted for weeks, and the response of listeners was enthusiastic (see "Il primo esperimento" 1927). In the course of 1927, and in the following years, *Venerdì 13* was rebroadcast with different companies by the other URI stations; the text was published in the journal *Illustrazione Teatrale* in July 1927.

17   These words were taken up almost verbatim in a statement present in a contemporary French publication: "Comme les 'Symboles' de l'art scénique, la musique reste le premier véhicule de sensations de l'art invisible" (Cusy and Germinet 1926: 19).

radio drama.[18] In the second one, expressed by the Italian radio theorist Enrico Rocca, any arbitrary use of sound was rejected in favour of a use of music that would serve to reinforce the message and the "inner drama" of the text, i.e., to emphasise, enhance or even transfigure it. Far from being a "simple matter of taste", for Rocca the choice and presence of music in a radio drama had to be indicated right from the writing of the script itself. Rocca identified one of the main specificities of the new genre precisely in this "word-sound" binomial (1938: 161f.):

> Whoever writes for radio-theatre will have not only to emphasise the word as the main dramatic element, but also to be able to indicate, as concretely as possible, the indispensable sound effects and the nature of any sound commentaries, linking or concluding music [...]. Only specially written music, which adheres to the text and in its own way takes up the interrupted motifs, fulfils this purpose. (Ibid.: 163)

As far as we know from contemporary accounts and original radio scripts that have survived, it seems that, beyond the theoretical validity of individual positions, the practice described by Arnheim was far more widespread in Italy than the second one advocated by Rocca. In this regard, it should also be remembered that, even up until the end of the 1940s, radio drama was essentially a live broadcast event and was only rarely recorded (at that time in Italy recording media were privileged for political and sporting events). To better fit into their role, actors not infrequently acted in costume.[19] The wait between the various scene changes – a rather complex operation back then that required strategies of true 'radio stagecraft' – was filled with sound curtains or by real musical interludes, played live in the same room where the radio drama was being performed, or (more often) taken from the gramophone. In the latter case, the function of the music as a caesura was, for the listeners, much more evident. Even on this level, the gap between Italian radio and the major European broadcasting stations was evident: in the BBC's radio drama productions, for example, the problem of waiting between scene changes had been overcome as early as 1928 with the introduction of the dramatic control panel, a

---

18   The first edition of Rudolf Arnheim's *Radio* (London: Faber and Faber, 1936) was translated and published in Italian (with the title *La radio cerca la sua forma*) by Hoepli in 1938.
19   This custom is attested in Italy until the period preceding the Second World War. Later on, the costumes were used for some photographic shots aimed at articles published in the *Radiocorriere* and other magazines, with the purpose of giving readers an ideal visual frame of the radio drama. The custom of broadcasting comedies in costume was also in vogue in Britain during the 1930s and 1940s; see Drakakis (1981: 4).

coordinated broadcasting system that allowed live events to be transmitted using several studios at the same time. Although increasingly present as a soundscape, a background and a psychological or situational projection, music was mostly considered as a complement to the text and, when composed specifically for radio productions (i.e., when it was not taken from classical repertoire or records), it was commissioned almost exclusively to composers within the radio corporation and, even today, unknow to most.[20]

Among the radio works produced with the contribution of musicians who enjoyed a certain fame during the fascist period, it is worth mentioning two examples: *Scalo di fortuna* (*Lucky Stopover*, 1937), scenario by Cesare Meano, music by Armando La Rosa Parodi), one of the first attempts in Italy to blend music with dramatic language in an organic and integrated way; and *E un uomo vinse lo spazio* (*And a Man Conquered the Space*, 1938; by Ettore Giannini, music by Ennio Porrino), the first experiment in Italy of '*oratorio radiofonico*' ('radio oratory'). These are, however, rare exceptions: the sustained rhythm of production, dictated by the need to put on the air at least one new radio drama every two weeks, favoured the use of preexisting music. In this case, it was a musical consultant who, on the director's instructions, would select from the classical or light repertoire pieces that could support dramatic feelings and contexts. The music contributed from time to time to make the 'acoustic images' incisive, to sustain the rhythm of the narration, or to create evocations and reflections on the plot through the use of specific instrumental timbres. Nevertheless, during the 1940s the importance of so-called 'sound commentaries' grew to such an extent that it led composers active in radio environments to predict: "The Radio and only the Radio is able to bring together poetry and music in an understandable and pleasant way. [...] It will no longer be possible to conceive of concepts expressed in words as separate from those expressed in sounds." (Modigliani 1947: 4)[21]

---

20 Between 1934 and the end of the 1940s, among the composers of music for radio plays in Italy we can find the names of Carlo Allietti, Pippo Barzizza, Vincenzo Davico, Rodolfo del Corona, Raffaele Gervasio, Armando La Rosa Parodi, Franco Leoni, Enzo Masetti, Gino Modigliani, Tito Petralia, Ennio Porrino, Egidio Storaci and Guido Turchi, just to mention a few of the best known.

21 Gino Modigliani was responsible for the music of *Il teatro dell'Usignolo*, a cultural appointment broadcast weekly from 1947 to 1949 and later transformed into *I notturni dell'usignolo*. These broadcasts were true milestones in the journey made by Italian radio towards the search for a specific language.

3 Radio Drama vs. Radio Opera

Based on what has been stated so far, it will not be surprising to learn that, up until the end of the Second World War, the two spheres of so-called *radiodramma* (in which the spoken word dominated) and *radio opera* (based on music) followed within the EIAR (then RAI) quite distinct channels of research, production and promotion. In the sphere of *radio opera*, at the beginning of the 1950s, the RAI sought to stimulate the creation of new experimental compositions for radio by commissioning radio operas from selected composers, leaving them free to choose their own subject matter. Such an enterprise might be viewed as meritorious if the composers had not been chosen in recognition of their popularity (earned often during the fascist regime) or based on favouritism, as is immediately obvious from the roll call of those selected. To promote in Italy the 'birth' of a new and experimental radio art, the RAI turned to such establishment figures as Giorgio Federico Ghedini (1892–1965), Gian Francesco Malipiero (1882–1973) and Ildebrando Pizzetti (1880–1968). All of them were composers in their sixties or seventies, without the least familiarity with the medium or its technology, and moreover entrenched in openly conservative positions. These names are even more astonishing if one recalls that only a few years earlier Malipiero and Pizzetti had actually taken a public stand *against* the possibility of an art form in radio. What had changed some fifteen years later, leading them to accept a commission from the RAI (which in the meantime, on an artistic level, had remained basically unchanged)?

The key aspect, or the persuading factor, of the whole question proves to be an economic one. It must be remembered that it was not until the postwar years that both the RAI as an institution and the music composed for radio broadcasts were finally recognised as coming under the auspices of the SIAE (Società Italiana degli Autori ed Editori), the Italian society of authors and publishers established in 1882 for the collective management of authors' rights. Writing radio operas or music for the radio suddenly took on a new allure for these composers, and given the high fees guaranteed from commissions, broadcasting became an irresistible proposition indeed. The genesis of many of the first Italian radio operas created specifically for the medium – such as Pizzetti's *Ifigenia* (1950), Franco Alfano's *Vesuvius* (1949),[22] and Ghedini's *Lord*

---

[22] Alfano's *Vesuvius* was actually a reworking of a ballet composed in 1933 (cf. De Benedictis 2004: 19); for more information about the radio works by Pizzetti and Ghedini cited in the text, see ibid. (16–25).

Inferno (1952), to name but three – seems not to have been linked particularly to the technical peculiarities of the microphone. Far from being experimental works, created with an eye to the medium's resources and instruments, these radio works can be seen quite simply as extensions of a tried and trusted theatrical (i.e., operatic) *métier*. Even listening to short excerpts from works such as the aforementioned *Ifigenia* (a "radio musical tragedy" which won the Prix Italia in 1950), or *Lord Inferno* (winner of the same prestigious prize for radio broadcasting in 1952), is enough to understand that at best they provided something like '*bel canto* for the radio'.[23]

In the same years, however, a true form of musical experimentation was beginning almost imperceptibly to sneak into the world of Italian radio in the sector of drama and fiction, precisely thanks to the aforementioned 'sound commentaries' and incidental music. The resumption of regular radio programming after the war made the production of radio plays (adaptations or originals) even more massive. Because of its many functions (both expressive and structural), music became – along with sound effects and noises – an indispensable element of building radio scenarios that were at once imaginary and intelligible. As early as 1946, the name Bruno Maderna emerged on the anonymous horizon of musical composers for radio plays, as the author of the soundtrack of a radio documentary dedicated to the Resistance (*Poesia della Resistenza*). In 1949, at the invitation of Alessandro Piovesan, then director of the prose department of the RAI-Rome, he composed the music for the 'radio ballad' *Il mio cuore è nel Sud* (*My Heart is in the South*), one of the first examples of a genuine acoustic art form devised for an imaginary stage.[24] In 1950, the ballad won the RAI's 'Silver Microphone' award, considered at the time to be a kind of radio Oscar; and in 1957, under the title *Stadt im Süden* (*City in the South*), it was presented with the prestigious Karl-Sczuka-Preis at the Südwestfunk in Baden-Baden. In December 1953, Luciano Berio, in turn, made his radio play debut with a soundtrack composed for the 'tragicomedy' *Il trifoglio fiorito* (*The Flowering Clover*).

Thus, while the RAI was commissioning radio operas from traditional composers who had no grasp of the medium's creative potential, the more youthful musical avant-garde was making its way into RAI, entering it through the back door of radio drama. Indeed, the more farsighted of them quite deliberately

---

23   Both works were readapted for theatrical scenes shortly after. The version of *Ifigenia* presented by Pizzetti at the Prix Italia is published in Antonucci (1998). See also De Benedictis (2020: 88).

24   Text by Giuseppe Patroni Griffi. Maderna's score is published by the Edizioni Suvini Zerboni, Milan.

took advantage of this 'service hallway', since they knew that in Italy – unlike America and Germany, for example – the only chance for young composers to be able to experiment with technologically advanced equipment of audio production and reproduction was to gain admission to the RAI environment. Perhaps the best example of this pragmatic approach is Luciano Berio: no sooner had he secured a contract in RAI as a music consultant and dubbing assistant in 1953,[25] than he began experimenting in the radio studios, manipulating oscillators, scissors and tape recorders, often in a semi-clandestine way. It was thus that, in December of that year, he succeeded in creating his first completed electroacoustic work, *Mimusique*, a kind of private étude of *musique concrète* lasting barely 2 minutes.[26] He produced it using the scant technical equipment that was available to him, which included some filters, a tape recorder, a white noise generator and a speed control device, basing the piece's whole development on the continual transformation of just three sound materials: a gunshot, a tam-tam strike and a sound produced by a human voice.

Quite apart from the artistic and documentary value of such experimentations, it is important to bear in mind that, while engaging in this unofficial activity, Berio began to create a network of diplomatic relations in the RAI hierarchy with a view to setting up a Studio for electronic music in Italy, along the lines of those already established in Paris and Cologne. The outcome of this diplomatic activity was the launch, at the end of 1954, of what officially became known, in 1956, as the Studio di Fonologia Musicale di Milano della RAI, cofounded by Berio and Maderna. With the creation of this Studio within the Italian broadcasting corporation a "principle of the non-innocence of technique" (Pasolini 1972: 230) was revealed in all its startling clarity.[27] Albeit considerably later than in other countries, in Italy, too, radio stopped being just a means for reproduction and became a vehicle for linguistic, expressive and ideological choices, through its own technological specificity. As Berio himself put it in his "Project for the constitution of an 'Experimental Centre for

---

25   Berio obtained this engagement also thanks to the encouragement and suggestions of Luigi Dallapiccola (cf. De Benedictis 2004: 189).
26   On this short piece, which is still unpublished, see De Benedictis and Rizzardi (2000: 162–164). *Mimusique* was included in the programme *La Musica Concreta*, curated by Berio himself in 1955 and broadcast on 13 July of the same year (cf. the listing in *Radiocorriere* 32/28: 24). The recording is preserved in the sound archive of the Studio di Fonologia Musicale (tapes Fon. 019 and Fon. 020); see Novati and Dack (2012: 180).
27   Pier Paolo Pasolini, in reference to cinematography and audiovisual techniques, spoke of the need to demystify an alleged "innocenza della tecnica". I take this concept freely to underline the non-neutrality of technological devices in the development of a radio art (see later in the text).

Radio Research'", presented in 1954 to the General Director of the RAI, Filiberto Guala, the future electronic laboratory was intended as the

> first Italian centre of organic research into and study of expression in radio. Its creation must respond to the need both for systematic experimentation with the expressive possibilities of radio and to become more aware of the phenomenon of radio broadcasting by studying its many aspects. (qtd. in Santi 1984: 170f.)

Among its main aims, the first three enumerated by Berio were:

1. The production of concrete and electronic music [...];
2. The creation of soundtracks for radio and television;
3. The making of special broadcasts featuring drama and documentaries with the aim of achieving a form of expression specific to radio. (Ibid.)

4 New Sonic Horizons in Italian Radio

Nowadays any reference to the Studio di Fonologia di Milano della Rai immediately evokes one of the most important European laboratories of electronic music of the fifties and sixties, able to hold its own against counterparts in Europe and on the other side of the Atlantic. But at the time of its creation, matters stood very differently. For the RAI, the principal purpose of this famous Studio of electronic music was to be an 'in-house laboratory' designed to provide the music, soundtrack, effects and any sound engineering for radio dramas and for adaptations of plays for radio and television. It was not a coincidence that Berio and Maderna convinced the management of the RAI to authorise the constitution of the electronic Studio at the RAI headquarters in Milan with an example of 'artistic sound engineering'. This was the radio documentary *Ritratto di città (Portrait of a City)* – subtitled "studio per una rappresentazione radiofonica" ('study for a radiophonic portrayal')[28] – achieved at the end of 1954, based on a script by Roberto Leydi. In this acoustic portrait of a city environment – commonly recognised as the Studio di Fonologia's "Opus 1" – the authors intended to provide a documentary featuring Milan in which sight was completely replaced by sounds.

---

28 The subtitle could alternatively be translated as "study for a radio play", "study for a radio performance" or "study for a radio representation". The term "portrayal" is preferred, however, due its semantic resonance with the *Ritratto (Portrait)*.

Within the panorama of Italian radio at the time, the formula of this audio portrayal was indeed highly innovative: the description was entrusted to two male speakers who, together with sounds and noises, comment on the activities of the city from dawn to dusk. The voices, in a slow, non-timbred and unemphatic pace, narrate and occasionally describe, but the real action is in the music and the electronic sounds, which 'translate' the words into acoustic 'images' for the listener.[29] In this purely acoustic rendering, Milan is described as a city suspended between reality and dream. Nineteen sound panels articulate single temporal moments, situations, places and emotions that accompany a metropolitan day.[30] The silence of dawn closes in a circle with the silence of the night, and between these two poles we get the following succession: the awakening, the fog, the monotonous and repetitive work of an accountant, the crazy urban alienation, the magnificence of the Duomo, the first lights of the evening, the frenetic life of the railway station, the description of the Navigli canals, the often secret deaths of anonymous people, the twilight. There are no characters or a true narrator unfolding the story. The described contexts are to be understood as 'snapshots' taken from above and edited with an implicit sequentiality. It is the power of the sounds (concrete, electronic or mixed) that clarify the spoken words and describe the urban scene, giving it a vibrant contour that even goes so far as to amplify the meaning of the text. In fact, in *Ritratto di città* the text is indeed a clue, a pretext to be elaborated in order to achieve "the first complete attempt of radio representation entirely obtained with the means of concrete and electronic music [...], and with frequencies produced by a generator".[31] This goal was achieved, considering that

---

29   The radio documentary *Ritratto di città* was published in 2000 on the CD accompanying De Benedictis and Rizzardi (2000). The speakers were Nando Gazzolo and Ottavio Fanfani, very well know actors in the Italian radio scene of the time. Roberto Leydi recalled that it was Maderna and Berio who requested an almost monotonous and colourless reading from the two actors, in order to increase the strength of the sounds (conversation, 24 July 1999; recording in my private archive).

30   The trend of urban description had acquired a privileged reputation above all in historic avant-garde cinema (in the specific genre of the documentary). Among the earliest and most significant examples we may count *Rien que les heures* (1926) by Alberto Cavalcanti, an evocation of a Parisian day; *Berlin, Symphonie einer Grosstadt* (1927) by Walter Ruttmann, a 'symphony' of images illustrating the daily life of a big city; and *Celovek s Kinoapparatom* (*The Man with a Movie Camera*) by Dziga Vertov (1929), a description of Moscow over the course of an entire day, mediated by the 'eyes' of a cinema operator.

31   Text taken from the opening announcement of *Ritratto di città* (original RAI reel); complete transcription in De Benedictis (2004: 197–198). For more in-depth information on *Ritratto di città*, see De Benedictis (2004: 192–202) and De Benedictis and Rizzardi (2000: 26–54).

through this radio documentary, with its overtly 'demonstrative' sounds, Berio and Maderna succeeded in convincing the radio establishment's heads of the need to open an electronic Studio within the RAI.

With the creation of the Studio di Fonologia in Milan, there was a turning point in Italy, both in the sphere of radio dramas and radio operas. Thanks to the new potential of the technologies for synthesising and electro-acoustic elaboration, music gained new importance in radio productions, and sound, which had been used as mere background and commentary until then, emerged as a protagonist in its own right. A synergetic relationship began to develop between the production of functional music and its art form counterpart: for composers like Berio and Maderna, the music they wrote for occasional radio dramas was *also* viewed as a laboratory for experimenting with acoustic solutions that could be taken further in their contemporary electronic or vocal/instrumental compositions. In 2000, urged to talk about his work at RAI in the beginning of his career, Berio recognised that with Maderna they "produced a great quantity of 'functional' music, not only because we needed money, but also because every time we wanted to try something new" (qtd. in De Benedictis and Rizzardi 2000: 166).

The data summarised in Table 4.1 conveys the intensity of their activities in the sphere of radio drama. The table lists the titles of all the radio productions with music that Berio and Maderna realised in the Studio di Fonologia from 1954 through to the mid-sixties.[32] The titles of electroacoustic works they produced in the same years (underlined and outlined in Table 4.1 in grey) offer a global perspective on their main experimentation conducted at the Milan-based Studio.

Many of the titles included in this list could be cited as examples of the best radio art in Italy from the fifties and sixties. In terms of style and quality, radio plays such as *Mi devi ascoltare* (*You Have to Listen to Me*), *Waterloo*, *La Loira* (*The Loire*), *La bella del bosco* (*Beauty of the Woods*), *L'Augellino belverde* (*The Green Bird*), *Il cavallo di Troia* (*The Trojan Horse*), *Aspetto Matilde* (*Waiting for Matilde*), *Mani* (*Hands*), *Ritratto di Erasmo* (*Portrait of Erasmus*), *Il malato immaginario* (*The Imaginary Invalid*) and many others were, in the end, decidedly superior to the radio plays that, in the same years, were turned out by the other RAI production headquarters in Rome, Turin, Florence and Naples.[33] The reasons for this 'superiority' must not be sought (or not only, at least) in

---

32 All the radio play cited in Table 4.1 are kept at the RAI archives and, in part, in Berio's and Maderna's bequests preserved at the Paul Sacher Foundation in Basel.

33 For an overview of the RAI radio drama productions in Italy from 1950 to 1974, see De Benedictis (2004: 56–60).

TABLE 4.1 List of the radio dramas and electronic works by Berio and Maderna produced at the Studio di Fonologia (RAI) from 1954 to 1975

Year	LUCIANO BERIO	Text/Direction	BRUNO MADERNA	Text/Direction
1954	*Ritratto di città*		*Ritratto di città*	Roberto Leydi (T)/B. Maderna - L. Berio (D)
1955			*Sequenze e strutture*	
	Morte di Wallenstein	F. Schiller - V. Sermonti (T)/E. Ferrieri (D)		
	Mi devi ascoltare	N. Kneal (T)/E. Convalli (D)		
	Annibale alle porte	R.E. Sherwood - G. Landi (T)/E. Convalli		
1955–56	*Mutazioni*			
1956			*Notturno*	
	Un caso clinico	D. Buzzati (T)/S. Bolchi (D)	*Uomo e superuomo*	G.B. Shaw - P. Ojetti (T)/A. Brissoni
	L'abito verde	N. Meloni (T)/A. Merlin (D)	*Brigida vuole sposarsi*	E. Labiche - A. Miserendino (T)/E. Convalli (D)
	Le cose in solitudine	M. Mattolini (T)/E. Convalli (D)		
	Santa Giovanna	G.B. Shaw - P. Ojetti (T)/S. Bolchi (D)		
	Torniamo a Matusalemme	G.B. Shaw - P. Ojetti (T)/G. Morandi (D)		

TABLE 4.1 List of the radio dramas and electronic works by Berio and Maderna (*cont.*)

Year	LUCIANO BERIO	Text/Direction	BRUNO MADERNA	Text/Direction
1957	*Perspectives*		*Syntaxis*	
	Waterloo	G.B. Angioletti - N. Saba (T)/G.B. Angioletti (D)		
	La Loira	A. Obey - A. Brissoni (T)/A. Brissoni (D)		
1958	*Thema (Omaggio a Joyce)*		*Continuo*	
	Omaggio a Joyce. Documenti sulla qualità onomatopeica del linguaggio poetico (with Umberto Eco)		*Musica su due dimensioni*	
	La bella del bosco	J. Supervielle - A. Savini (T)/A. Brissoni (D)	*L'Augellino belverde*	C. Gozzi - V. Sermonti (T)/V. Sermonti (D)
	La scampagnata		*La scampagnata*	E. Scribe - A. Brissoni (T)/A. Brissoni (D)
	La fanciulla di neve	A.N. Ostrovskij - E. Lo Gatto (T)/A. Brissoni (D)		
	Le 18 misure cantate sul corno unno	Tsai-Yen - C. Campo (T)/C. Campo (D)		
	L'uccellino azzurro	M. Maeterlinck - A. Savini (T)/A. Brissoni (D)		

TABLE 4.1   List of the radio dramas and electronic works by Berio and Maderna (*cont.*)

Year	LUCIANO BERIO	Text/Direction	BRUNO MADERNA	Text/Direction
1959	*Peter Pan*	J.M. Barrie - C. Ricono & F. Pucci (T)/A. Brissoni (D)		
	La bottiglia del diavolo	S. Basco (R.L. Stevenson) (T)/A. Brissoni (D)	*Il cavallo di Troia*	C. Morley - G. da Venezia & U. Liberatore (T)/M. Ferrero (D)
	Il viaggio impossibile del Sig. Flectar	A. Merlin (T)/U. Benedetto (D)	*Laure persécutée*	J. de Rotrou - V. Sereni (T)/V. Puecher (D)
	Luce nella notte di Solferino	G. Guerrieri (T)/G. Giagni (D)	*Mani*	R. Marinkovic - D. Cernecca (T)/A. Brissoni (D)
	Il professor Taranne	A. Adamov - G.R. Morteo (T)/A. Brissoni (D)	*Aspetto Matilde*	E. Maurri (T)/N. Meloni (D)
	Elettra	H. von Hofmannsthal - G. Bemporad (T)/M. Ferrero (D)	*L'altro mondo ovvero Gli stati e imperi della luna*	C. de Bergerac - A. Brissoni (T)/A. Brissoni (D)
1960	*Différences*		*L'altro mondo ovvero Gli stati e imperi del sole*	C. de Bergerac - A. Brissoni (T)/A. Brissoni (D)
			Invenzione su una voce	
	Momenti			
	Johnny e i pescecani	V.G. Rossi - A. Brissoni (T)/A. Brissoni (D)	*Amor di violino*	E. Carsana (T)/A. Brissoni (D)

TABLE 4.1 List of the radio dramas and electronic works by Berio and Maderna (*cont.*)

Year	LUCIANO BERIO	Text/Direction	BRUNO MADERNA	Text/Direction
			Il puff	E. Scribe - A. Mori (T)/A. Brissoni (D)
			Macbeth	Shakespeare - S. Quasimodo (T)/M. Ferrero (D)
1961	*Visage*		*Serenata III*	
	Don Giovanni	Molière - C. Vico Lodovici (T)/M. Ferrero (D)	*Don Perlimplin*	F.G. Lorca - V. Bodini & B. Maderna (T)/B. Maderna (D)
1962			*Le rire*	
1963	*Esposizione*			
1964 [1968]			[Tape for *Hyperion*]	
1969	*Questo vuol dire che...*		*Ritratto di Erasmo*	B. Maderna (T/D)
1971			*Tempo libero*	
1972			*Ages*	Shakespeare/G. Pressburger (T/D)
1971–73			[Tape for *Satyricon*]	
1973	*Il malato immaginario*	Molière - V. Sermonti & L. Diemoz (T)/G. Pressburger (D)		
1975	*Diario immaginario*	Molière - V. Sermonti (T)/G. Pressburger (D)		

a peculiar quality of the music composed by prominent figures like Berio and Maderna. In fact, by virtue of its functional dimension, the quality of the music written for these radio plays was not always of the highest (indeed, it was very often decidedly banal or even worthless from an artistic point of view). The two musicians managed instead to achieve acoustic works in which a perfect interaction between text, music and the technology offered by a radio studio prevailed. They were well aware that radio technology – its 'lutherie' and instrumentation – exerted a strong influence on the dramaturgical features of dramatic and musical productions realised for broadcasting. Berio and Maderna knew that a language or specific art for radio could be reinforced thanks to the possibilities made available by the recording and modification of sound on tape, by mixing and splicing different acoustic elements, by stereophony, by the use of the echo chamber and filters for transforming sounds, by the technique of crossfade and much more. All these resources played a part in the creation of radio works as listed in Table 4.1, for which the (implicit) role of technology was as important as the (explicit) roles of the musician, the director and the author of the text.[34]

Among the aforementioned techniques, particular mention should be made of stereophony. The first experiments with it were conducted in Italy in the early fifties, although it did not become a feature of public broadcasting until late in 1964; in an international context, by contrast, stereophonic radio works had already been produced for several years, and the category had been included in 1962 among the works competing for the Prix Italia (cf. De Benedictis 2020: 91). The possibility of locating and distinguishing the perception of acoustic events through the distribution of sound in different channels – in other words, of achieving a plastic listening experience – made it possible to set up previously unimaginable acoustic structures that revolutionised the very concept of 'space' and radio listening. In the German context, for example, it was precisely the use of stereophony that marked the watershed between old (*traditionelles*) and new (*neues*) *Hörspiel* (see Schöning 1969, 1982; Lermen 1975). In Italy, one of the first – and still perhaps best – examples of the use of stereophony for dramaturgical purposes can be found in *Don Perlimplin, ovvero il trionfo dell'Amore e dell'Immaginazione* (*Don Perlimplin, or the Triumph of Love and Imagination*) by Bruno Maderna,[35] a radio drama composed in 1961 (see Table 4.1) based on the eponymous play written by Federico

---

34 All these roles could sometimes be assumed by the same person, as for example in Maderna's *Ritratto di Erasmo*. For more information about this radio drama, see Romito (2012: 227–260; with original recording on CD 4).
35 Score published by the Edizioni Suvini Zerboni, Milan.

García Lorca in 1928. As Maderna himself wrote in a sketch preserved among his manuscripts at the Paul Sacher Foundation, *Don Perlimplin*

> is a work conceived and realised specifically for Radio – The sound recording was achieved with a 4-track tape recorder so as to make perception of the separation of the instruments into 4 distinct groups as clear as possible:
> **1st Group** – 5 Saxophones (also 4 Clarinets plus Bass Clarinet) 1 Bassoon, 1 Horn in F
> **2nd Group** – 1 Fl. (soloist), 1 Cl., plus 2 Vl, 1 Vla, 1 Cello, 2 CBasses [...]
> **3rd Group** – Guitar (with and without amplifier) Mandolin, Marimba, Vibraphone, Harp, Piano
> **4th Group** – 3 Trumpets, 3 Trombones.
> In the Studio di Fonologia of the RAI (headquarters of Milan) the individual tracks were recopied and carefully elaborated with the addition of filters, echoes, interpolations of parts of the recited text, so that the latter never had the music as 'background' but as completion and a 'real' part. The whole work aims at a new form of symbiosis between sound and words.[36]

With this radio drama, Maderna radically innovated both the concept of radio dramaturgy and that of 'setting up imaginary spaces'. Listening to the original (i.e., the original RAI tape) shows just how far the whole work was influenced by the resource of stereophony.[37] As summarised in the diagram reproduced in Figure 4.1, the distribution between left and right channels, or the simultaneous use of both, closely mirrors the progress of the drama. The protagonist, the elderly bachelor Don Perlimplin – interpreted not by an actor but by the 'voice' of a flute (the soloist of the "2nd Group" mentioned by Maderna in his note) – is always located in the *right* channel. The young and beautiful bride-to-be, Belisa, and her mother (interpreted by the intriguing sound of a saxophone quartet) are instead on the other side of the imaginary scene, in the *left* channel. After the wedding, the bride moves across to join her husband on the *right*. Marcolfa, the scheming old governess, who persuades Don Perlimplin to get married to the unsuitable Belisa, is relayed through both channels, so *left* and *right*, acoustically 'invading' all available space – exactly as, in the original play, she conditions and even directs the lives of all the other characters. However, when she confers or confabulates *sotto voce* with Don Perlimplin, or whenever she speaks loudly to his

---

36 The complete text (original in Italian) is published in De Benedictis (2004: 256f.).
37 The original tape of *Don Perlimplin* is published in De Benedictis and Novati (2012: CD 3).

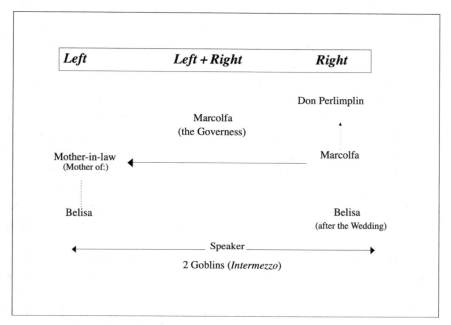

FIGURE 4.1 'Stereophonic dramaturgy' in Bruno Maderna's *Don Perlimplin*

mother-in-law, apparently acting in the interest of her master, she is located on the *right* (on the same side as Don Perlimplin). The speaker's voice fills both channels in a metaphorically neutral way, while the central Intermezzo of the two goblins ('*folletti*') – who comment on events from the standpoint of mischievous onlookers – is a real gem of stereophonic mixing technique, with various transitions between left and right channels according to the events and characters being referred to.

It may come as quite a surprise that such an important aspect in dramaturgical terms does not figure in either of the two recordings of *Don Perlimplin* currently available.[38] Rather than being based on Maderna's original recording, both of them were made on the basis of a score (published for copyright filing reasons) which continues to be mistaken for the prescriptive version of the work, complete in all its parts. The score of *Don Perlimplin* – like almost all scores of music written for the radio – should instead be regarded as merely a guide or author's script for the assemblage and realisation of a work whose definitive version (the true 'text') can only be identified as the last tape finalised and produced by the composer in the studio. It is indeed important to bear

---

[38] CD Stradivarius 33436, 1996 (conducted by Sandro Gorli), and CD Arts Music 47692-2, 2005 (conducted by Mauro Ceccanti 2005).

in mind that, for works genuinely conceived as 'acoustic art', the existence of a score (as in the case of *Don Perlimplin*) should not be perceived as a 'closed' or 'complete' performative basis. Concepts such as definitiveness, stability and performability can sometimes openly conflict with the nature of these particular sources. Because of its characteristics of realisation, and because all the operations allowed for by the radio equipment, which become an integral part of the work's conception, the final artistic product (i.e., the 'auratic' work) is to be understood as a whole formed by text, music *and* technology. Moreover, the operations of sound manipulation or mixing constitute, in radio works, a parameter that cannot be visualised with traditional writing (see Figure 4.2).

Used as a means of mixing music and words in a new way and creating imaginary spaces, even simultaneously, stereophony plays a pre-eminent role in at least two other radio productions listed in Table 4.1: *Ages* by Maderna, which won the Prix Italia in 1972, and *Il malato immaginario* by Berio, a long radio drama, based on Molière, produced in 1973 and subsequently reworked into the radio opera *Diario immaginario* (*Imaginary Diary*), winner of the Prix Italia in 1975.[39] In *Ages*, an "invenzione radiofonica" ('invention for radio') based on Shakespeare's *As You Like It*, Maderna went one step further in transforming an obligatory element of radio productions – the presentation of the opening credits – into a structural component of the work. In this case, the broadcast is not preceded, as usual, by an announcer who gives listeners information about what they are going to hear over the next half hour, but instead the technical information and the credits become an integral part of the composition. As the sketch "progetto di montaggio" ('editing project') reproduced in Figure 4.3 shows, prior to beginning his composition Maderna had already decided to insert the credits – "TITOLI (ANNUNCI)" – once the radio opera had started, making functional use of this structural element as a 'window' or 'curtain' separating an opening introductory part from the beginning of the dramatisation proper of Shakespeare's text. The outline sketched in Figure 4.3 refers to the first 5 minutes of the work; in fact, on the definitive tape the opening credits come exactly 4 and a half minutes into the programme.

In the case of both *Il malato immaginario* and the subsequent *Diario immaginario*, Berio made highly innovative use of another typical feature of the radio medium: noise. In this radio adaptation of Molière's *The Imaginary Invalid* noises go considerably beyond the descriptive or evocative functions of setting. They are used instead as true protagonists who can even 'substitute'

---

39   The original recordings of both works (*Ages* and *Diario immaginario*) are published in De Benedictis and Novati (2012: CD 5).

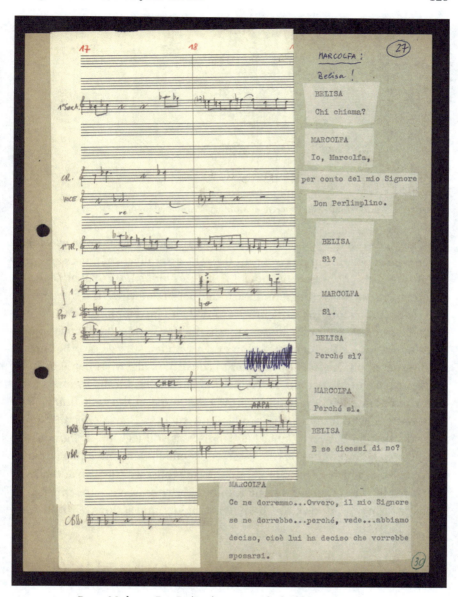

FIGURE 4.2   Bruno Maderna, *Don Perlimplin,* autograph, double-numbered page; p. 9 of the manuscript

the character with whom that particular noise is associated. Moreover, they become thematic material that can be treated and organised like music. Thus the coughing of the hypochondriac and of other characters may not only symbolise a metaphorical presence (the sickness), but can also be

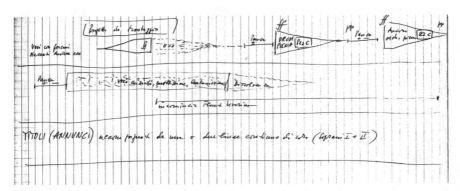

FIGURE 4.3   Bruno Maderna, 'Progetto di Montaggio' sketched for *Ages*

interspersed with the words they speak so as to constitute a canon or a fugue (even with exposition and closing stretto). The assemblage of noises and fragments of words or phrases that begins *Il malato immaginario* can be seen as a genuine Overture, or a programmatic introduction, in which the themes that will recur throughout the work are presented and mixed up. Thus, the initial sounds of someone limping by, the splash of a jet of urine, flatulence, coughs of different intensities, hammer blows on a wooden surface or other noises are presented polyphonically in order to constitute, like what happens in an Ouverture, a sort of 'memory reservoir' that anticipates for the listeners their occurrence and their development during the course of the radio drama. One may wonder whether, in radio productions such as *Diario immaginario*, a clear distinction between 'music' and 'noises' is still legitimate. Perhaps we should speak more properly of a 'syncretic sonic dimension', going so far as to conceive of music as a set of parameters to which we can also add noises, organised by the composer – along with notes, rhythms, etc. – to represent in acoustic form sensations, thoughts, environments, and actions of the characters on stage.

5   Conclusion

From the analysis of these and other productions made in the Studio di Fonologia of RAI-Milano, and their comparison with other contemporary radio works, it is possible to understand to what extent they proved influential in the wider context of how the 'radio drama' and 'radio opera' genres developed in Italy. The new impetus that can be identified in this field during the sixties undoubtedly owes much to many of these programmes (and to the people who, alongside the composers, contributed to their realisation, such as technicians, authors of the scripts and producers). Even though this electronic Studio has its own vital importance for music historians in a field different from radiodramatic art – namely, the field of electronic and electroacoustic music – we can nonetheless state that right from its creation, and thanks also to the work carried out by musicians like Berio and Maderna in the field of 'functional music', Italy could at last witness the emergence of a genuine acoustic art or, to put it in Berio's words, of a "theatre of the ears" (1995: 99).[40]

References

Antonucci, Giovanni (1998). *PRIXITALIA19481999. La radio e la televisione nel mondo*. Roma: Eri-Rai.

Berio, Luciano (1995). "A-Ronne". Enzo Restagno, ed. *Berio*. Torino: Edt. 99.

Brech, Martha (2000). "New Technology – New Artistic Genres: Changes in the Concept and Aesthetic of Music". Hans-Joachim Braun, ed. *"I Sing the Body Electric": Music and Technology in the 20th Century*. Hofheim: Wolke. 219–234.

Cusy, Pierre, Gabriel Germinet (1926). *Théâtre radiophonique. Mode nouveau d'expression artistique*. Paris: Étienne Chiron.

De Benedictis, Angela Ida (2004). *Radiodramma e arte radiofonica. Storia e funzioni della musica per radio in Italia*. Torino: De Sono-Edt.

De Benedictis, Angela Ida (2012). "'A Meeting of Music and the New Possibilities of Technology': The Beginnings of the Studio di Fonologia Musicale di Milano della Rai". Maria Madalena Novati, John Dack, eds. *The Studio di Fonologia. A Musical Journey 1954–1983. Update 2008–2012*. Milano: Ricordi. 3–18.

De Benedictis, Angela Ida (2018). "Radiokunst und 'Radiodramma' in Italien (mit Beispielen von Berio und Maderna)". Ute Holl, ed. *Radiophonic Cultures*. Berlin: Kehrer. 21–37.

De Benedictis, Angela Ida (2020). "Between Art and Promotion: The Prix Italia, Its Historical Context and Aims in the First Fifty Years 1949–1998". Jarmila Mildorf, Pim Verhulst, eds. *Radio Art and Music: Culture, Aesthetics, Politics*. Lanham, MD: Lexington Books. 85–97.

De Benedictis, Angela Ida, Maria Maddalena Novati, eds. (2012). *Imagination at Play: The Prix Italia and Radiophonic Experimentation*. Milan: Rai Trade/Die Schachtel.

---

40 See also http://www.lucianoberio.org/node/1420?1747386730=1 [01/04/2022].

De Benedictis, Angela Ida, Veniero Rizzardi (2000). "A Conversation with Luciano Berio". Angela Ida De Benedictis, Veniero Rizzardi, eds. *New Music on the Radio: Experiences at the Studio di Fonologia of the Rai, Milan 1954–1959*. Roma: Rai/Cidim. 160–175.

De Benedictis, Angela Ida, Veniero Rizzardi, eds. (2000) *New Music on the Radio: Experiences at the Studio di Fonologia of the Rai, Milan 1954–1959*. Roma: Rai/Cidim.

Drakakis, John (1981). "Introduction". John Drakakis, ed. *British Radio Drama*. Cambridge: CUP. 1–36.

Glandien, Kersten (2000). "Art on Air: A Profile of New Radio Art in Music". Simon Emmerson, ed. *Electronic Media and Culture*. Burlington, VT: Ashgate. 167–193.

"Il primo esperimento di teatro radiofonico" (1927). *Radio Orario* 3/5: 1–3.

"*La Musica Concreta*" (1955). *Radiocorriere* 32/28: 24.

"La radio e la musica" (1937). *La Rassegna Musicale* 10/9–10: 301–328.

Lermen, Birgit (1975). *Das traditionelle und neue Hörspiel im Deutschunterricht. Strukturen, Beispiele und didaktisch-methodische Aspekte*. Paderborn: Ferdinand Schöningh.

Luisetti, Federico (2012). *A Vitalist Art: Filippo Tommaso Marinetti's sintesi radiofoniche*. Geert Buelens, Harald Hendrix, Monica Jansen, eds. *The History of Futurism: The Precursors, Protagonists, and Legacies*. Lanham, MD: Lexington Books. 283–296.

Marinetti, Francesco Tommaso (1941). *Il teatro futurista. Sintetico (dinamico-alogico-autonomo-simultaneo-visionico). A sorpresa. Aeroradiotelevisivo. Caffè Concerto. Radiofonico*. Napoli: CLET.

Marinetti, Francesco Tommaso, Pino Masnata (2009) "The Radia: Futurist Manifesto (1933)". Lawrence Rainey, Christine Poggi, Laura Wittman, eds. *Futurism: An Anthology*. New Haven, CT: Yale Univ. Press. 293–295.

Mila, Massimo (1952). "La musica e la radio". *RAI. Radio Italiana. Annuario 1952. Relazioni e bilancio dell'esercizio 1951*. Torino: Edizioni Radio Italiana. 89–102.

Modigliani, Gino (1947). "Teatro dell'Usignolo". *Radiocorriere* 24/40: 4.

Nicolodi, Fiamma, ed. (1975). *Luigi Dallapiccola. Saggi, testimonianze, carteggio, biografia e bibliografia*. Milano: Suvini Zerboni. 92–93.

Novati, Maria Maddalena, John Dack, eds. (2012). *The Studio di Fonologia: A Musical Journey 1954–1983*. Milano: Ricordo.

Ohmer, Anja, Hans Kiefer (2013). *Das deutsche Hörspiel*. Essen: Oldib.

Pasolini, Pier Paolo (1972). *Empirismo eretico*. Milano: Garzanti.

Rocca, Enrico (1938). *Panorama dell'arte radiofonica*. Milano: Bompiani.

Romito, Maurizio (2012). "*Ritratto di Erasmo* by Bruno Maderna". Angela Ida De Benedictis, Maria Maddalena Novati, eds. *Imagination at Play: The Prix Italia and Radiophonic Experimentation*. Milan: Rai Trade/Die Schachtel. 227–260.

Santi, Piero (1984). "La nascita dello 'Studio di Fonologia Musicale' di Milano". *Musica/Realtà* 5/14: 167–188.

Savinio, Alberto (1989). "È lo strumento che crea la musica". Leonardo Sciascia, Franco De Maria, eds. *Opere. Scritti dispersi tra guerra e dopoguerra.* Milano: Bompiani. 975–978.

Schöning, Klaus, ed. (1969). *Neues Hörspiel. Texte, Partituren.* Frankfurt am Main: Suhrkamp.

Schöning, Klaus, ed. (1974). *Neues Hörspiel O-Ton: Der Konsument als Produzent. Versuche. Arbeitberichte.* Frankfurt am Main: Suhrkamp.

Schöning, Klaus (1982). *Spuren des Neuen Hörspiels.* Frankfurt am Main: Suhrkamp.

Schöning, Klaus, Nadja Schöning, eds. (2021). *Vom Neuen Hörspiel zur Akustischen Kunst zur Ars Acustica als Ars Intermedia: Erinnerungen. Essays, Vorträge, Reflexionen, Sendungen, Porträts und Gespräche.* Würzburg: Königshausen & Neumann.

Vowinckel, Antje (1995). *Collagen im Hörspiel. Die Entwicklung einer radiophonen Kunst.* Würzburg: Königshausen & Neumann.

Vugliano, Mario (1926). "Il teatro radiofonico". *Radio Orario* 2/36: 4–5.

CHAPTER 5

Composing the Radio: Musical Collaborations and Border Crossings in Drama and Features at the Australian Public Service Broadcaster

Virginia M. Madsen

Abstract

This chapter charts the role of music and 'composition' in radio 'plays', 'features' and associated forms made for the Australian Broadcasting Corporation (ABC) from inception to the early 2000s. Evolving 'radio-labs' for radiophonic creation at the ABC, BBC and beyond (often in both formal and informal dialogue), allowed expressive forms of audio literature and performance to flourish and develop to a sophisticated level. Historically and formally, 'features' were highly conducive sites for creative exploration, from auteur documentaries to 'reality-fictions' and provocative performance works involving writers, producers, performers, and composers. These nourished future imaginaries for radio and its listeners, inspiring an ongoing adventure in sound.

Until recently, the Australian Broadcasting Corporation (ABC), like the UK's BBC and its equivalents in Europe, has had a long tradition of producing and broadcasting original radio plays, audio theatre and performance, audio arts, features, serials and fictions. This output has included adaptations of dramatic, musical and poetic texts, novels and short stories, an activity which was considered part of the ABC's core business from its inception in 1932, through to its effective cessation (as core output) in 2012. From the late 1940s, the ABC also supported the production of related genres, mainly dramatised non-fiction and other documentary forms, known after the BBC nomenclature as 'radio features'.[1] By the 1960s, the ABC was producing special works of 'radio music', 'radio opera' and other hybrid forms of performance in addition

---

1 The term 'feature' was in use as early as 1924 in British radio, but had referred to 'miscellanies' rather than the experimental and later creative documentary and poetic forms it became most known for (cf. Coulton 1980: 40). The cinematic metaphor is prominent in this 1930 descriptor: "A 'Feature programme' [...] can only be described as an unseen but heard moving picture." (BBC 1930: 168f.)

to more traditional radio plays in a mix with the evolving fields encapsulated by the ideas of audio arts (*ars acustica*) and 'radio art'. Writers and composers (Australian and international) developed original work, oftentimes in collaboration with staff producers from specialised departments and 'units'.

By the early 1970s, members of historically discrete institutional areas within ABC Radio (Music, Drama and Features, Talks) came together to form new programmes, mixing genres and forms, and working across national networks. With the creation of *The Listening Room* (*TLR*) programme in 1988, the ABC emerged as a world leader in the audio arts and in engaging cross-genre interdisciplinary collaborations involving writers, composers, musicians, performers, dramatists and artists of all kinds. Here was a chance to play with and provoke radio's expressive and dramatic forms whether as fiction, nonfiction or something in-between. This period in particular is noteworthy, as the *TLR* programme marked a high point in the creative and collaborative participation of composers in radio performance works, in addition to related dramatic and poetic feature work.[2] This was also a remarkable time for experiment and increased international collaboration, as well as for ABC producers being more exposed to work from beyond the familiar BBC. The seeds of this renewal had germinated in the 1970s as producers opened to work from around the world, discovered new freedoms crossing genre boundaries, and benefited from critical advancements in audio technologies. We can hear the effects of increased circulation of material coming from non-Anglophone producers and centres via cassettes, and through participation in festivals and competitions.

Cutting, mixing and 'writing on tape', these audio arts pioneers would sound hitherto untapped spaces for radiophonic 'play'. Such encounters might lead to 'composing for the radio', or 'composing with the radio'. By the mid-1980s at the ABC, management was persuaded by these developments to increase their commitment to this work, with producers writing about and promoting their works as "new adventures in sound" (see Madsen 2009). Even the radio play or the radio feature would no longer be delineated as the established parameters for creative radio. Instead, a forging of new forms and revisiting and unearthing of older traditions and genres came together as new spaces were launched, first *Surface Tension*, then *The Listening Room*, then *Radio Eye*. These

---

2   "During the period 1988 to 1997 [...] TLR drew on works by composers of 28 different nationalities for presentation in its programs. Features were drawn not only from composers in Europe [...] but also from countries such as Greece, Croatia, Poland and Tibet, where contact, to say the least, was not so regular [...]. During the period 1988 to 1997 TLR broadcast 600 pieces of which 215 were by Australian composers. Excluding time taken up by introductions, fades and other presentational material, the Australian component represents about 75% of total broadcast time devoted by TLR to compositions." (Richards 2003: 171, 196)

sites were all poised towards dialogue with, or reinvention of, the much earlier radio labs that had been first imagined or supported in multiple broadcasting organisations from as early as the 1920s and 30s.

1 An Idea for a Radio Laboratory at the ABC Inspired by the Early BBC?

Very early in the ABC's history as Australia's first 'public service broadcaster' an idea circulated: could a space be created which would encourage experiment and creativity of all kinds in this newly emergent mass medium? Could this space be thought of as something like a 'research section' or 'lab'? In 1934, the respected British poet laureate John Masefield (then visiting Australia) wrote to the ABC's Melbourne Director Herbert Brookes after earlier discussions the two had been having on the subject of creative radio programmes. Masefield suggested to Brookes: "clever men should experiment in order to discover what kinds of narrative and drama are suited to broadcasting", even specifying that the ABC "should employ clever men and women writers for not less than three years" to allow them "to make experiments over the air". Moreover, they should be so free in their ideas or expression as to "infuriate the multitude" (Masefield 1934). Brookes forwarded these musings to Frank Clewlow (then National Manager of ABC Programs) and Clewlow in turn wrote to the ABC's Managing Director, Charles Moses, seizing the opportunity to raise the profile of drama within the new organisation. Drawing on Masefield's suggestions, Clewlow proposed a space dedicated to the production of new kinds of sound play and dramatic forms made specifically for the ear. He stressed the "importance of spoken word in broadcasting" and the "comparative neglect of development of new forms of its use in Australia" (Clewlow 1934). He suggested the ABC could have "the foundation of a laboratory, where several young writers [...] work and experiment [...] in different genres [...] [in] light and 'special feature programs'" (ibid.). He also imagined "one or more young composers of serious and light music" joining, in addition to "technical experimenters who would follow up the ideas of writers and musicians as to effects, microphone placings, and general technical development" (ibid.). His conclusion was clear: "Such a laboratory seems an urgent necessity." (ibid.)

Clewlow was certainly convinced by the visiting poet's proposals, who in turn appears to have reflected a programme development already established inside the BBC, the world's first public service broadcaster (PSB). Drawing on BBC history in this area, and reading these documents – held by the National Archives of Australia (NAA) – of early Australian Broadcasting Commission correspondence (Head Office, Drama 1933–37 SP1558/2 127/18/3/3-3), it is evident there was an awareness within ABC of BBC early drama and features experiments, and its first 'laboratory' for exploring new forms. Only a few years prior to this correspondence, the BBC had founded its pioneering Program Research Section in July 1928 (under John Reith, inaugural Director-General) as just the kind of incubator for new expression in sound broadcasting. This Section enabled a group of writer-producers to experiment with technologies and techniques, play with forms and encourage a host of other artists to work on their productions as collaborators. As Masefield wrote to Brookes (citing W.B. Yeats), "all art is a collaboration" and "this is especially true of dramatic and narrative art" (Masefield 1934).

Serving the cause of invention and cross-pollination, the BBC's first Research Section was launched with just a small band of producers. They gathered an array of notable and aspiring writers, composers and other artists into their orbit (e.g., the young Benjamin Britten), both men and women. Notably, the style of production used in this first BBC 'lab', and in the many novel drama productions and multi-form 'features' to emerge from it, had distinctive musical as well as cinematic and poetic aspects, even at this very early stage of development. This kind of new 'play' was also registering beyond the BBC, and certainly by the time the ABC was launched. These kinds of experiments forged in that BBC Section continued to resonate even after the group was merged into the BBC Drama Department,[3] and later also after a separate Features Department was formed.

What were these new 'features'? And why might we include them in the context of a discussion on radio drama and music at the ABC? To gain a better idea of these kinds of early programmes which did come to influence ABC drama and feature traditions and forms, as well as the potential for music and musicality to be prominent in them, it is helpful to touch on the features and plays of one of the pioneers of the group. Lance Sieveking experimented with kaleidophonic 'rhapsodies' and 'mosaics' in sound (e.g., his *Kaleidoscope*), fading in and out performers and effects from multiple studios employing the prototype of the contemporary audio mixing desk, first dubbed the Dramatic Control Panel, and which he helped develop with BBC engineers. In his book *The Stuff of Radio* (1934: 26), Sieveking recalled how he utilised seven or eight studios and over 100 people for just one of these "mosaic features" (i.e., for

---

3   Tyrone Guthrie reported that the BBC was experimenting and reacting against naturalism, envisaging a new "microphone drama" form: this radio drama might concentrate less on conveying to the audience "a series of mind pictures" and, instead, explore the "symphonic possibilities of the medium – vocal rhythms, colours, tempos, pitch" (1931: 189).

Kaleidoscope, broadcast by the BBC on 4 September 1928).[4] As a former pilot, we might imagine Sieveking 'playing' this panel as a navigator of the air, but also as a conductor-composer. With his fade-ins and -outs and turning of dials, bringing up as many as six studios and more microphoned sources in rapid succession, he also conjured cinema-like imagery out of the voices and words, waves and air, inviting listeners to be carried on his flights of fantasy. The words were arranged like music mixed with reality, and the microphone channelled sounds and scenes from the outside world too, as well as via *trompe l'oreille* created by Sound Effects operators. With palpable exhilaration he recalled the thrill of 'conducting' these elaborate concoctions made of voices, orchestras and sound effects: "[T]he river rushes by, it makes you wet to listen to it." Or: "Flick Studio 2. Now Studio 4. Now 1. Crossfade. […] (How they are howling and whining like lost souls down in the effects studio!)" (ibid.: 22f.) This description feels like theatre, opera and early modernist cinema score rolled into one, presaging something closer to cinema sound design and radio creation as these developed in the post war electronic period. We might even later encounter these forms across twentieth-century radio art and the German *Neues Hörspiel*. The main difference with the early Research Section productions was that all this effort could only be towards a live emission; broadcasts at that stage could not be recorded easily, so ultimately they were ephemeral, evanescent.

Nevertheless, these early BBC experimental features were performed works, usually of words, music and sound effects arranged for live broadcast. Later they would also be recorded. Unlike early radio plays mostly adapted from theatre, the use of music was not primarily functional (musical breaks and bridges, the familiar musicalised changes-of-scene), or even employed to act as a motif, or to carry or heighten emotion. In this emerging work from the BBC Research Section (and this continued after the Section was concluded), composers might also be invited to be fellow explorers in the still nascent medium, collaborating with writers in the creation of dramatic and poetic works, as well as in a variety of collaged features which did not need to fit into one genre, narrative or dramatic structure. The composer could be a co-director, and the producer (a new role) could also be understood here as an author-artist, with lines blurring between the roles of engineer, director or composer-conductor.

---

4 Sieveking worked with writers such as Edith Sitwell, and composers including Constant Lambert and William Walton. *Kaleidoscope* employed music as a "character", according to *Radio Times*: "Good and evil influences are whirled round in a kaleidoscope of sound during the crises in a man's life." See the listing for its repeat on 27 October 1933 as part of the BBC's *Twelve Plays for Broadcasting* series: https://genome.ch.bbc.co.uk/94d46c7c7a4747fa921a6fa81cb5d0d3 [23/04/2022].

This allowed producers to work with their 'materials'[5] in ways that might be considered as much musical as dramatic as they composed forms also influenced by wider modernist arts, and related literary and cinema movements.

2   An ABC Drama Department as a First Bid for a Radio Lab

Meanwhile in Australia, jumping from Sieveking's exploratory workshop for radio play to 1936 and Clewlow's bid for a similar experimental space, what eventuated for the ABC? Even as the Australian broadcaster was modelled after the BBC (albeit much smaller), and for many decades maintained close links with its British counterpart sharing programme traditions, receiving BBC programmes on 'discs', and staff participating in exchanges, the ABC differed in significant ways from its British progenitor. These divergences had a noticeable impact on the kinds and ambitions of productions attempted in the early ABC. This played out as the ABC commenced its experiments in radio drama and the broadcasting of original performative and other creative works. Most crucially, tighter funding for the ABC in this area had a significant impact on the ABC's ability to engage and commission new Australian radio plays and creative feature works. Even more challenging to produce would be the much more expensive collaborations with composers, conductors and musicians, or other artists as were part of the BBC's offering. While the ABC shared similar organisational structures, programme types and departments to the BBC, the ABC was not given monopoly status as a national public service broadcaster, thus always commanding less from the license fee and later government allocation. With substantially less funds available to employ staff, or for technical equipment/facilities, there was no equivalent to the BBC's developing features and experimental programme culture. Drawing on multiple sources, it also appears that ABC producer-writers of the time had less creative control over their productions from the technical side, certainly not in the way Sieveking and others were working with less interference or oversight (see Madsen 2017).

A radio lab imagined along the lines in which John Masefield relayed it to his host did not materialise at the ABC in those pre-war years, and for two decades there would be markedly fewer opportunities to devote the resources needed to productions of a similarly ambitious, experimental or collaborative nature as we find in the BBC. From 1936, however, and for at least the next thirty years, the ABC would go on to produce thousands of plays, dramatic

---

5 Sound effects were high in their creative thinking.

and poetic works, serials or book readings – and music works too as part of its core output.[6] It would do this contributing to the nurture of a homegrown Australian theatre industry and culture,[7] and with the hope that Australians who had formerly little access to these arts could now at least hear them.[8] But compared to the BBC, from its inauguration the ABC had to contend with the additional challenges of servicing a growing network of far flung stations and transmitters. It is not hard to understand why there was lower priority given at the ABC to the kinds of ambitious collaborative works involving composers and writers developed by BBC drama and features – and which attained notable recognition plus huge audiences from the Second World War to the onset of the Cold War.

Even so, those early exchanges between the poet Masefield and Brookes, then also with Clewlow, had struck a chord: a new radio site for creativity and ambition was brought into being, precipitating the closest thing to that BBC lab the ABC would be granted for decades to come: the first Federal ABC Drama Department (Fehlberg 1964: 36). Launched in 1936 and directed by the ABC's first Controller of Productions (i.e., Clewlow), hope was sown in this new Department that suitable and adventurous radio performance, writing and features might soon be developed for Australian listeners, and opportunities would be provided for collaborations between 'creatives' to influence techniques and technologies as well as forms into the future. Radio dramas at the ABC would be made in increasing numbers from that founding moment, expanding through the war years, attracting writers (young and established), some experimenting with new poetic forms of audio literature and drama – already a characteristic of BBC features.

The 'verse drama' pioneered in the BBC but also in the Columbia Broadcasting System (CBS), or Columbia Workshop, found admirers and adherents in Australia, reaching a high level in the work of poet Douglas Stewart, for

---

6 Already in 1933 the new Commission boasted it had "employed thousands of Australian musical, dramatic and literary artists [...] at a critical stage in our country's history" (ABC 1933: 8). A few years on, Frank Clewlow reported that "over 70% of the dramatic material broadcast during 1937 was written in Australia" (1940).

7 Clewlow wrote: "We are building up a library of plays about Australian conditions and character, which would have had little opportunity of being heard but for broadcasting." (1940) See also Indyk (1990).

8 It did this with the understanding that the ABC's role and mission was from the outset considered to be a cultural undertaking. Like the BBC, the ABC understood itself as fundamentally a cultural institution first (a place to cultivate the arts, music and ideas across all fields); and secondly, it also realised its mission was democratic: to inform, enlighten and educate all who might listen, from the most to the least educated, employing 'talks', 'features', educational programming, and later also news and topical programmes.

example. His *Fire on the Snow*, based on Robert Falcon Scott's expedition to the South Pole, premiered on ABC's National Program on 6 June 1941. ABC producers were experimenting in ways akin to their BBC or CBS counterparts. In the verse play they found a form which might act as a main site for this experiment. The ABC commissioned original works (e.g., Stewart's), and produced adaptations of some of the most celebrated of this 1930s genre: Clewlow produced the CBS verse play *The Fall of the City* (7 July 1938) by Archibald MacLeish a little over a year after its US premiere (11 April 1937). It was, Clewlow reported, a "new landmark in the progress of radio drama" (1938). In an article headed "ABC Plays for July", *The Telegraph* (Brisbane, June 25, 1938) hailed the Australian version in the same terms. The original, described as a "news broadcast in verse about a city that is conquered from within when its inhabitants invent and believe in their oppressors", had featured music composed and directed by the young Bernard Herrmann, who would work on many other CBS radio drama productions.[9] The ABC sought musical direction for these new forms too. Cecil Fraser was the musical director-composer for the ABC's own production of the MacLeish play. He conducted the ABC dance band and composed playful musical treatments for ABC Children's Sessions. Clewlow was further inspired to produce homegrown works himself of this genre in Alexander Turner's *Australian Stages* (1945), employing chorused voices (as heard in *The Fall of the City*) to evoke the rhythm of a train journey (Rees 1945: 211).

One of the problems in trying to assess this work and the quality of the collaborations is that few ABC recordings survive to give contemporary listeners an accurate sense of how the majority sounded. In contrast, similar works from the USA and the BBC are preserved.[10] Scripts held at the NAA archives and some commentaries from those playing key roles in ABC drama and features

---

9   Much more remembered were Herrmann's film collaborations. His first film score was for Orson Welles' *Citizen Kane*, and for Alfred Hitchcock's *The Birds* he played with *musique concrète* techniques and electronic effects (with Oskar Sala). Herrmann worked on thousands of radio dramas for CBS. Two notable examples are Welles' *War of the Worlds* (1938) and Norman Corwin's *We Hold These Truths* (1941), the latter purportedly heard by more Americans than any other radio drama until that time (60 million). This was a dramatised documentary-feature with Herrmann conducting. See UC Santa Barbara's guide: http://findaid.oac.cdlib.org/findaid/ark:/13030/tf438nb3jd/ [02/04/2022].

10 A work of this kind by Pare Lorentz, known for his film documentaries, was broadcast in 1938 (CBS, Columbia Workshop), then for the BBC. Both versions of *Ecce Homo* (or "Job To Be Done" in the BBC *Experimental Hour* version directed by Laurence Gilliam) survive. Also categorised a 'feature', this CBS play had a special musical score by Herrmann, with William Robson directing. *Radio Times* described Robson as a "leader of the most advanced school of American radio drama producers". See https://genome.ch.bbc.co.uk/4fec1b3de734437886ec4a71037bc41d [23/04/2022].

are helpful, nonetheless, and I draw on these along with listening to comparable British and American works of the period.[11] What is evident is that specially composed music only rarely played a significant role in early ABC dramatic productions, a notable contrast to the BBC or CBS output. Even as the ABC in its first 50 years prioritised music as a core part of its programming to Australians, offering listeners 'fine music' and popular forms alike, there were less of the kinds of plays and features which called for composers and conductors to work collaboratively to author original works. The ABC Drama Department produced many more adaptations from theatre. Original Australian work increased steadily from the war years on, but this was heavily word- and dialogue-based.

While ABC radio did not have the resources to attempt so many experiments with live music as the BBC or CBS from the late 1930s, it is important to underline that these kinds of musical collaborations and scores for drama or features were rare right across the Australian radio industry in this period. Lynn Foster, an accomplished writer for commercial radio in the 1940s making features and adaptations for the Lux Radio Theatre (and some ABC drama), remarked how in US radio "they use live musicians, not recordings" (qtd. in "Women in Radio" 1947: 9). The Columbia Workshop[12] golden age was continued to some extent in the postwar period, Foster observed, as "[e]very show has its own orchestra – or at least an organ – and music specially written for it" (ibid.). "Here", she lamented, "we are dependent on recordings that everyone else must use too" (ibid.). Certain special writers – she cited Corwin – have "the entire script [...] specially orchestrated" (ibid.). The ABC could not, for instance, employ a "staff conductor" (McGill 1940: 33) like Bernard Herrmann, who regularly directed and composed for CBS plays. Herrmann introduced contemporary composers like Arnold Schoenberg and Charles Ives to CBS listeners too, drawing from them new ways to work with music and words

---

11 Very few recordings before 1960 of this kind of work were kept by the ABC or are extant in other collections. These works were often not recorded onto discs or may have been lost. This absence helps to explain why such a large variety of productions, including notable examples written by distinguished writers and composers, could be extinguished from the memory of the institution. They do not stand out in institutional histories and are barely acknowledged in most critical literature on the ABC.

12 Rarely did a Columbia Workshop programme rely solely on words for its impact, writes Jeff Porter: "Instead, producers preferred an acoustic chorus: voice, ambience, musical motifs, and effects. The Workshop saw sound-making as part of its mandate to be 'experimental' – and vital to the 'magic of radio' as the show's announcer promised each week." (2016: 33)

whether for cinema or radio. He innovated as he replaced literal 'effects' with something closer to musicalised 'design'.[13]

The impact of the loss of composed music in drama for audiences of 'Golden Age' radio in Australia, and thus for the ABC, is highlighted well in an example from September 1942, when the broadcaster received the scripts for Norman Corwin's feature *An American in England*. Arthur Mason, the ABC's London Representative organising the contract, noted – even as the ABC was receiving these scripts to broadcast "free of charge" (with thanks to CBS) – that "[i]t will be difficult, if not impossible, to secure for the ABC, Benjamin Britten's incidental music" (1941). The rep hoped "there would not be any objection" to the ABC using "incidental music of their own", and that it would be "regarded by them as suitable?" (ibid.) This problematic lack of resources, and thus loss of the special music this anecdote identifies, comes with consequences. Deprived of this score, the work Corwin imagined, and as it was aired on the ABC, becomes a different, potentially lesser feature: producers and audiences alike miss out on the fruits of an original collaboration which is closer to a composition made specially for the radio.[14] Audiences may also not have understood the extent of the aesthetic loss, as there was nothing public to compare with the ABC's adaptation.[15]

Predominantly, the way music was used in ABC radio drama production right up until the 1970s was via licensed 'production discs', which offered producers thousands of choices for different musics (to match mood, convey tension, deliver pace). These were easy to incorporate technically, although this is not to say producers could not be creative with them, and their use continued well into the 1980s in ABC radio drama. Housed in the ABC's then Sound Effects library, a small group of 'effects operators' held the keys to their secrets as they selected tracks or played with mixing and layering them together, creating their own tailored sounds. Copyright free, this music was economical and could conjure mood, provoke emotion, change pace, separate scenes, bring tension or realism, signify location, occasion or historical period (much as it

---

13 Herrmann joined CBS in 1933 conducting and, while still in his mid-twenties, became the head of serious music and musical director of the CBS symphony.
14 Good writing, while essential, Porter writes, "would be empty without the radiophonic innovations of Orson Welles, Arch Oboler, Norman Corwin, the Columbia Workshop, and others who mined the tension between sound and sense. Their intuitive understanding of how to exploit radio's semiotic quirks, particularly the slippage between words and nonverbal signs, opened up radio as an artistic form" (2016: 36).
15 Britten, of course, had been a frequent collaborator on BBC features before the war, and continued to work on these with the BBC's newly established Features Department after the war ended.

is used now in podcasts). This music provided emphasis or punctuation, and could even be a commentator on the action and more besides (Crook 1999: 92). There were drawbacks associated with production music, however: the risk of sounding formulaic, predictable, artificial. Arguably this kind of music usage led to a number of ABC Features producers minimising music in their drama and features productions, or going so far as to avoid its use almost completely (Wetherell qtd. in Madsen 2003b).

3 Postwar Dramatised Features, Documentary Sound Pictures and Symphonies

In 1945, reporting on the dramatised feature series that the ABC had just produced (*Theirs Be the Glory*), which drew on soldier and prisoner of war witness experiences in New Guinea fighting the Japanese, Clewlow confirms how the ABC rarely relied on the input of a composer: "There is little doubt that the composition of special music for certain features is a thing we should do more if our allotment only allowed." (Clewlow 1945) However, for this production, it had been his desire to do exactly that. *Theirs Be the Glory* marked an exception to the rule, and the considerable investment in this series prepared the way for the launch of a separate Features Department three years later, based on the BBC's. This department, as it was imagined and conceived, might be at least equipped to attempt more of these ambitious special programmes where composition and original music played an essential creative and affective role.[16] By the war's end, these composed features were also attracting larger audiences and critical attention in both the UK and the USA.

The 13-part series – or "Radio Saga of the New Guinea Campaign", as it was also called – received 'special mention' by critics for its music after the first episode aired. Performed by the ABC's own Sydney orchestra, broadcasts commenced in October 1945[17] featuring Cecil Fraser's 'special jungle music': the "thematic and atmospheric pieces" were composed "to heighten and sustain

---

16 Laurence Gilliam described how Features Department should make "specially created radio programmes employing writers and musicians of the highest calibre". However: "This should not be confused with radio opera which would lead to inhibiting misunderstanding with the music world, but should be an unrestricted exploration of the combined use of words and music." (1953)

17 Compiled with official cooperation of the navy, army and air force authorities, the actuality documentation was in the form of "recorded first hand interviews with the men who created history in the New Guinea jungle". Recordings were also sourced from "the ABC's own library of historic recordings" with "some of these interviews […] obtained in the

the dramatic content of the story" ("New Guinea Documentary" 1945: 4). Writer James Donnelly, recently released from his normal role as ABC's NSW State Program Director, described the work as: "The biggest documentary job ever tackled by Australian radio. It tells of the toughest job Australians ever did." (qtd. in "Canned History" 1945) While critics praised the music, actuality and effects, and sounds were researched on location in order to be as 'authentic' as possible, reviews of the actors were less effusive – not an uncommon complaint for radio drama, critics reacted to what they described as 'artificial' voices and the failure of radio to provide here something closer to the real experience, authentic documentary *actuality* being more associated, at least in Australia, with cinema.

Donnelly also tried his hand at the 'city symphony', a genre already part of film and radio's formal vocabulary explored in the 1920s but by no means exhausted as a sonic form by that time.[18] Donnelly's symphony feature or 'sound picture' broadcast November 1947 was titled "Sydney: Symphony of a Great City" and part of the newly created ABC *Australian Walkabout* feature documentary series. This series, designed to take the listener to towns, cities and even remote Indigenous settlements all over Australia, would be transferred to the new Features Department once established in 1948. ABC publicity reported how Donnelly's sound 'picture' "will call the tribes to Corroboree at Bra-yak-alung (Land Belong The East Men)" to tell the story "of the Big Smoke, Sydney today" (ABC 1947). This broadcast would also "attempt to portray the personality of the metropolis in terms of some of the multitudinous sounds that voices its life-activity" (ibid.). The publicity described the programme as "[d]esigned in symphonic form [...] in four movements, 'The Stalwart City', 'The Dreaming City', 'The Happy City', 'The Creative City'" (ibid.). The programme also "feature[d] a number of recordings not heard before. Against a background of 'photography in sound', the programme invited the listener to travel on Sydney's underground railways, as well as her trams and ferries" (ibid.). There was a barely disguised call to the listener to visit the beaches,

---

field by ABC war correspondents, especially for this series of historical presentations" ("New Guinea Documentary" 1945: 4).

18   Much later, in the 1980s, Australian listeners would get to hear a series of city sound portraits made by composers and sound artists. These were not live but rather made for and with tape, commissioned by the Acoustic Art Studio (WDR, Cologne) and broadcast on Radio National and ABC FM. Part of the Metropolis series produced by Klaus Schöning, these programmes varied greatly, some more sculptural than musical and encompassed by the term *Neues Horspiel*. Artists included *musique concrète* pioneer Pierre Henri (*La Ville. Die Stadt*, 1984) and Australian composer Vincent Plush's *Metropolis Sydney* was added in 1988 (see Kreutzfeldt 2018).

playgrounds and nightspots. Amongst the "patterns of opinion of free speaking men and women" we might also hear those "interviewed by Douglas Channel, Sydney's popular 'Man in the Street'" (ibid.). Here was specially featured music by "Sydney composers, and Sydney orchestras and ensembles, including excerpts of [one of the most celebrated Australian musical and dance works of the time], *Corroboree* by John Antill" (ibid.). This kind of potpourri-montage programme sounds somewhat quaint today, but it connects the ABC's work with those early BBC experiments, and reminds us how even here we cannot assume the work existed or was produced as a recorded programme. While more portable recording machines were becoming available thanks to the German invention of the *Magnetophon* at the end of the war, and portable disc recording was used to make 'radio features' and war reports, this symphony may have only been produced live, since no recording is extant. Ultimately, these questions cannot be answered and sounding out becomes impossible. Today, the task of historical re-instatement of this sound and musical moment is therefore as much a question for the imagination as it is of documentary evidence. I would hazard that this symphony was 'composed' live, as operators cued in their discs containing 'sound photographs' in between Donnelly voicing his commentary, with the orchestra parts stitched together as was the case with most ABC radio drama of the time. ABC features here remained as evanescent as Sieveking's pioneering 'sound pictures' and recall these earlier works.[19]

At this same time, revered American radio writer, broadcaster and producer Norman Corwin had just completed a new kind of feature-documentary series incorporating a ground-breaking form for the recording of interview-actuality (onto tape), but still including his familiar narration and live composed music. Corwin was reasonably well known in Australia, attracting significant press and listeners. The ABC aired multiple renditions of his work,[20] including the original *One World Flight* series (1946). As noted, Corwin was always trying for new effects and understood the emotional power of music in these productions. For his *One World Flight*, he told Australian audiences he had a fresh technique to use paper tape for recording and editing interviews. As he travelled around the globe recording leaders and ordinary people in multiple countries to paint a portrait of a devastated yet newly hopeful world at war's end, he innovated a form of composed documentary feature from thousands

---

19   This also reveals differences in national radio operational structures as well as technical capacities and hierarchies.

20   Cecil Fraser also created 'special music' for the ABC version (February 1947) of Corwin's *The Undecided Molecule* feature, a reflection on atomic energy and the atom bomb in the wake of Hiroshima.

of pieces of edited tape; these then played or 'mixed' as 'voices' of a new kind, and actuality matched with music here to construct a new experience of actuality performance, no less perhaps a radio symphony or sound picture of the world able to be transported via the microphone. Corwin also wanted "to use music as more than the mortar between the bricks" (qtd. in Zinnamon 1984: 313), claiming he was the first to do this, even as he was coming out of a strong tradition that had developed in CBS and BBC 'Golden Age' radio of employing musicians and orchestras for radio plays with significant experimentation, as we have seen.

4 Opportunities Open: Rhapsodies and Reveries with a New ABC Features Department

No doubt, D.G. Bridson, the BBC Assistant Head of the Features Department who was invited to Australia and by the ABC to spend 9 months in the country, brought some of these ideas with him when he was asked to advise the ABC as it prepared its own stand-alone department modelled on the BBC's.[21] He produced programmes over the course of many months, working with Australian actors and composers, and took these back to the BBC. He gave workshops to local staff, allowing them to hear examples from the BBC's Features Department. As *ABC Weekly* reported, he produced "the first Australian feature of its kind written and produced by a BBC staff man to be heard in both Australia and Britain, and the first 'Walkabout' for which special music (with the Sydney Symphony Orchestra as interpreter) has been written" (Bridson qtd. in "BBC Man's Walkabout" 1948: 14). The composer was the same John Antill who not long before had received acclaim for his *Corroboree Suite*. Antill wrote the music for two collaborations with Bridson, describing how he wanted "to try to capture in a tone poem the story of the Murray River: its beneficence to the land through which it flows, until grown perhaps a little weary of its labours, it escapes thankfully to the sea" (qtd. in ibid.) Bridson's fully scored radio 'panorama' feature *Australian Rhapsody* was another opportunity for Antill, as well as for the voice of rising Australian star Peter Finch.[22] Bridson made a point to

---

21 "Features Department was created on a temporary basis in order to take advantage of Mr Bridson's presence in Australia", wrote ABC's Charles Moses to Clewlow: "The amount of work done by this Department will be strictly limited [...], the matter will come up for review at the end of the experimental 6 months." (1948)

22 The programme supplied most of the BBC's 1949 Australia Day feature programme from London. The music by John Antill, ABC music supervisor for New South Wales, was recorded for the broadcast by the Scottish Orchestra in Edinburgh, while the voice had been recorded for the first ABC version in the Sydney studios (1948).

say, however, that "Australia does not appreciate their own composers", thus he was "taking back to London [...] John Antill's special incidental music for [...] *Australian Rhapsody*" (Bridson 1948: 16). Somewhat oddly – and here we find another of these ABC losses of memory – the Australian version of this feature would not include Antill's specially composed music when it aired. Bridson noted the irony: "It is curious but true that Londoners will hear that music – and Australians will not!" (ibid.) Fortunately, the BBC Archives have retained a recording of this feature, but no trace exists in Australian repositories.

After listening to this sound work many times, it is hard to imagine as a voice piece *sans music*: the words of the narrator (Finch) speak intimately to us, and sounds closely recorded as we imagine the pilot in his small plane looking down on 'the great south land' and its people. The music helps to evoke an almost dreamlike state in those who might have listened in, capturing the plane moving in and out of its trajectory, the drone of propeller and the lone voice casting their spell on us, then the musical interpretation bringing us out of inner reverie as if from the clouds. This effect is produced not only through the way Finch speaks this soliloquy – slowly, quietly, closely miked and in such measured tones as to leave us space to imagine what he is seeing below and within – but also because Antill's music acts as a gentle enough stream to carry the words forward, and with such subtlety as to make the inner 'thoughts' seem as if they were one mind speaking to another. We almost feel as if inside the cabin with this pilot, and the music takes us equally from the inner sanctum of thought to the outer bigger story of Australia, carrying the rhapsody forward. While the words today appear naïvely optimistic of this 'young land' – still named as a 'Dominion' and barely responsive to the voices of Australia's disinherited Indigenous peoples – the reverie asks us to imagine futures for this land of relative newcomers, basking in the sun of its luck and almost accidental freedoms – and which, it must have seemed to Bridson in 1948, issued forth from a continent but minimally scarred by the war. In this Antipodean reverie, the annihilation, darkness and barbarity which in 1948 still confronted Europeans wherever they turned, could be kept at bay, a distant chimera.

The treatment of music and plane effects held under the words of Peter Finch also recalls philosopher Gaston Bachelard's musings from that same time (a moment of new hope, and radio as a part of that). He writes on the potential of the radiophonic imaginary and what these new forms of sounding expression and voices from the 'logosphere' could offer as they might speak intimately one to one. Bachelard described how the radio might induce states of active reverie in the listener. Radio producers likewise might be thought of as 'psychic engineers', their work activating the imagination in ways that might promote thought, and perhaps also, healing. Radio drama, or feature poetry, could emerge in certain kinds of works to present the listener with spaces in which to dream and co-create. Sound plays like this one might also address the listener less from an imagined proscenium, opening the 'old world' theatre arts to re-composition. Word and music can be freed from old meanings and tired arrangements as radio calls on new imaginaries: unbounded spaces to liberate listeners and the radio from propaganda and censorship, the medium no longer being the monstrous site of terrifying dictator phantoms, the scream of sirens and hate, or the fabrication of fake realities to suit the perverted idea that was national socialism. For Bachelard, the radio here might even be a 'storehouse' for creativity that each person can draw upon (see Bachelard 1971; my translation).

Bridson called his and Antill's feature a 'rhapsody', and perhaps this similarly awakened 'vision' was imbued with something not so far from the Bachelardian 'radio reverie'? This was a 'play' less interested in plot turns or characters, and more in provisioning, even nourishing future imaginaries for both radio and its listeners.

5   The Radio Play Versus the Feature in Compositional Experiments at the ABC

From 1948 we can also gauge the impact of new access to international works of features and drama, as well as interest in radio music work as the world's first media prize, the Prix Italia, was launched by Italian national radio (later also television). Between 1948 and 1965 the BBC entered and won numerous prizes for its radio features and plays.[23] Once the ABC joined, also becoming part of the jury, producers were given the chance to submit and to hear international work, much of it also from Europe. They grasped that new approaches and technologies were transforming 'radio creation' as they had known it. The techniques and creativity of winning entries inspired some ABC broadcasters, also alerting them to the re-invigorated spirit of experimentation in European radio from the mid 1950s, as new 'radio labs' and 'workshops'[24] formed in Italy, France, Germany and the UK. The BBC's Third Programme cultural channel (launched in 1946) also created more room for modernist experiments and new literary forms, plus ambitious features, documentaries and new radio

---

23   Oddly, between 1949 and 1955 all BBC Prix Italia entries bar one were Features Department productions.

24   Examples include the Club d'Essai, and later Atelier de Création Radiophonique (France). Electronic music workshops were also established in Finland, Italy, Poland, Denmark and Sweden.

drama.²⁵ This work ruffled old feathers perhaps, but captured attention both inside and beyond the BBC. Douglas Cleverdon not only produced Dylan Thomas's *Under Milk Wood* (1954), taking more than 4 years in the making, but can be understood as one of its creators (if we understand a work like this as the product of a very specific ecology and collaboration, at that time almost without international parallel).

A feature like this one opened the possibilities for not only documentary forms but creative radio 'play', and this included radio plays more traditionally understood in theatrical terms. The features space was also not defined by genre and seemed to allow more room to imagine and craft entirely new kinds of radio experiences or listening events, composers as co-authors not being an exception.²⁶ It was perhaps the first place to comprehend the radio itself as being compositional, performative, generative, not as a mere matter of story or voicing of naturalistic drama. The 'play' here (but also in documentary) engaged with inherent musical and sonic attributes as well as forms (of voices, with their cadences in performance, as words sounded in spaces or as treated by electronics, recurring in patterns and with other sounds in counterpoint, or as chorus). Cleverdon described "Features" as "the main channel for experimental or creative radio" (Cleverdon n.d.),²⁷ recounting how the feature-drama "masterpiece" *In Parenthesis* (1942), by David Jones, was of no interest to BBC Drama producers when offered to them, mainly because they would always be "too busy producing plays, and play readers too busy supplying them, for an experimental work of this kind to receive the loving care it demands" (ibid.).²⁸ This same point was made by one of the creative new "feature writers" employed in 1952

---

25 The flowering of these forms reached new heights with Samuel Beckett's radio plays, produced by Donald McWhinnie.

26 Benjamin Britten created the music for one of BBC's most revered features, Louis MacNeice's 'feature-play' *The Dark Tower* (1946). So important was this contribution for its author that he dedicated the published script to Britten (see MacNeice 1947). As John Drakakis points out: "Dramatists such as Edward Sackville-West [...] sought in his play *The Rescue* [1943] to give music itself (provided especially for the production by again Benjamin Britten) a status coequal with poetic dialogue." (1981: 89) Here the writer also imagined the place of music in the work, which is why Sackville-West called his play "melodrama in the traditional sense of a drama incorporating music" (Sackville-West and Britten 1945: 8).

27 Cleverdon then indicates how much of a difference this approach will be to its different components: "It would be unrealistic to expect [...] the Drama Producer to take as much interest in the musical as in the dramatic side of a production; the Features producer, however, is equally interested in every aspect which will lead to a better piece of radio." (ibid.)

28 The epic poem is here described as an adaptation of a war novel.

after the ABC's first Features Department was established on the BBC model (1948).[29] One can find many correspondences like this comparing the two histories and departments in the postwar period. Mungo MacCallum described the new openness of the 'radio feature', revealing that ABC Drama, as its BBC counterpart, remained less likely to move beyond the boundaries it prescribed for the 'radio play'. MacCallum's words echo Cleverdon's:

> A duologue or a dialogue for two voices which could be described as experimental theatre is not normally radio drama, it is a radio feature [...]. Drama has primarily been adaptations of theatre drama [...] or [...] proscenium drama, i.e., orthodox drama [...] or dramatizations in serial form of books, things of that sort [...]. Drama has limited itself with those fields. (qtd. in Lunney 1973)

These feature plays as explored in the BBC Features environment (as 'sound play'), and less so but also in the ABC, would not be restricted to story or narrative, or naturalism: they could be free to engage with the medium itself, and its poetic and dramatic performance forms, even borrow from musical or cinematic craft, thinking and metaphors.[30] As Rudolf Arnheim had suggested in his book *Radio* (1936), the medium had the potential to be *Hörkunst* ('hearing art'), a term that encompasses and connects well this art of sounding with an art of listening (listening being active, generative for the listener as well as for the performer).

6   Features, Composing New Sound Plays and 'Writing on Tape'

As the electronic age of *musique concrète* dawned, experiments in drama and features were capturing the imagination of writers and audiences at the BBC and elsewhere. During the heights of Features Department productions, Douglas Cleverdon wrote: "Music: killed in theatre: too lavish in film [...] [but] just enough money in radio for us to use it effectively. 40–50 composers within last 2 or 3 years [...]. Unlike music in film, not subservient to visual image. It is

---

29   In the end, the broadcaster would only briefly follow Bridson's and the BBC's example. ABC's Features Department was established in 1948, but merged back into a Drama and Features department only a few years later.
30   In 1946, riding a wave of fame and success, the BBC granted new scope to features, and thus also to creative approaches to radio by agreeing to a separate Features Department under the leadership of Laurence Gilliam. The department grew until 1965 when it was absorbed into Drama again while some work moved to Talks.

sound in its dramatic own right." (Cleverdon n.d.) What traces of this are there at the ABC? Where might the ABC's ambitions for these new forms be found in radio's awakening to a new era of television, but also tape, and how were they expressed in new commissions and creativity?

While the ABC was not quite on the cusp of revolution here, an apparent *coup d'état* had come for ABC radio features with (writer-producer) Ivan Smith and (composer) George Selwyn English's 1959 Prix Italia win for *Death of a Wombat*. Here was an ABC production that emulated the BBC features tradition but was homegrown, with a subject familiar to any Australian: the natural landscape and its terrible propensity to burn. At its heart was the humble native marsupial wombat, struggling for survival against the furies of nature unleashed as fire, and as these forces ravaged a drought-stricken environment left all the more vulnerable because of the onslaughts of man. The feature was spare, composed of two 'voices': that of a narrator in interplay with the Sinfonietta orchestral score delivered by a group of ten players.[31] A memory, however, seeps through this feature, of Bridson's and Antill's much earlier (lost) *Rhapsody*, and the tradition which it engendered at the ABC. Described as 'an impression' and 'allegory' the work won the documentary category of the Prix Italia, a first for the ABC.

Drama and features producer Andrew McLennan, who joined the ABC in the mid-1970s and was to work with many artists and composers on new radio features, plays and cross-genre experiments, recalls the programme being not "wildly experimental" but "moving", part of the prehistory of ABC musical collaborations nudging radio features and plays into new territory. The ABC described features broadly at this time as "programs that use music, dialogue, narration and actuality and combines them in such a way as to produce a form of reporting unique to radio" (ABC 1959: 38). The word "reporting" seems a strange frame for *Death of a Wombat*. It is as far from 'reporting' understood in journalistic terms as might be an impressionist painting of a similar scene, although if we think of long-form documentary films, particularly of the *auteur* kind, the connection makes sense. A feature's subjects might also be "history, the local or contemporary scene, biography, adventure, satire, fantasy or poetry" (ibid.); thus, the 'report' descriptor might just as well refer us

---

31   A recording was released (R.C.A. L16233) in 1961 with Alastair Duncan as the Narrator. The Sydney Symphony Orchestra was conducted by Nicolai Malko. See https://www.youtube.com/watch?v=xEpJU3I37qI [06/04/2022]. The cover notes described it as "a story of suffering, terror and devastation, told in such starkly simple and realistic phrases that any listener, from seven to 70, falls under its spell and feels in sympathetic rapport with the wildly fleeing animals" ("The Death of a Wombat").

COMPOSING THE RADIO   149

to writerly features or literary journalism, as cinema's essaying. Richard Connolly, a drama and features producer in the ABC of this period, and also a composer himself (later to become Head of Radio Drama) recalled "the wombat"; he credits it and its producer, Ivan Smith, with helping to keep "features alive" at the ABC, providing space for new writers "like Colin Free to enter the ABC, and break rules" (qtd. in Madsen 2003a). The ABC's first fully stereophonic play (i.e., especially written for stereo) was a 'space drama' by Colin Free, *The People Out There* (1964), as Connolly recalls. It was produced by Ivan Smith, who likened the stereo production "in technique to the making of a film" ("Radio Drama" 1964: 1).[32]

But more often than not, ABC radio's experiments were predominantly the work of ABC "features staff" rather than those of Drama (McLennan qtd. in Madsen 2007). Echoing Cleverdon again, McLennan explains how Drama producers were too busy churning out plays and continuing to use tried and true old methods, which linked Drama to the fading 'Golden Age' of radio. Almost two years into the 1960s, critic John Croyston, writing in his column for *The Bulletin* ("Radio: Too Timid"), described "radio in Australia" as "only slowly emerging from its traditional role" (1961: 34). He lamented ABC's cautious response as the 1960s arrived for him, not with a bang but a whimper:

> Radio appears to be at a public discount in Australia [...]. Overseas the shock [apropos television] merely shifted the pieces into new places, and radio emerged stronger and more identifiable [...]. Realising that radio [...] had not realised its potential, the BBC, for instance, found works from those writers who were working at the most imaginative level, Pinter, Ionesco, Beckett. The results were more than satisfying [...]. The process lead [sic] to the establishment of a new art. (Ibid.)

As McLennan intimated, *The Wombat*, though beautiful as a reverie on Australian fire with a protean environmental message, was hardly a major provocation. It did take the form beyond the boundaries of the radio play, however, while nevertheless being a fully realised musical and dramatic work, and it is one of few works from this period which was aired repeatedly by the ABC (up until 2009), having attained the status of a radio classic. Croyston may not have

---

32   To experience the full effects of the broadcast, listeners needed two receivers, and the two outlets of each city ABC offering at the time: "The sets should be positioned 8ft to 12ft apart, the right one turned to [station] AR, the left to [station] LO [i.e., the two Melbourne ABC stations]. With the sets forming the base of a theoretical triangle the listener should then position himself at the apex." (ibid.)

concurred with this attachment to "the wombat", as he pressed his point about the need for wilder things at the ABC:

> At this stage in its development radio needs the courage to test these new techniques [...]. It is concerned with the word rather than the situation. Beckett's *Embers* has, as its situation, a man sitting by the beach thinking. That is situation enough. What is needed now is the further experiment. Who can say where it could lead? For being nonphysical, the experience is as wide as the imagination and as limited as Time. (Ibid.)

Internationally, there was a lot of experimentation as the sixties heated up. New cultural programming was being picked up in the ABC during the later 1960s and into the 1970s. The Italian and French labs or ateliers visited by some ABC staff in the 1970s allowed a new way of thinking about radio 'creation' – as composition, but also as 'writing on tape' – and here we can think of the *microstylo* ('microphone pen', after the *caméra-stylo* or 'camera pen' proclaimed by the French New Wave cineastes).[33] In 1972, drama producer Richard Connolly, returning to the ABC from a fellowship spent in Europe, brought home this idea for radio, but as expressed to him by a RAI Drama producer, Franco Malatini. Malatini spoke of the work they were doing in Milan and Rome in drama and features as "writing on tape" (Connolly 1972: 1). The microphone, formerly confined to the studio except for outside broadcasts and some 'actualities' or 'actuality features', now also roamed with the producer-composer. Music, channelled in the soundscape as much as in a sound effect, also entered the drama and features lexicon and could be used in a naturalistic denotative mode, or in more complex ways for metaphoric-symbolic, musicalised and psychological effects. All of this kind of thinking began to enter the ABC by the early 1970s. Thus, when Andrew McLennan – a young actor performing in experimental productions like Alfred Jarry's *Ubu Roi* – joined the ABC not long out of university, he had wondered, he recalls, "where all *that* stuff was: all the fun stuff? Where was all the new stuff?" (McLennan qtd. in Madsen 2007)

Louis Nowra, arguably one of Australia's leading playwrights, "one of a handful of mainstream dramatists who, when writing for radio, are interested in exploring sound as a unique dramatic medium" (Hillel 1997: 68), was encouraged in this direction first by McLennan (e.g., *The Song Room*), and then by producer Jane Ulman, who went on to work for *TLR* and author many diverse

---

33   See Alexandre Astruc's 1948 essay "Naissance d'une nouvelle avant-garde: la caméra-stylo", first published in *L'Écran*; English translation ("The Birth of a New Avant-Garde: La Caméra-Stylo") available in Graham and Vincendeau (2009: 31–36).

and accomplished works for the sound medium. With production from Ulman on Nowra's *Summer of the Aliens* play (BBC/ABC 1989) this became the first Australian drama to win the Prix Italia (drama category). For this playwright, after initially rejecting ABC radio drama norms (mid-1970s), he turned to McLennan first as a producer most open to experiment, and who considered music and the role of composition in drama as integral. We find that Nowra, with his previous wife Sarah de Jong (a composer and later collaborator on ABC radio dramas), had worked in Germany, where "they had been subject to listening to bits of German experimental radio – which is a very eruptive and a very strong tradition" (McLennan qtd. in ibid.: 69). Nowra's collaboration with McLennan involved new techniques of recording actors on location, akin to filmmaking, and use of different realistic 'acoustics' – an apparent rejection of 'Golden Age' radio drama methods (at least of those more the norm in ABC studio-based radio dramas until the 1980s). However, in *Summer of the Aliens* and other plays, Nowra used the device of a narrator; he had heard Orson Welles, recalling: "The only radio plays I have ever listened to all the way through" (qtd. in ibid.: 78).

McLennan worked with Australian novelist David Foster to make other wilder rides than Nowra's (for ABC FM's *The Stereo Play*), e.g., "Knight's Move" (1987). This was far from proscenium theatre, as musical as it was theatrical, described as a "drummer in search of his own musical identity and on a quest for the 'real Australian rhythm'".[34] The production was virtuosic with a schizophrenic as hero, and should be understood as the work of McLennan as much as Foster.[35] McLennan was able to play with sound effects not only for their denotative meanings to represent invisible things and actions in the drama, but for their surreal and comic qualities and musicality. This included how they might work with voices and in the arrangements of sounds in interplay with one another; music and sound effects used musically, performed also here as voices in the head. They acted as a kind of meta-play the audience could perceive as operating inside the main character's mind. This was the goal as the play's subject was schizophrenia, with the playing of this second soundtrack inside the head of the main character being a brilliant and memorable 'move'. Foster, a former scientist and musician, created his protagonist also as a

---

34   See http://www.abc.net.au/rn/arts/preview/sep97/block31.htm [05/08/2003]. ABC's webpage listing for the production is unfortunately no longer available online.

35   Audio examples of the founding Executive Producer of *Surface Tension* and *The Listening Room* can be heard in this homage to McLennan: "Never M.O.R. The Audacious Audio of Andrew McLennan" (28 April 2020). See https://www.abc.net.au/radionational/programs/the-history-listen/never-m.o.r-andrew-mclennan/12092358 [06/04/2022].

musician, and this choice was deliberate: "I was able to avail myself of musical metaphors", he said, "while at the same time highlighting the kind of crisis I believe responsible for inducing symptoms in people genetically disposed to schizophrenia". Music and schizophrenia might then be authoritatively linked, since music was integral to this work from its very conception in the writer's mind, as well as a suite of music being specially composed for the play.[36]

In *Sunday Night Radio 2* (SNR2) (1973–1980), a little before this production, you could have heard similarly strange soundings and juxtapositions, both within a play and in the line-up of this new itinerary for the ears: traditional dramatised literary features could be curated with new expressive forms and 'reality-fictions' (see Madsen 2013b), for example as explored by producer-artist Kaye Mortley; or an interview with a French philosopher, say Georges Bataille, might be followed by a new Australian author's radio drama. The old staid type of radio play was discreetly shown the exit in John Blay's study "Aubrey D", as humorous alienation Australian-style took centre stage in his provocation. Canberran critic Maurice Dunlevy savoured one night's delights in his review:

> Conventional dialogue is given a very small role. Rock music, radio commercials and sound effects are far more important. When Aubrey screams, "This whole bloody suburb. Everybody knows everything. You can't move. I wanna be Who I Am! I wanna be SOMEBODY", we are prepared for it not by conventional dramatic development but by the mood that sound effects and rock music have created. (1974: 10)

Enraptured, Dunlevy hailed Blay as having "brought a new dimension to the creative side of Australian radio", opening up "great possibilities for other Australian writers" (ibid.). Dunlevy was no less smitten with SNR2, calling it the "best thing to happen in the electronic media in years" (ibid.). At last, here was an "opportunity for steam radio to find new energy and new directions" (ibid.). Boundaries between genres were now malleable as discussion, music, poetry, features, interviews and drama could all be heard in one 'curated' space. The old traditional PSB cultural outlet had finally embraced the new wave.[37]

---

36 This 'Gondwana' suite was performed by Phil Treloar (percussion) and Roger Frampton (soprano saxophone).

37 As broadcasting turned fifty in Australia, the Commission argued that the traditional cultural role of radio "should not be minimised". It also announced bold new steps: Radio 2's "format" was "re-fashioned" in the evenings offering more "opportunities for new developments, new ideas, new writing and for experiment in the use of radio itself as an art form, in programmes which seek to extend the frontiers of radio" (ABC 1973: 7).

Naturally enough new ABC producers and writers to the medium from the early 1970s also sought their own ways forward as part of this gathering 'new wave' (see Madsen 2013b). Innovative sound and recording technologies revolutionising both production and listening were a key part of a new radio imaginary emerging almost exclusively now from State broadcasters and PSBs. The CBS experiments were a distant memory, if they were remembered at all. The more literary-imagined 'sound play' and the dramatised documentary feature here could also become re-invigorated sites for audio-visionary exploration, as creators engendered new art forms from these spaces and from the cross-fertilisation between forms, organisations and individuals. Music here could have remained primarily 'incidental', conforming to dominant theatrical conventions in radio drama and plays, and subservient to words, voice and narrative; or, the whole sonic dimension (including music) could have become something much more integral, and potentially also provocative or activating as to how a work might be now received, appreciated or communicated. Although limited by the perennial problem of inadequate funding, a new group of artists, audio dramatists and performer artists were here invited to enter the expanded radio spaces and studios of the ABC; as they did so, they too made discoveries and forged original works for broadcast. Klaus Schöning and Mauricio Kagel's work was brought to the ABC in the late 1970s. As composer Richard Toop wrote in an interview with Kagel, the "medium that has particularly attracted Kagel since its inception in the sixties [was] Hörspiel, a cross-disciplinary radio genre poised between music, drama and sound art familiar in Australia through ABC-FM's The Listening Room" (1997/2004). This programme became a major site for radio art, performance and *Neues Hörspiele* like Kagel's, with his *Soundtrack* and *Der Tribun* both adapted for Australian audiences by Andrew McLennan. Former ABC colleague and drama producer Jane Ulman wrote: "In Australia, the more adventurous producers at the ABC began to use the word Hörspiel to denote the experimental possibilities of the radiophonic medium." (2018: 314).

McLennan visited WDR's Studio Akustischer Kunst in Cologne and Klaus Schöning, its director from 1969 to 1996. Numerous works were created between the two sites after this connection was made.[38] McLennan,

---

38   McLennan recalled: "it seemed to me there was a moment in the early seventies when we were beginning to say to ourselves: 'How would we do this properly?', and a number of us had gone overseas at that time and seen European studios in operation [...]. What we were astounded by was the equipment they had at their disposal to make these pieces. What went on here [...] in the late sixties, early seventies, was as if it was still a live radio drama. Everything was done in real time." (qtd. in Hillel 1997: 69)

for example, produced English language versions of German work, such as Gerhard Rühm's 1972 *Ophelia und die Wörter* (*Ophelia and the Words*) with the renowned Australian actor Judy Davis.[39] McLennan also adapted or commissioned productions from Argentinian composer and *Hörspielmacher* Mauricio Kagel, whose ambitious sound-text works won him international acclaim.[40] For Schöning, old style radio drama or *Hörspiel* of the 1950s "encapsulated itself as a creature of text-based literature" (Schöning 1991: 317). Here, "SFX [sound effects] and music were subordinated as illustrative acoustic crutches for the word, for plot" and "field recording was relegated to reporters" (ibid.). In Schöning's experience, it was "only music departments [...] [who] seized the opportunity to develop radio as a center of the avant-garde for their art" (ibid.). One therefore, he stressed, "had to wait for the 60s before real change and mixing of genres could occur" (ibid.). Here the idea of the *Hörspielmacher* and composer-director becomes a new model for the composer-producer of *Neue Hörspiele* (ibid.: 322).

Kagel and Schöning also worked with Australian composer-writer Moya Henderson, but it is not well known that this highly awarded composer produced several highly distinguished works for ABC radio. The score for her first commission, *Split Seconds* (1977), described as a "radio play", a "music play" and "ear theatre" all in the one manuscript, was influenced by an earlier musical fellowship in Germany. The document is of great interest as a visual score, while the work employs highly accomplished electronics and radiophonics.[41] With original instrumental sound effects and other concrete sounds it could only be "realised through the medium of electronics", Henderson wrote, "properly presented only on radio".[42] She also authored a virtuosic "Hörspiel", as she described it, about the life and death by suicide of Belgian Jeannine

---

39   The piece is based on the complete text of Ophelia in Shakespeare's *Hamlet*: "All nouns and verbs were extracted from this text and lined up in their root form", says Rühm (qtd. in Schöning 1971: 208). The play is comprised of these words as if they were swirling around her head, but imprisoning her in her own world and that of fate. McLennan's production (1987) used multitracking and stereo, so that her words appear to move in space a circular movement.

40   Kagel emigrated to Europe in 1957, where he discovered *Hörspiel* and began to make his own new forms. His students included composer Moya Henderson, who wrote an obituary for Kagel (2009). For more of his comments on music in radio drama, see Toop and Kagel (1997/2004).

41   Using 16-track stereo, actors and instruments, 600 different items were combined and balanced together in the studio.

42   Moya Henderson, *Split Seconds* (Prix Italia Manuscript Score and Notes). 1977–1978: Henderson and John Harper, ABC Archives No 80/10/113.

Deckers, better known as the 'Singing Nun'.⁴³ Written, performed, composed and directed by Henderson with music for six sopranos and folk instruments, the play (1990) was recorded as a feature for ABC's *TLR* in locations such as Rose Bay Convent, Sydney, and the Devil's Coach House, Jenolan Caves, NSW.⁴⁴ Both works received special commendations at the Prix Italia competition in 1978 and 1990.⁴⁵

Another composer to return to the ABC after exposure to German music and radio labs was David Ahern. The ABC commissioned him to commemorate the Captain Cook Bicentenary, and his *Journal* was recorded in April 1969 with three actors, three actresses, ring modulator (doubling violin), and didgeridoo (doubling double bass). It was also an ABC Prix Italia entry. Ahern had returned to Australia from working with composers Cornelius Cardew in London and for two years had been a personal assistant to Karlheinz Stockhausen.⁴⁶ He had many ideas for ABC radio at this time of electronic discovery, as McLennan discovered when Ahern was employed producing "talks and discussions about avant-garde music as well as his own original sound-works" (McLennan 1994). Ahern, McLennan noted, "desperately tried to get the ABC to give him something like an electronic studio, a version of the radiophonic workshop [i.e., at the BBC]" (qtd. in Madsen 2007). McLennan says Ahern had "very modest requests [...] based on what he'd seen in Europe. You know he'd walked into Stockhausen's class [in Darmstadt] and he'd never seen or heard anything like it – sound running around the hall [...] this figure looming over a huge [mixing] board" (ibid.). But the time was not ripe for Ahern's 'lab' in 1969; the idea received a very negative response from ABC Music, who did not see what all the fuss was about.

---

43   Deckers was known in Francophone countries as 'Soeur Sourire'. The full title of Henderson's documentary drama is *Meditations and Distractions on the Theme of the Singing Nun*.
44   In the 1960s, Deckers achieved pop star status with her hit "Dominique". This made millions of dollars in royalties but none went to Deckers. The convent superior distributed proceeds instead to the bishops, priests, missions and charitable institutions. Despite this, when leaving the Order, Deckers incurred the entire tax debt for the royalties. As Sally MacCarthur writes: "With her long-time friend, Annie Percher, Jeannine Deckers committed suicide in 1985, in penury and in despair". While the story was tragic, exploring also lesbian love in the church, and incurring criticism as well as high praise, "Henderson's treatment of it is brilliant. Through her use of music and the medium of radio, Henderson herself performs as actor, vocalist and instrumentalist in its production." (1994: 144)
45   The play received its Special Commendation in the documentary category. For all of her radio plays, see https://www.moyahenderson.com/categories/radio-plays [07/04/2022]. Henderson was also awarded Order of Australia Membership in 1996.
46   He later became a music critic at *The Sydney Daily Telegraph*.

McLennan with others would go on to make a new bid for a lab – this time with much more luck and traction. When ABC established a new Arts Unit in 1987, arguably this was that chance to install the kind of radio lab or workshop long dreamed of since early in the ABC's history, although diverging in significant ways from those that had gone before or were still funded, operating at the same time (in France and Germany, for example). The new Unit was initiated after "some serious attempts internally to capitalise on home grown talent and ideas", and it aimed to "break down the silos" (see Harrison et al. 1987). It also hoped to offer a response to the continuing and compelling international creativity in radio out there, and now able to be heard much more strongly by both producers inside the ABC and collaborators outside it wishing to make new kinds of radio art, performance and writing for the ear. These collaborators did not want to be confined to one genre, fact or fiction. They were boundary riders now crossing between older categories of drama, features, poetry, reportage, documentary and music (see MacGregor et al. 1987).

7 Adventures in Sound and Re-Composing Radio Play

With the hybrid and upstart ABC Arts Unit, creative personnel moved from Features, Talks and Drama to the new space, and their first show, *Surface Tension*. Geraldine Brooks, excited about its entrance into the radio schedule of Radio 2 in 1986, enthused: "Surface Tension demands the old fashioned intensity of wireless days: you really have to sit down and do nothing but stare at the radio in order to catch all that's going on. Surface Tension is leaning on the limits of radio, as much a fascinating exploration of its own medium as it is a conveyor of information on other kinds of art." (Brooks 1986: 73) She found it "so good it makes everything else on radio suddenly seem intensely ordinary" (ibid.). Running for 90 minutes on Saturday afternoons, *Surface Tension* "hurls ideas out on the airwaves" exploring and experimenting "with the spaces between documentary, drama, music and play" (ibid.). When Geraldine Brooks wrote that high praise, she was only starting her career with the *Sydney Morning Herald*. Later she relocated to the USA as a journalist and novelist, winning the 2005 Pulitzer Prize for Fiction for her novel *March*. Here is a description of one daring radio play part of *Surface Tension,* instigated and performed by poet Chris Mann. Andrew McLennan, the producer, recalls the poet creating "a 4-channel mix for Australia Day, 1986, using 17th and 18th century texts" (McLennan 1994). These were Jonathon Swift's *Gulliver's Travels*, Daniel Defoe's *Robinson Crusoe* and English playwright Richard Broome's *The Antipodes*. The fourth text was William Dampier's journal from his charting of the West Australian coast. "These speculated on the existence of an Australian continent" and

> were read not by professional actors, but by leading figures from some of the country's better known radical and conservative lobby groups: a trade union official, a leader of an ex-servicemen's league and a fashion photographer. The play was performed by ABC announcers, each reading their parts in isolation, the final version being a splicing together of their various performances. The "Quadrophonic Cocktail", as it was called, was broadcast via the four channels of the ABC's combined Metropolitan, National and Fine Music networks. (Ibid.)

The audience was invited to "mix your own audio adventure" (ibid.). McLennan aptly describes Mann as "a poet/musician whose written works have been compared by John Cage to the work of James Joyce" (ibid.).

Surface Tension lasted a mere couple of years and made an impression on critics and public, but it soon managed to "infuriate the multitudes" listening to prime-time Saturday afternoon ABC. Managers wrapped the show up, but agreed to a new programme: *The Listening Room* (1988–2003). Alluded to before, this was to be the last of the ABC's big commitments to radio features and performance (in a truly exploratory sense), and to engaging in an interplay with other forms of radio performativity and 'play'. This is not to say more interesting and productive programmes and spaces did not come after, but all of this subsequent work was built on these two programmes which established a viable ecosystem for production of originally composed or written, radiogenic creation and collaboration, as well as an ecology that promoted and nurtured genuine research into radio as a site for artistic invention, creativity and surprise – surely the essence of any adventure. The question of music, performance and narrative in this 'play' comes up again and again, and sits in tension with the various kinds of works which found a niche in Australia (see McLennan 1994; Madsen 2009).

There are important impacts of *The Listening Room*, too, which might productively be added to the history and 'mix' explored here, and which touch on musical interpretation and artistic collaboration in a radio performance work and 'play'. One such example is an ABC work called "If" (2001). Originally made for *TLR* by staff producer and artist Sherre DeLys, the short piece is worth bringing into the lineage of examples from the ABC's past that this chapter has tried to restitute from the vaults and archives of history and oblivion. Though a small work among so many examples we could pick from *TLR*, many more conventionally like a radio play or drama and many also collaborations with musician-composer-artists, "If" provided an original musical epiphany for the would-be producer-hosts of a renowned American podcast 'show', perhaps not so oddly titled *Radiolab,* launched in 2002. "If" influenced the style and approach taken to their hugely successful nonfiction stories, now known globally and still featuring as one of the most downloaded podcasts in the world. This was also a collaboration between a seasoned journalist-host (NPR) and a composer-experimenter with radio's forms.

These founding producer-presenters of the American podcast *Radiolab* first imagined and devised their show from a word and music perspective in an act of 'composition'. Here, they drew on a specific hearing of an experimental radio feature by DeLys. "If" became the 'catalyser' for the kind of playful essaying in sound and word they would go on to pursue. The reaction from *Radiolab* co-founder and host Robert Krulwich on first hearing this little ABC piece (at a festival in 2002) is worth recalling because it shows how a musical listening and composing can transform what was at the start a piece of reportage and interviewing:

> I could see there was this kind of *ignition* for something [...]. You see, what you need to do is hear new ways of doing old things: it's a subtle business, you can borrow from other cultures [...] or, with the "If" program, there was a marriage of music directly onto content: sometimes it was the music carrying the content and sometimes it was the kid's [words]. The two were somehow merged, each equally important. (qtd. in Madsen 2013a)

Krulwich of WNYC (New York) continues: "This wonderful little boy [at the programme's centre] was in a cancer ward [...] and, in spite of the tribulations of being a cancer patient, he was dreaming. The key word [we hear] was 'If,' and it was captured musically." (ibid.) The word 'if', said by the boy, is first encountered as he speaks to the interviewer (although no interviewer is ever heard). The child speaks in short verse-like sections about being in hospital, about all the tests he has had, his attempts at play, the frustration of painting when all colours seem to turn to brown, etc. His 'ifs' articulate the subjunctives: "If I were a fish [...]", "If I were a kid in the children's ward [...]", and they are then transformed by the musical manipulations of this uncategorisable work. The sounded word 'if' is treated musically and extended machinically, becoming sung speech – and more than symbol it soon comes across as pure creativity.

We also hear joy – bursting out against all the constraints imposed on this child by his medical situation and by, what can we call it, 'an ordinary boredom'? The voicing shuttles us back and forth between reality and fiction, actuality and artiface, and the words are again extended and manipulated, but they never alienate, feel artificial or unnecesarily 'treated'. The *musique concrète* techniques allow the listener to hear all the 'play' in a heightened way, taking us and the space to a higher, deeper and more moving level, merging reality and the imagination, materialising words into more than simple vehicles for communication or semantic transfer. 'Iiiiiiifffffffffffff' transformed into the new sung form, then triggers a duet with a cello. Entering the fray, the cello is joined by an accompanist, improvising around a central theme of this boy's words, to leave us transformed in the process. The writer-sculptor-composer artist Sherre DeLys is also, on another level, playing the studio and the radio lab here. She has been given a licence to do so in this (formerly) protected space (TLR was cut in 2003), and simply follows the boy's already free form association. He leads in what is now a play or dance between the unordinary poetry of his words and the music it now releases. We have moved beyond the sound bite currency and sociology of daily journalism and talk to "adventures in sound" (see Madsen 2009). The flow here is rewound and replayed, the ordinary made strange, improvisation turned towards other objectives. The talk, once perhaps 'banal', of the 'everyday' is now experienced as a gifting to us of music, poetry – art.

8   A Final Word on Musical Play in the ABC's Continuing Journey in Sound

This chapter has recalled specific instances and periods in the ABC's radiophonic history of 'play' and 'adventures in sound', in order to address some of the spectra of productions and programmes that emerged, and to allow for an encounter with a space opened to, and refreshed by, new kinds of work and invention, be it musical, dramatic or literary. Here sonic and musical composition could be posed as a key part of radio's 'play' to affect a range of audio effects, and new approaches to form and production. I have also focused on some historical works in which composers and musicians mixed ideas, and were brought together to contribute as authors, collaborators and co-creators. I have offered this kind of contextual framework in part as a way to encounter forgotten Australian works anew, but also as a way to understand the impact of behind-the-scenes workings and workings-out of these forms and experiments, in particular relating these to the local situation but also to transnational contexts. That still hard to define audio field and form called 'features', often overlooked when the focus is restricted or limited to radio drama, becomes an illuminating and creatively alive space here. In the current moment, however, features and composing with sound radio drawing on multiple tools and audio-visionary thinking seem very hard to find in the ABC (the last of the radio labs, the Creative Audio Unit, was axed in 2016). There has been a break in the journey, at least in Australian radio, and a huge loss of memory (again). While podcasting has opened the radio to new forms and expansions of audio, certainly sound design, and the 'sound rich' category is there in the new mix at the ABC as in international contexts, the legacy of radio features and the radio labs they inhabited and engendered, the richness of ideas and a sense of exploration in this field, have been largely silenced now in ABC radio and podcasting. The 'adventures' and moves towards more experimental gestures and 'play' of the past are now at risk of being disconnected from current and future sounding.

References

ABC (1933). *The First Annual Report of the Australian Broadcasting Commission* (ABC), *1932–1933*. Sydney, NSW: Australian Broadcasting Commission.

ABC (1947). "Sydney Symphony of a Great City". 16 October. ABC Publicity material, NAA: ABC Collection: Australian Walkabout Series C678T1.

ABC (1959). *The 27th Annual Report of the ABC, 1958–1959*. Sydney, NSW: Australian Broadcasting Commission.

ABC (1973). *Annual Report 1972–1973*. Sydney, NSW: Australian Broadcasting Commission.

"ABC Plays For July" (1938). *The Telegraph*, 25 June: 18.

Arnheim, Rudolf (1936). *Radio*. Margaret Ludwig, Herbert Read, transl. London: Faber and Faber.

Bachelard, Gaston (1951/1970). "Rêverie et radio". *Le Droit de rêver*. 2nd ed. Philippe Garcin, ed. Paris: Presses Universitaires de France. 216–223.

BBC (1930). *BBC Year Book*. London: British Broadcasting Corporation.

"BBC Man's Walkabout on the Murray River Miracle" (1948). *ABC Weekly*, 20 March: 14.

Bridson, Geoffrey (1948). "BBC Man's Candid Comments on Our Radio Programmes". *ABC Weekly*, 25 September: 16.

Brooks, Geraldine (1986). "An Arts Show That's State-of-the-Art". *The Sydney Morning Herald*, 10 March: 73.

"Canned History Would Live Forever" (1945). *Sunday Telegraph*, 28 October. Clipping, ABC Collection, NAA: Series SP767/1 Item 131, "Theirs be the Glory".

Cleverdon, Douglas (n.d.). Lectures. Lilly Library, Bloomington, Indiana, Cleverdon mss II, Box 5.

Clewlow, Frank Dawson (1934). "Mr Clewlow's Memo Re Drama". 26 November. NAA: Australian Broadcasting Commission Head Office Correspondence File Drama 1933–37, SP1558/2 127/18/3/3-3.

Clewlow, Frank Dawson (1938). "Note on Australian artists, writers, musicians". 16 May. NAA: ABC Head Office Correspondence File Drama 1938–30, SP1558/2/919.

Clewlow, Frank Dawson (1940). "Frank Dawson Clewlow: Federal Controller of productions". NAA: SP1558 127/18/3/3-3, "1940 Drama".
Clewlow, Frank Dawson (n.d.). "Monthly Reports Drama & Features 1937–39". SP1558/5 Box 3.
Clewlow, Frank Dawson (n.d.). "Monthly Reports Drama & Features 1940–1945". SP1558/5 Box 3.
Connolly, Richard (1972). *Churchill Fellowship Report*. Sydney. Author's private collection. Unpublished.
Coulton, Barbara (1980). *Louis MacNeice in the BBC*. London: Faber.
Crook, Tim (1999). *Radio Drama: Theory and Practice*. London and New York: Routledge.
Croyston, John (1961). "Radio: Too Timid". *The Bulletin*, 11 November: 34.
Drakakis, John (1981). *British Radio Drama*. Cambridge: CUP.
Dunlevy, Maurice (1974). "A Literary Board Plunge on Radio That Paid Off". *Canberra Times*, 3 May: 10.
Fehlberg, Tasman (1964). *The Australian Broadcasting Commission: A National Service*. Renee Erdos, ed. Australian Landmarks. Croyden: Longmans.
Gilliam, Laurence (1953). "Experimental Production Work". Memo, 16 April. BBC WAC R19/354/8 Ent Features memos File 7 1952–3 File 6.
Graham, Peter, Ginette Vincendeau, eds. (2009). *The French New Wave: Critical Landmarks*. London: British Film Institute.
Guthrie, Tyrone (1931). "Future of Broadcast Drama". *BBC Handbook 1931*. London: BBC. 185–190.
Harrison, Martin, Anthony MacGregor, Andrew McLennan, Virginia Madsen, Robyn Raylich (1987). "High Performance Radio, Surface Tension Returns to Radio National". Press Release for ABC Radio National. Sydney. Author's private collection.
Henderson, Moya (2009). "Mr Kagel, 1974–1976: Much Larger Than Life". *Musicology Australia* 31/1: 101–107.
Hillel, John (1997). "Screenplays for Radio: The Radio Drama of Louis Nowra". *Australasian Drama Studies* 30: 68–86.
Indyk, Ivor (1990). "The ABC and Australian Literature 1939–1945". *Meanjin* 49/3: 576–588.
Kreutzfeldt, Jacob (2018). "Radiophonic Cities: The City Portrait in Transnational Radio Collaborations". Golo Föllmer, Alexander Badenoch, eds. *Transnationalizing Radio Research: New Approaches to an Old Medium*. Bielefeld: Transcript. 143–153.
Lunney, Suzanne (1973 online). Interview with Mungo MacCallum. Edgecliff, New South Wales, 11 July. National Library of Australia, audio recording nla.obj-214942889, transcript ORAL TRC 206. https://nla.gov.au/nla.obj-214942889/listen/1-3373 [23/04/2022].
MacCarthur, Sally (1994). "Moya Henderson". *Contemporary Music Review* 11: 141–146.

MacGregor, Anthony, Andrew MacLennan, Virginia Madsen, Robin Ravlich (1987). "The Listening Room Program Statement of Aims". ABC Sydney. Author's private collection.

MacNeice, Louis (1947). *The Dark Tower and Other Radio Scripts*. London: Faber and Faber.

Madsen, Virginia (2003a). Interview with Richard Connolly. Sydney, 25 June. Audio recording/transcript. Unpublished.

Madsen, Virginia (2003b). Interview with ABC Drama and Features Producer, Rodney Wetherell. Melbourne, 20 August. Audio recording/transcript. Unpublished.

Madsen, Virginia (2007). Interview with ABC Arts Producer, Andrew McLennan. Sydney, 20 November. Audio recording/transcript. Unpublished.

Madsen, Virginia (2009). "Written in Air: Experiments in Radio". Gail Priest, ed. *Experimental Music: Audio Explorations in Australia*. Sydney, NSW: UNSW Press. 154–174.

Madsen, Virginia (2013a). Interview with Robert Krulwich. New York, 18 December. Audio recording. Unpublished.

Madsen, Virginia (2013b). "'Your Ears Are a Portal to Another World': The New Radio Documentary Imagination and the Digital Domain". Jason Loviglio, Michele Hilmes, eds. *Radio's New Wave: Global Sound in the Digital Era*. Abingdon and New York, NY: Routledge. 126–144.

Madsen, Virginia (2017). "Innovation, Women's Work and the Documentary Impulse: Pioneering Moments and Stalled Opportunities in Public Service Broadcasting in Australia and Britain". *Media International Australia* (MIA) 162/1: 19–32.

Masefield, John (1934). "Letter to Director ABC, Melbourne". 10 November. NAA Australian Broadcasting Commission Head Office Correspondence File: Drama 1933–37, SP1558/2 127/18/3/3-3.

Mason, Arthur (1942). "ABC Letter to Kathyrn Campbell CBS, London Office". 25 September. Thousand Oaks Library, California, Special Collections, Norman Corwin Collection, General Correspondence: An American in England.

McGill, Earle (1940). *Radio Directing*. London and New York, NY: McGraw Hill.

McLennan, Andrew (1994). "A Brief Topology of Australian Sound Art and Experimental Broadcasting". *Continuum* 8/1: 302–317. (Reprint: McLennan Andrew (n.d. online). "A Brief Topology of Australian Sound Art and Experimental Broadcasting". http://www.kunstradio.at/AUSTRALIA/lennon_topology.htm [24/04/2022].)

Moses, Charles (1948). Memo to Frank Dawson Clewlow (Features). 25 March. NAA SP613//1/0 Item 12/1/1.

"New Guinea Documentary" (1945). *ABC Weekly*, 6 October: 4.

Porter, Jeff (2016). *Lost Sound: The Forgotten Art of Radio Storytelling*. Chapel Hill, NC: Univ. of North Carolina Press.

"Radio Drama in Two Dimensions" (1964). *The Age*, 3–9 July: 1.

Rees, Leslie (1945). "Drama Chronicle". *Meanjin* 4/3: 210–211.

Richards, Donald (2003). "The Creative Ear". PhD Thesis. Univ. of Western Sydney. Unpublished.
Sackville-West, Edward, Benjamin Britten (1945). *The Rescue: A Melodrama for Broadcasting Based on Homer's* Odyssey. London: Secker & Warburg.
Schöning, Klaus (1971). *Sound Journey*. Judith Rosenthal, transl. Cologne: West German Radio.
Schöning, Klaus (1991). "The Contours of Acoustic Art". *Theatre Journal* 43/3: 307–324.
Sieveking, Lance (1934). *The Stuff of Radio*. London: Cassell & Co.
"The Death of a Wombat" (1972). *The Canberra Times*, 20 July: 3.
Toop, Richard, Mauricio Kagel (1997/2004). "Playing Back Reality". Richard Toop, transl. *Trove*, archived webpage. https://webarchive.nla.gov.au/awa/20040915234410/http://pandora.nla.gov.au/pan/12750/20030529-0000/au.geocities.com/masthead_2/issue1/kagel.html [29/04/2022].
Ulman, Jane (2018). "Changing the Record – Rose Radiophony". *Contemporary Music Review* 37/4: 313–325.
"Women in Radio" (1947). *ABC Weekly*, 16 August: 9.
Zinnamon, Jerrold (1984). "Norman Corwin: A Study of Selected Radio Plays by the Noted Author and Dramatist". PhD Thesis. Univ. of Oregon. Unpublished.

PART 2

Case Studies of Radio Drama

CHAPTER 6

Experiments in 'Symphonic Drama' on the US Radio (1937–1938)

Tim Carter

Abstract

The US Federal Theatre Project was established in 1935 as part of President Roosevelt's 'New Deal' to alleviate the Great Depression. In addition to experimenting in live theatre, the FTP created a Radio Division to extend its reach nationwide. Its broadcasts in 1937–1938 included two series of 'symphonic dramas'; for the second, playwrights were commissioned to 'interpret' classical orchestral works by way of a matching 'original dramatisation'. The choice of pieces and the scenarios attached to them were both timely and topical. They also reveal the importance of radio in fostering various vernacular modernisms in a peculiarly American context.

One of the more enlightened acts under US President Franklin D. Roosevelt's 'New Deal' in response to the Great Depression was the establishment in 1935 of four national 'arts' organisations grouped as 'Federal One' under the umbrella of the Works Progress Administration (WPA).[1] The Federal Art, Music, Theater, and Writers' Projects were each mandated to offer training and 'relief' to the unemployed in their respective professions who would thus be better equipped to return to, or enter, the commercial marketplace (see McDonald 1969). However, the Projects each in their various ways became cultural mobilisers for a particularly American form of vernacular modernism that also sought to mediate between presumed high- and lowbrow cultural consumption. There was

---

[1] I am grateful to David Seubert for his advice on recordings, and to Mark Evan Bonds for his comments on a draft of this essay. It draws on materials surviving in the New York Public Library for the Performing Arts, Billy Rose Theater Division (henceforth NYPL), also with reference to those in the National Archives and Records Administration in College Park, MD, Record Group 69, Federal Theatre Project Collection (NARA/FTP), as well as to contemporary newspapers such as the *New York Times* (NYT) and similar sources. In my transcriptions I have silently modified the styling, added editorial punctuation where needed for sense, and corrected obvious typographical errors. Editorial additions are placed in square brackets.

a strong degree of idealism behind the creation of Federal One: that the arts could serve the nation in harsh economic times by way of social and cultural uplift. Its legacy remains in the murals decorating federal buildings across the country, and the civic orchestras founded under its auspices (see Bindas 2003). But its impact was strongest in the case of the Federal Theatre Project (FTP) which, under the leadership of Hallie Flanagan, became a powerhouse for new trends in the creation and production of a wide range of dramatic forms (see Witham 2003; Osborne 2011).

The Projects generated a remarkable degree of creative energy but also prompted significant complaints from the private sector, which felt threatened by competitors with the benefit of public subsidy. More troublesome still were the patent left-wing sympathies of most involved in their administrations: Hallie Flanagan, for example, was a strong devotee of progressive trends in European theatre as a result of a Guggenheim Fellowship (1926) spent abroad, and she became a particular advocate of dramatic developments in the Soviet Union. Opponents of Federal One were quick to accuse the Projects of Socialism or Communism, and while the weight of those labels varied widely within the fluctuating political climate of the 1930s, they eventually led to a series of painful investigations by the US Congress. The FTP was terminated on 30 June 1939, and the Writers' Project lost its federal funding that same year, although it continued under state sponsorship until 1943, by which time the other Projects had also fizzled out. The United States was now at war, so different priorities were in play.

The FTP sought a broad reach across the nation: its masterstroke was the simultaneous staging in twenty-one US cities of Sinclair Lewis and John C. Moffitt's anti-fascist play, *It Can't Happen Here*, based on Lewis's novel of 1935, on Tuesday 27 October 1936, precisely one week before the 1936 presidential election. But in addition to producing old and new plays in particularly creative ways – always with low ticket prices and often in non-traditional locations – the FTP supported vaudeville, circus and marionette productions, explored new theatrical forms such as the controversial *Living Newspapers*, and gave significant opportunities to African American performers. Less well known, however, is the FTP's involvement in radio broadcasts by way of the Federal Theatre of the Air, which was inaugurated on 15 March 1936 and grew by offering regular programming to the major networks and to local commercial stations on the East and West coasts, also with additional radio divisions created in eleven states.

This was a logical extension of the FTP's mission to act as a national provider of culture. In addition to creating studio performances of classic and modern plays and light opera (for example, the complete works of Gilbert and Sullivan), plus a pioneering series devoted to Black gospel music, poetry and writers, the

Federal Theatre of the Air extended its reach into arts programming more broadly, plus lectures and the like on history, broadcasts for children, and even public-service segments on health and safety, thereby making it one public voice of the WPA.² It tended to favour serial formats – as with the airing of James Truslow Adams's *Epic of America* in episodes from 28 November 1937 to 27 February 1938 (with a 'postlogue' on 21 April) – because they established a regular time slot and audience. Thus it ran thirteen weekly programmes titled *Exploring the Seven Arts*, presented largely by Leah Plotkin on Wednesday evenings (9:45–10:00) from 7 April to 25 August 1937 (with presentations on "New Trends in the Dance", "The Future of American Art", "The Writer and His Audience", etc., to cite the first three). This then led to a long-running sequence of 15-minute programmes on *Exploring the Arts and Sciences* (5 November 1937 to 16 January 1939), in which leading figures spoke on their areas of expertise: the first was a talk on "Why Music Is the Greatest of All the Arts" by Carleton Sprague Smith, Chief of the Music Division of the New York Public Library.

My present argument, however, concerns two other such series, one called *The Symphonic Drama Hour*, which ran from 20 April to 22 June 1937 (repeated the following year), and the other, *Experiments in Symphonic Drama* (4 July to 26 September 1938). Each involved plays that were performed with recordings of classical music as underscoring, though they were quite different in design. Like the Federal Theatre of the Air broadcasts in general, they were geared to a number of elements within the FTP's core mission: new ways of conceiving drama and its modes of presentation, and some manner of cultural education. They also used a label that was gaining significant kudos in the mid-1930s.

1   Symphonic Drama

Composers had used versions of the term 'symphonic drama' previously to signify works that did not fit neatly into preexisting genres, or somehow sought to transcend them: take, for example, Hector Berlioz's *Roméo et Juliette* for choir and orchestra of 1839, a "symphonie dramatique", or Erik Satie's *Socrate* (1920), a "drame symphonique" setting texts by Plato for female soloist(s) and orchestra that made a splash with its US premiere at the Wadsworth Atheneum in

---

2   Flanagan (1940/1965: 267–269) offers a useful, if obviously biased, account of the Federal Theatre of the Air. A large number of scripts for its programming survive in NYPL, WPA Radio Scripts, *T-Mss 2000–005; the collection is organised in 121 series (see the finding aid at http://archives.nypl.org/the/21674 [14/04/2021]). A seemingly less complete collection (not examined in detail for the present essay) survives in NARA/FTP.

Hartford, CT, on 14 February 1936 (as part of a festival sponsored by the so-called Friends and Enemies of Modern Music) in a double-bill alongside Stravinsky's *Les Noces* (1923), with modernist sets by Alexander Calder. The term also became a bone of contention among supporters or opponents of Wagnerian opera. But there was a longer history to the notion that symphonies themselves, despite seeming concerned just with abstract musical form, nevertheless contained some manner of drama within them, often expressed as a struggle for reconciliation between themes or keys. This led easily enough to the invention of stories that might lie behind them, whether imagined serving as the composer's inspiration, or in order to elucidate these works for lay audiences. Beethoven became the test case in the nineteenth century, given that he was a musical titan who needed to be worshipped but also brought more down to earth for the benefit of mortal ears. His Symphony No. 7 in A Major (1813), for example, attracted a host of narratives ranging from a peasant wedding through a Moorish fantasy to Wagner's "apotheosis of the dance", but even the earliest of them (purportedly from 1819) could also take a distinctly political turn:

> The sign of revolt is given; there is a rushing and running about of the multitude; an innocent man, or party, is surrounded, overpowered after a struggle and haled before a legal tribunal. Innocency weeps; the judge pronounces a harsh sentence; sympathetic voices mingle in laments and denunciations – they are those of widows and orphans; in the second part of the first movement the parties have become equal in numbers and the magistrates are now scarcely able to quiet the wild tumult. The uprising is suppressed, but the people are not quieted; hope smiles cheeringly and suddenly the voice of the people pronounces the decision in harmonious agreement [...]. (Forbes 1967: 765)

Beethoven's erstwhile assistant, Anton Schindler, claimed much later (in 1860) that the composer himself strongly disapproved of this hermeneutic strategy.[3] As we shall see in the case of the FTP's *Experiments in Symphonic Drama*, however, it remained a common one, as it does today in many circles.

By the 1930s, the label 'symphonic' became something of a fad across the arts. Choreographer Léonide Massine's work for the Ballet Russe de Monte Carlo included his first "symphonic ballet", *Les Présages* (1933), to Tchaikovsky's Symphony No. 5 in E Minor (1888), which was quickly followed that same year

---

3 This reading of the Seventh Symphony by Karl Iken, editor of the *Bremer Zeitung* in 1819–1820, first appeared in the last (1860) edition of Schindler's biography of Beethoven (Schindler 1966/1996: 399f.). However, Schindler has been exposed as a notorious fraudster.

by *Choreartium*, to Brahms's Symphony No. 4 in E Minor (1885), and then by *Symphonie fantastique* (1936), to the eponymous work by Berlioz (1830). (All three of those symphonies will return in a different context, below.) The prominent North Carolina playwright Paul Green produced a series of "symphonic dramas" (cf. Green 1958: 17) including his outdoor pageant, *The Lost Colony*, staged in Manteo, NC, on 4 July 1937 to celebrate the 350th anniversary of the first British settlement established in the New World, on Roanoke Island (President Roosevelt attended a performance in August). Film critic Frank S. Nugent also reported that the film musical *High, Wide, and Handsome* (Paramount Pictures, 1937) – depicting life in the Pennsylvania oilfields in 1859 – by Oscar Hammerstein II and Jerome Kern was being labeled a "symphonic drama" given that "musical romance" or "operetta" had "too tinkling a connotation to be applied to a rugged and virile historical saga" (Nugent 1937: 15). Nugent was worried that the term had "a slightly esthetic sound" (ibid.), but this is clearly what helped popularise it in so many quarters at the time, even if no one could quite work out what it meant.

The FTP viewed Green's *The Lost Colony* with some enthusiasm. Its African American unit based in Birmingham, AL, had already staged two "symphonic dramas" (so the newspapers called them) in June and July 1936, one titled *Home in Glory* – after the gospel hymn – and the other, Harold Coulander's *Swamp Mud*, dealing with prisoners on a chain gang (cf. "Second Production" 1936: 2; cf. "Home in Glory" 1936: A3). Hallie Flanagan then commissioned Green and the German émigré composer, Kurt Weill, to write another 'symphonic drama', *The Common Glory*, for its celebrations in 1937–1938 of the sesquicentenary of the signing and ratification of the US constitution. The plan was to stage it in multiple cities, although the project foundered, in part because Green and Weill could not decide whether the music was to be incidental to the play (as it was in *The Lost Colony*) or to have a more prominent role.[4] However, one can see why a 'symphonic drama' might have appealed to the FTP with regard to its mission to promote large-scale forms and to engage in theatrical innovation that would not compete directly with commercial enterprises. In the end, it did not have much luck with staging such works in the larger cities. But the radio may have seemed a more favourable medium for the genre: the Federal Theatre of the Air took it up with some enthusiasm.

---

4 For *The Lost Colony*, *The Common Glory* and other similar FTP projects, see Carter (2011). Brooks Atkinson provided a largely positive review of *The Lost Colony*: he, too, was not very clear on what 'symphonic drama' might mean, although he expressed some skepticism over whether Green had risen to its challenges (1937: 139).

2   *The Symphonic Drama Hour*

In mid-1937, residents of New York City could tune in to no fewer than thirteen radio stations (at least, according to the regular listings in the newspapers), including those affiliated with the 'big four' national networks – WEAF (the National Broadcasting Company's Red Network), WJZ (NBC Blue), WOR (Mutual Broadcasting System) and WABC (Columbia Broadcasting System) – plus others with a more regional reach. In keeping with their presumed responsibility to inform and educate as well as entertain, these stations offered significant amounts of 'classical' music amid their daily fare, whether through live performance or by way of recordings (see Crum 2009): the regular Saturday matinee broadcasts from the Metropolitan Opera House on the NBC Blue Network, inaugurated in 1931, were by no means untypical. Such programming was also bolstered by talks and interviews: Walter Damrosch's long-running series of user-friendly lectures on classical music for NBC's *Music Appreciation Hour* (1928–1942) is the most obvious case in point (see Howe 2003). Thus, when the FTP began planning its radio operation in 1936, it hoped to secure regular spots on one of the major networks. But perhaps inevitably, its niche activities tended to end up on local stations, including New York's WQXR, founded that year by John V.L. Hogan and Elliott Sanger as part of their Interstate Broadcasting Company (based in Long Island City). WQXR took advantage of newly emerging 'high fidelity' technologies to focus largely on classical music, interspersed with news and informative presentations. It was generally regarded as a "class" station catering to listeners of "more intellectual and sterner musical tastes" ("New York Studio" 1937: 4) – it also broadcast the FTP's *Exploring the Arts* starting on 7 April 1937 – and thus was an obvious place for a series initially called *The Symphonic Drama Hour*.

The FTP launched the first of its 'symphonic dramas' with Ibsen's *Peer Gynt* (1867), to the music provided by Grieg for its premiere in 1876, on Tuesday 20 April 1937 at 9:00–10:00 p.m., and the series continued in the same day/time slot with nine or ten more plays until 22 June; the FTP seems to have kept the slot thereafter but shifted in late June through July to a separate run of plays by Ibsen. No recordings of these broadcasts survive, to the best of my knowledge, nor would one expect them to: even if the (somewhat basic) technology was available, it was more in the FTP's interest to support further live broadcasts than to reuse recordings. There is also some confusion over the sequence given that the surviving scripts of *The Symphonic Drama Hour* mostly document the rerun of the series beginning in early April 1938, with six or seven additional programmes.[5] But the format is clear: with just two exceptions,

---

5   The 1938 scripts for *The Symphonic Drama Hour* are in NYPL, WPA Radio Scripts, *T-Mss 2000–005, Series XCVIII, with the 1937 *A Midsummer Night's Dream* in Series XCIX. There is

these were abridged plays done live in the studio "with WPA players" (as was sometimes listed in the papers) and with incidental music played from 78 rpm records. According to the text of the announcement prefacing each broadcast, these productions were created by "weaving together the works of great composers and the literature of famous writers". This rather grandiose claim was also reinforced by the theme music for the series (at least in its 1938 iteration), drawn from the Prelude to Wagner's *Die Meistersinger von Nürnberg* (1868). But some of this weaving had already occurred, given that in the case of *Peer Gynt*, Alphonse Daudet's play *L'Arlésienne* (1872, based on his short story from 1869) and Shakespeare's *A Midsummer Night's Dream*, the relevant "great composers" had provided incidental music specific to them (Grieg, Bizet and Mendelssohn respectively).

In terms of plays, the 1937 series tended to stick with nineteenth-century fare save for *A Midsummer Night's Dream*; they also included *La Dame aux camélias* (1852) by Alexandre Dumas *fils*, W.S. Gilbert's *Pygmalion and Galatea* (1871), Edmond Rostand's *Cyrano de Bergerac* (1897) and Oscar Wilde's *Salome* (first performed in 1896). But when the series was rerun in 1938, earlier works were added, going back to Sophocles's *Oedipus Rex* and running through the medieval morality play *Everyman* (15th century), Shakespeare's *Henry VIII* (ca. 1613), Dryden's *All for Love* (1677) and Goldoni's *The Mistress of the Inn* (that is, his *La locandiera* of 1753). More Ibsen was added as well, with *Romersholm* (1887), *A Doll's House* (1879) and *The Lady from the Sea* (1889). All these works had a strong degree of literary prestige, and the 1937 broadcasts were often given special mention by the *New York Times* among the top-billed "Outstanding Events on All Stations" in its daily radio listings.

The choice of accompanying music is fairly predictable, for example Ibsen's *A Doll's House* with piano music (or its orchestral arrangements) by Grieg, or *La Dame aux camélias* with Verdi – presumably drawing somehow on *La traviata* (1853), the opera based on the play. Shakespeare's *Henry VIII* was paired with Tchaikovsky (although which of his works is unclear), but other of the earlier plays had music better fitting their purpose: *Everyman* with unspecified pieces by J.S. Bach, and Edmond Rostand's *Cyrano de Bergerac* with seventeenth-century music loosely related to the period in which the play is set (1640–1655) that had been selected by Walter Damrosch, presumably from the various recordings available from the early 1930s of arrangements of music by Lully and similar composers.

Two of the 1937 broadcasts worked differently, however. All these plays were adapted by in-house scriptwriters attached to the Federal Theatre of the

---

an additional complication that these scripts variously stem from the WNYC broadcasts and the later KFAC (Los Angeles) ones in a different order.

Air (and presumably on the unemployment relief scheme), including Ysobel (Isobel) Martin and Lewis W. Moyer.[6] But Moyer was also commissioned to write two new ones to be paired with Rimsky-Korsakov's *Scheherazade* (1888) and with Rachmaninoff's *Isle of the Dead* (1908). For *Scheherazade*, Moyer drew – predictably enough – on the *Arabian Nights* stories that had prompted Rimsky-Korsakov to write his suite in the first place. In the case of *Isle of the Dead*, he came up with a more creative approach, using Marie Berna's commission of the second version of Arnold Böcklin's famous painting (now in the Metropolitan Museum of Art) to enable a flashback of the artist's life, thereby concocting a story to explain the painting's mysterious subject that, in turn, had inspired Rachmaninoff's symphonic poem. This hints at a different approach to 'symphonic drama' that would soon become more firmly established.

When the FTP reran the 1937 series with additional programmes starting on 4 April 1938 (each Monday at 2:00–3:00 p.m.), it switched New York radio stations to WNYC, which was now receiving a significant injection of funds from the WPA; it was also a major outlet for the Federal Music Project.[7] A further advantage was the station's links to the Intercity Network, enabling WNYC programmes to reach listeners further afield, including Boston (WMEX), Pittsburgh (KQV) and Philadelphia (WIP). In October–December 1938, the extended series was also broadcast on station KFAC in Los Angeles.[8] However, the FTP already had plans for a much more substantial sequence of symphonic dramas that worked in different ways. The WNYC rerun petered out (it may never have been completed) given that starting on 4 July 1938 the station gave the FTP a different Monday time slot at 5:00–5:45 p.m., just before the earlyevening news broadcast. Now the plan was for what was announced in the *New York Times* as "a series of original stories written to music masterpieces under the direction of the Federal Theatre": "The program planners will take symphonies and tone poems such as Mozart's Symphony No. 1 [*sic*] in C major, Tchaikovsky's 'Nutcracker Suite', Sibelius's 'Finlandia', etc., and present them in conjunction with dramas written especially for them."[9] ("Shows" 1938: 106) The details here are not quite correct: plans were clearly still in flux when the FTP created the press release on which this notice was based. But the general principle was clear: the approach that Lewis Moyer had taken with

---

6 Martin was perhaps the actor who had a small role in Edmond Rostand's *L'Aiglon* (1900) on Broadway in late 1934.
7 See Scher (1965) and https://www.wnyc.org/story/121668-the-federal-wpa-music-project-is-a-major-presence-at-wnyc/ [14/04/2021].
8 The KFAC sequence was certainly done live (which one would expect) – the credits in the scripts involve different directors, etc. – as also seems most likely for the WNYC one.
9 The Mozart work was presumably his Symphony No. 41 in C Major, K. 551 (*Jupiter*).

Rimsky-Korsakov and Rachmaninoff in 1937 was now being developed on a much more ambitious scale.

3 Experiments in Symphonic Drama

When the Federal Theatre of the Air celebrated its second anniversary in 1938, the *New York Times* summarised a report by its director, Leslie Evan Roberts, as follows:

> the project has found employment for numerous actors, directors, technicians, script writers, sound effects experts, singers and a production staff. Thirty-eight series of programs, chiefly drama, have been produced and adapted for broadcasting, including many noted stage and screen plays, novels and short stories. All time on the networks and over local stations is given gratis [...]. ("Behind the Scenes" 1938: 160)

Roberts noted that the value of this airtime had reached more than $2 million by 1 January 1938, with another $1.5 million expected by 30 June; he also said that "approximately 50 per cent of the performers employed since the project started two years ago have been returned to private employment" (ibid.). This was regarded as a significant success given that one "of the primary purposes of the Federal Theatre Radio Division is the preserving of the skills and the reemployment of the people in the theatrical profession" (ibid.). But in addition,

> An almost equally primary purpose is the production of educational and cultural programs which will familiarize the radio public with the best in drama, art, history and music in order to advance the general cultural level of the American people and further the significant progress of radio. (Ibid.)

A similar account of the Federal Theatre of the Air's successes had already appeared in the leftist *Daily Worker*, which noted the conservative estimate that its broadcasts were reaching 10 million listeners each week ("W.P.A." 1938: 7).[10] Now it was time to produce 'symphonic drama' of a different kind.

The series of thirteen *Experiments in Symphonic Drama* that began on 4 July 1938 took the opposite approach to the 1937 one (see Table 4.1). Some of the same production staff involved in the latter's 1938 iteration remained,

---

10   The 10 million figure is repeated in Flanagan (1940/1965: 269).

including Jane Kim as director and Evelyn Schonmann on the production side working under the supervision of Charles Crumpton. As with the earlier series, the broadcasts were also done live from the studio. But adding 'experiments' to the title offered a sense of innovation, and also an excuse should it fail. The new plan was to start with the music rather than with classic plays: various scriptwriters attached (it seems) to the FTP's New York Radio Division were each allocated specific orchestral works in a particular recording and asked to create a new dramatic treatment for which the music would act as underscoring. In principle, the work was to be played continuously and in sequence, and while fading up and under was allowed, it needed to remain a constant presence. In practice, however, the writers tended to insist on a more flexible approach – especially as the series progressed – to suit their narratives: for example, by switching the order of movements or even their segments. This may also have been prompted by the sequencing issues raised by playing works from multiple double-sided 78 rpm recordings, whether exchanging them manually or by way of one or other automatic system.[11]

For the rest, however, the writers were given free rein to respond as they thought best to their assigned pieces. Thus, Cecil Stevenson explained his approach to Beethoven's Symphony No. 3 in E Flat Major (*Eroica*) in a note added at the end of the typescript of his text:

> The author can truly say that the Music was the inspiration for the following script. He listened to the music for hours in order to get full benefit from it. The story follows the music, with the low passages under dialogue and the natural crescendos coming up between scenes. The moods of the music have been very carefully studied and will be found to coincide with the moods in the story.[12] (60)

This statement was no doubt well intentioned, but it reveals the inherent problems of the exercise. Some listeners also seem to have been confused: the text of the initial announcement prefacing each programme referred to "experiments in interpreting symphonic music with synchronized dialogue", which was then explained further: "Each symphonic work presented on this series will have a dramatization which has been inspired by the musical work." From

---

11 For automatic systems, see http://gasdisc.oakapplepress.com/introcoupling.htm [14/04/2021]. The scripts sometimes suggest that such automatic systems (or rather, recordings designed for them) in 'drop' or 'slide' formats were intended, although very occasionally the side-to-side cues do not seem to be correct.

12 All quotations are taken from the scripts as listed in Table 6.1.

TABLE 6.1   Overview of the Federal Theatre Project's thirteen *Experiments in Symphonic Drama* (1938)

The scripts survive complete in NYPL, WPA Radio Scripts, *T-Mss 2000-005, Series XXVII, in numbered folders as indicated here. Broadcasts were on WNYC (and sometimes other stations on its Intercity Network) on Mondays, 5:00–5:45 p.m. Newspaper listings occasionally identify different works, as detailed in the notes. The recordings used are identified in the scripts (which sometimes also provide alternatives, though only the primary one is given here); they can usually be identified by reference to the *Discography of American Historical Recordings* at https://adp.library.ucsb.edu/index.php.

	Music (recording [Victor Red Seal save where noted])	Date	Dramatist	Plot outline
1	Kodály, *Háry János Suite* (Minneapolis Symphony Orchestra, cond. Eugene Ormandy)	4 July	Leslie Balogh Bain	An abridged version of the opera (about the fantastical exploits of Háry János in the Napoleonic era), with some variants.
2	Tchaikovsky, *Nutcracker Suite* (Philadelphia Symphony Orchestra, cond. Leopold Stokowski)	11 July	S.J. Shumer	An ageing Pierrot and Pierrette reminisce over their theatrical careers.
3	Brahms, Symphony No. 4 in E Minor (Philadelphia Orchestra, cond. Leopold Stokowski)	18 July[a]	S.I. Nawler	John, a war reporter traumatised and disillusioned by his experiences on the battlefields of Spain and China, escapes his engagement to socialite Lynn to become a farmer.

a   Advertised in *New York Herald Tribune*, 18 July 1938, p. 22, as Elgar, *Enigma Variations* (broadcast on 25 July); NYT lists just "Symphonic Drama". Listings for 25 July do not identify the work.

TABLE 6.1   Overview of the Federal Theatre Project's thirteen *Experiments* (*cont.*)

	Music (recording [Victor Red Seal save where noted])	Date	Dramatist	Plot outline
4	Elgar, *Variations on an Original Theme* (*'Enigma'*) (Halle Orchestra, cond. Hamilton Harty [Columbia Masterworks])	25 July	William B. Farrell	A Civil War blockade runner lives the high life in New York but eventually returns to the South.
5	Grofé, *Grand Canyon Suite* and *Mississippi Suite* (Paul Whiteman and his Concert Orchestra [Victor Black Seal])	1 Aug.[b]	Edward Ray Downes	A city-slicker couple experience the rigors of life in the Wild West as they contemplate moving there.
6	Beethoven, Symphony No. 3 in E Flat Major (*Eroica*; London Philharmonic Orchestra, cond. Serge Koussevitzky)	8 Aug.[c]	Cecil Stevenson	A Hero is imprisoned by the Minister of Propaganda and befriended by jailor Daniel. War is declared; the Minister is ineffectual; Daniel frees the Hero who brings victory; the Minister is assassinated.

b   Advertised in *NYT*, 1 Aug. 1938, p. 10, as Wagner's *Tristan and Isolde* (also *New York Herald Tribune*, 1 Aug. 1938, p. 24; *Philadelphia Inquirer*, 1 Aug. 1938, p. 28 [on station WIP]).
c   Advertised in *NYT*, 8 Aug. 1938, p. 27, as *The Age of Steel* (broadcast on 12 Sept.); see also *New York Herald Tribune*, 8 Aug. 1938, p. 26. But *New York Herald Tribune*, 12 Sept. 1938, p. 28, lists it correctly, as does *Philadelphia Inquirer*, 12 Sept. 1938, p. 18 (for station WIP).

TABLE 6.1   Overview of the Federal Theatre Project's thirteen *Experiments* (cont.)

	Music (recording [Victor Red Seal save where noted])	Date	Dramatist	Plot outline
7	Debussy, *Prélude à l'après-midi d'un faune* (Philadelphia Symphony Orchestra, cond. Leopold Stokowski)	15 Aug.[d]	William B. Farrell	Two parallel stories as the satyr, Pan, and modern-day Tom court successive women but are rejected.
8	Berlioz, *Symphonie fantastique* (Symphony Orchestra of Paris, cond. Pierre Monteux)	22 Aug.[e]	Leslie Balogh Bain	Beelzebub allows a Poet (Paul), who has taken hashish, to foresee the disastrous consequences of his love for the fickle Clarisse. Then he must return and decide either to stay with the demons or to live his life as it is ordained. Although Paul views himself murdering Clarisse and being executed for the crime, he chooses to return.
9	Liszt, *Les Préludes* (San Francisco Symphony Orchestra, cond. Alfred Hertz)	29 Aug.[f]	Harold Hartogensis	A Wall Street stockbroker wants to retire to the village in Pennsylvania where he was born. He meets his long-lost sweetheart, but she eventually rejects his marriage proposal. He returns to the city where at least he still has his work to do.

---

[d]   Advertised in *NYT*, 14 Aug. 1938, p. 136 (and 15 Aug. 1938, p. 29; *New York Herald Tribune*, 15 Aug. 1938, p. 24), as Debussy's *La Mer*.
[e]   Advertised in *NYT*, 22 Aug. 1938, p. 27, as *Romeo and Juliet* (presumably Tchaikovsky); see also *New York Herald Tribune*, 22 Aug. 1938, p. 24.
[f]   Advertised in *NYT*, 29 Aug. 1938, p. 9 as the *Grand Canyon Suite* (broadcast on 1 August); see also *New York Herald Tribune*, 29 Aug. 1938, p. 24.

TABLE 6.1   Overview of the Federal Theatre Project's thirteen *Experiments* (*cont.*)

	Music (recording [Victor Red Seal save where noted])	Date	Dramatist	Plot outline
10	Tchaikovsky, Symphony No. 6 in B Minor (*Pathétique*; Philadelphia Orchestra, cond. Eugene Ormandy)	5 Sept.	George Thorp	A Mother asks her son, John (a priest), to bring home his wandering brothers, Peter (a poet) and Philip (a soldier). They return but find her dead.
11	Prokofiev, *The Age of Steel* (London Symphony Orchestra, cond. Albert Coates)	12 Sept.	Harold Hartogensis	Praise of steel for its contributions to transport, construction, agricultural machines, etc., switches to blame as workers die in accidents, and then 'thinking machines' take over the world.
12	Tchaikovsky, Symphony No. 5 in E Minor (Philadelphia Symphony Orchestra, cond. Leopold Stokowski)	19 Sept.	George Thorp	Anton and Paula, farmers of land destroyed by evil wind, winter freezes, drought and locusts, lead a march to seek new life in the golden city on the hill, but they are denied entry.
13	Rachmaninoff, Piano Concerto No. 2 in C Minor (Philadelphia Symphony Orchestra, cond. Leopold Stokowski)	26 Sept.	Harold Hartogensis	Zacharias and his children, David, Miriam and Joseph (married to Sarah), are dissatisfied with life in the valley. They are led by the old Eupheme to what he promises will be a magic land of plenty, which turns out to be where they currently live.

the fourth programme on, however, there was an addition: "Often that dramatization will not coincide with the composer's program notes. However, it will be a sincere effort at interpreting the mood the music inspires in the individual writer."

The scripts thus prepared were typed in duplicate copies within the offices of the Radio Division, usually less than a week before their intended broadcast (so it seems from the dates on their first pages). The fact that things moved so quickly appears to have created occasional confusion in the Division's press office as it communicated programme listings to WNYC and to the newspapers (as noted in Table 6.1, not everything matches up neatly). There also appear to have been changes of plan: the initial announcement of the series mentioned a Mozart symphony and Sibelius's *Finlandia*; broadcast schedules in the newspapers also refer to Wagner's *Tristan und Isolde* (1865; probably the "Prelude" and "Liebestod"), Debussy's *La Mer* (1905), and *Romeo and Juliet* (presumably Tchaikovsky's *Overture-Fantasy*; 1870). None of them was used.

These scripts needed to be compiled with some care, also including timings for the music for the benefit of the sound engineer operating the turntable. A straightforward example is provided by S.I. Nawler's play for Brahms's Symphony No. 4 in E Minor (Programme 3). The following extract covered the beginning of the third movement (Allegro giocoso). 'John' is a war correspondent newly returned to the United States and traumatised by battlefield events he has seen in Spain and China. He has also realised how war operates to the benefit of the military-industrial complex, and now he urges a public boycott of stores attached to it, leading to his arrest, trial and imprisonment, although he is then transferred to an institution for the insane. The Brahms performance used here was by Leopold Stokowski and the Philadelphia Symphony Orchestra recorded in March 1933, and the timings (allowing an additional one second for each fade under or up) fit perfectly the 2' 46" taken up by disc 4, side 1:[13]

> *Music [0' 00"]: 18 seconds. Then fade and hold under [0' 19"] 1 minute.*
> Sound: Crowd noises... subsiding, as John speaks.
> JOHN: I know what I'm talking about, when I tell you not to patronize this store or others like it. I'm not a wild-eyed radical. I've seen the things I talk about. I've seen war. I've seen men and women just like yourselves suffer and

---

13   For the recording (Victor Red-Seal Album M-185), see https://adp.library.ucsb.edu/index.php/objects/detail/50003/Victor_7825 [14/04/2021]; the third movement is available at https://www.youtube.com/watch?v=TLmQl3ElopU [14/04/2021].

	lose all hope. I've seen what has happened to their children. You can stop all that. I tell you can [sic] stop all that! Boycott these stores! Boycott these goods! Cut off the money that feeds the war gods! In the name of God and humanity, I ask you to do your part! I ask you to...
POLICEMAN:	I ask you to shut up. And quick, buddy!
Sound:	*Crowd murmur under.*
JOHN:	I have a right to talk here.
POLICEMAN:	Where's your permit?
JOHN:	I haven't any.
POLICEMAN:	Where's your flag?
JOHN:	I haven't got one.
POLICEMAN:	Come along with me!
JOHN:	I'm an American citizen!
POLICEMAN:	You're a public nuisance! Now, come along!
Sound:	*Crowd noise fade up and out.*

Music [1' 19"]: Fade up and hold [1' 20"] for 14 seconds. Then fade [1' 34"] and hold under [1' 35"] for 8 seconds.

JUDGE:	Either pay the fine or go to jail.
JOHN:	I haven't the money.
JUDGE:	Got anybody whom you might call on for help?
JOHN:	Yes, there's... No, no one to call on for help.

Music [1' 43"]: Fade up and hold [1' 44"] for 1 minute, 2 seconds... that is, to the end of Disc Four, Side One [2' 46"]. (21–23)

The three segments where the music is 'up' correspond to most of the *fortissimo* passages in this first part of the movement (mm. 1–19; 80–94 [*fortissimo* at m. 89]; 101–167). Another *fortissimo* passage occurs while the music is "under" (at m. 35; 0' 34"), roughly where John would have declared "You can stop all that", although it seems unlikely that such precise coordination was intended or even possible: the music just stays in the background during the spoken dialogue. However, there is certainly a sizeable chunk of the Brahms on its own at the end of this passage: a minute is a long time on the radio.

4   Thematic Choices

Nawler's dialogue here is fairly jejune. But what is most intriguing about these symphonic dramas is how and why their writers might have chosen particular scenarios to match the music they were assigned. Their hands were somewhat tied by works that already adhered to a clear programme. For example, it would have been hard for Leslie Balogh Bain to use Zoltán Kodály's *Háry János Suite* (1927; Programme 1) for anything other than an abridged version of the action of the composer's eponymous opera from 1926 (although the latter was not performed in the United States until the New York World's Fair in 1939).[14] Likewise, Edward Ray Downes's opportunities for Ferde Grofé's *Grand Canyon Suite* (1931; Programme 5) were limited by its five movements ("Sunrise", "Painted Desert", "On the Trail", "Sunset", "Cloudburst") even with various additions from his *Mississippi Suite* (1926: "Father of the Waters", "Huckleberry Finn", "Old Creole Days", "Mardi Gras"). Thus, Downes's opening narration is predictable, as are his sententious trochaic tetrameters echoing Henry Longfellow's *Song of Hiawatha* (1855):

> Cloudless sky and painted desert – hoofbeats ringing down the trails – mountebanks and painted ladies – desert towns and wooden jails – heat and hate and love and laughter – cowboy songs, the friendly jest – raise their voice in mighty chorus – to sing the Saga of the West! [*20 seconds of music*] Ferde Grofe, in his "Grand Canyon" and "Mississippi" Suites, has painted a musical picture with a sweepingly colourful brush. And now we attempt to add words to Grofe's superb musical story. We bring you a yarn as simple and ageless as time itself. A tale of a boy – and a girl – and the West! Perhaps it was yesterday – it may be today – it could be tomorrow. Our locale is the desert. The time – just before dawn – (3)

On the other hand, Leslie Bain took a slightly more creative approach with Berlioz's *Symphonie fantastique* (Programme 8): this work already had a programme (the five movements represent various opium-induced fantasies of an artist suffering from unrequited love), but Bain added a twist: the Devil gives Paul (a poet) the chance to see his future life with his fickle beloved, Clarisse – whom he murders in a fit of jealous rage – but he ends up deciding to live it anyway.

Other programmatic musical works in the series allowed greater freedom. For Tchaikovsky's *Nutcracker Suite* (1892; Programme 2), S.J. Shumer concocted a dialogue between an ageing Pierrot and Pierrette reminiscing about theatrical careers that were varied enough to allow (at a stretch) the inclusion of

---

14   The *Suite* itself was well enough known, however: Macklin Marrow was to conduct it at Lewisohn Stadium five days after the broadcast of Programme 1, on 9 July 1938 (cf. "Music Notes" 1938: 10), although rain forced the concert to play in the Great Hall of City College instead (cf. J.D.B. 1938: 21).

the suite's "Russian", "Arabian" and "Chinese" dances. In the case of Debussy's *Prélude à l'après-midi d'un faune* (1894; Programme 7), William B. Farrell took advantage of the fact that the piece was too short by playing its two segments (sides A and B of the 1927 Stokowski recording) multiple times, neatly intersecting two separate narratives concerning unsuccessful attempts to find a female companion by the mythological Pan (who stands in for the faun in Stéphane Mallarmé's poem on which Debussy's work is based) and a modern New Yorker in Central Park.

Perhaps the most adventurous handling of an original programme, however, was Harold Hartogensis's treatment of Prokofiev's *Le Pas d'acier* (*The Age of Steel*), using eight of the eleven movements of the ballet premiered in Paris in 1927 (Programme 11). Prokofiev's work was an exercise in praise of Soviet industrialisation: it was commissioned by Sergei Diaghilev in response to the International Exposition of Modern Industrial and Decorative Arts at the 1925 Paris World's Fair. However, when it was done at the Metropolitan Opera House on 21–22 April 1931, in a double-bill also marking the US premiere of Stravinsky's *Oedipus Rex* (1927), it was given a new scenario by stage-designer Lee Simonson and choreographer Edwin Strawbridge in what was advertised as a "dramatized polemic against the brutal rhythm of manual labor" ("Pas d'Acier" 1931: G9).[15] Hartogensis took a similarly ambivalent view. His play (mixing rhymed and blank verse with prose) starts out by extolling the benefits of steel for modern transport, industry and agriculture, but the tone changes as workers die in horrific accidents in a foundry and then at the construction site of a New York skyscraper, at which point the perils of industrialisation come to the fore. As the Narrator says:

> Production for use. That's the name they gave it. They cluttered up the earth with things. With things of steel. Man grew soft. The barbarian became tame. Science then gave steel a brain – a brain to think for man. And with the Thinking Machine, man's fall began. (42)

The play ends with a convention of the National Federation of Thinking Machines voting in favour of the downfall of humanity. The mechanical assembly cheers, repeating what was a positive refrain earlier in the text now turned into a threat: "The age of steel has just begun!" It was a timely warning: there was much speculation in the newspapers over the development since the late 1920s of various forms of 'thinking machines' (that is, early analogue computers) at

---

15   This programme (first heard in Philadelphia on 10 April 1931) was done under the aegis of the League of Composers and the Philadelphia Orchestra Association, with Leopold Stokowski conducting.

the Massachusetts Institute of Technology. For his play, Hartogensis also took a leaf from a dramatic genre that had become closely identified with the FTP in general: the so-called *Living Newspapers*, focusing in episodic form on political and social issues of the day.

The question of the extent to which these symphonic dramas should engage with such contemporary anxieties came to the fore particularly in the case of more abstract musical works that otherwise offered little programmatic guidance to their content. Elgar's *Variations on an Original Theme ('Enigma')*, from 1899, and Liszt's symphonic poem, *Les Préludes* (1854), in Programmes 4 and 9, appear to have challenged their writers given the odd stories they attached to them (respectively, about a Civil War blockade runner and a jaded stockbroker). But for Beethoven's *Eroica* Symphony (1805; Programme 6), Cecil Stevenson took advantage of its obvious associations to hark back to another successful venture for the FTP, Lewis and Moffitt's *It Can't Happen Here*: an unnamed 'hero' falls victim to a corrupt Minister of Propaganda and profiteering statesmen who stir up the populace against him until he is once more needed to lead the army in a successful victory in battle against (unnamed) foes.

5   War and Exile

Such references to war are not surprising for 1938. We have already seen that Brahms's Fourth Symphony (Programme 3) was attached to a story about a newspaper correspondent traumatised by his experiences in the Spanish Civil War and in China: 'John' breaks off his engagement with his socialite fiancée – who cannot comprehend his newfound beliefs – and finds refuge on a farm. The FTP had itself promoted a series of anti-war plays to be staged between 6 April 1937 (the anniversary of the US entry into World War I) and Memorial Day on 30 May (cf. Weill and Green 2012: 20–23). But on his farm, John introduces a more ambivalent message about fighting for what is right:

> Look around and you'll find a world of paradoxes: – songs from sorrow, laughter out of tears, life from death... and so, I've found peace is something we must fight for! But a fight to build, not destroy: – from the dark into the light; to live and not to die! Peace doesn't come as we wait passively. If it is worth having... if we are worthy of it... we must fight for it. (43)

By mid-1938, the FTP was under significant attack from the political Right for its left-wing tendencies and for being a not-so-tacit supporter of the Roosevelt administration, as well as from the Left for not in fact being radical enough.

Despite the President's landslide victory in the 1936 election, the tide started to turn in the first half of 1937 given Roosevelt's misjudged attempt to reform the Supreme Court and then a series of vicious labour disputes in the steel industry: he later paid the price in the 1938 mid-term elections. The FTP itself also became embroiled in the well-known public-relations disaster of Marc Blitzstein's controversial musical-theatre piece and anti-capitalist diatribe, *The Cradle Will Rock*, in the summer of 1937 (see Pollack 2012: 150–194; Wright 2016). It is not surprising, then, that some of these symphonic dramas tended to muddy the political waters.

This is clearer still in a second prominent war-related theme in these broadcasts. Three of the last four programmes in the series dealt with exile and diaspora, issues that had come to a head in the so-called Évian Conference, an international meeting convened in France from 5 to 16 July 1938 in an attempt to address the global problem of relocating Jewish refugees fleeing the Nazi regime: the conference ended in ignominious failure, and with disastrous consequences. It is also probably no coincidence that these three programmes are all based on seemingly soul-searching works by Russian composers. For example, there was an obvious degree of national stereotyping in George Thorp's treatment of Tchaikovsky's Symphony No. 6 in B Minor (*Pathétique*; 1893) in Programme 11. Here a 'Mother' sends her son, John (a priest), to find his brothers Peter (a poet) and Philip (a soldier) who have gone to seek their fortunes in the world: Peter is on a quest for the meaning of life, while Philip is wracked with guilt at having killed in battle. The three brothers eventually cross paths in 'a great city' and return home to the sound of bells that, it emerges, are for mourning: their mother (Mother Russia?) is dead.

Thorp took an even more painful turn in his script for another Tchaikovsky symphony, the Fifth in E minor (Programme 12). Anton and Paula seek to leave their farm devastated by the harsh climate and plagues of locusts to reach "a bright new world shining with hope" beyond the hills (6). They are joined by a beggar, a prostitute and a thief. As they reach the wall of the golden city, they find a crowd gathered around a bright fire, a 'Leader' at its head:

> See them, Anton – from all corners of the earth they have gathered here before the Great Wall – from the North – the South – the East and West – black and white – yellow and red – the hungry and oppressed – the dreamer and the just – all hoping for the answer to their lot. Look about you – how they gaze with eager eyes to realize the hope that lies beyond. (14)

But no one has yet been able to pass the barrier because the powers that guard it are too strong. Anton tries to break down the wall and is captured by those who control it. They tell him to speak, but while they see his lips move, no sound reaches their ears. Anton cries out:

> You cannot hear me – you cannot hear a million voices roaring out – and the cries of a million babies. You will not hear a world that pleads for the better life – and of hope that will not die. Voices raised sing into the sky – from a sea of oppressed – yet you cannot hear – not one of you – for the voices here are hushed. (19)

The inhabitants of the golden city demand Anton's execution, but first he is sent to trial, where a judge accuses him of threatening the peace that reigns behind the wall. Anton makes an impassioned response:

> You call this peace – when men bend low – hunger stalks the land – and misery runs riot. – You call this peace when injustice rules – and greed is everywhere – you call this peace – that we suffer thus and over all a few command. No – this is no peace that you pretend – give us our share in this world about – and a glimpse at the sun and stars – give us the right to serve our faiths – and worship what they are – give us that which you possess – and possessing crave to keep – give us those things you claim your birthright – and we no more will weep. (30f.)

Despite this powerfully poetic entreaty, the play ends up in the air, as the Narrator concludes: "But the long night was still with the troubled thoughts of man – for there was none to find the answer." (32)

The timely Dustbowl narrative here is clear enough, but Anton's plea for "the right to serve our faiths – and worship what they are" gives it a different, more powerful emphasis, and for obvious reasons. The results of an opinion poll conducted in the United States in July 1938 make depressing reading: 67.4 per cent were in favour of excluding European refugees under any circumstances (the figure was even higher in polls in 1939), and only 23.1 per cent supported welcoming them.[16] Of that latter figure, only 4.9 per cent advocated raising immigration quotas; 18.2 per cent wanted to stick with them. But those quotas were already wholly inadequate. In June 1938, the waiting list for US visas amounted to almost 140,000 from Germany (against a quota of 27,370 immigrants from Germany and Austria), and that figure stood at 220,000 by

---

16   Most of the results of the poll (which also covered a wide range of other issues) were published in the July 1938 issue of the monthly *Fortune* magazine, see http://fortune.com/2015/11/18/fortune-survey-jewish-refugees/#jewish-refugees [14/04/2021]. Of the respondents to the refugee question, 9.5 per cent were 'Don't Knows'.

September.[17] The humanitarian crisis deteriorated still further, leading to the appalling treatment of (mostly Jewish) refugees on the German ocean liner MS *St. Louis*, denied entrance successively to Cuba, the United States and Canada in May–June 1939, and thus forced to return to Europe. It is unfortunate that the very last programme in the series was Harold Hartogensis's Old Testament-style handling of Rachmaninoff's Piano Concerto No. 2 in C Minor (1901; Programme 13): Zacharias and his children, David, Miriam and Joseph, are dissatisfied with life in their valley and are guided by the old Eupheme to what he promises will be a land of plenty, which turns out to be where they started. It was not that easy in the real world of the late 1930s.

It would probably be no less unfair to condemn the FTP for political naivety than to accuse it of cultural snobbery: Hallie Flanagan and her colleagues were more well-meaning than that. These *Experiments in Symphonic Drama* were typical of the rather earnest programming of the Federal Theatre of the Air, and one has to acknowledge the attempt to engage with highbrow musical works while softening their demands on the audience and using dramatic narrative to prompt new ways of engaging with them. One suspects, too, that they were an attempt to counter radio's inherent tendency to encourage "distracted listening", which was becoming a concern in the 1930s (see Goodman 2010). But if this reinterpretation of musical classics fits into a long tradition of reading 'abstract' music in programmatic terms, it also brought a modernist twist to the enterprise while demonstrating that the arts could indeed be relevant in what was proving to be a resonant decade.

References

Atkinson, Brooks (1937). "Founding Fathers: Paul Green's 'The Lost Colony' Performed on Roanoke Island". *New York Times*, 15 August: 139.

"Behind the Scenes: Federal Theatre Radio Project Reports on Results of 2 Years on the Air" (1938). *New York Times*, 1 May: 160.

Bindas, Kenneth J. (2003). *All of This Music Belongs to the Nation: The WPA's Federal Music Project and American Society*. Knoxville, TN: Univ. of Tennessee Press, 2003.

Carter, Tim (2011). "Celebrating the Nation: Kurt Weill, Paul Green, and the Federal Theatre Project (1937)". *Journal of the Society for American Music* 5: 297–334.

---

17 I take these figures from https://encyclopedia.ushmm.org/content/en/article/the-united-states-and-the-refugee-crisis-1938–41 [14/04/2021].

Crum, Jason R. (2009). *Complex Harmonies: United States Radio Culture, Modern Literature, and National Identity, 1919–1945*. PhD Thesis. Univ. of California San Diego.

Flanagan, Hallie (1940/1965). *Arena: The History of the Federal Theatre*. New York, NY: Benjamin Blom.

Forbes, Elliot, ed. (1967). *Thayer's Life of Beethoven*. Vol. 2. Princeton, NJ: Princeton Univ. Press.

Goodman, David (2010). "Distracted Listening: On Not Making Sound Choices in the 1930s". David Suisman, Susan Strasser, eds. *Sound in the Age of Mechanical Reproduction*. Philadelphia, PA: Univ. of Pennsylvania Press. 15–46.

Green, Paul (1958). "Symphonic Outdoor Drama: A Search for New Theatre Forms". *Drama and the Weather: Some Notes and Papers on Life and the Theatre*. New York, NY: Samuel French. 1–44.

"Home in Glory" (1936). *Atlanta Daily World*, 28 June: A3.

Howe, Sondra Wieland (2003). "The NBC Music Appreciation Hour: Radio Broadcasts of Walter Damrosch, 1928–1942". *Journal of Research in Music Education* 51: 64–77.

J.D.B. (1938). "Marrow Leads Orchestra in Great Hall Concert: Philharmonic Shuns Stadium as Rain Threatens". *New York Herald Tribune*, 10 July: 21.

McDonald, William F. (1969). *Federal Relief Administration and the Arts: The Origins and Administrative History of the Arts Projects of the Works Progress Administration*. Columbus, OH: Ohio State Univ. Press.

"Music Notes" (1938). *New York Times*, 9 July: 10.

"New York Studio Specializes in High Quality Radiocasts" (1937). *The Christian Science Monitor*, 7 April: 4.

Nugent, Frank S. (1937). "The Screen: 'High, Wide and Handsome,' a Story of the Oil Rush, Opens at the Astor". *New York Times*, 22 July: 15.

Osborne, Elizabeth A. (2011). *Staging the People: Community and Identity in the Federal Theatre Project*. New York, NY: Palgrave Macmillan.

"'Pas d'Acier': Symbolical American Scene for Prokofieff Music" (1931). *New York Herald Tribune*, 29 March: G9.

Pollack, Howard (2012). *Marc Blitzstein: His Life, His Work, His World*. Oxford and New York, NY: OUP.

"Second Production of WPA Theatre Slated for IHS" (1936). *Atlanta Daily World*, 23 June: 2.

Scher, Saul Nathaniel (1965). "Voice of the City: The History Of WNYC, New York City's Municipal Radio Station, 1924–1962". PhD Thesis. New York Univ.

Schindler, Anton Felix (1966/1996). *Beethoven As I Knew Him*. Donald W. MacArdle, ed. New York, NY: Dover.

"Shows the Microphone Will Present: Musical Salutes to the Fourth of July – Concerts Booked for This Week" (1938). *New York Times*, 3 July: 106.

Weill, Kurt, Paul Green (2012). *"Johnny Johnson": A Play with Music in Three Acts*. Tim Carter, ed. The Kurt Weill Edition I: 13. New York, NY: Kurt Weill Foundation for Music/European American Music Corporation.

Witham, Barry B. (2003). *The Federal Theatre Project: A Case Study*. Cambridge: CUP.

"W.P.A. on the Air-Waves" (1938). *Daily Worker*, 23 March: 7.

Wright, Trudi (2016). "Lost in *The Cradle:* The Reconstruction and Meaning of Marc Blitzstein's 'FTP Plowed Under' (1937)". *American Music* 34: 344–364.

CHAPTER 7

The *Radiokapellmeister* at Work in Danish National Radio: Oscar Wilde's *Salome* as Radio Drama with Symphonic Orchestra (1930)

Michael Fjeldsøe

Abstract

In 1930, Danish National Radio presented a live broadcast of Oscar Wilde's play *Salome* as radio drama with symphonic music by Emil Reesen (1887–1964). The score and the parts make it possible to look into the specific procedures that were used in order to adapt a text to radio and to the requirements of radio drama. This chapter argues that Reesen as a *Radiokapellmeister*, i.e., the conductor of a radio orchestra and intimately familiar with the technique as well as the limitations of radio broadcasting, was key to the success of the broadcast. Furthermore, it shows what the music adds to the radio play.

In 1930, Danish National Radio presented a live broadcast of Oscar Wilde's play *Salome* as radio drama with symphonic music composed and conducted by Emil Reesen (1887–1964). This remarkable production represents an attempt to adapt a genre to radio that is not just a broadcast play but a large-scale dramatic piece for radio accompanied by symphonic music specifically composed to suit the combined dramatic and technical demands of live broadcasting. Wilde's text was used with minor cuts and a few added sentences to explain unseen action. The first broadcast was on 22 August 1930 and, according to the files in the Danish Radio Archives, lasted 1 hour and 15 minutes. A second live broadcast took place on 20 May 1932.[1] The composer, Emil Reesen, had since 1927 been one of the two *Kapellmeister* or principal conductors in

---

[1] The score (137 pages) and the parts used for these performances have been transferred from the Danish Radio Music Archives to the Royal Library: Emil Reesen, *Salome*, DK-Kk, Orkesterbiblioteket. Hørespil 140. The title page reads: 'Emil Reesen (1930). Musik til Salome. Sørgespil i 1 Akt af Oscar Wilde. Oversat af Aage Hertel. (Beregnet til Radio-Udsendelse.)' [Emil Reesen (1930). Music for Salome. Tragedy in One Act by Oscar Wilde. Translated by Aage Hertel. (Intended for radio broadcast.)] Two copies of the text, typescript, 'Salome. Sørgespil i een Akt. Oversat og bearbejdet af Aage Hertel, Musikken af Emil Reesen', DK-Kk, Danmarks Radio. Hørespil 413. Along with the text, a photocopy of the ledger [regiprotokol]

charge of the Radio Orchestra.[2] The main characters of the play were prominent actors from the Royal Danish Theatre, which added to the notion of a prestigious production for the still rather new media of radio. The famous Poul Reumert played the part of Herod and Salome was played by Else Skouboe. Indeed, it was an ambitious enterprise as both Wilde's play and Richard Strauss's opera were known in Copenhagen. In this chapter, I will analyse this production focusing on the role of the *Radiokapellmeister* as a figure combining technical and musical expertise, and discuss the question of what the application of a large-scale musical composition of this sort adds to the genre of radio play. I will argue that the figure of the *Radiokapellmeister*, who was both a conductor of a radio orchestra and intimately familiar with the technique and the limitations of broadcasting, was a key figure in early radio history, as he would combine the competences needed for choosing, adapting and performing music adequately for broadcasting. My second aim is to relate how music in this kind of radio play is used to establish large-scale formal unity and cross references between characters and sections of the play. This is different from the traditional use of music for plays as prelude and entr'actes, accompaniment for songs or background music creating a specific atmosphere. Here, music also supplies a separate layer of interrelations that work together with the dramatic course of events.

1   Early Broadcasting Practices and their Challenges

In the early days of public radio, it was a major issue that the technological equipment for recording and broadcasting music, as well as the receivers used by listeners, had severe difficulties in coping with complex sounding bodies like symphony orchestras. High and low frequencies did not transmit well and the blended sound of instruments in the Romantic orchestra turned into a blurred muddle. This meant that specific means had to be employed in order to cope with this situation. At a time when broadcasting almost exclusively meant the transmission of live performances, there were several options. One was to choose from an existing repertoire that seemed suitable for radio;

---

from the Danish Radio Archives refers to the exact length of the first performance. The ledger also contains a full list of the cast for each performance.

2 Danish National Radio was established in 1925. For a short overview of Danish radio history, see Michelsen et al. (2018b: 29–45); for a broader presentation, see Michelsen et al. (2018a), which also contains a short discussion of the present case (cf. 212–215).

another was to adapt or re-arrange music to fit the requirements of broadcasting; and a third option was to compose music with the specific conditions of radio transmission in mind. The latter option was at that time referred to as 'radio music', considering it a specific genre (see Fjeldsøe 2016). On a regular day of broadcasting, the first two options were of course those covering most of the music played. The performance or commission of new compositions required a special effort and a lot more resources in the form of money and rehearsal hours.

That this refers to common practice is clear from a statement by the Danish composer Knudåge Riisager in the journal *Radiolytteren* in 1928:

> It is well known that not all music is suited for radio broadcasting, whether this is to blame on the music or on the current technical state of radio. It has almost become a commonplace to say that Kammersanger Holm [i.e., honorary chamber singer Emil Holm, the head of Danish National Radio] allegedly said that Brahms is not 'suited' for radio. [...] In such cases there are two ways to proceed: Either you change the methods used for broadcasting based on accumulated experiences, and this might require the technician and the musician to work closer together than they do now, or one must, in ways similar to gramophone recordings, rearrange and adapt existing scores for the specific purpose of radio broadcasting.[3] (1928: 1)

In the same vein, it is interesting to note how another composer, Ludolf Nielsen, who in 1926 was employed as the first music consultant in the Danish National Radio, presented his line of duties:

> There was plenty to do; the orchestra, which at that time [April 1926] was expanded to sixteen musicians, needed a repertoire; there was nothing but a few borrowed scores and the difficulty was that it mostly had to be

---

3 "Det er en kendt Sag, at ikke al Musik i lige Grad egner sig til Udsendelse paa Radio, hvad enten dette nu er Musikens eller den forhaandenværende Radiotekniks Fejl. Det er næsten blevet et Slagord, at Kammersanger Holm skal have udtalt, at Brahms ikke "egner sig" for Radioen. [...] Man kan her gaa to Veje: enten kan Udsendelsesmetoderne ændres paa Basis af indvundne Erfaringer, og her maa vistnok ogsaa Teknikeren og Musikeren i højere Grad end før se at komme til at arbejde Haand i Haand, eller ogsaa maa man på lignende Vis, som Tilfældet er med Hensyn til Grammofonindspilningerne, instrumentere og tilrettelægge den bestaaende Litteratur for det specielle Radioformat." Unless otherwise stated, all translations from Danish are my own.

arrangements, which meant that one had to refrain from using many an orchestral piece [...].[4] (1929: 81)

Providing a repertoire was his main job. For some young composers this would have been an area of experiments, which they willingly took on without being sure of the outcome. If one wanted to minimise the risk of failure, experience and routine could be useful. It is thus of interest that one of the reasons to choose Ludolf Nielsen for this post seems to have been his experience from playing in the symphony orchestra of the Tivoli Gardens. These musicians were used to playing a wide range of music and several concerts a day with a minimum of rehearsal time, conditions that were similar to those of the early radio orchestra. And, as a composer, Nielsen also supplied multiple pieces for radio himself, using a pseudonym when it was in the lighter genres. Indeed, he was one of the first Danish composers to produce music for a radio play, when in 1928 he provided a score for the historical play *Dyveke* (cf. Cornelius 2018: 100).

The Radio Orchestra was established in 1925 with just eleven musicians and was gradually expanded over the next few years. By 1930, it had reached the size of twenty-eight full-time musicians and thirty assistants hired in for symphonic concerts. This would have been the orchestra performing the radio drama at stake. It was only in 1931 that a full-time orchestra with fifty-eight musicians was realised (cf. Granau 2000: 45, 58, 85–88).

2 The *Radiokapellmeister*

As a *Radiokapellmeister*, Emil Reesen was one of those key figures of early radio who was both a conductor and responsible for the quality of the sound in music broadcasting. Thus, he would have been well aware of the technological limitations of broadcasting. Such experienced people of the trade represent a specific kind of radio professional who knew how to adapt to the conditions of radio broadcasting in their performance of musical works. Besides optimising technical solutions, a skilled conductor was able to influence the result by stressing a clear and distinct performance style and by keeping the radio audience in mind. In those cases where such a person was a composer as well, he

---

4 "Der var nok at tage fat paa; Orkestret, som nu udvidedes til 16 Mand, skulde have Repertoire, der var kun nogle faa laante Noder, og Vanskeligheden laa i, at det for største Delen skulde være Arrangementer, saa man maatte resignere overfor mangt et Orkesterværk [...]."

would have been able to provide new music for radio based on all the necessary experience and skills acquired from his day-to-day work with a radio orchestra. A composer of this kind would have known how to include such musical features that worked well in broadcasting already during the process of composing. That Reesen was just such a figure is stressed in an article leading up to the broadcast of *Salome*, which argued that it had been of vital importance to choose him:

> It was then decided to let Emil Reesen compose the music for the play, as he was considered qualified precisely because of his profound experience with scenic-orchestral music and his insight into radio-technical matters. [...] Absolute clarity in the music was the aim; sounds that were unfit for broadcasting because they were too compact were omitted. In fact, all considerations have been made keeping radio and nothing but radio in mind. The music is extremely concise and focuses entirely on providing a full musical image of the quintessence of the tragedy, and apart from a very short prelude there is only one piece of music with an independent character, namely, the Dance of the Seven Veils.[5] ("Musiken" 1930: 15, 42)

Reesen's father was a musician in the military band of the First Regiment based in Copenhagen, of which he later became the music director, and as a child Reesen himself learned to play several instruments, including the violin, but he trained mainly as a pianist. His teacher was Siegfried Langgaard, who had studied with Franz Liszt. Although a talented classical pianist, he played from an early age at restaurants and in theatre orchestras. He also took up composition, and from 1919 onwards he had posts as a conductor at Copenhagen theatres and revues. In this capacity, he also arranged and composed scores, so he knew how to provide music for all purposes with a sense for what would work well with the audience. In 1925, he left Copenhagen for Paris, adding a flair of French music to his repertoire, but when he was offered a permanent position

---

5 "Man valgte da at lade Emil Reesen komponere Musiken dertil, idet man mente, at netop han, med sin rige Erfaring for scenisk-orkestral Musik og sit Indblik i det radio-tekniske, matte være kvalificeret dertil. [...] Der er tilstræbt en absolut Klarhed i Musiken, Klange, der ikke egnede sig til Radiooverføring – fordi de var for kompakte, er udgaaede. Ja alle Hensyn er taget med Radio – og kun med Radio for Øre. Musikken er uhyre prægnant og koncentrerer sig udelukkende om at give et musikalsk afsluttet Billede af Sørgespillets Kvintessens, og rent bortset fra et ganske kort Forspil, findes der kun et Stykke Musik af selvstændig Art, nemlig de syv Slørs Dans."

as conductor at the Danish Radio in 1927, he was keen to return (cf. Granau 2000: 77; see Cornelius 2015).

3   Criteria of 'Radio Music'

The need to provide music tailored for radio was a major issue in the latter part of the 1920s all over Europe. The first commissions from radio stations were offered during 1928, and in 1929 the influential Baden-Baden contemporary music festival, whose board included Paul Hindemith, announced 'Original music for radio' as one of the featured topics (cf. Häusler 1996: 102–107; Stapper 2001: 136–143). Kurt Weill, one of the composers contributing to the festival, was also an early radio critic, and thus he was used to evaluating music according to how it worked in broadcasting. His list of demands for composers of radio music includes knowledge of the acoustic requirements of the studio, the possibilities of microphones regarding orchestra and instruments, how to distribute high, low and middle voices, and the need to avoid complex harmony. He also states the necessity to provide clear-cut musical forms that correspond to the inner logic of the play (see Weill 1929/2000). These criteria are not very specific and address mainly technical rather than aesthetic matters.

To be more specific, it is useful to consult Michael Stapper, who analysed a large body of early works conceived of as radio music and concludes by listing a number of features characteristic of radio-specific musical works. One is the limited size of the orchestra, as it was much easier to control the sound of a smaller ensemble; another is the composition of the ensemble, with the sinfonietta becoming a kind of model with few strings and a preponderance of wind instruments. In many cases, saxophones were added, and the sound tended towards that of a jazz band. A third feature was the compositional technique and the instrumentation. In order to obtain a clear sound, musical lines were often presented by a few solo instruments or played in unison by the full orchestra; contrapuntal settings were preferred to blended chords; pizzicato and distinct playing techniques were favoured; and special attention was given to the audibility of bass lines. Short and clear-cut forms were used like in classical suites or in popular dance music. Other features were the preference for distinct and clear rhythms, and not least a specific culture of interpretation, shunning all Romantic traits and aiming at strict, unsentimental, objective modes of playing (cf. Stapper 2001: 158–282). In short, the German term *Sachlichkeit* ('objectivity') covers the overall approach, not in the sense of a preferred style, but as a specific result of prerequisites required by the radio as a medium (see Grosch 1999).

4 The Production of *Salome*

Such criteria, though, only address one set of challenges posed by the production of a radio play. Besides requirements common to all kinds of radio music, Reesen also had to cope with the task of providing music for a dramatic piece of considerable length. It had to work as a radio play. First, it was of great importance that the text would be heard throughout. The piece works with sections of melodrama alternating with sections of spoken theatre. The technique of melodrama implies that the text is recited accompanied by music, but not in the style of a song or an opera. The text is spoken and there is no specified melody or demands for a specific rhythm apart from that immanent in the wording. Thus, music and words correspond in a less strict sense, defined by common beginnings and additional meeting points to co-ordinate the course of the play. Other sections are spoken theatre without use of the orchestra except for occasional sound effects. This is a different approach than in traditional theatre where music – besides providing a prelude and interludes – mainly adds sound effects, offers an occasional background and maybe accompanies songs during the play. *Salome* is more like a melodrama with symphonic music, where the music has a much more prominent role in providing a large-scale form and cross-references between scenes (see below). On the other hand, the absence of distinct melodies makes this music a kind of accompaniment without an upper voice that demands detailed shifts in harmony to fit the melody. There is no singing at all, so any resemblance to opera is avoided. Neither does a choir occur, except as a choir of 'mumblers' used as a sound effect to give the illusion of a crowd of people that at times is heard from inside the palace.

The choice of Oscar Wilde's play attests to the ambitions of the Danish Radio; it shows courage to pick a text that was already well known and contested for its frivolity and decadence. *Salome* had been performed in Copenhagen both as a play and in Richard Strauss's version as an opera. Inevitably, this production would be compared to both. As a play, it had been performed at the Dagmar Theatre in the 1903–1904 season (cf. Dahl [1933]: 31). The opera premiered in Dresden in 1905, and in May 1913 the Kiel opera presented it in Copenhagen and gave three performances at the Casino Theatre. The role of Salome was performed by Aline Sanden, an opera singer from Leipzig who had performed in a number of Strauss's works. She was clearly the star, and despite some reviews that foregrounded the play's terror and depravity, it was clear that it was a good performance with excellent protagonists.[6] In 1919, the Royal

---

6 See ("Rædslernes Opera" 1913; "Tysk Opera" 1913). *Salome* was performed on 17, 19 and 21 May 1913.

Theatre made its own production which ran twelve times, with Mikhail Fokin as choreographer (cf. Leicht and Hallar 1977: 250). In a widely read, popular book by Anna Erslev, *Tonekunstens Mestre* (Great Composers), one reads what was most likely a common opinion among the mainstream audience:

> Wilde has added to the plot that the tyrant Herod, dissipated and half-insane from drinking, is in love with his stepdaughter Salome. Disgustingly, his and the completely corrupted girl's carnal desires are elaborated in detail, as is the jealousy of the mother. Nothing as brutal as the final stroke, where Salome greedily kisses the chopped-off head of the prophet, has ever been seen anywhere in our time. The music of Strauss is far from soothing the nastiness, glaring and provocative as it is.[7]
> (1914/1923: 273)

5 Musical Means

5.1 *Instrumentation and Settings*

How can one recognise the means of composition and instrumentation that Reesen put into use in order to obtain a piece suited for the radio? First, we must consider the size of the orchestra. It is clear from the parts used for the production that the number of strings was reduced compared with the number of string players otherwise deployed for symphonic music by the Radio Orchestra. The title page indicates the use of six first violins, four second violins, four violas, two cellos and two basses, in all eighteen string players. This is consistent with the number of parts in the original set. It is also clear that the number of strings used in regular symphonic concerts would have been thirty (distributed ten, eight, six, four, two), as extra copies of the string parts were prepared in case The Dance of the Seven Veils was performed as a concert piece. As the woodwind and brass sections were of normal size, with two flutes, oboes, clarinets, bassoons, trumpets and French horns, the balance of the sound shifts in favour of wind instruments.[8] No trombones were used, but some of the woodwind players could change to the deeper-sounding

---

[7] "Wilde har tildigtet, at den udsvævende, af Drik halvt vanvittige Tyran Kong Herodes er forelsket i Stifdatteren Salome. Modbydeligt udmales hans og den totalt fordærvede unge Piges Sanselighed, ligesom Moderens Skinsyge. Noget saa raat som Slutningseffekten, hvor Salome graadigt kysser Profetens afhuggede Hoved, er næppe før set i Nutiden. Strausz' Musik mildner langtfra paa Ækelheden, grel og sansepirrende som den er."

[8] The extra parts were copied later and a note was added on the cover containing the parts: "Salomes Dans 5-4-3-2-2".

instruments such as the English horn, bass clarinet and contrabassoon for special effects. Besides the twelve wind players, a harp, a celesta and two percussionists were also required. Additionally, a part was prepared called 'Contento', which is unusual. This is not an instrument, but the part used for the person in charge of sound effects. He would produce noise from inside the banquet hall when the doors opened, as the whole play is set on the square in front of Herod's palace.[9]

Throughout the piece, the very quiet quality of playing pianissimo (pp) is common, and the strings are playing with sordini for long stretches. This not only affects the volume of the sound, but adds a tense and airy quality to it as well. It is like lowering your voice in order to make the audience listen carefully. One distinct feature is the fabric of the E flat minor sound that the orchestra produces in the prelude. The strings are divided into seven voices laid out like a tapestry of sound, playing the same harmony but slightly displaced in time and rhythm. All are playing very quietly, pp and muted; and when small melodic phrases are given to the French horn, they add pitches in between the notes of the harmony (see Figure 7.1). This music, as is the case with other characteristic settings of music, reappears several times during the piece. It connects to the figures of Narrabot and the Page, and to that specific air of anxiety and dangerous attraction that their conversation is about. In this way, Reesen is able to establish long-term references, to recall certain moods or to refer to earlier situations with musical means.

Most often, each part in the orchestra is playing its own melodic line to the effect that the compact sound of the full orchestra is rare. Each of the musical settings requires a new combination of instruments, producing a distinct sound. When the Prophet appears, he is accompanied by a slow march-like music played in pp by clarinets, bassoons and French horns in their low register, accompanied by timpani and muted strings (see Figure 7.2). This music recurs when the Prophet appears throughout the piece, although in different instrumentations. By comparison, when Salome enters or is the protagonist,

---

9   Sigurd Wantzin, who produced radio plays in Danish National Radio, explains: 'Another and no less important factor in theatre broadcasts are the so-called "sounds" – I prefer the proper term [in Danish:] "Kontentum", an established term in theatre, probably from Latin "Contentus" – which is to [...] substitute what one cannot provide in a natural way and Kontentum in radio is much more difficult to produce than at the theatre' (1929: 78f.). ("En anden og ikke mindre betydningsfuld Faktor ved Skuespiludsendelserne er de saakaldte 'Lyde' – jeg vil nu foretrække at benævne dem ved deres rette Navn 'Kontentum', et i Teatersproget hævdvundet Udtryk, der formentlig har sin Oprindelse i fra det latinske Ord 'Contentus' – hvilket er [...] en Erstatning for, hvad man ikke ad naturlig Vej kan fremskaffe og Kontentum er i Radioen langt vanskeligere at fremstille end paa Teatret.")

FIGURE 7.1   Emil Reesen, *Salome*, No. 1, mm. 6–10. This fabric of sound connects to the characters of Narrabot and the Page, and their sense of anxiety about the dangerous attraction of Salome. Note that the E flat minor notation with six flats is not repeated on each page. The melody is played by a French horn (in F) which plays the notes F and A flat

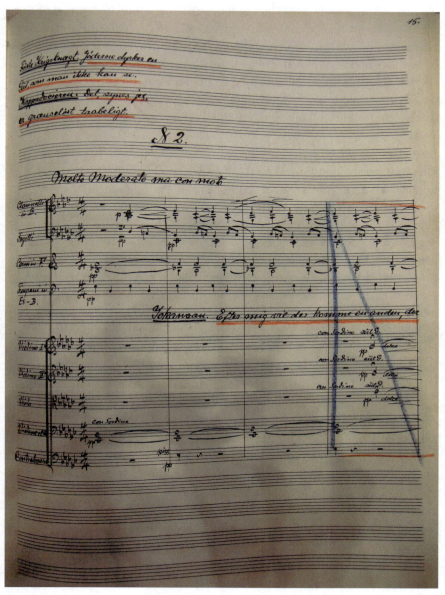

FIGURE 7.2 Emil Reesen, *Salome*, No. 2, mm. 1–4. The music accompanies the first occurrence of the voice of the Prophet. Here one can see how Reesen worked in order to establish coherence in the length of the music and the spoken lines, as he cancelled m. 4 along with m. 5 on the next page. This occurred during rehearsals when the original score did not fit the time needed for the spoken text

we hear the full orchestra. The sparse use of the full orchestra makes these occasions stand out as a contrast and marks Salome as a powerful and dynamic character. She is not just the protagonist; she also provides the energy needed to instigate action. When Herod appears for the first time at the beginning of Section 2, he, too, is introduced by the full orchestra. He enters accompanied by a martial theme, played loud and in a contrasting tonality, so that precisely this theme and this tonality come to signify Herod.

5.2 Large-scale Form

This leads to the question of how the music provides form and creates additional meaning. Table 7.1 gives an account of the relationship between the music, the characters and the action in Reesen's score to *Salome* (see Table 7.1). One of the strengths of musical composition is the ability to establish large-scale form. By means of music it is possible to establish coherence – that is, using cross-references and recurrences, tonality, themes and characteristic settings or types of sound – or, just as important, to set off different sections from each other through contrast and non-identity. Such large-scale formal procedures are much less prominent in plays without music; in theatre, form is to a large degree produced by the staging, shifts of scene, lights or other visual effects not available in radio plays. Thus, music can be used to bring forward the latent form of the drama, but music can also establish connections or contrasts that are not necessarily given in the text.

Salome is a tragedy in one act with no change of location; there is, however, a change in the dramatic setup based on which characters are in action. Reesen uses this to mark up three sections. Interestingly, he does not do that just by dividing the music into three movements, as would be the case in a purely musical composition. Rather, he sets off the three sections from each other by changing the way the parts with music and those with spoken text alone interact. He composed the play using the parts without music as formal elements. In the first section, music dominates with short intersections of unaccompanied dialogue. In the second section, the spoken parts rule with short intersections of music. The third section consists of only three elements, i.e., two long musical settings with a long, spoken scene in the middle.

In the first section, Narrabot, the young Syrian who is captain of the Guard, is talking to the Page of Herodias outside the palace. Their conversation on the pale moon and on Salome circles around Narrabot's fascination with Salome and their fear of what terrible things could happen if he does not resist her. The music accompanying this situation of anxiety and desire is always in E flat minor, either in the form of a static fabric of sound surrounded by small melodies (see Figure 7.1) or of ephemeral music for five solo strings (first heard at No. 1, ⑤). After a while, the Prophet, Jokanaan, is heard from his prison, and at each occurrence he is accompanied by his own music, which is sombre and slow, first presented in low pitched wind instruments and strings (No. 2; see Figure 7.2). This music is also in E flat minor, which adds to the unity of the sound. When Salome comes out from inside the Palace (at No. 4, ⑧), the full orchestra is heard for the first time, which characterises the moments where she is in focus. This goes on until Salome at last succeeds in talking Narrabot into releasing Jokanaan from the pit. At this point, there is a sudden shift in tonality to F sharp major, and the music consists of dramatic glissando strokes divided by dramatically spoken lines during fermatas. This marks the moment of fateful decision, a fatal turn. Due to the shift of tonality, this moment stands out. When the Prophet appears, he and Salome perform what would be the great love duet in an opera, had it not been for his hating and detesting her. This dialogue goes on until Narrabot kills himself as he recognises what he has caused. At that point (marked '†'), the tonality of C sharp minor is heard for the first time. All action mentioned above is accompanied by music.

Parallel to that, there is a layer of unaccompanied short dialogues between the musical numbers and during the fermatas within the numbers. Here we have two soldiers and a stranger, a Cappadocian who gives an account of what happens, who is who and what happened earlier. Most of their dialogue is in Wilde's text, where they already have this function of commenting on and explaining the situation; however, in a few cases a sentence or two is added in order to explain something that would be obvious on a stage but needs to be said when no visuals are available. The first section provides a sense of unity because the music accompanies most of the text and thus dominates the spoken parts. Until the fateful F sharp major occurs, it would be fair to regard E flat minor as a stable tonality. After that moment, the music moves more freely, which corresponds to the fact that Salome is the main character here.

The beginning of the second section is marked by the sudden appearance of Herod. His entrance is accompanied by a strong, march-like music for full orchestra playing in their low register. This music and the main motif follow Herod, and it is always in C sharp minor, which marks a strong contrast to the previous section. Another contrast occurs due to the fact that in this section the parts with music are much shorter and those without considerably longer. This turns the tables, so now the unaccompanied parts work as the main line of action and the parts with music as intersections. As a result, this section, where Herod is present throughout, has its own sound, leaving most of his lines unaccompanied. An additional reason for this might be that the male voice would otherwise be difficult to hear on radio. In this second section, the main plot is the triangular situation where Herod tries to persuade Salome to dance while

TABLE 7.1 Correspondences of music, characters and action in Emil Reesen's music for Oscar Wilde's *Salome*

Section 1

Music	No. 1					No. 2	No. 3	No. 4				
	①②	ᵃ	④	ᵇ	⑤				⑧			
Tonality	Ebm		Ebm		Ebm	Ebm	Ebm	Ebm	Moving	Ebm	Ebm	Ebm
Qualities	Fabric		Fab.		Str.	Prophet	=⑤	=⑤	Full orch.	=①	=⑤	Pr.
Characters												
Salome												
Jokanaan												
Narrabot												
The Page												
Two Soldiers												
A Capadocian												

a   Narrabot gives in and orders the Prophet to be released from the pit.
b   Narrabot kills himself.

Section 2

Music	No. 7		No. 8	No. 9		No. 10		No. 11	
	Pomposo			Lento				Adagio	
Tonality	C♯m		C♯m	Bb - Gm		Ebm		Am	
Qualities	Herodes		'Cold wind'	Hymnic		=④ + Proph.		Flageolet 'Messias'	
Characters									
Salome									
Jokanaan									
Herodes	(enters)								
Herodias									
Two Soldiers									
Other			Tigellius		Jew Second Jew		Jew	Tigel.	Nazarean Jew

a   Herodes promises Salome whatever she wants, and she agrees to dance.

No. 5	No. 6										
							ᴖ	⑰			
E♭m	B♭m	G°	Mov.	E♭m	E♭m	E♭m		F♯	E – C – E C♯m – moving	C♯m	Bm
Proph.	Low winds		=⑧	=④	Pr.			gliss. Fate	Full orch.	trem.	
									"Love/hate dialogue"		
								a		b	

No. 12		No. 13		No. 14	No. 15	
		Pomposo	24			
E♭m	E♭m	C♯m	E♭m	E♭m	F♯	C♯m
=④ + Prop.	=④ + No.9	Herodes	Proph.	Proph.	=⑰ Fate	trem.
				a		

TABLE 7.1   Correspondences of music, characters and action in Emil Reesen's music (cont.)

Section 3

Music	No. 16					
			Dance of the Seven Veils	c		
Tonality	Ebm	Ebm	C#m - moving		F#	C#m
Qualities	=②	=② + Proph.			=⑰ Fate	Herod. trem.
Characters						
Salome						
Jokanaan						
Herodes				a		b
Herodias						
Other						

a   Herodes asks for her request.
b   After his attempt to persuade Salome to wish for something else, Herodes eventually gives in.
c   Herodes orders Salome to be killed.

his wife, Herodias, tries to prevent it. Herod is the protagonist in this section, and the tonality of C sharp minor is prominent; when Jokanaan is heard, he is still marked by his own music and his own tonality. At the fatal moment when Herod promises Salome that she will get whatever she wants if she agrees to dance, the F sharp major glissandos return and mark this as a second fatal moment.

The third section has yet another structure. First, a long section with music contains Salome's Dance of the Seven Veils. When she finishes, we hear for the third time the fatal F sharp major glissandos when she is asked what she demands and then requests Jokanaan's head on a silver plate. Following that, a short passage with Herod's music played tremolo (where fast movements of the bow produce a trembling sound) underscores the tenseness of the moment. This is followed by a long scene without any music that could be regarded as a dramatic effect: at the height of the radio play there is only spoken dialogue, as if the music holds its breath. Here, Herod tries to persuade Salome to change her mind. This has the effect of suspending the action, literally creating suspense. At the exact moment where he gives in and says 'Let her have it', music reoccurs. This music starts and begins in C sharp minor, and in the middle, where Salome has her long, ecstatic monologue, celebrating that she gets to kiss Jokanaan's mouth, the full orchestra is used and the music moves freely

No. 17						
C♯m	Moving		C♯m	C♯m	𝄐	C♯m
Herod. slowly	Full orch.		trem.	trem.		
	Salome's monologue				c	
Nazar.						

again. At the end, Herod takes control, orders her to be killed and the music fades out. This last musical number (No. 17) is framed in C sharp minor, which adds stability. At the same time, it marks who is in charge. At the end, Herod is the last man standing.

5.3   Dramatic Implications

These basic ideas of themes, settings and tonality relating to certain characters and moods make it possible to recognise by ear who is on stage. The relative stability of E flat minor in the first section applies both to Narrabot/The Page and to the Prophet. As a result, they are set on the same 'level', which is not obvious from the text, and another composer might have made a different choice and turned their relationship into a contrast. It underscores their common resistance, or at least reluctance, to giving in to the erotic attraction of Salome. The return of music from Nos. 1 and 2 in the rest of the first section works as a well-known musical procedure without referring to a specific musical form. Tonal contrast, which in classical musical forms would have been expected between the 'First theme' of Narrabot/Page and the 'Second theme' of the Prophet, is instead found between the tonal stability of their music and the unstable music of Salome. Her music moves around between tonalities, which also, together with the use of the full orchestra, gives her appearance a dynamic note. She represents a dynamic force and, in fact, her actions drive the drama forwards. It also marks Salome as unstable und unpredictable herself. Interestingly, the use of music, too, gives account of the balance of power. In No. 4, after the powerful entrance of Salome, the music shifts back to the music of Narrabot and the Page, as their resistance is still stronger than the will of Salome. Later, after the fatal moment in No. 6, where Narrabot gives in and releases the Prophet from the pit, it is Salome's music that sets the scene.

In the second section, musical procedures open up to even more subtle references, as when Herod considers whether the Prophet might be right after all; during the spoken dialogue, Herodias accuses Herod of being scared of the Prophet, which he denies. The music suggests otherwise, as the second appearance of the Prophet (No. 10) combines Jokanaan's music with the music of anxiety (No. 1, ④). Since neither Narrabot nor the Page are present, it functions here as a reference to Herod's state of mind. This happens again in No. 12, where it transforms into a combination of the music of anxiety and the hymn-like music of No. 9, which accompanied the prophecy of the Second Coming. Later, at the very beginning of the third section (No. 16), Herod is worried because Salome is going to dance in the blood of Narrabot, which to Herod confirms a prophecy made by Jokanaan. Again, the E flat minor music of anxiety is included in the setting.

After the second section, in which the passages of C sharp minor relating to Herod and those of E flat minor are still in balance, section three makes a sharp turn just after the beginning, leaving us only with the dynamic music of Salome in contrast to the C sharp minor of Herod. The piece ends in his tonality, which at the same time indicates that Herod has taken charge and that the tragedy has been fulfilled.

6 Conclusion

There was quite a lot of publicity leading up to the production of *Salome*, as it was the first radio play of the season and it was widely reported that Reesen was composing new music, but also the fact that Wilde's play would be broadcast was regarded as a major event. Radio drama did not regularly get reviewed in the papers, but in this case it was. One review in particular testifies to the significance of the music:

> Some might certainly find that Oscar Wilde's 'Salome' does not belong in the repertoire of Danish State Radio. But *everyone* would agree that the way in which this task was solved at the broadcast last night was

artistically splendid. The tragedy is not in the best of taste; however, it seemed as if the radio elevated it, due to the excellent performance of the actors, but also because the accompanying music had a brilliant effect.[10] (pe-de 1930)

This comment attests to the success of providing a radio play that functioned well both in terms of drama and in terms of broadcasting. Any difficulty in hearing the actors or the quality of the transmission of the music would certainly have been noted. The decision to make a second live broadcast in 1932 also indicates that the play was regarded as successful. I would suggest that Emil Reesen being an experienced *Radiokapellmeister* was a key factor of the radio play's success.

Another important finding is to acknowledge the importance of scores and parts in the radio archives, as they are sources revealing the practices of early broadcasting. They give an otherwise inaccessible account of what were the means used to provide the qualities needed for broadcasting at a time when technical standards were still an obstacle. Not least the music for radio plays is a valuable source, as much of this music was composed specifically for the medium. More than a hundred such scores from the Danish National Radio are preserved, and for researchers it is an advantage that they do not have a long performance history. Often, they are in a pristine state, only documenting one or two early performances. Radio music archives might also provide sources to study how music was arranged or adapted for early radio broadcasts, for example by making changes in scoring or instrumentation. Such sources represent more than a musical work; they provide insight into practices of broadcasting music on the radio, often as part of radio drama.

Reesen's score for Oscar Wilde's *Salome* shows how he, a *Radiokapellmeister* by trade, was able to adhere to the demands of the technical limitations, and at the same time to adapt to the rules of radio drama. As a live broadcast, the radio play had to work without retakes. First, he knew how to co-ordinate music and speech in a live performance by using fermatas and other means that may add flexibility to the timing. It is visible in the score, too, how Reesen during rehearsals cut single bars or short sections in order to fit the music to

---

10 "Der er maaske dem, der vil synes at Oscar Wildes "Salome" ikke absolut hører hjemme paa Statsradiofoniens Repertoire. Men *alle* vil kunne være enige om, at den Maade, hvorpaa Opgaven var løst ved Udsendelsen i Aftes, var kunstnerisk fortræffelig. Helt smagfuld er Tragedien ikke, men det var ligesom Radioen hævede den op, bl.a. paa Grund af det udmærkede Spil, der blev ydet, men ogsaa fordi den ledsagende Musik var af glimrende Virkning."

the length of the text. Second, his music was transparent, distinct and quiet, which makes the text audible and the music well fitted for broadcasting. Third, he was able to establish a large-scale form through means of tonality, themes and settings – means that are specific musical features working independently of the text. To that end, he also included the length of the spoken passages as a formal element. Fourth, he succeeded in adding meaning to the play that is not by default given in the text. This is done by aligning, contrasting or combining music that refers to characters, former action or sentiments. Taken together, Reesen's music provides a good example of how musical composition contributes to the genre of the radio play. It shows how music adds to the unity, form and meaning of the piece in a way that spoken theatre with musical effects might not be able to do on its own.

References

Cornelius, Jens (2015 online). "Emil Reesen – en biografi". http://www.jenscornelius.dk/emil-reesen-dansk-musiks-altmuligmand [04/06/2021].

Cornelius, Jens (2018). *Ludolf Nielsen*. Copenhagen: Multivers.

Dahl, Helge, ed. ([1933]). *Dagmarteatret 1883 – 7. Marts – 1933*. Copenhagen.

Erslev, Anna (1914/1923). *Tonekunstens Mestre*. 4th ed. Copenhagen: H. Hagerups Forlag.

Fjeldsøe, Michael (2016). "The Concept of 'Radio Music'". *Danish Yearbook of Musicology* 40: 69–78.

Granau, Martin (2000). *Holms Vision: Radiosymfoniorkestret 75 år*. Vol. 1. Copenhagen: Danmarks Radio.

Grosch, Nils (1999). *Die Musik der Neuen Sachlichkeit*. Stuttgart: Metzler.

Häusler, Josef (1996). *Spiegel der Neuen Musik: Donaueschingen. Chronik – Tendenzen – Werkbesprechungen*. Kassel: Bärenreiter.

Leicht, Georg, Marianne Hallar (1977). *Det kongelige Teaters repertoire 1889–1975*. Copenhagen: Bibliotekscentralens forlag.

Michelsen, Morten, Iben Have, Anja Mølle Lindelof, Charlotte Rørdam Larsen, Henrik Smith-Sivertsen, eds. (2018a). *Stil nu ind... Danmarks Radio og musikken*. Aarhus: Aarhus Univ. Press.

Michelsen, Morten, Iben Have, Mads Krogh, Steen Kaargaard Nielsen, eds. (2018b). *Tunes for All? Music on Danish Radio*. Aarhus: Aarhus Univ. Press.

"Musiken til 'Salome'" (1930). *Radiolytteren* 5/33: 15, 42.

Nielsen, Ludolf (1929). "Musikkonsulentens Arbejde". Oluf Lund-Johansen, ed. *Radiofoniens Aarbog 1929*. Copenhagen: Radiolytteren's Forlag. 81.

pe-de (1930). "Radio-Komedie. Oscar Wildes 'Salome'". *Fyens Stiftstidende*, 23 August.

"Rædslernes Opera i Kjøbenhavn" (1913). *Berlingske Tidende*, 15 May.

Riisager, Knudåge (1928). "Radiomusik". *Radiolytteren* 4/1: 1.
Stapper, Michael (2001). *Unterhaltungsmusik im Rundfunk der Weimarer Republik.* Tutzing: Hans Schneider.
"Tysk Opera paa Kasino. Salome" (1913). *Social-Demokraten*, 18 May.
Wantzin, Sigurd (1929). "Hvordan man tilrettelægger et Radio-Skuespil". O. Lund-Johansen, ed. *Radiofoniens Aarbog 1930.* Copenhagen: Radiolytteren's Forlag. 76–80.
Weill, Kurt. (1929/2000). "Zu meiner Kantate *Das Berliner Requiem*". Stephen Hinton, Jürgen Schebera, eds. *Kurt Weill, Musik und musikalisches Theater: Gesammelte Schriften.* Ext. and rev. ed. Mainz: Schott. 90–92.

CHAPTER 8

Our Language Beats against Its Limitations: Music, Musicality and Musicalisation in Norman Corwin's *They Fly through the Air with the Greatest of Ease* (1939)

Troy Cummings

Abstract

Through the lens of musicology, this chapter provides a much needed historical context and critical analysis of Norman Corwin's understudied and most significant early radio play, *They Fly through the Air with the Greatest of Ease* (1939), an acerbic rebuttal of fascist militarism that also ironically echoes avant-garde Italian Futurist musical ideas. This chapter further contributes and exemplifies a practical and repeatable three-pronged musicological approach to radio play analysis which (1) isolates overt music for analysis, (2) treats the entire piece as a work of electroacoustic music, and (3) explores key points of potential semantic guidance of musical experience.

Obsessed with the sounds, speed and awesome power of weaponised aviation, Filippo Tommaso Marinetti (1876–1944) dreamed of a radically new kind of music – mechanical anthems "thunderously arousing the optimistic and active pride of living in the great Italy of Mussolini" (qtd. in Slonimsky 1994: 392). Marinetti and the composer Aldo Giuntini (1896–1969) described this new music in the *Manifesto della aeromusica* (*Manifesto of Aeromusic*, 1934), which includes a list of poetic metaphors to guide composition:

> We shall have the following types of syntheses, which will enable us to live sanely in speed, to fly, and to win in the greatest war of tomorrow.
> Sonorous block of feelings. Decisive crash. Spatial harmony. Howling interrogation. Decision framed by notes. The regularity of the air motor. The caprice of the air motor. Interpenetration of joyful notes. Triangle of songs suspended at a thousand metres. Musical ascension. Fresh fan of notes over the sea. Aerial simultaneity of harmonies. Anti-human and anti-impressionist expression of the forces of nature. Coupling of echoes. (Ibid.)

In Marinetti's personal scrapbook documenting Futurism, he pasted a collage of an orchestra playing in the clouds, directly next to a clipping about Italian air raids in Ethiopia (Marinetti 1936: 79). He clearly wanted 'aeromusic' to not only be innovative musically but also politically charged.

Giuntini and a few other Italian composers wrote aeromusic for piano, programmatic pieces which evoked airplane acrobatics with crashing chords, quick, fluttering patterns and rests resonating with echoes. However, these pieces only imitate airplane flight; they do not explore the musical use of machine noise that the manifesto suggests. Earlier Futurist music by Luigi Russolo (1885–1947), with custom built noise machines, did achieve a synthesis of noise and music, including airplane-themed compositions, but the music itself did not inspire patriotism as the manifesto hoped. On the contrary, audiences in Milan rioted when they heard the music.

Norman Corwin's (1910–2011) politically charged radio play *They Fly through the Air with the Greatest of Ease* (1939) both explored airplane noise as music and aroused affect in hundreds of thousands of listeners. Ironically, *They Fly* is frankly anti-fascist, denigrates aerial warfare and is directly linked to Italy's air raid campaigns in Abyssinia via Vittorio Mussolini (1916–1997), Benito Mussolini's son, who Corwin credited as the inspiration of *They Fly*. Vittorio, who praised aerial warfare, in true Futurist fashion, as the "quintessence of beauty", was an amateur pilot, aspiring film producer and author ("Vittorio's Beauties" 1937: 15). Recounting an air raid of Ethiopian cavalry in the Second Italo-Ethiopian War (1935–1937), he wrote: "We arrived upon them unobserved, and immediately dropped our loads of explosives ... I remember one group of horsemen gave me the impression of a budding rose as the bombs fell in their midst. It was exceptionally good fun." (ibid.; ellipsis in original)

These words, from the book *Voli Sulle Ambe* (*Flights over Both*, 1937), which was published in Germany bluntly as *Bomber über Abessinien* (*Bomber over Abyssinia*), led to a flood of newspaper articles in the United States decrying the light-hearted descriptions of the death of the out-matched Ethiopians. On 23 September 1937, protestors set up loudspeakers in New York harbor shouting "deport Mussolini's son" at Vittorio's incoming liner ("Mussolini's Son 'Spirited'" 1937: 6). Two days later, full page adds in film trade magazines protested his arrival in Hollywood. Vittorio became associated with air raids on civilian targets like the bombing of Guernica, Spain in April 1937, and was asked on his USA visit if he would support a global ban on civilian air raids. "Such an international agreement among aviators would be unnecessary because no civilized nation would think of bombing civilian populations", he replied (ibid.: 3). In July 1937, Japan began bombing civilian targets in China, sparking international outcry.

Corwin was producing the poetry program *Poetic License* (1937–1938) on WQXR in New York City in 1937. On the episode of 23 August 1937, he noted the air raids in China and Spain saying: "I walked the sidewalks of New York without fearing that at any moment I might be strewn around the avenue by a bomb from heaven" (1). A year later, in August of 1938, after being hired at the Columbia Broadcasting System, he proposed a radio play on the subject:

> It occurred to me, during the height of the Spanish and Chinese bombings, that nobody has yet done a good air raid job – in spite of the fact that people are reading about air attacks in every morning's news. And it seemed to me that a gripping job might be done without resorting to exploding bombs, wailing sirens or general shrieking. How do you like this synopsis for a show you could call OUT OF A CLEAR SKY (1938a: 1; underlining and upper casing in original).

Corwin then went on to describe a rough version of what would become the radio play *They Fly*. However, Archibald MacLeish (1892–1982) beat him to it with *Air Raid* (1938), a verse radio drama about the aerial bombing of civilians, broadcast on CBS's flagship programme, Columbia Workshop, on 27 October 1938. Corwin had a choice to make: either abandon his earlier idea of a radio play on the same theme, or continue and have his work blatantly compared to *Air Raid* and its author, a famous poet and successful radio playwright. Corwin chose to write his radio play anyway.

His audacious decision paid off. On 19 February 1939, the day *They Fly* aired, William Robson, who directed *Air Raid*, "rushed into the control room after the broadcast and said, gripping [Corwin's] hand, 'Norman, you're a major American poet'" (Corwin 1939e). Days later, William Lewis, vice president of programming at CBS, admitted to Corwin that *They Fly* "topped" *Air Raid* (ibid., 23 February). The Institute for Education by Radio awarded *They Fly* first prize in radio drama. The attention that *They Fly* received put Corwin on the nation's radar as a silver-tongued anti-fascist voice, and it was a turning point in his career. This radio play's basic themes – the perils of war, the evils of fascism and the hope of world peace – became the defining themes of Corwin's radio art.

They Fly had an encore performance on 10 April 1939. A third was planned on 7 September 1939, but that week Germany began air raids in Poland, and Britain responded with airborne leaflet dropping in Germany. What was supposed to be *They Fly*'s third broadcast began as follows:

> Tonight the Columbia Workshop was to have repeated *They Fly through the Air with the Greatest of Ease*, Norman Corwin's verse drama about

> the aerial bombardment of civilian populations. The performance was scheduled two months ago, but since that time the war tactics, which the author indicted with such emotional force, have become an actuality, so that we are reminded only too vividly everyday of the point of the play. For this reason we are indefinitely postponing tonight's performance of *They Fly through the Air*. (Corwin 1939c)

Since *They Fly* was an episode on his poetry programme *Words Without Music*, there was no budget for a musical score, only for sound effects. The result was a radio play that relied on airplane sounds similar to the way that many of his later radio plays relied on a musical score. Corwin called sound technician Ray Kremer "the Matulay of the broadcasts", referring to Laszlo Matulay, the illustrator of the first publication of *They Fly* (cf. Corwin 1939a: 10). Kremer interpreted Corwin's sound cues to create a single aural bomber plane from multiple disc recordings, cueing the records live on air.

Corwin wrote only one brief passage of instrumental music into *They Fly*, the first minute and a half of a Chopin piano étude, yet he explored music from various angles in the radio play, making it ideal for musicological techniques that not only examine traditional music but also address sound organisation, modes of listening and techniques which direct listeners into musical experiences. To illustrate this, I delineate three musicological approaches to radio play analysis – music, musicality and musicalisation.

Here is a thought experiment to clarify the differences in these approaches. Imagine a radio programme of a live broadcast of Beethoven's 1808 *Pastoral Symphony*. The announcer introduces the symphony, the performers and location over the sounds of the orchestra tuning, audience noise, the scuffling of chairs and sheet music. We hear the applause when the conductor takes the podium, the silence before the first notes, the movements of Beethoven's symphony and the ending applause of the audience. Now I will quickly run through three potential analyses of this imagined radio programme using the methods which I label music, musicality and musicalisation.

The first method, music, would isolate the symphony, discuss the history of its composition, details about Beethoven's life, theoretical analyses of the music, information about this specific performance, orchestra and conductor, or this music's context in the history of broadcast radio. The second method, musicality, would analyse the orchestral music, all of the voices, applause, tuning up and concert hall noises and resonance as a sonic whole. This method would look for insights into the visceral aural experience of the programme's sound design distanced momentarily from the semantic experience. The third method, musicalisation, would address how both the experience of the music and experience of the overall musicality of the programme are potentially affected by semantic elements.

Imagine that the announcer discusses the concert hall of the performance, saying 'the resonance of this great hall makes the tuning up and the shuffling of stands and sheet music sound fascinating'. Immediately the listener is likely to become more aware of these sounds. This awareness can expand their euphonic sensitivity to include noises that they may not have considered musical or sonically interesting before. The sounds may be no different, but the context in which they are listened to has changed. The extra symphonic noises have been musicalised through verbal directions on how to listen to or how to identify them.

In a similar way, the experience of Beethoven's music can be affected if the announcer gives the programmatic titles for the movements, like "Scene by the Brook" for the slower second movement or "Thunder, Storm" for the tempestuous fourth movement. These titles add a layer of accompanying images and feelings to the music that can become an indelible part of the listener's experience of that music. Musicalisation is happening through the juxtaposition of the programmatic titles and the symphonic movements.

1 Music

The first method I will apply to *They Fly*, which again I simply call 'music', focuses on overt instrumental music. Corwin's radio play follows the doomed mission of a warplane and its civilian targets. After the bomber crew prepare for takeoff and begin their flight we hear the sounds of civilians in an apartment building. One family is busy arguing at breakfast, someone is practicing piano in another flat, parents comfort a crying baby in another, all busily unaware of their fate – the "antithesis of abstract" Corwin wrote, noting the mundane realism (1942a: 81). The air raid happens from the perspective of the bomber crew, and the civilians die below in the distant thuds of explosions. The bomber goes on to incinerate a warehouse full of workers and bomb a group of refugees, after which the crew discuss lunch plans. Corwin alludes to Vittorio Mussolini's infamous lines in the dialogue. As the refugees explode, the pilot exclaims: "Gee, that's fascinating! What a spread! Looks just like a budding rose, unfolding!" (1939a: 37) Then the gunner shoots down the scattered survivors. After the air raid the bomber is shot down by an enemy aircraft.

The piano music, an excerpt from Chopin's (1810–1849) Étude Op. 10, No. 3, is the only music cue in *They Fly*. After listening in on a family's breakfast conversation, the Narrator transitions the scene to the next apartment. In the 5 to 10 second pauses between stanzas the piano volume swells to fill the spaces:

> As the quarrel at the breakfast table fades out, we hear piano music fading in. It is the Chopin Etude in E major. Some moments elapse before the Narrator speaks:
>
> NARRATOR
> (Over music)
> Are these your drums and trumpets, enemy?
> Is this your war song, coming from a baby grand?
> Is this your reveille, your charge, your anthem?
>
> What kind of soldier trains
> By practicing an etude in the morning?
>
> Play on:
> The movement ends before it's meant to end.
> A great fortissimo
> Will twist your hands
> Inextricably in the strings. (1939a: 26f.)

The final sentence, which begins "A great fortissimo", ends before the first beat of bar 17, which Chopin marked fortissimo. This is a significant musical moment in the étude, a melodic high point and a break in the established accompanimental pattern, a freezing of tension, which is followed by a descending melodic relaxation. During this descent, the scene crossfades into the crying baby of the next scene. Corwin could not afford to commission unique music for this scene, yet he still wanted integration between the words and music. His solution was to choreograph his poetry and Chopin's music, lining up key moments in both and directing the voice actors and live musician himself.

Corwin had years of experience combining solo piano music with poetry on the radio. This was the basis of his first radio series, *Rhymes and Cadences* (1934–1935), which alternated between poems and solo piano pieces of complimentary moods. Two episodes of his next series, *Poetic License*, included Corwin's original piano compositions played after the poems that inspired them. The music cue in *They Fly* was initially a Beethoven sonata, but during a late rehearsal he changed it to the Chopin étude (cf. 1939b: 11). Perhaps he had trouble lining up the Beethoven sonata with his text, but there is evidence that he preferred the placid reputation of Chopin in this context over the bold tropes of Beethoven.

Corwin was initially critical of music as a method for political protest. In August 1937, during a programme of poetry on the subject of war, he wrote that "music is generally so abstract that it can't be bothered", yet he championed the power of poetry as protest (2). By the time he came to write *They Fly*, this characterisation had not changed much, since the baby grand piano dies as easily as the crying baby. The Chopin étude offers no symbolic defence, but Corwin's portrayal of music in his radio plays changed swiftly as worldwide tensions grew. By April 1939, a month after the broadcast of *They Fly*, in *Seems Radio is Here to Stay* (1939), Beethoven's ghost is summoned to hear how popular he is on the radio. "How restful is your rest there in Vienna anyway?", Corwin asks, referring to the war, sure that Beethoven "must be out assembling harmonies somewhere", fighting in his own way (1942a: 221f.). Later in the radio play, musical composition is set on a par with the free press as means of protest:

> Narrator: (*with rising inflection to ride over the timpani*).
> The air we listen to must be as free as that we breathe
> Or there will arise such dissonance and such cacophony
> As will stave in the eardrum!
>
> Damn the very thought!
>
> *There'll be no muffing of the ear, no licking of the boot*
> *In this America!*
>
> (*Defiantly.*) Come now, you men who make our music!
> Beat *that* out in harmonies for all to hear!
>
> *Music. Timpani alone up to great peak; then orchestra*
> *Concludes with spirited, defiant passage.* (Ibid.: 237)

In September 1939, in an episode of Corwin's *So This is Radio* series, the orchestra becomes a battalion: "I've no more right to ask to conduct this orchestra than I would have to ask a general if I could lead his army through a battle." (1939c)

In the *This is War* series from 1942, the Chopin étude returns, this time in Nazi-occupied Poland:

MUSIC: Piano ... fade in tuneful melodic Chopin etude and hold for about ten seconds ... suddenly ... Smash down on keyboard with both forearms.
GIRL: I was playing Chopin until you slapped your filthy hands on the keyboard. (1942b: 203)

The young woman is then sent to a brothel for German soldiers, followed by a "distorted variation of the Chopin theme" (ibid.). This time the musician protests but still is as defenceless as the pianist in *They Fly*. The solo pianist, the piano and the Chopin étude – feminine, vulnerable and alone – are propagandistically valuable to the fight, not in their strength but in their ability to incite anger at their violation or distortion as victims. In contrast, Beethoven and the orchestra are symbols of masculine strength, victors and active fighters. What started as a revision to a music cue in *They Fly* became a musical exposition heard by millions over several radio plays, an exploration of musical icons as weaponised radiophonic symbols.

This kind of analysis, which focuses on overt music, is an obvious place to begin a discussion of music in *They Fly*. However, it has an effect that I would like to highlight. As it isolates the music in a radio play for analysis, it reinforces the separations between the "old radio art trinity" of music, words and sound effects (Glandien 2000: 170). Scripts need these divisions to communicate authors' intentions to directors, producers and performers. The result is that each line of a script – each instance of any sound – must be clearly sorted into one of these three categories. Yet this categorisation does not necessarily dictate how a radio play is heard. Music may be heard where there is no music cue, and radio playwrights often approach the choice and organisation of sounds in ways that verge on and cross over into musical composition. Types of analysis that also explore a radio play's sound organisation and visceral experience are equally vital to the musicological purview. *They Fly*'s solitary music cue lasts less than a minute and a half. An exploration of its poetic and musical timing and its symbolic weaponisation enriches our understanding of this radio play, but the bulk of its musicality is still to be explored.

2 Musicality

The second approach I use in this chapter, called 'musicality', analyses a radio play as if any of its sounds can be heard as musical. In *Music and Discourse* (1990), Jean-Jacques Nattiez directly addresses this move from music to musicality. He writes, "the transition from the noun 'music' to the adjective 'musical' seems to me both fundamental and telling: that transition allows us to escape a totality wrongly conceived as unique, and to recognize the 'musical' aspects of a whole range of sound phenomena" (60). In radio play analysis one totality that the musicologist must escape is the certainty that music exists only after cues marked 'music'.

Euphony, in a broad sense, is synonymous to what I mean by musicality. This term, which refers to the pleasing sound of words and voices, implies a divorce of a sound from its meaning and a focus on aural aesthetics, and can be broadened to encompass all sounds. Euphony focuses on traditional musical concepts, like pitch, rhythm, motif, timbre, and dynamics, in nontraditionally musical sounds, like admiring the sound of a language one does not understand or being enthralled by the noises of a waterfall – or indeed the dynamic sound of an airplane engine. Euphonic listening also meshes with the concept of reduced listening. The electroacoustic composer and radio artist Pierre Schaeffer (1910–1995) advocated and coined the term 'reduced listening' ('écoute réduite') to describe listening which focuses on the qualities of sounds and divorces them from their meanings and sources (see 1966).

It helps to treat radio plays as a type of electroacoustic music, a style of music where any sound is potential musical material and where traditional "lattices" of harmony, metred rhythm and pitch become optional (Wishart 1996: 23). Electroacoustic music has a close historical relationship with radio drama. The first national centres of electroacoustic music were most often founded in the sound departments of radio stations with equipment made for sound effects turned to musical composition. There is an aesthetic relationship as well, since both are aural media dependent on electroacoustic technology, and both have a potentially universal sound palette. These reasons make electroacoustic scholarship a potential boon to radio play scholarship.

By treating radio plays as electroacoustic music we can take advantage of the established theories in a field which has wrestled with musical materials beyond the sounds made by traditional musical instruments and singing voices. Electroacoustic music ranges from purely synthesised soundscapes, wholly alien to many listeners, to field recordings of urban or natural settings, and narrative works indistinguishable from radio plays. Some electroacoustic music scholarship is intended to help mysterious sound atmospheres become graspable to the listener, to give language to novel abstractness, and can give listeners what Leigh Landy calls "something to hold on to" in often enigmatic seas of sound (2007: 52). Dennis Smalley's essay "Spectromorphology: Explaining Sound Shapes" is an attempt to establish some vocabulary for electroacoustic music, but he makes the caveat that spectromorphology is "more concerned to account for sounds whose sources and causes are relatively mysterious or ambiguous rather than blatantly obvious" (1997: 109). However, methods like Smalley's can help us grapple with the sound design of a radio play apart from semantic narrative. We need to be able to discuss the euphonic experience of words and sounds not intended for music per se, to describe the visceral aural experience that happens in tandem with semantic understanding.

Corwin's radio play *They Fly* is a good example of the blatantly obvious category. Its sound sources, i.e., voices, airplane engines, explosions, etc., are causally and semantically straightforward. Yet he consciously composed his radio plays with broad musicality in mind, once saying at a talk: "I was at some pains not to tax the patience of the listener with too much of the same color, not to be monotonous. I made more, I think, of the mosaic structure for that reason. I was careful not to bog down." (2006)

Corwin's phrase "mosaic structure" refers to building a radio play with acoustically eclectic dramatic vignettes connected with narration that is often paired with background music. Narration inherently creates different dynamics, timbres and tempos than dramatic scenes. These differences have been expertly explained in electroacoustic music scholarship. Smalley writes about the general classifications of gesture and texture:

> Musical gesture, derived from our experience of physical gesture, is concerned with the tendency for sound shapes to move towards or away from goals in the musical structure; it is concerned with growth, temporal evolution, sense of forward direction, the impact of events, dramatic surface. Texture, however, is more about interior activity, the patterns inside sounds, about encouraging the ear to contemplate inner details; it is often more about standing still and observing the behaviors of sounds rather than pressing onwards through time. Gesture can be textured, and textures can be formed from gestures – the interplay and balance between them lie at the heart of our experiences in musical time. (1992: 14)

They Fly's narration is marked by constancy, repetition and returning, while its scenes are marked by variation, novelty and forward motion. The interplay of these different zones is a definitive characteristic of *They Fly*'s sound organisation, and Smalley's concepts of texture and gesture are useful tools to describe this dynamic.

The Narrator's unaccompanied voice opens, fills a central interlude, and ends *They Fly*. These one-voice sonic environments allow for a relaxed awareness of Jameson's vocal intricacies at structurally important moments. The sound quality of Jameson's narration, its alliteration, selective iambic pentameter and minute changes of tempo and dynamics, mesh nicely with Smalley's concept of texture. The instrumentation of the narration is relatively static, a single voice at times heard over scenes fading in and out, over the humming of engines, or briefly over piano music. The voice has a limited pitch range. It does not sustain long enough to approach singing, which keeps the words granular, the open vowel sounds broken continually with consonants, pauses and breaths. Only in the climactic finale is this stylistic consistency interrupted, when the Narrator shouts to be heard over the rising volume of the engine.

Repetition is a prominent euphonic element of the narration – repetition of the same voice, repetition of words, phrases and pauses or repetitions of questions, with their final upward inflections. Listen to the following block of narration soon after the "steady drone" of the engine first joins Jameson's voice (Corwin 1939a: 20). 'And' is repeated seven times, always preceded by a pause. Scattered alliteration as well as 'm' and 'b' opening sounds – another form of repetition – are clear compositional elements:

> And all those mornings that we spoke about,
> And mists and clouds and lightnings,
> And moons enough to burst the oceans bubble-like,
> And galaxies slow wheeling in the boundless skies
> And meteors, auroras, rainbows, nimbuses ....
> All these the earth has seen, but never, until now
> A bombing plane. (Ibid.: 21)

This segment is followed by a volley of phrases ending in upward inflections:

> How looks the morning to you, gentlemen?
> You there, gunner in the turning tip-up seat,
> Were you admiring the sunlight on that river to the north?
> And you, with earphones on, what thoughts think you between them?
> Of life? Of death? Of poker hands?
> Of breasts? Of thighs? Of furbelows?
> Spaghetti? Of your leader? Of the enemy? (ibid.: 21f.)

Now contrast this with the dramatic scene that follows the above examples with its rapid interruptions, varied sound sources and overlapping sounds:

> We hear table sounds of crockery and cutlery, with conversation, fading in. The first clearly audible voice is that of the father:

Father: Just the same, you had no business telling him he could take the car.
Mother: Oh, he's old enough to be treated like an adult. For heaven's sake, think of the time when you –
Daughter: That's right, Dad. Jack's –
Father: Nobody asked your opinion, Elly. Pass the toast, please. (Ibid.: 24f.)

They Fly's dramatic scenes align with Smalley's notion of gesture. Changing timbres and rhythms and abrupt dynamic extremes create a forward momentum, what Landy calls "narrative discourse" in electroacoustic music (2007: 74). "'Narrative' here is by no means to be taken literally", he explains; "instead, it concerns the notion of a piece's taking the listener on a sort of voyage, one in which exact repetition of longer segments is rare" (ibid.). Repetition forces one to move backwards in time, to remember a former sound, rhythm or inflection and connect that with a present one for effect. *They Fly*'s gestural scenes utilise non-repetitive eclectic variety for effect, which encourages forward movement or forward listening.

The following is a loose synopsis of *They Fly*'s sound organisation inspired by reduced listening. Notice how each scene adds new sounds, perspectives, rhythms or timbres. The cockpit scenes are immersed in engine noises, yet each adds a new element, like explosions, gunfire or dramatic changes in vocal patter. All the while the narration stays subdued until the unhinged climax.

They Fly begins with the Narrator's unaccompanied voice in a calm, slow tempo for some time. The first dramatic scene is the crew of Bomber No. 6 preparing for flight and the levelling out of the engines after takeoff. The preflight banter shifts from the established slow vocal rhythm of the Narrator to the short syncopated phrases of the distinct voices of the Pilot, Gunner, Radioman and Mechanic. The first non-vocal sound is a slamming door, heard when the crew boards the plane. With this cue, Corwin begins to introduce more extra-linguistic elements. First, there is a spatial dimension as the Mechanic asks from a distance: "Switch off? Gas on?" As the motor starts we hear raised voices from close and far as the crew yells their preflight checklist (Corwin 1939a: 19). As the first scene ends, the motor's sound becomes a drone and a dominant steady stream of sound which Jameson's voice joins for a second length of narration.

The next dramatic scene is a montage of three contrasting domestic atmospheres, each fading in and out, overlapped by the Narrator's voice. The first has breakfast table sounds, the second piano music, and a baby crying marks the third. The first and last sections include the only female voices in the radio play. The delicate clinking of utensils and dishes, the slow, low arpeggios and harmonised melody of the Chopin étude, and the voices of the mother and father comforting their baby form a calm, slow-paced trio. The baby's wailing draws us out of the calm, the cry crossfading into engine sound.

The final three scenes have the voices of the Pilot, Gunner, Radioman and Headquarter Voice "as heard through earphones", interspersed with explosions and gunfire (ibid.: 33). The first segment features two bomb releases. An explosion follows the clank of the first salvo; the second salvo is followed by a different muffled explosion. The scene after this has a single bomb explosion with bursts of sustained gunfire.

Calm crew voices surround the explosions and gunshots. The explosions are the loudest notes so far in the radio play, emphasised through contrast with the relaxed volume and tempo of the voices. The last scene, an air battle between Bomber No. 6 and an attacking plane, is preceded by the longest Narrator speech, a portion of which is given in silence, without engine noise. The battle scene's bursts of loud, fast voices approach the tone of the machine gun fire. Random, short bursts issue from two separate guns at different distances, which cease with the grunts of pain from the Pilot as he is shot. Narration and scene crescendo together as Jameson's shouting fights to be heard over the engine's rising pitch and volume. After three seconds of solo engine noise there is a rumbling crash that suddenly cuts to silence, followed by a calm, slow tempo in the voice of the Narrator, unaccompanied – the same atmosphere that opened the radio play.

Analysing with reduced listening techniques can help us approach a radio play from a fresh angle. Here it gives the distance from *They Fly*'s imposing and figuratively loud plot to hear aspects of the sound organisation beneath that might go unnoticed. The dramatic scenes form a narrative of acoustic variety heard over the length of the radio play, while the narration embraces a more limited sonic range and instrumentation, building cohesion from diverse types of repetition within those limits.

This dichotomy is echoed in the way Corwin explained his sound organisation process. *They Fly* was an original radio poem in a radio series of experimental poem adaptations. Referring to himself in the third person in the introduction to the first episode of this series, he described his procedure of setting a poem for radio, which included adding sound effects, multiple reading voices, short dramatic scenes or choral recitation, as expressly musical:

> Columbia offers a different treatment of the very old art of Song – *Words Without Music*. This experimental program is based on the theory that words, when arranged in the right way, are music in themselves; and to

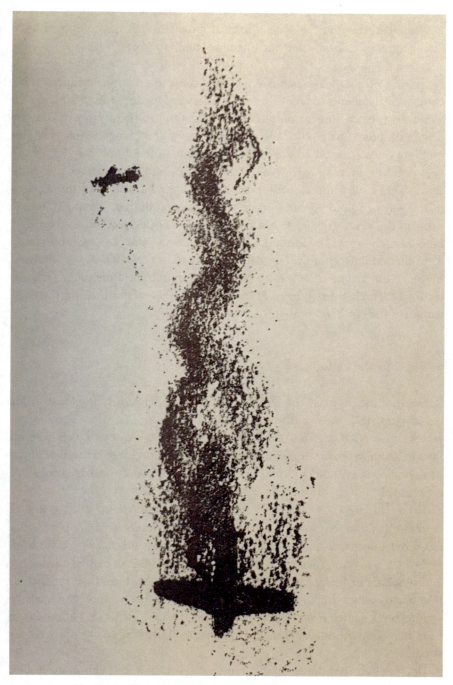

FIGURE 8.1   The Crash of Bomber No. 6 by Laszlo Matulay (Corwin 1939a: 55)

> support this theory Norman Corwin has taken a number of poems and applied them to the special uses of radio through the combined techniques of orchestration and augmentation. (1938b: 1)

He started with a spoken poem as a textual sonic foundation and then added contrasting elements to break up a straightforward reading and to explore new sonic territory, creating a compositional dichotomy of texture/poem and gesture/extra-poetic material. *They Fly*'s form is simply a longer version of this method. Corwin noted an approximate analogy in the graphic design of the 1939 publication of *They Fly*. He called the black and white charcoal illustrations "sound-substitutes", writing that "what may be lost from these pages in the way of sound effects is more than regained through Laszlo Matulay's brilliant drawings" (1939a: 9). His comparison is not perfect, but he reveals a familiar dichotomy. The implication is that spoken words can be represented as printed text acceptably. The visual texture on the printed page somewhat mimics aural textures that spoken words make, but "translating sound [effects] into sight" (ibid.: 10) requires a dramatic break, a visual gesture, like the illustration of the crash of Bomber No. 6 (see Figure 8.1).

3   Musicalisation

'Musicalisation', as I use the term in this chapter, is when sounds and words become music or musical through semantic processes. I explore two ways in which this can happen in a radio play. The first way is via verbal directions on how to listen to or how to identify a sound. The second way is through juxtapositions of words and music that imply that the two are working together expressively.

The word musicalisation has a history in radio and sound studies. Rudolf Arnheim (1904–2007) used the term to describe sounds in radio drama that cross the lines between realistic sound effects and musical expression (cf. 1936: 43). In a similar way, Landy writes about the axis of reduced listening and semantic or "heightened" listening (2007: 173). He states that "emancipation occurs when the known and the unknown are both appreciated, where synthesis takes over from thesis and antithesis" (ibid.). This axis of modes of listening is where musicalisation happens, as meanings create contexts for sounds.

Douglas Kahn continues this focus on modes of listening in his essay "Sound Art, Art, Music", in which he discusses the musicalisation of sound at length in the context of twentieth-century avant-garde art:

> In reality, sounds are never far enough above or below society to escape poetics, bodies, materials, technologies, discursive and institutional contexts or the beck-and-call of phenomenology's "auditory imagination". All that needs to happen is to admit that consciousness plays a part of auditory perception. Even if one wished to maintain a strict division between a type of musical listening that imagines to hear only sonic and phonic content and other types of listening that hear a range of other contents riding the vibrations of sound, then all that needs to happen is to admit the possibility of different modes of listening existing simultaneously or oscillating quickly. (2014: 345)

Sounds beat against ear drums, but musicalisation happens in the imagination. Arguably, it can happen without an actual sound present. Silence or the memory of a sound can be fused with the experience of musical meaning through verbal directions or contextual juxtaposition. Therefore, musicalisation of sound is musicalisation of the imagination.

For example, consider the Narrator's soliloquy on silence. This interlude, although in a central location, is the part of *They Fly* that was written last, a reflection on the work as a whole. To think more clearly the Narrator leaves the engines, saying "let us withdraw to some precinct of peace to meditate" (Corwin 1939a: 42).[1] In a new atmosphere of voice and silence, where all action and all noise has stopped, the Narrator tries to write an ode to the wartime murder of civilians. After failing he admits:

> Our language beats against its limitations [...]
> Our rhythms jangle at the very start [...]
> Our similes concede defeat [...]
> We cannot undertake this ode. (Ibid.: 43f.)

He then returns to the action, and the interlude ceases as he follows Bomber No. 6 to its destruction.

The Narrator begins the soliloquy by saying that he needs to get away from the motor noise to think, explaining, "the music of the motors is monotonous; our meter will be influenced" (ibid.: 42). In the August 1938 letter proposing "Out of a Clear Sky", Corwin directly linked music to the airplane engine noise:

---

1 Corwin wrote parts of *They Fly* during meditative walks in Riverside Park in New York City, trading his noisy typewriter for a pad and pencil. Once, in the night's relative quiet, he saw "the battle fleet display searchlights in the river" (1939e, 12 February 1939). He seems to summon these contemplative moments in this soliloquy.

In one apartment, a man and wife lie in bed, talking low of plans for the future. In another a party is going on; in a third, two newspapermen discuss everything but their assignment in the city; in a fourth, a student of music is trying to compose, and we hear fragments of melody within his head. Suddenly out of the pattern of music, but on the same pitch there is a flashback to the ominous drone of the bomber in flight – nothing but the long, sustained note of the motor boring through the night. (1938a: 1)

From an early point in the history of *They Fly*, Corwin planned to play with sound as music. The final radio play did not involve the musical note to airplane engine metamorphosis of "Out of a Clear Sky", but this soliloquy visits the idea from a different angle. Corwin describes the engine sound, brings attention to it and encourages the listener to identify it as music. We, as listeners, are perhaps more aware of the rattle of motor, which flares up for a moment, then fades away. This attention is important because Corwin wishes to construct silence. He tells us to listen musically, then takes away the sound. The sound cue reads: "The motors fade. Silence." (1939a: 42) After an abnormally long pause we hear "yes, this is better", followed by another pause; then, "it is silent here" followed by silence again (Corwin 1939d). Jameson draws in closer to the microphone, and his voice becomes clear and louder even though he is speaking more quietly. He then takes the silence into the imagination. "The cogwheels of the brain turn quietly", the Narrator says, suggesting a paradox: that we imagine not hearing a fantastical silence (cf. 1939a: 43). He then phonates "Mmm" – an audible breakdown of speech – noting that language is somehow inadequate in this new atmosphere of voice and silence, and he decides to return "to things we are sure about – to the familiarity of Bomber No. 6" (ibid.: 45). He returns to the motor noise and, with that underpinning of sound, his words flow unhindered for thirty lines.

"It's a sense or feeling that you have clothed something that is naked", Corwin would later say about writing music into his radio plays (qtd. in Cummings 2007). The slowly rising and falling pitch and timbral texture of the engine noise buoys Jameson's words and the spaces between his words. This is Corwin's aeromusic, military music built of military sound, and, in its simplicity, it has the unobtrusiveness necessary for sustained background music.[2] In this

---

2   Until *They Fly*, Corwin had resisted using background music, arguing that "I didn't want anything to distract from the music or from the text, and I thought the listener has work enough cut out to appreciate the words and music separately." (qtd. in Cummings 2008) Even in his early experiments combining piano music and poetry, *Rhymes and Cadences* and *Poetic*

interlude, Corwin takes away this supporting backdrop, points out the missing support and then emphasises the loss. This silence relies more on musical sound than anywhere else in *They Fly*, and this relationship highlights the ubiquitous phenomenon that happens when words and music work in tandem.

Layering sound and speech in a radio play pulls the listener in two directions at once. Lawrence Kramer calls the similar phenomenon in song "a volatile interplay between two attempts to be heard" (1984: 169). The music – motor sound primarily in *They Fly* – pulls the listener towards sonority and visceral experience, while the words guide the listener into semantic cognition. Many scholars have noted that these moments of cognitive interplay catalyse engaged listening. Brandon Labelle calls them "acts of charged listening" (2006: ix), John Hollander "great anatomized acts of listening" (1972: 59), and Kramer writes that they are postures "of intenser listening" (1984: 139). "It is from this blend of conflicting impressions that the sense of purification by catharsis may in certain circumstances arise", writes opera scholar Robert Donington (1990: 7). In the silence the Narrator asks, "can phrases tailored to a patch of earth be stretched to fit the sky?" (Corwin 1939a: 43) Yes, he seems to answer, with the catalyst of musical sound.

4   Conclusion

A musicological analysis of a radio play is not a straightforward endeavour. We must answer a complex question: which music? "The critical procedure", as Joseph Kerman writes about opera analysis, "involves a sharpening of musical awareness and an expansion of our range of imaginative response to drama" (1956: 7). Obviously, we must begin by addressing the overt instrumental music directly, a complex matter by itself because, as Nattiez points out, "a musical work is at once its genesis, its organization, and the way it is perceived" (1990: ix). This multilayered situation is complicated even more since radio plays can have music in them, are entirely made of sound which can be heard musically, and can directly influence the way that music and sound are heard while they are being heard. The musicological approaches of music, musicality and musicalisation begin to address this complexity, revealing that there are three types of music to analyse: the overt music, the electroacoustic entirety and

---

License, he always kept the two separate. This reluctance ended with *They Fly*, with its pervasive engine noise as background music and the brief overlapping of Chopin's étude and narration. He began his collaboration and friendship with Bernard Herrmann (1911–1975), who Corwin called the "dean of radio composers", weeks after *They Fly*'s success (ibid.).

the new music created in the imagination through semantic guidance and juxtaposition.

To end this chapter, I would like to go back to the beginning of *They Fly*, actually before the beginning and after the end. In both broadcasts we only hear the title in the announcements before and after the radio play itself. The title references the lyrics, "He'd fly thro' the air with the greatest of ease / A daring young man on the flying trapeze", of a nineteenth-century song that had a phenomenal surge of popularity in the USA during the 1930s, reflected in film, radio and literature (Leyborne 1868: 4f.). One example is William Saroyan's (1908–1981) short story "The Daring Young Man on the Flying Trapeze" (1934), a stream of consciousness piece about a struggling writer who dies of hunger alone in his flat, a victim of the Great Depression. The last paragraph begins: "then swiftly, neatly, with the grace of the young man on the trapeze, he was gone from his body" (25). As his consciousness unravels, "[t]he earth circled away, and knowing that he did so, he turned his lost face to the empty sky and became dreamless, unalive, perfect" (ibid.). Compare this death to *They Fly*'s ending. "Like a corkscrew in the sky", the warplane falls, and the sound cue reads: "there is a tremendous crash, followed by several seconds of silence" (Corwin 1939a: 54). As "a little oil and blood" quietly seep into the ground, the radio play ends:

> The sun has reached meridian.
> The day is warm.
> There's not a ripple in the air. (Ibid.: 56)

Both stories end with a spiraling to dead silence, and both stories repurpose the popular song in moods that matched the dark times they were written in. Unlike Saroyan's short story, *They Fly through the Air with the Greatest of Ease* does not reference the song's text or melody. Yet one can imagine the title summoning the tune in listeners' imaginations at the beginning and end of this radio play, as faint "vibrations in the chambers of imagination" but nonetheless a species of musical experience (Corwin 1942c: 245). This is an unintended plebeian mockery of Marinetti's grandiose aeromusic, and a direct nod perhaps to Vittorio Mussolini, to whom the radio play was dedicated, in hopes that the daring young man would fall to his death.

References

Arnheim, Rudolf (1936). *Radio*. Margaret Ludwig, Herbert Read, transl. London: Faber & Faber.

Chion, Michel (1990). *Audio Vision: Sound on Screen.* Claudia Gorbman, transl. New York, NY: Columbia Univ. Press.

Corwin, Norman (1937). "Poetic License 23 August 1937". TMS, American Radio Archives, Norman Corwin Collection, Thousand Oaks Public Library, Thousand Oaks, CA.

Corwin, Norman (1938a). CBS office communication to Max Wylie, COR 01056, American Radio Archives, Norman Corwin Collection, Thousand Oaks Public Library, Thousand Oaks, CA. 2 August.

Corwin, Norman (1938b). "Words Without Music 4 December 1938". TMS, American Radio Archives, Norman Corwin Collection, Thousand Oaks Public Library, Thousand Oaks, CA.

Corwin, Norman (1939a). *They Fly through the Air with the Greatest of Ease.* Weston, VT: Vrest Orton.

Corwin, Norman (1939b). "They Fly through the Air with the Greatest of Ease, late draft without station introduced". TMS, American Radio Archives, Norman Corwin Collection, Thousand Oaks Public Library, Thousand Oaks, CA.

Corwin, Norman (1939c). *So This is Radio*, Haendiges 89749A, 7 September 1939, cassette.

Corwin, Norman (1939d). Words Without Music No. 11 They Fly through the Air with the Greatest of Ease, 19 February 1939, Kansas City, MO: Marr Sound Archives, 46,427 Goldin, vinyl record.

Corwin, Norman (1939e). Bound hand-written diary. American Radio Archives, Norman Corwin Collection, Thousand Oaks Public Library, Thousand Oaks, CA.

Corwin, Norman (1942a). *Thirteen by Corwin.* New York, NY: Henry Holt and Company.

Corwin, Norman (1942b). *This is War: A Collection of Radio Plays about America on the March.* New York, NY: Dodd, Mead, and Co.

Corwin, Norman (1942c). *More by Corwin.* New York, NY: Henry Holt and Company.

Corwin, Norman (2006 online). "Encore Screening: A Note of Triumph: The Golden Age of Norman Corwin". Pre-screening talk, Univ. of Southern California Annenberg School for Communication. https://www.youtube.com/watch?v=Imb22SJcnDY [11/06/2021].

Cummings, Troy (2007). Interview with Norman Corwin. Los Angeles, 12 November. Unpublished.

Cummings, Troy (2008). Interview with Corwin, Norman. Los Angeles, 18 June. Unpublished.

Donington, Robert (1990). *Opera and Its Symbols: The Unity of Words, Music, and Staging.* New Haven, CT: Yale Univ. Press.

Giuntini, Aldo, F.T. Marinetti (1934). "Manifesto della aeromusica: sintetica, geometrica e curativa". *Stile futurista* 2: 14.

Glandien, Kersten (2000). "Art on Air: A Profile of New Radio Art". Simon Emmerson, ed. *Music, Electronic Media, and Culture.* Aldershot: Ashgate. 167–193.

Hollander, John (1972). "Wordsworth and the Music of Sound". Geoffrey Hartman, ed. *New Perspectives on Coleridge and Wordsworth*. New York, NY: Columbia Univ. Press. 41–84.

Kahn, Douglas (2014). "Sound Art, Art, Music". *Tacet 3*: 328–347.

Kerman, Joseph (1956). *Opera as Drama*. New York, NY: Knopf.

Kramer, Lawrence (1984). *Music and Poetry: The Nineteenth Century and After*. Berkeley, CA: Univ. of California Press.

Labelle, Brandon (2006). *Background Noise: Perspectives on Sound Art*. New York: Continuum International.

Landy, Leigh (2007). *Understanding the Art of Sound Organization*. London and Cambridge, MA: MIT Press.

Leyborne, George (1868). *The Flying Trapeze*. Boston: C.H. Ditson and Co. Sheet music.

MacLeish, Archibald (1938). *Air Raid: A Verse Play for Radio*. New York, NY: Harcourt, Brace and Co.

Marinetti, Filippo Tommaso (1936). Filippo Tommaso Marinetti Libroni on Futurism. GEN MSS 475. Box 101, slide 79. Beinecke Rare Book and Manuscript Library, Yale University.

"Mussolini's Son Scouts War Talk" (1937). *New York Times*, 9 October: 3.

"Mussolini's Son 'Spirited' Ashore Here, Closely Guarded Against Demonstrations" (1937). *New York Times*, 24 September: 6.

Nattiez, Jean-Jacques (1990). *Music and Discourse: Toward a Semiology of Music*. Carolyn Abbate, transl. Princeton, NJ: Princeton Univ. Press.

Saroyan, William (1934). *The Daring Young Man on the Flying Trapeze and Other Stories*. New York, NY: Random House.

Schaeffer, Pierre (1966). *Traité des objets musicaux*. Paris: Éditions du Seuil.

Slonimsky, Nicolas, Richard Kostelanetz, Joseph Darby (1994). *Nicolas Slonimsky: The First Hundred Years*. New York, NY: Schirmer.

Smalley, Denis (1992). Compact disc liner notes to *Impacts interieurs* by Dennis Smalley. Montreal: Diffusion I Media.

Smalley, Dennis (1997). "Spectromorphology: Explaining Sound Shapes". *Organised Sound* 2/2: 107–126.

"Vittorio's Beauties of War" (1937). *Daily News*, 27 November: 15.

Wishart, Trevor (1996). *On Sonic Art*. Amsterdam: Harwood Academic Publishers.

CHAPTER 9

Themes, Backgrounds, Bridges and Curtains: A New Musical Language for American Radio Dramas, 1930–1950

Peter Graff

Abstract

Music in radio dramas served four primary functions: what industry insiders referred to as themes, backgrounds, bridges and curtains. Each category inherited its form and function from earlier film and theatre traditions, yet the liveness of radio and its competing sonic elements necessitated that composers create a distinct musical language for the new medium. Utilising dozens of radio music anthologies and broadcasting manuals from the 1930s and 1940s, this chapter demonstrates how composers overcame the unique challenges posed by radio and ultimately grants a window into the ephemeral soundscape of early American radio dramas.

The American radio drama emerged in the 1920s under the shadow of its more mature sibling, silent film. Both mediums utilised music to compensate for a perceived lack – sonic in one and visual in the other.[1] Without an extant body of musical repertory for radio, early radio practitioners turned to film, inheriting not only its collections of incidental photoplay music but also its conventions and musical vocabulary. Borrowing from silent film was a logical solution for the nascent artform, principally because both had similar dramatic needs that music could efficiently carry out. These included establishing setting, conveying mood, commenting on dramatic action, and lending continuity across and between scenes.[2] Yet despite the similar functions of music in film and radio

---

1 On these sensory deficiencies, film critic Béla Balázs in 1924 called film the "art of the deaf" and radio drama the "art for the blind" (ca. 1924/2006: 48).
2 Claudia Gorbman outlines these functions in her foundational text on film music, *Unheard Melodies*. While Gorbman describes music's role in sound films, her principles equally apply to silent films and radio dramas, including signifying emotion, cueing narrative action, lending continuity between shots, and creating unity across the narrative (1987: 73–91). Radio treatises outline similar functions of music in radio dramas. David Mackey, for example,

drama, there are key differences that rendered film music unsuitable for the airwaves. In his 1944 essay recounting the early days of radio, music director for the Columbia Broadcasting System (CBS) Julius Mattfeld noted the industry's initial reliance on film music – a result of music directors and music libraries migrating from picture palaces to radio studios – but ultimately pointed to its inherent shortcomings: "The radio, operating on the basis of minutes and seconds, required briefer and more punctuated musical underscoring." (2)[3] In addition to the issue of timing, the primacy of spoken dialogue in radio dramas conflicted with the older musical repertory, which was designed to meet the demands of continuous musical accompaniment. Composers were thus tasked with creating a distinct musical language for this new medium. How did they rise to meet the new challenges set forth by radio? What aspects of silent film music informed the compositional language of the radio drama? And how did this new repertory operate within the live broadcast? These are the fundamental questions that I take up in this study.

In the past two decades, the radio drama has gained significant scholarly attention, with primary focus given to its literary merits and its role in shaping cultural politics (see Hand 2006; Huwiler 2005; Porter 2016; Verma 2012; Wedel 2011). The use of music in radio dramas, despite being an inseparable component from nearly the start, has evaded considerable study, with most scholars attending to original scores written by well-known composers like Bernard Herrmann and Kurt Weill (see Daniels 2017; Kosovsky 2000; Wissner 2013). Although major networks employed house composers to write for radio dramas, especially their prestige one-off broadcasts and some nationally-syndicated serials, they relied more so on in-house libraries of pre-composed music to more economically score their weekly productions.[4] On this point, American playwright and radio director Arch Oboler writes that, due to the costs associated with composing and arranging music, "radio plays with a complete, original music score are rare birds in the broadcast roost" (1940: xxiv). BBC radio producer Felix Felton similarly describes special scores as "economically impossible" given the rapid turnover rate of a new episode each week, which rarely received more than one broadcast (1949: 111). Thus, studies of

---

notes nine overlapping functions (cf. 1951: 36–38), Morris Mamorsky outlines four (cf. 1946: 50f.), and Max Wylie includes seven (cf. 1939: 357).

3 Mattfeld's contemporaries make similar claims, such as Albert Crews, who writes that early radio music cues "came out of the libraries of the old pit piano players who accompanied the silent films" (1944: 150).

4 As Mamorsky observes, there were at most fifty composers making a living solely through the industry in the 1940s, with the majority of radio composers working freelance in other arenas, including publishing anthologies of incidental music (1946: 48).

special scores or individual programmes tell only a partial story of how music lived in the world of the radio drama.

This study, by contrast, is grounded in close analysis of the anthologies of stock music that composers began generating in the 1930s and 1940s specifically for use in radio dramas. These anthologies became essential scoring aids that saved not only money, but considerable time – a primary concern in the broadcasting industry. According to former National Broadcasting Company (NBC) staff composer Morris Mamorsky, music directors typically had only three days in which to score a single show (1946: 48).[5] With a well-stocked library of radio-appropriate compositions, they could efficiently keep on top of such demanding schedules. Although these radio compositions functioned like photoplay music, they look and sound quite different. Relying on dozens of production treatises and music anthologies, I contend that these differences were a result of two constraints of the medium: the first concerns the liveness of radio broadcasts, in which timing was a significant limiting factor; the second, and perhaps more crucial, is that all narrative information in radio drama is communicated through sonic means, so that dialogue and sound effects compete with music for listener attention. In this essay, I demonstrate how American composers navigated these challenges through an analysis of the musical language preserved in radio music anthologies published in the United States. By considering these indispensable yet largely ignored resources, we gain a more complete understanding of the compositional practices and soundscape of the ephemeral radio drama.

1   Building a Musical Repertory for Radio

In the first decade of radio, studio music directors relied upon the so-called photoplay collections published for use in silent film. Oboler explains that this reliance was as much a practical matter as it was a convenient one: "when silent pictures went out of business, these great accumulative masses of movie

---

5   In her 1945 article on music in radio dramas, Rose Heylbut describes the typical scoring process: "When a script is assigned for production, the composer, the author, and the producer discuss how much music is to be used, what kind of music, and the exact spots where it is to go. Then the composer times the specified passages with a stop-watch and writes suitable cues or bridges of desired length. [...] After composer, author and producer have ironed out preliminary adjustments, the music goes to the copyist, and at last to the conductor. [...] Then joint rehearsals begin, the producer taking the dramatic actors through their lines, and the composer sitting by, stop-watch in hand, to time (and if necessary adjust) the coinciding of his cues with the dramatic entrances." (493f.)

cues moved over onto the racks of the radio stations to once again plague our collective ears" (1940: xiii).[6] Within roughly a decade, radio studios began to abandon silent film music libraries in favour of new compositions that were more responsive to the medium and more up to date with contemporary musical trends. Perhaps unsurprisingly, some of the earliest radio music collections were penned by former silent film composers and accompanists, such as Leo A. Kempinski and organist Jesse Crawford (see Kempinski 1938; Crawford 1940). Along with music and composers, radio also inherited the sound effects – along with their operators – from vaudeville and movie houses, where inventive techniques were developed to fill the large theatres; yet these practices similarly required adjustments due to the physical space of radio studios and the limits of recording technology. As former soundman Robert Turnbull writes, "a can of buckshot to simulate rain sounded like a hundred Niagaras when held close to the sensitive mike" (1951: 183). Thus, although the sonic traditions of silent film informed the early years of the radio drama, they required significant alterations for the airwaves. The adjustments composers made for radio dramas are evident across the many pages of extant radio music anthologies.

In my research, I surveyed twenty-six radio music collections published in the United States between 1938 and 1946, comprising over one thousand individual compositions.[7] Most collections are scored for piano or organ, but were intended to be orchestrated to fit the in-house studio ensemble. Adaptability was a major selling point of these books. The prefaces to Roy Shield's anthologies, for example, explain that users should feel free to modify not only instrumentation, but also dynamics, register and tempo (cf. 1946a; 1946b). Edward Truman's collection further explains how music directors can achieve different effects through the subtle change of a single cue: "a bar played full and $f\!f$ will present an exactly opposite mood when dolce with strings and an mp solo" (1943: 2). Although the four major American networks – CBS, NBC, the American Broadcasting Company (ABC) and the Mutual Broadcasting System (MBS) – employed large orchestras of fifteen to thirty members for their music programming, such groups were generally disadvantageous for the purpose of radio drama: they overpowered the voice, the familiar orchestral timbres

---

6   Oboler's negative opinion of photoplay music was a common one, and he goes on to advise other radio playwrights to indicate specific compositions or moods in their scripts to "prevent the revival of these trite tremolos [and to] forestall the use of a music theme which is completely out of the scene mood" (1940: xiii).
7   The collections for this study can be found at the Library of Congress, where most were deposited for copyright. These twenty-six anthologies represent only a fraction of the total number created in the United States and abroad.

distracted listeners, and they were expensive to manage.[8] Instead, music directors preferred smaller combinations for radio dramas. Radio playwright Norman Corwin, for instance, recounted offering Bernard Herrmann a large orchestra to score his drama *Samson* (1941), only to have the composer turn down the offer in favour of an ensemble consisting of flute, mandolin, guitar and four harps (cf. 1944: 228).[9] The most effective ensembles for radio drama ranged from the simple piano or organ, which were most common in daytime serial programmes, to small chamber combinations like Herrmann's score for *Samson* (cf. Crews 1944: 427).

Radio music anthologies typically grouped works based on the function they carried out in the dramatic broadcast, often coalescing into four broad categories referred to as *themes, backgrounds, bridges,* and *curtains*.[10] These categories were so codified that they often appeared in the titles of the collections themselves, such as *Dramatic Varieties: Themes for Radio Dramatic Shows* (Leibert 1941), *Interludes and Curtains* (Buhrman 1942), *Bridges Moods Interludes* (Katzman and Rettenberg 1943), and *Organ Backgrounds* (Gart 1945). Each category played a distinct role in the broadcast and each exhibited musical characteristics that were shaped by the demands of the artform.

2   Themes

In episodic serials, each programme had unique theme music that appeared at the opening of every broadcast. *Themes* (also called *opening themes, programme themes,* or *signatures*) were an exercise in branding, as their primary goal was to establish a sonic identity with a particular show. As broadcaster and educator David Mackey writes, "a strong opening theme makes for strong

---

[8]   Tom Bennett notes that the standard studio concert orchestra comprised approximately eighteen musicians: "three trumpets, two trombones, four saxophones, four rhythm, five strings (consisting of three violins, one viola, and one cello)" (1946: 82). He also claims that saxophones would often double on clarinet. Boris Kremenliev describes the average studio orchestra as between fifteen and thirty, being a "cross between a chamber orchestra and a dance band" (1949: 76f.). On the use of full orchestras, Kosovsky explains that, although Bernard Herrmann used lush Romantic scoring for his radio melodramas of the mid-1930s, he moved away from such thick scoring for his later radio work (cf. 2000: 144).

[9]   Felton echoes this sentiment in writing that "some of the most effective background music has been for a very small combination of instruments" (1949: 123).

[10] Both Kremenliev and George Davis describe these four categories (cf. Kremenliev 1949: 76; Davis 1947: 6–14). Alternatively, Crews outlines six: *themes, diegetic backgrounds, non-diegetic backgrounds, bridges, montages* and *sound effects* (cf. 1944: 424); and Mamorsky notes only *backgrounds* and *bridges* (cf. 1946: 48).

program identification" (1951: 35f.).[11] Themes were occasionally accompanied by an announcement of the show's title or a particular sponsor, which could receive their own fanfare calls. A musical lead-in and narration typically followed a theme as a way to establish the beginning of the story (cf. Davis 1947: 8). Themes oftentimes appeared again at the end of the broadcast as a 'cushion' if time permitted or if the studio needed to stretch for time.[12]

According to NBC production director Albert Crews, the use of themes began in the early days of radio when band leaders opened their broadcasts with the same short musical excerpt as a sort of programme trademark (cf. 1944: 149). This practice went on to influence all types of programming, commercials, and even stations themselves, as in the iconic three-note studio logo for NBC. Like the NBC chime, many series themes migrated to television along with the original show. When *Amos 'n' Andy* (1928–1960) transitioned from radio to television in 1951, for example, its theme, "The Perfect Song" by Joseph Carl Breil, followed suit. While not all radio series included background music or bridges, nearly all featured a theme.[13] Since themes would recur each episode, some productions invested in original compositions, while others took from the existing classical repertory – particularly works in the public domain. *Tarzan and the Diamond of Asher* (1934), for example, had a lengthy original theme written by Felix Mills. To reflect the series' exotic setting, Mills scored the theme for an equally exotic chamber ensemble that included bass flute, marimba and drums. *The Lone Ranger* (1933–1954), conversely, utilised Rossini's *William Tell Overture* to open the show for decades in radio and later on television. Because themes tended to either be original compositions or borrowed classics, they rarely appear in radio music anthologies.

Despite the compositional variety that themes represent, there are a few general characteristics they share with regard to timing and melodic content. In his 1947 treatise *Music-Cueing for Radio-Drama*, George Davis instructs that a show's theme must be short, 10 to 15 seconds, and be "outstandingly interesting

---

[11] Mackey was a speech professor at Pennsylvania State College specialising in areas of radio production and history. Sherman Paxton Lewton, professor of Radio and Visual Education at Stephens College, similarly instructs that themes should establish an association with the programme (cf. 1938: 290).

[12] 'Cushion' (also 'padding' or 'fill') is an industry term referring to the practice of padding the programme to avoid dead air. The theme song was often chosen for this purpose, but in some cases additional credits or narration would accomplish the task (Kremenliev 1949: 75; Turnbull 1951: 299). Cushioning your programme with dialogue, according to Norman Weiser, was referred to by some as 'drooling' (1942: 204, 207).

[13] Crews admits that in daytime serials, which were cheaply produced, "most music occurs in the theme" (1944: 149).

for its melody, or harmonic rhythmic effect, and it must bear a relation to the quality of the show: Romantic, Comedy, Mystery, etc." (1947: 8). Crews echoes this advice, calling for strong melodies that are hummable and recognisable (cf. 1944: 149). Regarding length, Crews indicates that the opening theme should last 20 to 25 seconds and match the overall tone of the programme. Emphasis on memorable melodies is one of the key features distinguishing themes from backgrounds, bridges and curtains.

3   Backgrounds

Background music (alternatively called *atmosphere*, *mood music* or *underscoring*) occurs beneath spoken dialogue and enhances emotion within a given scene. It can either be diegetic or non-diegetic (i.e., part of the narrative world or not), establish setting, intensify or clarify emotion, supply continuity to a scene or an entire series, and in some cases serve as a leitmotif or sound effect.[14] This category shares its purpose with other dramatic arts, most notably melodramatic theatre and film, but what marks radio as unique is that it communicates solely through sound. In radio, dialogue, dramatic action, movement and emotion are all conveyed through sonic means and require careful consideration when layering voices, music and sound effects. Of these three, the voice is the most important, with music and sound effects often mixed beneath dialogue and narration. As William Cordell and Kathryn Cordell wrote in 1936, "if the dialogue is the backbone of a stage play, it is the entire skeleton of a broadcast drama" (412). Yet words alone sometimes fail in communicating crucial information to the listener: foreshadowing dramatic events, revealing a character's sinister motives, or indicating physical actions, to name a few. A character's slurred speech may indicate drunkenness, but when coupled with the sound of a speeding car and a dissonant musical climax, the narrative becomes more complex. In most cases, however, music remains subservient. As NBC staff composer Leo Kempinski cautions, "it should never take away from the script – either for its goodness or its badness! If for any reason the music outshines the story, it isn't good background music." (qtd. in Heylbut 1945: 494)[15]

---

14 These functions are outlined by Mackey (cf. 1951: 36), Kremenliev (cf. 1949: 76) and Mamorsky, the last of whom offers a taxonomy of five types: "(1) Backgrounds based on the use of montages. (2) Backgrounds based on the use of leitmotifs. (3) Backgrounds based on the use of folk music. (4) Backgrounds based on the use of standard symphonic music. (5) Backgrounds based on the use of original symphonic music" (1946: 56).
15 Corwin similarly writes that "radio music is seldom noticed by critics save when it is shockingly bad" (1944: 92).

Music directors originally turned to the classical canon and to silent film music for their backgrounds, but beginning around 1930, according to journalist Rose Heylbut, scoring for radio shifted from a "digging-out of tunes to a valid and important medium of musical creation" (ibid.: 493). This was done for a few reasons. First, audience familiarity with musical works was potentially distracting, drawing the mind away from the programme at hand to recall previous association with such works (cf. Felton 1949: 123; Mamorsky 1946: 49). Because of this very issue, orchestrators even avoided familiar instrumental combinations in favour of smaller chamber ensembles: "[the symphonic sound] is too established. We know it too well", writes Max Wylie, concluding: "It distracts more than it enhances." (1939: 427) Additionally, classical works generally took too long to develop musical ideas. On this point, Crews writes that "in a dramatic program, the music must accomplish its purpose in a matter of seconds" (1944: 426). Heylbut also emphasises this idea by explaining that, although the Grand March from *Aida* may seem appropriate for a military scene, "five seconds of martial music might cut off *Aida* at the wrong point" (1945: 494). The industry therefore turned to less well-known compositions for its backgrounds, especially the short and flexible works contained in anthologies of incidental music.

Because music should never obscure the clarity of the voice, music directors used backgrounds less frequently than themes and bridges. Although there was debate among practitioners about the best use of backgrounds, most advocated using them sparingly, principally because they distracted the listener. James Whipple, former instructor of radio classes at the University of Chicago, claimed in 1938 that their use is "not good modern technique", but he also conceded that they had proved particularly useful in certain genres like comedy and fantasy programmes, verse dramas and allegorical plays (cf. 50).[16] A decade later, Davis similarly cautioned against overuse, but noted that backgrounds were helpful when a mood is not conveyed by the story-content alone. Such instances include "dream-sequences; enactment of the stream-of-consciousness; conversations of animals; the reading aloud of mail to oneself; a visit to Mars; montage effects" (1947: 9). Finally, Oboler warns that underscoring often punctures the believability of tense, realistic scenarios: "the moment music begins to play, a great part of the realism goes, and what comes through the loud-speaker is just voices of actors play-acting at life" (1940: xxiv).

---

16   Whipple also writes that there is "little excuse for introducing music as a background" (1938: 50). Whipple was a member of the radio division at the Lord & Thomas advertisement agency and taught radio courses at the University of Chicago.

For these reasons, few programmes employed backgrounds consistently and almost none used them continuously.[17]

To navigate the competing sonic elements of radio dramas, composers of background cues adjusted their approach to melody, harmony and rhythm. In his early writing on the industry, media theorist Rudolf Arnheim notes that radio composers in the early 1930s were indebted to the sound world of Wagner, Richard Strauss and Debussy for showing the "expressive potentialities of instruments and the subtleties of harmony" (1936: 41f.). He continues by also acknowledging the influence of jazz on radio dramas, particularly its emphasis on instrumental timbre, sound effects, and use of "expressive distortion" (ibid.). Within this sonic landscape, backgrounds generally avoided catchy melodies and energetic rhythmic figures so as to not distract from the dialogue.[18] In his 1939 treatise, Wylie castigates the overuse of melodies in film scoring (especially familiar material) and likewise advises against it in radio for fear of disrupting listener attention (cf. 357).[19] When featuring a melody, Felton suggests that orchestrators should avoid the pitch range of the voice actors to maintain clarity (cf. 1949: 123).[20] Melodies in backgrounds are often angular and unpredictable, and thus harmony takes on a greater role in conveying a general mood. The harmonic vocabulary of backgrounds leans toward late Romanticism and Expressionism by favouring chromatic elements, though never going full tilt into modernist or avant-garde territory. As industry veteran Boris Kremenliev points out, radio in the United States is a commercial industry and therefore American composers "cannot afford to bite the hands that feed" by indulging too much in modernist writing (1949: 80f.).[21] The angular and chromatic language of backgrounds, created to enhance mood while not distracting the listener, helped establish a musical vocabulary that was somewhat distinct from the related film industry.

---

17 On this point, Crews claims that the use of backgrounds in radio "lagged behind" its use in theatre and film (1944: 433).
18 Felton writes that backgrounds require "a special sort of 'underwriting'", and claims that traditional orchestral writing "may prove to be too strong for the program" (1949: 123).
19 On the distracting nature of melodies, Wylie argues that "our conscious mind is pulled away from the central purpose before us for its good taste or in terms of its disturbing us for its bad taste" (1939: 357).
20 Although radio music anthologies do not reflect this practice, music directors and orchestrators may have taken care to complement the voices in a given scene.
21 As Kremenliev writes with regard to the harmonic language used in radio dramas, "radio music leans chiefly on the idiom of the past, on imitative rather than creative writing. [...] I know only one Hollywood composer who freely indulges in atonal writing, modern techniques, and doublings usually labeled 'Oriental' by producer and sponsor alike" (1949: 80f.).

The anthologies of radio music abound with chromaticism, augmented intervals and added-tone chords. "Voice Background No. 1" from Jesse Crawford's *Radio Dramatic Series* (1940) features an unpredictable disjunct melody with constant chromatic alterations, while simultaneously connoting a generally uplifting mood through a constant upward motion and waltz-like rhythms (see Example 9.1). Muriel Pollock's "Rustic Revel" from her *Musical Moods* (1943) is marked "rollicking and gay" and achieves this effect through playful lilting figures, yet it too contains an erratic melody and a harmonic motion that sinks step by step over the span of one and a half octaves (see Example 9.2). As is common throughout these publications, radio composers aimed to achieve

EXAMPLE 9.1 Jesse Crawford, "Voice Background No. 1", from Jesse Crawford's Radio Dramatic Series (1940)

EXAMPLE 9.2 Muriel Pollock, "Rustic Revel" (mm. 9–24), from Muriel Pollock's Musical Moods Book 2 (19

a general emotional effect, but rarely did so through the reliance on traditional melodic and harmonic signifiers.

In *addition to melody and harmony, backgrounds also exhibit formal conventions that composers designed to accommodate the liveness of radio. Background compositions typically contain short melodic phrases that music directors could easily adapt to differing scene lengths.*[22] Optional repeats also appear throughout background excerpts for the performers or orchestrators to meet the needs of a dramatic moment. John Gart's "Expectation" from *Serial Moods* (1946), for example, changes melodic motion and accompanimental figuration every two or four measures, allowing orchestrators to repeat these segments as needed to fill the air time – the final two measures even include repeat signs for this purpose (see Example 9.3). Alexander Semmler (writing under the pseudonym Ralph Sandor) addresses this point in the preface to his 1941 anthology: "For background purposes, most pieces have convenient repeats, or can be repeated in their entirety" (2). This emphasis on adaptability is also a central feature of musical bridges – a category that carries out more narrative work by registering the mood of adjoining scenes.

EXAMPLE 9.3 *John Gart, "Expectation", from* Serial Moods *(1946)*

---

22   Kosovsky writes that Bernard Herrmann "eschewed traditional melodic patterns in order to be able to edit musical passages to a desired length with ease" (2000: 351).

4   Bridges

Bridges (also called *interludes*, *segues* or *transitions*) occur between scenes of a narrative programme and are essential for establishing context, as they convey changes in time or location, provide comic or emotional tags, or simply act as neutral bridges. There were a variety of methods radio producers used to transition between scenes, including music, narration, sound effects, fades in and out and silence – and of course producers employed these in various combinations.[23] Music was the most frequently used because of its ability to succinctly convey narrative information, such as a change in time, setting or mood.[24] This capacity to shift time or space in mere seconds is one benefit that radio had over the stage, where curtains must be raised and lowered and sets swapped out to achieve the same effect.[25] Although radio shares this ability with motion pictures, where music can carry out a similar effect between scenes, radio dramas were transmitted live and were not afforded the luxury of days of editing in post-production, nor did radio have visuals to confirm that such a change occurred. Bridges were thus of critical importance in radio. And yet, directors did not employ them in great number within a drama because scene lengths were generally long. As Crews writes: "There are seldom more than one or two transitions in the nine or ten minutes of dialogue in a [fifteen-minute daytime] serial program." (1944: 427)[26]

Early radio dramas used generic bridges that, according to the Cordells, were not connected to the theme of the production or action of the scene (cf. 1936: 413). Crews also recalls that most bridges in early dramas were adapted

---

23   Wylie outlines these five methods (cf. 1939: 72). Mackey describes similar methods for dividing scenes: "music, sound, silence, narration, or any combination of these" (1951: 81).

24   Mamorsky provides seven functions that bridges carry out: *passage of time, change of locale, emphasis, emotional tags, comic effects, gag bridges* that play on song titles or lyrics, and *neutral bridges* (cf. 1946: 54).

25   Arnheim even describes bridges as "acoustic curtains" (1936: 116f.). For more on the distinctions between radio and stage drama, see Lewton (cf. 1938: 10).

26   Commercial show lengths, according to Oboler, fell into three main categories: "the fifteen-minute daytime sketch known, to the trade, as 'soap operas' [...]; the half-hour, once-a-week play which is either complete in itself or part of a once-a-week serial; and the short playlet used, generally, to display the dramatic prowess of a 'star' as part of a variety hour" (1940: xxvii). The show itself, however, takes up less time than indicated as a result of commercials, announcements and opening or closing material. Oboler further explains that the half-hour programme runs between 21 and 24 minutes, while the 15-minute slots actually last anywhere from 7 to 12 minutes (cf. ibid.: xxviii). On the nature of radio transitions in daytime serials, Crews claims they are usually of the silent variety (cf. 1944: 427).

from existing orchestral repertory, which he describes as "a hold-over from legitimate theater practices, in which the orchestra would fill in between acts" (1944: 150). Although classical excerpts may have worked well in the world of theatre and film, they were, as previously noted, ill-equipped to meet the time demands of radio. The neutral, non-descriptive bridges that the Cordells describe were likewise quickly replaced in favour of cues that conveyed specific narrative information – in a time-sensitive production, one must not waste an opportunity to enhance the narrative. By the mid-1930s, music directors made greater efforts to match music to the drama, which is precisely when the first music anthologies for radio began to appear.

Charles Paul's *Radio Transitions* (1942) perfectly illustrates the ability for bridges to establish a new mood or setting in a matter of measures. His descriptive titles give us a clear window into the effects he was trying to achieve. For example, Paul indicates a change of emotion in "Home Sweet Home to Bustle", which partially quotes the popular ballad before growing more rhythmically active, culminating in an upward glissando (see Example 9.4). In "Climactic Moment to Hockey Game", the cue transitions to a new location, dissipating the tension of the previous scene and establishing a new setting, possibly around an ice rink (see Example 9.5). Paul's collection also contains cues to establish time, including a series of excerpts titled "Sucker for Xmas", which one could use to transition into a scene taking place during the Christmas season (see Example 9.6). Even when quoting familiar melodies like "Home, Sweet Home" or "Jingle Bells", Paul filters them through the same angular and chromatic musical language that is common in background cues – a feature that sets these categories apart from themes. Semmler's *Incidental Music Book*

EXAMPLE 9.4   Charles Paul, "Home Sweet Home to Bustle", from Charles Paul's *Radio Transitions* (1942)

EXAMPLE 9.5   Charles Paul, "Climactic Moment to Hockey Game", from Charles Paul's Radio Transitions (19

EXAMPLE 9.6   Charles Paul, "Sucker for Xmas No. 3", from Charles Paul's Radio Transitions (1942)

11 (1944), again published under his pseudonym Ralph Sandor, presents a particularly unique example of bridges by offering music directors multiple options for transitioning from a single mood. "Transition 1", for instance, begins in a style marked "Gay Mood" and can transition to either "Menace", "Hurry" or "Mystery", all without disrupting harmonic continuity (see Figure 9.1).

Like themes and backgrounds, bridges are principally concerned with timing. Kremenliev writes that a bridge is "seldom more than ten seconds long" (1949: 76), and NBC music director Frank Black adds that "a few seconds' difference in timing may either establish or dispel the illusion that you wish to create" (1946: 73).[27] Composers thus emphasised adaptability through short phrases and by employing repetitive 'vamp' sections – a device familiar to theatrical arts for fitting the desired length of a scene transition. A clear example of this is Paul's "Heavy Tension (Background) to Chord", a four-measure excerpt

---

27   Whipple alternatively writes that bridges should not exceed 30 seconds (1938: 45).

THEMES, BACKGROUND, BRIDGES AND CURTAINS

FIGURE 9.1 *Ralph Sandor [Alexander Semmler], "Transition No. 1", from* Incidental Music Book II *(1944)*

with repeats after each bar (see Example 9.7). Another good illustration is Harry Salter's "Mysterioso Creepy" from his *Airway Incidentals* (1942), which contains distinct two-measure phrases marked with rehearsal letters and repeat signs (see Example 9.8). Owing to the importance of timing, some collections even

EXAMPLE 9.7   Charles Paul, "Heavy Tension (Background) to Chord", from Charles Paul's Radio Transitions (1942)

EXAMPLE 9.8   Harry Salter, "Mysterioso Creepy", from Airway Incidentals (1942)

FIGURE 9.2   Louis Katzman and Milton Rettenberg, "Furioso" from Bridges Moods Interludes (1943)

printed timestamps in the margins to indicate how long a piece would last, such as Louis Katzman and Milton Rettenberg's *Bridges Moods Interludes* from 1943 (see Figure 9.2). In my survey of 438 bridges, the average length is 7.86 measures, with some as little as one measure or a single chord.

In addition to brevity, bridges also tend to evade clear resolution – a lack of finality that signals to listeners that the story has not yet finished. Harmonically, this is achieved by a lack of clear cadential figures, with many bridges ending on a diminished, augmented or especially dominant-seventh chord. Structurally, composers halted musical progress with fermatas, ostinatos, ritardandos or decrescendos, denying the completion of even, periodic phrases. In his "Dramatic Transition No. 48" (1946), for instance, Roy Shield ends the short bridge with a rhythmic ostinato that one can repeat as the volume peters out (see Example 9.9). Written in fade-outs were also common, as in Truman's "Interlude for Effect", which instructs "dim out", or Paul's "Closing in on Suspects to Motion", which indicates "bis to fade" (see Examples 9.10 and 9.11). Fade-outs were also accomplished by fermatas, decrescendos and/or through the technological intervention of a studio engineer – what Turnbull calls a "board fade" (1951: 294).[28] Of the 438 bridges that I surveyed, the most commonly used devices are the fermata and written-out pause, occurring in 240 and 107 examples, respectively. Nearly 80 per cent of bridges, then, rely on

---

28   Black notes how "the engineer can achieve a 'fake' crescendo from his control panel that would make Rossini green with envy" (1946: 68).

EXAMPLE 9.9   Roy Shield, "Dramatic Transition No. 48", from Roy Shield's Musical Transitions for Radio: Folio II (1946)

EXAMPLE 9.10   Edward Truman, "Interlude for Effect", from Broadcast Mood Music (1943)

EXAMPLE 9.11   Charles Paul, "Closing in on Suspects to Motion", from Charles Paul's Radio Transitions (194

a suspension (often over a dominant-seventh chord) coupled with a fade out in order to indicate the continuance of a story. Composers Elliott Jacoby and Vaughn de Leath acknowledge this feature on the cover of their 1940 collection *50 Dramatic Moods*: "You will observe that most of the themes end with a suspension diminishing in tone volume until fade-out so that the dialogue may be resumed over the last chord."

5   Curtains

Curtains (also referred to as *bumpers*, *play-offs*, or *act-ins* and *act-outs*) are related to bridges – often presented in treatises as a subcategory – but do not transition between scenes; rather, they open or close off a scene with a clean break, either buttressed up against another scene, credits or commercials.[29] The term comes from stage plays and melodramatic theatre, where music would accompany the opening or closing of the physical curtain. Curtains share some functions and musical characteristics with bridges, but are distinct in important ways. Unlike a bridge, which can help usher listeners from one mood to another, the curtain's primary responsibility is to set the scene or wrap up the previous one by commenting on the action. They therefore lend continuity to a broadcast by extending the mood before and after a given segment or episode. If the curtain music opens a scene, Mackey writes that it should "reflect the nature or mood of the coming play", and if the curtain closes a scene, it should "carr[y] the last scene and the play to its proper emotional conclusion" (1951: 35f.). This makes such compositions much more emotionally consistent than bridges, as they do not segue between contrasting scenes. An opening curtain (or 'act-in'), however, still sets the tone, establishes setting, and occasionally foreshadows events to come like a bridge. A closing curtain (also called a 'tag') offers a clean break before the next unit of the programme, whether it be a commercial, end credits or station announcement. And as a practical measure, Kremenliev notes that a close-curtain cue can also contribute a definitive ending to dramatic moments that "might otherwise lack finality" (1949: 76).

These distinct functions are reflected in the musical characteristics of curtains. Like backgrounds and bridges, curtains rely on a somewhat expressionist palette that features disjunct melodies and chromaticism. Unlike background cues, however, curtains are meant to be heard, and unlike bridges, they primarily feature one mood and offer a clear sense of resolution – especially close curtains or 'act-outs'. As one might expect, resolution often comes by way of a major or minor triad in the home key. If writing in a major key, composers often add a major sixth (occasionally a major second), which fits

---

29   Curtains are presented as a separate category by Cordell (1936), Kremenliev (1949), Mackey (1951), Oboler (1940) and Turnbull (1951).

EXAMPLE 9.12 *John Gart, "Money Curtain", from* Serial Moods *(1946)*

EXAMPLE 9.13 *Burt Buhrman, "Curtain No. 4", from* Interludes and Curtains *(1942)*

comfortably in the sound world of popular music in the 1930s and 1940s. John Gart's *Organ Backgrounds* (1945) offers several cues marked "curtain" or "tag" and they all end with this major-sixth chord. The same can be said about his subsequent publication, *Serial Moods for Radio* (1946), which includes "Money Curtain", a piece that quotes the chorus to "The Gold Diggers' Song" (commonly known by its chorus "We're in the Money") and ends with the expected consonant sonority (see Example 9.12). Bert Buhrman's *Interludes and Curtains* (1942) also contains many curtains that end with the major-sixth chord, such as "Curtain No. 4", which manages to offer a resolution in only two measures (see Example 9.13). In addition to tonal closure, a sense of finality is also frequently communicated through the use of a crescendo and either an accelerando or ritardando, such as Lew White's "Curtain Music No. 11" (see Example 9.14).

6 Conclusion

The new musical language that I have outlined came about as a result of two aspects inherent to the broadcast medium. First, the supremacy of voice in radio dramas prompted composers and music directors to stray from distracting or familiar instrumental combinations and rely on angular melodies as well as a more chromatic harmonic vocabulary; it also encouraged them to avoid

EXAMPLE 9.14 Lew White, "Curtain Music No. 11", from Lew White's Dramatic and Novelty Folio (1939).

well-known tunes and reduce rhythmic activity specifically in background cues. Second, concerns over the timing of live broadcasts gave rise to short, sectional compositions that emphasised adaptability through ostinatos, vamp sections, fermatas and fade-outs. Although I claim this to be a new musical language, I acknowledge that radio inherited much of its structure from other dramatic arts dating back centuries, especially opera, melodrama and film. A few of the collection titles even betray this lineage, such as *Songs and Themes for the Screen, Radio and Stage* (1937) or *Musicue Library: A Series of Compositions for Radio, Theatre and Motion Pictures* (1944). But as the compositions in these collections reveal, music for radio drama responded to the unique format and constraints of the industry.

As the distant sound world of American radio dramas comes closer into focus, its legacy beyond the airwaves grows more apparent. The musical conventions of radio were solidifying just as television was coming into prominence. Radio dramas provided a suitable scoring model for the episodic structure of TV, which still relies on catchy theme songs, background music, bridges between scenes or curtains to and from commercials. Whipple noted this comparison with television as early as 1938:

> Writing for television broadcasts will closely approximate playwriting, but the time element, that bugaboo of all radio writers, will not be eliminated by this coming scientific device and the writer who learns radio

technique will find a place in this field more readily than one who knows only playwriting. (7)

Several radio music anthologies indicate their usefulness to the televised medium, including *Modern Compositions for Radio, Screen, Television* (1946) and *Corelli-Jacobs Mood Music: For Film, Television, Radio, and General Performance* (1959). Today, while some shows invest in original music, many continue to rely on similar production music libraries – now available through digital subscriptions. And, with the growing use of music in serialised podcasts, radio's musical aesthetics are returning to the medium for which they were originally crafted nearly a century ago.

References

Arnheim, Rudolf (1936). *Radio*. Margaret Ludwig, Herbert Read, transl. London: Faber & Faber.

Balázs, Béla (ca. 1924/2006). Transl. Russell Stockman. "Radio Drama". *October* 115: 47–48.

Bennett, Tom (1946). "Arranging Music for Radio". Gilbert Chase, ed. *Music in Radio Broadcasting: NBC-Columbia University Broadcasting Series*. New York, NY: McGraw-Hill. 76–90.

Black, Frank (1946). "Conducting for Radio". Gilbert Chase, ed. *Music in Radio Broadcasting: NBC-Columbia University Broadcasting Series*. New York, NY: McGraw-Hill. 66–75.

Buhrman, Bert (1942). *Interludes and Curtains*. New York, NY: Emil Ascher.

Cordell, William H., Kathryn Coe Cordell (1936). "The Future Theatre of the Air". *Sewanee Review* 44/4: 405–419.

Corwin, Norman (1944). *More by Corwin: 16 Radio Dramas by Norman Corwin*. New York, NY: Henry Holt.

Crawford, Jesse (1940). *Jesse Crawford's Radio Dramatic Series*. New York, NY: Emil Ascher.

Crews, Albert (1944). *Radio Production Directing*. Boston, MA: Houghton Mifflin.

Daniels, Dieter (2017). "Absolute Sounding Images: Abstract Film and Radio Drama of the 1920s as Complementary Forms of a Media-Specific Art". Holly Rogers, Jeremy Barham, eds. *The Music and Sound of Experimental Film*. Oxford: OUP. 23–44.

Davis, George (1947). *Music-Cueing for Radio-Drama: A Practical Treatise on the Application of Music to the Radio-Script*. New York, NY: Boosey & Hawkes.

Felton, Felix (1949). *The Radio-Play: Its Technique and Possibilities*. London: Sylvan Press.

Gart, John (1945). *Organ Backgrounds*. New York, NY: Emil Ascher.

Gart, John (1946). *Serial Moods: A Collection of 54 Dramatic Cues for Radio Shows.* New York, NY: Emil Ascher.

Gorbman, Claudia (1987). *Unheard Melodies: Narrative Film Music.* Bloomington, IN: Indiana Univ. Press.

Hand, Richard J. (2006). *Terror on the Air!: Horror Radio in America, 1931–1952.* Jefferson, NC: McFarland.

Heylbut, Rose (1945). "Background on Background Music: How NBC's Experts Fit Music to the Mood and Action of Dramatic Shows". *Etude* 63: 493–494.

Huwiler, Elke (2005). "Storytelling by Sound: A Theoretical Frame for Radio Drama Analysis". *Radio Journal: International Studies in Broadcast and Audio Media* 3/1: 45–59.

Jacoby, Elliott, Vaughn de Leath (1940). *50 Dramatic Moods for Background Use with Dramatic Radio Scripts or Sketches for Piano.* New York, NY: Alfred Music.

Katzman, Louis, Milton Rettenberg (1943). *Bridges Moods Interludes: Original Incidental and Background Music for Radio Drama and Professional or Amateur Theatrical Productions.* New York, NY: Broadcast Music.

Kempinski, Leo A. (1938). *Radio Drama Series.* New York, NY: Photo-Play Music.

Kosovsky, Robert (2000). "Bernard Herrmann's Radio Music for the Columbia Workshop". PhD Thesis. City Univ. of New York. Unpublished.

Kremenliev, Boris (1949). "Background Music for Radio Drama". *Hollywood Quarterly* 4/1: 75–83.

Leibert, Richard W. (1941). *Dramatic Varieties: Themes for Radio Dramatic Shows.* New York, NY: Emil Ascher.

Lewton, Sherman Paxton (1938). *Radio Drama.* Boston, MA: Expression Company.

Mackey, David R. (1951). *Drama on the Air.* New York, NY: Prentice Hall.

Mamorsky, Morris (1946). "Composing for Radio". Gilbert Chase, ed. *Music in Radio Broadcasting: NBC-Columbia University Broadcasting Series.* New York, NY: McGraw-Hill. 47–65.

Mattfeld, Julius (1944). "Introduction". *Incidental Music Book II by Ralph Sandor.* New York, NY: Alpha Music. 2.

Oboler, Arch (1940). *Fourteen Radio Plays.* New York, NY: Random House.

Paul, Charles (1942). *Charles Paul's Radio Transitions.* New York, NY: Emil Ascher.

Pollock, Muriel (1943). *Muriel Pollock's Musical Moods Book 2.* New York, NY: Bob Miller.

Porter, Jeffrey L. (2016). *Lost Sound: The Forgotten Art of Radio Storytelling.* Chapel Hill, NC: Univ. of North Carolina Press.

Salter, Harry (1942). *Airway Incidentals: A Collection of Musical Themes for Radio.* New York, NY: Emil Ascher.

Sandor, Ralph [Alexander Semmler] (1941). *Incidental Music.* New York, NY: Alpha Music.

Sandor, Ralph [Alexander Semmler] (1944). *Incidental Music Book II*. New York, NY: Alpha Music.

Sessions, Kenn, George F. Briegel (1944). *Musicue Library: A Series of Compositions for Radio, Theatre and Motion Pictures*. New York, NY: George F. Briegel.

Shield, Roy (1946a). *Roy Shield's Musical Transitions for Radio: Folio I*. New York, NY: Bergman, Vocco and Conn.

Shield, Roy (1946b). *Roy Shield's Musical Transitions for Radio: Folio II*. New York, NY: Bergman, Vocco and Conn.

Truman, Edward (1943). *Broadcast Mood Music: For Organ and Other Instruments*. Hollywood, CA: Van Brunt.

Turnbull, Robert B. (1951). *Radio and Television Sound Effects*. New York, NY: Rinehart.

Verma, Neil (2012). *Theater of the Mind: Imagination, Aesthetics, and American Radio Drama*. Chicago, IL: Univ. of Chicago Press.

Wedel, Kip A. (2011). "One Nation on the Air: The Centripetalism of Radio Drama and American Civil Religion, 1929–1962". PhD Thesis. Kansas State Univ. Unpublished.

Weiser, Norman S. (1942). *The Writer's Radio Theatre, 1941: Outstanding Plays of the Year*. London and New York, NY: Harper & Brothers.

Whipple, James (1938). *How to Write for Radio*. London and New York, NY: McGraw-Hill.

White, Lew (1939). *Lew White's Dramatic and Novelty Folio: Especially Compiled for Dramatic Radio Sketches and Background Use*. New York, NY: Emil Ascher.

Wissner, Reba (2013). *A Dimension of Sound: Music in the Twilight Zone*. Hillsdale, NY: Pendragon Press.

Wylie, Max (1939). *Radio Writing*. Toronto and New York, NY: Farrar & Rinehart.

CHAPTER 10

Referenced Music in Radio Drama: Jef Geeraerts' *Concerto* (1970) and Samuel Vriezen's *Schade* (2017)

Siebe Bluijs

Abstract

Radio drama has two possibilities to include music: (1) the music is part of the soundtrack; (2) the characters or the narrator explicitly refer to music by means of language. Because of its medial affordances, the radio play can evoke both possibilities simultaneously. This chapter looks at the productive interaction between the semiotic systems of language and music in two radio plays. Both case studies conceptualise music as a locus to address and think through political-ideological issues that are indicative of the different political contexts in which these radio plays were conceived.

Other than the sound film, a medium that also emerged in the 1920s, the radio play has hardly been considered as an autonomous art form.[1] Only rarely do the other arts refer to the radio play; usually, it is the other way around. In its approximately hundred-year history, however, the radio play has taken full advantage of its status as an intermediate form. Relying on practices of 'remediation' (see Bolter and Grusin 1999), it has constantly appropriated techniques and conventions from other art forms and genres, making listeners rely on their knowledge of other media to decode radio play signs. It has, for instance, adopted literary conventions such as the use of a third-person narrator (or, in more precise narratological terms, a heterodiegetic narrator).[2] In the words of radio play scholar Lars Bernaerts, "conventions circulate between

---

1 This statement specifically pertains to Flanders and the Netherlands. Although the art form has gained a more prominent status in Austria, Germany and the United Kingdom, it can be said that the radio play is often overlooked in these countries too.
2 The narratologist Gérard Genette distinguishes between different types of narrators. A heterodiegetic narrator is a narrator who is not part of the storyworld. A homodiegetic narrator, by contrast, is a narrator who is also one of the characters and thus exists on the level of the storyworld (cf. 1972/1980: 248).

media. For a relatively marginal medium like that of the radio play, this circulation is vital" (2019: 317).[3] It can be argued that the radio play derives its identity precisely from this dynamic interaction. Intermediality is at the heart of its history: the first radio plays were live theatre performances on the radio, and the radio play developed unique forms of expression after the introduction of montage, a technique that the radio play shares with film (cf. Arnheim 1936: 132; Hand and Traynor 2011: 17f; Drakakis 1981: 5).

The fact that the radio play is particularly susceptible to the dynamics of remediation is especially interesting with regard to music. Music, an (auditory) art form in its own right, is also one of the semiotic elements that the radio play has at its disposal (more on this below). As such, it can employ several narrative functions. Music in the radio play often functions similarly to its use in film: it can establish an atmosphere, create suspense, illustrate the inner life of the characters, contribute to characterisation, etc. It can also be used to put the listener on the wrong track. The music can be intradiegetic, meaning it is heard on the level of the storyworld, for instance when it is being played on a radio owned by one of the characters. It can also be extradiegetic, meaning it is part of the narration, for instance when it is used in a fashion that is similar to that of the curtain in theatre: to indicate scenic transitions. The music can be composed especially for the radio play – such as Benjamin Britten's original score for *The Dark Tower* by Louis MacNeice (cf. Van Puymbroeck 2019: 246) – or it can be a piece that is already well-known.

The double position of music in the radio play – as a semiotic element and as a medium in and of itself – can be narratively productive, as I aim to demonstrate in this chapter. Besides the inclusion of music in the overall composition, the radio play has another semiotic system at its disposal to 'incorporate' music. Like in narrative prose, such as a novel or a short story, music can become part of the storyworld by being referenced (cf. Hallett 2015: 607), for instance when a character or a narrator mentions a musical work.[4] Comparable to music that

---

3   Of course, the radio play influences other media and genres as well. We can think of the use of sound in film and theatre, and the use of medium-specific narrative techniques in the radio documentary and the radio commercial. According to the German radio play researcher Eugen Kurt Fischer: "Die Beschränkung auf das Hörerlebnis hat eine rundfunkeigene Dramaturgie ins Leben gerufen, die keineswegs auf das Hörspiel beschränkt ist." ('The fact that radio drama limits one's experience to listening only has led to the creation of a specific radiophonic dramaturgy – one which is by no means restricted to the radio play.' (1964: 10))

4   Theoretically, music can be invoked by other semiotic means in the radio play. A melody can be mimicked through the electro-acoustic manipulation of the pitch, changes in volume can create rhythmic patterns, etc. For the purposes of this chapter, I leave these possibilities aside.

is added to the sound layer, music that is being referred to by characters or a narrator can function as a means of characterisation or as a *mise en abyme*, among other options. Or in the words of Hallett: "It may contribute to equipping a character with certain features or experiences or illustrate and contextualize the world in which the story is set." (ibid.) Additionally, it is possible for a character or a narrator to not only mention a musical work, but also to provide commentary on it or to present an interpretation of the music. The radio play offers the possibility to present music and the commentary on that music simultaneously.[5] Put more generally: the radio play can make intermedial references to music, but it also has the ability of "intermedial reproduction" (Wolf 2015: 462f.).

This chapter's central focus is the productive interaction between the two semiotic systems of music and language in the radio play. In order to flesh out this interaction, I turn to audionarratology, a subdiscipline of (transmedial) narratology that "attends to sound narratives as a network of oral and/or aural semiotic systems" (Mildorf and Kinzel 2016b: 12).[6] This research discipline considers language as one meaningful sign system among others. The other semiotic elements that the radio play has at its disposal are: voice, sound, music, silence, electroacoustic manipulation, stereophony, mix/montage and 'actuality' (cf. Huwiler 2005a: 57f; see 2005b; Schmedes 2002).[7] Audionarratology offers helpful tools to distinguish between the different sign systems

---

5   For more on the question of simultaneity in radio drama, see Kita (2021).
6   Audionarratology starts out from the observation that classical narratology, relying heavily on visual metaphors, lacks a proper vocabulary and a clear methodology to consider the narrative aspects of sound. Audionarratologists argue that the same holds true for transmedial narratology, which is mainly focused on (audio)visual media, such as films, video games and graphic novels (see Thon 2016, for instance). That is why audionarratology reverts to sound studies and studies of oral narrative culture, in which the spoken word plays a central role (cf. Mildorf and Kinzel 2016b: 1f, 4). Some publications that are at the basis of this research discipline are: Mildorf and Kinzel (2016a, 2017), Mildorf (2019), and Bernaerts and Mildorf (2021).
7   Because of language's expressive qualities some radio play scholars have assigned a privileged status to it (cf. Huwiler 2005b: 46). Although the words uttered by the narrator and the characters are often central to conveying the radio play's story, audionarratology insists that other elements are equally important. So, even though some of these elements are used in almost every radio play (such as voice), while others are used more rarely (silence, for example), there is principally no hierarchy between them. Not all radio plays employ all semiotic elements or use them in the same measure. Andrew Sachs's *The Revenge* (BBC, 1973) is famous because it is a radio play that lacks language altogether: the story about a prison escape is told entirely by means of (paraverbal) sounds, electroacoustic manipulation, stereophony and montage. On the other side of the spectrum are radio plays that only use one voice, in which case they closely resemble an audio book. It is therefore useful to speak of the prototypical radio play, which commonly uses several voices, music and diegetic sounds to evoke a storyworld.

of language and music, and to consider how they interact within a narrative context. This chapter considers two radio plays in which a musical piece is explicitly referenced by means of language. In these case studies, a narrator or a character analyses, comments on or interprets a musical work. They invoke music ranging from the Classical and the Romantic era to pop music and contemporary classical music.[8] In both case studies music is conceptualised as a locus to address and think through political-ideological issues that are particular for and representative of the specific political contexts and periods in which these radio plays were conceived (1970 and 2017, respectively). They concern the countercultural revolution of the sixties and the ecological crisis of the present moment. The referenced musical compositions in these radio plays are instrumental in making one consider alternatives to the status quo. The first case study incorporates music (and commentary by the characters on that music) in the story, making music an intrinsic part of the narrative progression. The second radio play references a musical piece by means of language, presenting its compositional principles as an alternative way to consider (dominant) narratives around ecological issues. In both cases, the musical references are a two-way-street: on the one hand, the radio play offers an interpretation of the musical piece; on the other hand, the interpretation of the musical piece provides an entrance to interpreting the radio play itself.

1   Jef Geeraerts – *Concerto*

The radio play *Concerto* (1970)[9] by the Flemish author Jef Geeraerts is about the relationship between Walter and his mother, who is morbidly obese and, consequently, bedridden. The mother is 'pathologically sensitive towards sounds. [...] A trauma with historical dimensions: her place of birth was ravaged twice by aerial bombardments' (1970: 5).[10] Therefore, mother and son live in a house devoid of resonances from the outside world. The secluded domestic

---

8   Not coincidentally, the authors of these radio plays have distinct musical backgrounds: Samuel Vriezen is a composer and a performer, and Jef Geeraerts has written extensively on music (see Geeraerts 2009).

9   Two radio play productions were made: one by the Flemish broadcasting corporation BRT (Geeraerts and Joos 1970), and one by the Dutch broadcasting corporation KRO (Geeraerts and Tollenaar 1970), which are both based on the same (unpublished) radio play script (Geeraerts 1970).

10 The translations of the radio plays are my own. The page numbers refer to the (unpublished) radio play scripts, which can be found in the archives of the broadcasting corporations.

sphere is a locus for tyranny. Mother wants Walter to keep the door of her room open at all times, so she can see what he is up to. She does not trust him after he got involved with a woman of his own age. Walter disobeys his mother's orders by closing the door while she is sleeping. These are the only times he is alone. Walter is the narrator and main character of the story – in narratological terms he is the homodiegetic narrator. While talking to himself Walter alternately talks about his mother in the third and the second person. The grammatical changes are often accompanied by a shift in tone: when he speaks 'to' his mother his voice sounds tender – 'why did you have to become sick, mother?' (ibid.: 2) – and when he talks *about* her, his voice sounds remote.

Concerto plays out several topoi of classical psychoanalysis. It makes extensive intermedial references to Alfred Hitchcock's movie *Psycho* (1960) to characterise Walter's psychological state. While his mother is sleeping, he plays back in his mind the scene of her kicking his girlfriend out of the house. This scene is followed by the famous screeching violin music from *Psycho*'s shower scene by the American composer Bernard Herrmann. Through intermedial reference, the music becomes part of the narration. In Hitchcock's film, the music is heard when a young woman gets murdered. The fact that we hear the same music in the radio play suggests that Walter interprets his mother's actions as murder. The music thus provides a commentary on the fragment and contributes to the characterisation of Walter. The reference to *Psycho* is further made explicit when Walter retells the story of the movie's most important scenes. The radio play particularly employs the semiotic element of voice, which is also a crucial element in Hitchcock's film. Walter imitates the voice of *Psycho*'s main character, Norman Bates, and Norman's mother (whose voice, as we find out at the end of *Psycho*, is actually Norman's). Likewise, Walter imitates his own mother's voice in his soliloquies. This doubling indicates that the movie's Oedipal theme is an entrance to understanding the radio play. It is suggested that Walter has not completed the Oedipal phase, as he has not successfully transferred the love for his mother to another woman. At the same time, his mother is a figure of (patriarchal) authority, whose rule Walter is unable to escape.

Concerto's psychoanalytical motives are connected to political-ideological issues. Read more generally, the story of Walter's relationship to his mother is about the installation and breach of power relations. This reading is activated by the radio play's musical title. The etymological roots of 'concerto' presumably go back to the Latin words *concertare* (meaning to join or to bind together) and *certare* (competition, fight).[11] The inherent contradiction between these

---

11   See the *Online Etymology Dictionary*, https://www.etymonline.com/word/concert#etymonline_v_17309 [02/06/2021].

two meanings is applicable to the musical form. In a concerto, the solo instrument alternately blends in with the orchestra or stands out in relation to it. The tension between these two seemingly opposite poles is also the driving force of the narrative: Walter acts according to his mother's will, but he wishes to break away from her as well. Therefore, the musical term of the radio play's title is an indication of the play's overall structure. Additionally, the radio play activates the musical form of the concerto by including several concertos in its soundtrack. Apart from caretaking, one of Walter's tasks is to compile a daily collection of music for his mother. She only wants to hear music that eases her nerves and she claims that she is only allowed, on doctor's orders, to listen to certain composers (Brahms, Tchaikovsky and Chopin). Despite these strict preferences, she pronounces their names incorrectly and she does not recognise their music: she thinks Chopin is Brahms and vice versa. By contrast, Walter demonstrates that he has extensive musical knowledge. When it comes to music, he clearly has the upper hand. Therefore, music becomes the locus for opposition to his mother's reign.

Walter increasingly tries to gain control over her by offering commentary on the pieces. Accompanying the first few musical fragments, he provides (mostly made-up or apocryphal) biographical details about the composers. Recurrent themes in these commentaries are death and illness. He remarks that César Franck wrote the *Variations Symphoniques* (1885) for his sick daughter, and that the little girl died at the premiere. About Frédéric Chopin's Nocturne Op. 9, No. 1 (1830) Walter notes that the composer wrote the piece while he was dying from tuberculosis. Through these comments, Walter suggests that the music his mother listens to is linked to death and decay. When he finds out that his words have no effect on her, he shifts to a more explicit approach. Chopin's Étude Op. 10, No. 2 (1836)[12] is accompanied by Walter's commentary on the composer's appearance. According to him, the man was bald, carried thick glasses and had a crooked walk. He says Chopin wrote the piece for his mother, who dressed him badly. As the Étude op. 10, No. 2 is replaced by the more 'aggressive'-sounding Étude Op. 10, No. 5 (1830), he goes on to say that Chopin's mother became too heavy and bedridden, so the composer had to stay home to take care of her, having to use his musical talent to record and play classical recordings. The implication is clear: Walter, like his fictitious Chopin, could have been a great musician, like the real Chopin, but his mother stood in the way. Walter's words are lost on her, however: she thinks he is joking and believes he is flattering her.

---

12   In a performance by Kurt Leimer, as the script indicates.

Because Walter is unable to deface his mother's beloved Chopin by means of language, he decides to bring her favourite composers into contrast with other music. The radio play thus enacts a collision of musical poetics, evoking Walter's struggle to overcome his mother's tyranny. After playing Chopin he plays Bach's Concerto for Violin, Oboe and Strings in D Minor (ca. 1730). Mother complains that it is plain noise to her, but Walter does not give in. According to him, it is music's task to address the profound questions of life and to 'open up consciousness' (Geeraerts, 1970: 19), which he feels Bach's Concerto does. To illustrate his point, he then plays Tchaikovsky's Violin Concerto in D Major (1878), which he nicknames the 'Kitsch Concerto' and calls 'bourgeois' (ibid.). Walter explains that the concerto conveys the notion that life is good as it is: 'Nothing can disturb our perfect happiness. Ours is the best of all possible worlds.' (ibid.: 20) This Leibnizian proclamation is applicable to Walter's situation as well: his mother does not allow an alternative for their seclusion (such as Walter sharing his life with a woman). Walter wishes for (the possibility of) another world. He projects his unbearable suffering onto the music: he brings it to his mother's (and to the listener's) attention that the director accentuates the sentimental passages and the overabundant tremolos of the violins.

To understand how music can express a 'bourgeois' world view, it is useful to turn to the work of the French political economist Jacques Attali. The central premise of his book *Bruits: essai sur l'économie politique de la musique* (1977) is that music is intrinsically tied up with society's modes of production, which means that "[a]ll music, any organization of sounds is then a tool for the creation or consolidation of a community, of a totality. It is what links a power center to its subjects, and thus, more generally, it is an attribute of power in all of its forms." (1985: 6) So, according to Attali, music that, for instance, relies on harmonic structures, embodies the "bourgeoisie's dream of harmony" (ibid.: 5f.). By historicising and reading dominant musical forms, Attali aims to uncover societal structures: "music runs parallel to human society, is structured like it, and changes when it does. It does not evolve in a linear fashion, but is caught up in the complexity and circularity of the movements of history." (ibid.: 10) At the same time, Attali argues, music is not merely a representation or an expression of its time, but also a locus for societal change: "Music is prophecy. Its styles and economic organization are ahead of the rest of society because it explores, much faster than material reality can, the entire range of possibilities in a given code." (ibid.: 11)

For Walter, music's ability to foreshadow and to spark (societal) change is central in his wish for emancipation. Since he fails to make his point through language, he changes his strategy by making the music speak *for* him. Walter has great knowledge of classical music, but we also find out that he was a musical prodigy as a child. Because he had to take care of his mother at an early age, however, his musical talent could never come to fruition. For Walter, curating and playing recorded concerts is a sad substitute for his destroyed musical ambitions. Instead of having a musical career, Walter has to play disk jockey for the single-member audience of his mother. He finds a way, however, to put the technology to use for his emancipation. He goes against his mother's wishes by including all kinds of musical pieces in the sound collage. Following Tchaikovsky's concerto, he plays "El paso del ebro" (ca. 1938), an anti-fascist song from the Spanish Civil War by the Spanish composer Rodolfo Halffter. According to Walter, this music illustrates the political power of music. When he plays the song, he proclaims: 'this music is testament to the vivacious power of the artful combination of do, re, mi, fa, sol, la, si!!'[13] (Geeraerts 1970: 21) The Spanish song almost brings his mother to a nervous breakdown: we hear her gasping and moaning. This reaction suggests that a musico-political revolution against authoritarian regimes corresponds to a rebellion against parental authority. What matters perhaps more than the historical context of the song, however, is Walter's conceptualisation of music as the 'artful combination' of separate elements. Considered as such, Walter's sound collages can be regarded as a form of musical expression.

Since Walter's musical approach seems to finally affect his mother, he pushes through. What follows is an audiophonic bombardment consisting of a quick succession of fragments from orchestral works, among which are Bach's Toccata and Fugue in D Minor (early 18th century); Stravinsky's *Le Sacre du Printemps* (1913); Prokofiev's Suite from *The Love for Three Oranges* (1919); Albinoni's Adagio for Organ and Strings (presumably early 18th century); and Beethoven's Fifth Symphony (1808). Considering his mother's sensitivity towards sound, it is no surprise to find she is horrified by this onslaught of loud orchestral works. Notably, most of the musical works referenced in the radio play have become canonised because of their revolutionary musical qualities at a certain moment in musical history. Within the context of the radio play, however, the true revolutionary quality is not in the works themselves but in their skillful combination. Played shortly after one another, and even simultaneously, their individual harmonic qualities get lost in the cacophonous whole. If, according to Attali, harmonic musical structures embody a bourgeois mentality, the disintegration of harmony into tumultuous dissonance corresponds to an anti-bourgeois revolution.

---

13   In Flanders, it is common to use the solfège or solmisation syllables 'do, re, mi, fa, sol, la, si' to indicate the major scale (which in C-major would be C-D-E-F-G-A-B-(C)).

As his mother loses consciousness, other fragments enter the collage. Music by Wagner is heard alongside the sounds of bombs and Nazi radio propaganda – e.g., "das Oberkommando der Wehrmacht gibt bekannt"[14] (ibid.: 23). This juxtaposition underscores the historical relation between music and politics. Since the sound collage has its desired effect, Walter finally musters the courage to tell his mother about his true feelings:

> Why did you always insist that I had talent to play the piano, mother, even to play Chopin, while in reality I only had time to develop my talents to scrub the furniture, to sweep the floors, to pour coffee, to eat cottage cheese, and to say yes? Why have you fooled me my whole life, mother – me, the gifted audio technician, who had to use an expensive stereo to glue together music performed by others for the daily con cer to? (ibid.: 27)

Walter is condemned to use the technology that his mother has bought for him, but he uses that equipment to his advantage by making it speak for him. Through the act of cutting and pasting he rewrites his own situation and is able to claim a subjectivity of his own.

As Walter's rebellion against his mother is played out by references to the history of Western music, the radio play's psychoanalytical theme gives way to a more general political interpretation. The climax of the musical onslaught is a Dutch pop song that continues to play as we hear the mother suffering a stroke. "Het land van Maas en Waal" (1966) by Boudewijn de Groot[15] is a carnivalesque song about the 'tin harmonic orchestra of Circus Hieronymus Bosch', that is modeled after Bob Dylan's "Rainy Day Women #12 & 35" of the same year. Its nonsensical lyrics about rabbits with funnels on their heads and roosters laying glass eggs make it a prominent product of the countercultural and psychedelic revolution of the sixties. Walter's personal battle for individuality is indicative of a generational struggle against parental authority that occurred during the sixties, as "pop music became a particularly salient site for the exploration of identity" (Hertz and Roessner 2014: 4). The fact that a pop song is the culmination point in a series of classical works is testament to Walter's successful struggle for freedom – in Attali's words: "Janis Joplin, Bob Dylan and Jimi Hendrix say more about the liberatory dream of the 1960s than any theory

---

14 'the high command of the Wehrmacht announces'.
15 Because of the song's success in the Dutch pop charts, Boudewijn de Groot released an English version of the song as well, titled "The Land at Rainbow's End", which can be found on YouTube and Spotify.

of crisis." (1985: 5f.) The breach of parental authority at the level of the story reflects a larger shift in the social order. Jef Geeraerts' radio play thus indicates that music can be a site for political, ideological or generational struggle. It shows that some music validates dominant bourgeois ideologies, while other music can go against these ideologies, potentially even overthrow tyrannical regimes.

2   Samuel Vriezen – *Schade (Damage)*

Schade (Vriezen and Hendrix 2017)[16] by the Dutch poet and composer Samuel Vriezen consists of two alternating – seemingly unrelated – parts (see Table 10.1).

TABLE 10.1   The composition of the radio play *Schade* by Samuel Vriezen

Part I	Part II
Voice A (*low female*): speaking on behalf of a member of the Goi community (Niger Delta).	**Voice B** (*high female*): describing a performance of *Ins Ungebundene* (1998) by the contemporary Dutch composer Antoine Beuger.
Voices X, Y and Z (*male*): reflecting on issues surrounding the Niger Delta in unfinished conditional clauses.	
Underlying both parts (heavily distorted in Part II): A soundtrack of ambient noises: natural sounds, animals, people shouting at a stock market, chain saws, oil rigs, a city soundscape, etc.	

In the first part we hear a female voice (A) that speaks on behalf of an anonymous member of the Goi community in the Niger Delta. All of her utterances start with the words 'someone says…', followed by direct speech – for example: 'someone says "here we were fishermen and farmers"' (Vriezen 2017a: I).[17] These sentences are followed by a group of male voices (X, Y, Z) that bring up issues concerning the ecological consequences of massive oil extraction in the Niger Delta by the Royal Dutch oil company Shell. They speak of international

---

16   I would like to thank Samuel Vriezen for sending me the unpublished radio play script (Vriezen 2017a) and his helpful comments on his creative process.
17   The Roman numerals correspond to the scenes that are indicated in the radio play scenario (which lacks page numbers).

treaties, colonial history, the sabotage of the pipelines, the Nigerian government, the rise of militias and fighting gangs, the West's dependence on the oil industry, the mass immigration that is the result of destroyed landscapes, the history of the science of extraction, the shareholders' (lack of) responsibility, etc. By bringing together juridical, ideological, historical, scientific, economic, ethical and other questions, the radio play traces centuries of entangled issues that are related to the ecology of the Niger Delta.

In the second part of the radio play, a female voice (B) describes a performance of the composition *Ins Ungebundene* (1998) by the contemporary Dutch composer Antoine Beuger (1955), a founding member of the Düsseldorf-based Wandelweiser Composer's Ensemble.[18] In their work, Beuger and his associates try to think through John Cage's critique on the presumed dichotomy between music and silence.[19] *Ins Ungebundene* is an example of Beuger's approach to music. The piece consists of one D-note that contains a theoretically endless variety of overtones, resulting in a musical composition "that is permanently on the verge of disappearing" (qtd. in Saunders 2009). During both parts of the radio play we hear a soundtrack of ambient noises, such as animals and water, children's voices, people shouting at a stock market, the sounds of drilling rigs and chain saws, and the soundscape of a city. In part II this soundtrack becomes distorted (more about this below). As the three male voices speak, the sound collage undergoes a crescendo, before it suddenly stops, invoking the notion that the oil extraction will eventually come to a (possibly catastrophic) end.[20]

The radio play provides alternative scenarios to this outcome. Every sentence of the male voices is a conditional clause that is left unfinished ('If...', without the resolving 'then...'). Because the sentences are not concluded, they are possibilities without a definitive ending; they are kept lingering. The radio play presents a succession of probabilities and possibilities that can be categorised along axiological lines: regarding morality, e.g., 'If oil companies did

---

18 For more information about the ensemble's members, their history and their ideas on music, see the ensemble's website: https://www.wandelweiser.de/_texte/erstw-engl.html [02/06/2021].

19 In an interview, Beuger explains his approach to music: "[I]nstead of assuming music to have some finite number of basic elements to start with, I am suggesting the opposite: the matter of music is 'all that is (sounding)'. The form of a specific music, then, is the way it cuts into this infinitely dense continuum. [...] [K]nowing that even the smallest slice one carves out, again, contains an infinite number of elements. [...] So, asking someone to play an 'a' of a certain duration, a certain volume and a certain tone colour is like asking him to write the number pi: he'll do something more or less approaching something else, which is more or less close to something else again, etc." (qtd. in Saunders 2009)

20 When voice A is speaking there is no background sound. The sound collage is continued where it is left off after the male voices resume their talk.

more for communities than pay taxes' (I); deontic lines, regarding norms and laws, e.g., 'If Shell D'Arcy didn't get concessions from the Brits in 1937' (XX); and alethic lines, regarding truth, e.g., 'If oil wasn't fluid' (I) or 'If oil would never run out' (XXI).[21]

To understand this sequence of possibilities, I find it useful to turn to the work of literary scholar Gary Saul Morson. According to Morson (1998), narrative fiction is often read as ontologically closed, which means that every event in the narrative world stands in relation to the story's progression. Every small detail can be considered significant because it potentially foreshadows the story's outcome. This reading attitude is especially activated 'in hindsight', as novels are reread or read in a community of (professional) readers. That this attitude is particularly employed in relation to so-called 'realist' fiction is ironic, since it runs counter to our experience of the 'real' world: there are all kinds of incidents to which we do not ascribe a purpose. To go against this bias towards closure, Morson presents the term 'sideshadowing' as an alternative to the reading strategy of foreshadowing. If foreshadowing presents the actuality of the present as inevitable, sideshadowing draws attention to its intrinsic contingency:

> Instead of casting a shadow from the future, it casts a shadow 'from the side', that is, from the other possibilities. Along with an event, we see its alternatives, with each present, another possible present. Sideshadows conjure the ghostly presence of might-have-been or might-bes. In this way, the hypothetical shows through the actual and so achieves its own shadowy kind of existence in the text. (Ibid.: 601f.)

So, whereas foreshadowing closes off the plethora of possible outcomes, sideshadowing leaves these possibilities intact. This has fundamental implications for the "temporal legitimacy" (ibid: 602) of the present, as it undermines its inevitability: "Whereas *fore*shadowing works by revealing apparent alternatives to be mere illusions, *side*shadowing conveys the sense that actual events might just as well not have happened." (ibid.: 601)

By posing a series of hypothetical scenarios that are left unresolved, Vriezen's radio play goes against the conventional bias toward closure. By evoking a series of unfinished conditional clauses, it uses sideshadowing to consider other possible outcomes to the initial real-world conditions. Since Morson's argumentation relies heavily on visual metaphors, his notion of sideshadowing as

---

21 For more information on these 'modalitities' and their relevance for narrative theory, see Doležel (1976), Bell and Ryan (2019).

conjuring the 'ghostly presence' of other outcomes is perhaps a more apt metaphor in the context of my argument. Considering radio's historical connection to the otherworldly,[22] I wish to argue that *Schade* exploits an affordance of the audiophonic medium. If, according to Morson, "[t]he other possibilities usually appear invisible or distorted to later observers" (ibid.: 603) in conventional narratives, they are made audible in *Schade*. The invisible (but imaginable) possibilities are evoked by means of language, while the physical world is made present by the sound collage of ambient noises, through the materiality that is inherent to sound's reliance on indexical signs.

The ambient soundtrack of chainsaws and city noises is an audiophonic representation of the pollution of the Niger Delta. It also conveys how our ability to think about these ecological issues is 'polluted'. According to Roland Barthes, noise pollution, quite literally, stands in the way of thinking: "there is an audio-pollution which everyone [...] feels [...] is deleterious to the living being's very intelligence, which is, *stricto sensu*, its power of communicating effectively with its *Umwelt*: pollution prevents listening" (1976/1991: 247). According to Barthes, listening can be considered as a kind of thinking since it is concerned with focusing and decoding:

> Listening is henceforth linked (in a thousand varied, indirect forms) to a hermeneutics: to listen is to adopt an attitude of decoding what is obscure, blurred, or mute, in order to make available to consciousness the 'underside' of meaning (what is experienced, postulated, internalized as hidden). (Ibid.: 249)

What is made obscure or muted in dominant discourses on the pollution of the Niger Delta is exactly the possibility of different outcomes. Politicians and shareholders make a claim on 'realism': they hold that there is simply no alternative to the capitalist notion of extraction (which is legitimised through all kinds of laws and treaties).[23] The pollution of the region and the exploitation of its people are regarded as sad but ultimately inevitable outcomes of a system that is considered 'closed' by its apologists.

The description of Beuger's composition in part II points to a listening practice to deal with the kinds of pollution that such a capitalist logic installs (both of the ecology and of thought). Before I go into more detail, however, it is important to note that the music referred to in the radio play is not actually

---

22 Since the radiophonic voice is a 'disembodied' one, radio has often been considered a 'ghostlike' medium (cf. Sterne 2003: 290; see Whitehead 1992; Weiss 1995).
23 For more on the notion of 'capitalist realism', see Fisher (2009).

played. Instead, the female voice (B) provides an explanation of the effects of a performance of the piece. During this description, the soundtrack of ambient noises is distorted and temporarily slowed down. The distorted sounds more or less correspond to the description of the musical composition. The female voice says that the overtones emerge one by one: first the dominant overtones of the third and the fifth are heard, then the less dominant seventh, and eventually even overtones that escape the interval of a single octave:

> The tone is alive. A poignant overtone, the third, pulses. A lower, the fifth, is soft and stable. And higher, softly whistling, the seventh – a sultry color that now emerges. [...] The whole world is surrounded by this simplest of harmonies. If you want, you can even hear higher partial tones, the ninth, the tenth, eleventh, twelfth, thirteenth. This one D contains ranges of hidden melodies. (Vriezen 2017a: 9)

The description of *Ins Ungebundene* thus provides a starting point for developing a radical listening practice based on attention and the suppression of dominant overtones, so that usually unheard overtones, such as the thirteenth, can come to the foreground. The female voice says about the single D-note: 'It lasts, the sound penetrates your thinking. This harmony does not have a limit.' (ibid.: 12f) Limitless thinking, the radio play suggests, is needed to gain an overview of the seemingly limitless issues surrounding the extraction of oil in the Delta.

Therefore, Beuger's composition offers a model to restructure listening itself. Dominic Pettman's notion of the *vox mundi* provides a theoretical framework for understanding such a listening practice in relation to ecological issues. The *vox mundi* is "the sum total of cacophonous, heterogeneous, incommensurate, and unsynthesizable sounds of the postnatural world" (2017: 8). Pettman claims – following Barthes' conception of listening – that the world contains a multitude of voices, and that we need to learn to listen to them by allowing "specific voices to emerge from the disharmonic choir" (ibid.: 83). Listening to the *vox mundi* is to recognise that we are interpellated by these voices, obliging us to rethink our notion of being together with radically other and non-human entities (ibid.: 92).

The radio play makes this point, as the female voice (B) reflects on the effects of the composition after it has been performed:

> She must have moved, the organist, but she is still sitting, now with her hands on her lap. The tone is gone and the world stays. An awakening. The large space in which you sit with the audience is abandoned by the tone. A new reality. The ranges of the hidden melody are still there. They

resound in the memory. But you no longer hear the third pulsing. (Vriezen 2017a: 15; Vriezen and Hendrix 2017: 14' 05"–15' 06")

One of the effects of the composition is that the third (a dominant overtone) is no longer heard. The undoing of the third is a metaphor for the wish to escape the dominant discourses surrounding the Niger Delta. What one hears, instead of the dominant overtones, are the acoustics of the space itself. As Vriezen writes in an essay that resembles Beuger's musical poetics: 'In theory, even one impulse [...] contains all frequencies. After transmitting such an impulse, you do not hear voices, but only, in the resonances, the harmonic characteristics of the room's acoustics'. (2017b: 21) These characteristics are what gives a certain room its particularity. In analogy to this musical practice, Vriezen's radio play tries to find the characteristics of the space of the Niger Delta. This space is not a single acoustic room, but it contains subtones, overtones and resonances of unheard voices and unknown practices from the past and the present that the radio play tries to uncover, in order to find other possible outcomes to the catastrophic present.

Instead of offering clear-cut answers, Vriezen's piece uncovers the unheard voices (human and non-human) of this ecological disaster. The dominant narrative on this issue, the radio play implies, is inherently reductionist: it provides an illusion of 'oneness' and 'wholeness' by suppressing so-called minor or unrelated issues that do not fit into its logic. *Schade*'s ambition is to break open such a deterministic worldview. Since these voices are obscured and muted in the dominant discourse, they can be linked to the sideshadowing that the voices X, Y and Z evoke by means of language, because, as Morson remarks: "Sideshadowing restores the possibility of possibility. Its most fundamental lesson is: *To understand a moment is to grasp not only what did happen but also what else might have happened.*" (1998: 602, emphasis in original) Beuger's *Ins Ungebundene*, a composition without harmony, melody or clear progression, offers an effective model to address the ideological-political and ecological issues that the radio play is concerned with, as the female voice explains: 'No more harmony, no hidden range of melody. You open yourself up to the harmonyless, tangible, loose reality that you are in.' (Vriezen 2017a: 20)

3 Conclusion

If music is a locus for ideological and political struggle, different times and different situations call for different kinds of music – and different approaches to that music. The case studies employ different strategies in their use of musical references. In Jef Geeraerts' *Concerto*, music is presented as an emancipatory instrument to rebel against parental authority, and by extension against power relations in general. This capacity is explicitly brought to the foreground by the character's discourse. The radio play presents a succession of musical fragments to drive the narrative forward. This progression culminates in a musical revolution (the emergence of rock music) that mirrors a cultural revolution: the insurrection against (parental) authority. Therefore, this rebellion can be regarded within the larger cultural context of the sixties' counterculture. Whereas Geeraerts' radio play shows how music can be instrumental in providing an alternative to the status quo, Vriezen's radio play employs a musical composition that challenges the status quo's claim on closure. In *Schade* the referenced music offers a model to retrace the fleeting and suppressed circumstances that surround the massive oil extraction in the Niger Delta. Rather counterintuitively, the radio play does not include the music that is being referred to by the narrator. Instead, it uses electroacoustic manipulation and stereophony to re-enact the effects of the music that are described by the narrator. By blending the boundaries between music and ambient sounds, the radio play is true to the Cagean poetics of Beuger's composition. By evoking possible scenarios and by bringing voices to the foreground that are drowned out in (dominant) discourses, it offers an alternative listening (or reading) practice that insists on the possibility of alternatives.

References

Arnheim, Rudolf (1936). *Radio*. Margaret Ludwig, Henry Read, transl. London: Faber & Faber.

Attali, Jacques (1985). *Noise: The Political Economy of Music*. Brian Massumi, transl. London and Minneapolis, MN: Univ. of Minnesota Press.

Barthes, Roland (1976/1991). "Listening". Richard Howard, transl. *The Responsibility of Forms: Critical Essays on Music, Art and Representation*. Berkeley, CA: Univ. of California Press. 245–260.

Bell, Alice, Marie-Laure Ryan, eds. (2019). *Possible Worlds Theory and Contemporary Narratology*. Lincoln, NE: Univ. of Nebraska Press.

Bernaerts, Lars (2019). "The Multimodal Evocation of Minds in Audio Drama". *CounterText* 5/3: 312–331.

Bernaerts, Lars, Jarmila Mildorf, eds. (2021). *Audionarratology: Lessons from Radio Drama*. Columbus, OH: Ohio State Univ. Press.

Bolter, Jay David, Richard Grusin (1999). *Remediation: Understanding New Media*. Cambridge, MA: MIT Press.

Doležel, Lubomír (1976). "Narrative Modalities". *Journal of Literary Semantics* 5: 5–14.
Drakakis, John (1981). *British Radio Drama.* Cambridge: CUP.
Fischer, Kurt Eugen (1964). *Das Hörspiel: Form und Funktion.* Stuttgart: A. Kröner.
Fisher, Marc (2009). *Capitalist Realism: Is There no Alternative?* Winchester and Washington, DC: Zero Books.
Geeraerts, Jef (1970). *Concerto.* Brussels: VRT. Unpublished radio play script.
Geeraerts, Jef (2009). *Muziek & emotie.* Amsterdam: Meulenhoff/Manteau.
Geeraerts, Jef, Jos Joos (1970). *Concerto.* Brussels: VRT. First broadcast 15/11/1970. Radio play.
Geeraerts, Jef, Willem Tollenaar (1970). *Concerto.* Hilversum: KRO. Radio play.
Genette, Gérard (1972/1980). *Narrative Discourse.* Jane E. Lewin, transl. Oxford: Basil Blackwell.
Hallett, Wolfgang (2015). "A Methodology of Intermediality in Literary Studies". Gabriele Rippl, ed. *Handbook of Intermediality: Literature – Image – Sound – Music.* Berlin: De Gruyter. 605–618.
Hand, Richard J., Mary Traynor (2011). *The Radio Drama Handbook: Audio Drama in Practice and Context.* London: Continuum.
Hertz, Erich, Jeffrey Roessner (2014). "Introduction". *Write in Tune: Contemporary Music in Fiction.* London: Bloomsbury. 1–16.
Huwiler, Elke (2005a). *Erzähl-Ströme im Hörspiel: Zur Narratologie der elektroakustischen Kunst.* Paderborn: Mentis.
Huwiler, Elke (2005b). "Storytelling by Sound: A Theoretical Frame for Radio Drama Analysis". *The Radio Journal* 3/1: 45–59.
Kita, Caroline (2021). "Simultaneity and the Soundscapes of Audio Fiction". Lars Bernaerts, Jarmila Mildorf, eds. *Audionarratology: Lessons from Radio Drama.* Columbus, OH: Ohio State Univ. Press. 101–117.
Mildorf, Jarmila (2019). "Aural Worldmaking: Introduction". *CounterText* 5/3: 290–293.
Mildorf, Jarmila, Till Kinzel, eds. (2016a). *Audionarratology. Interfaces of Sound and Narrative.* Berlin: De Gruyter.
Mildorf, Jarmila, Till Kinzel (2016b). "Audionarratology: Prolegomena to a Research Paradigm Exploring Sound and Narrative". Jarmila Mildorf, Till Kinzel, eds. *Audionarratology: Interfaces of Sound and Narrative.* Berlin: De Gruyter. 1–26.
Mildorf, Jarmila, Till Kinzel (2017). "Narrating Sounds: Introduction to the Forum". *Partial Answers* 15/1: 61–67.
Morson, Gary Saul (1998). "Sideshadowing and Tempics". *New Literary History* 29/4: 599–624.
Pettman, Dominic (2017). *Sonic Intimacy: Voice, Species, Technics (Or, How to Listen to the World).* Stanford, CA: Stanford Univ. Press.
Saunders, James (2009 online). "Interview with Antoine Bueger". http://www.james-saunders.com/interview-with-antoine-beuger/ [02/06/2021].

Schmedes, Götz (2002). *Medientext Hörspiel: Einsätze einer Hörspielsemiotik am Beispiel der Radioarbeiten von Alfred Behrens*. Münster: Waxmann.

Sterne, Jonathan (2003). *The Audible Past: Cultural Origins of Sound Reproduction*. Durham, NC: Duke Univ. Press.

Thon, Jan-Noël (2016). *Transmedial Narratology and Contemporary Media Culture*. Lincoln, NE: Univ. of Nebraska Press.

Van Puymbroeck, Birgit (2019). "'Magie der verbeelding!' Louis MacNeice' *The Dark Tower* en Edward Sackville-Wests *The Rescue* op de Vlaamse radio". Lars Bernaerts, Siebe Bluijs, eds. *Luisterrijk der letteren: Hoorspel en literatuur in Nederland en Vlaanderen*. Ghent: Academia Press. 245–262.

Vriezen, Samuel (2017a). *Schade*. Hilversum: VPRO. Unpublished radio play script.

Vriezen, Samuel (2017b). "Meerstemmig, ongelijktijdig. Tien variaties op geen begin". *nY* 34: 19–34.

Vriezen, Samuel, Hanneke Hendrix (2017). *Schade*. Hilversum: VPRO. 16 December. Radio play.

Weiss, Allen S. (1995). "Preface: Radio Phantasms, Phantasmic Radio". *Phantasmic Radio*. Durham, NC: Duke Univ. Press. 1–8.

Whitehead, Gregory (1992). "Out of the Dark: Notes on the Nobodies of Radio Art". Douglas Kahn, Gregory Whitehead, eds. *Wireless Imagination: Sound, Radio, and the Avant-Garde*. Cambridge, MA: MIT Press. 253–264.

Wolf, Werner (2015). "Literature and Music: Theory". Gabriele Rippl, ed. *Handbook of Intermediality: Literature – Image – Sound – Music*. Berlin: De Gruyter: 459–474.

CHAPTER 11

Functions of Music in the 1992 German Radio Play Adaptation of J.R.R. Tolkien's *The Lord of the Rings*

Jarmila Mildorf

Abstract

Drawing from research on music in radio drama and on audionarratology, this chapter discusses various functions of music in the German radio play adaptation of J.R.R. Tolkien's *The Lord of the Rings*. Composed by Peter Zwetkoff, the music does not function as a simple backdrop to the unfolding storyworld but actively participates in the construction of plot, suspense, characters, settings, moods and overall narrative coherence. Zwetkoff's special musical style is contextualised with reference to developments in music (*Neue Musik*) and radio art experiments in Germany.

J.R.R. Tolkien's *The Lord of the Rings* trilogy (1954a/1991a, 1954b/1991b, 1955/1991c) is beloved by fans of fantasy literature and many others and has consequently attracted not only a wide readership worldwide but also extensive scholarly attention. A subsection of Tolkien scholarship has focused on music in his works (see, for example, Eden 2014; Flieger 2005; Jorgensen 2006; Steimel and Schneidewind 2010). This is hardly surprising given the fact that Tolkien's mythological storyworlds are informed by the medieval "music of the spheres" concept (Larsen 2010) and are replete with songs and ditties[1] that are derived from folk tunes as well as Gregorian chant (cf. Eden 2014: 511). Less attention has been given to how this music is actualised in transmedial adaptations of Tolkien's text or even how music more generally is used in these contexts (see, however, Adams 2002; Arnold 2017; Young 2007). In this chapter, I will focus on the German radio play adaptation of Tolkien's trilogy, *Der Herr der Ringe*, and look more closely at which functions music fulfils in this adaptation.

In late 1991 and early 1992, the Westdeutscher Rundfunk (WDR) and the Südwestdeutscher Rundfunk (SWR) together produced Peter Steinbach's radio

---

1 For a list of the songs presented in *The Lord of the Rings*, see Jorgensen (2006: 3).

play adaptation of *The Lord of the Rings*, which was directed by Bernd Lau and first broadcast in 30 instalments between January and April 1992. At 756 minutes in total, this is one of Germany's longest radio play productions, and it is also credited with being its first digital radio play (cf. Lücke 2011: 15). The music for this production was composed by Peter Zwetkoff (1925–2012),[2] who was awarded several radio art prizes in his lifetime, among them the *Hörspielpreis der Kriegsblinden* (Radio Play Prize of the War Blind) and the *Prix Italia* (Italian television, radio-broadcasting and website award; see De Benedictis 2020). The music is particularly impressive for its sheer range of different styles. Employing, among other things, choral, symphonic and vocal music,[3] the radio play anticipates the monumental quality that the film music was to display in the early 2000s. At the same time, unusual and unexpected musical phrases that shift back and forth between atmospheric sound tapestry and structured sound remind one of the experiments of the 'new music' of the early twentieth century, which sought to renew musical patterns and sounds by exploring their limits (see Bekker 1923/2014; Blumröder 1981). And it has to be noted that experimentation with sounds and music was already present in radio play or sound art productions in Germany in the late 1920s, e.g., in Walter Ruttmann's *Weekend* (1930) or Fritz Walter Bischoff's audiosymphony ("Hörsymphonie") *Hallo! Hier Welle Erdball* (1928; literally *Hello! Radio Wave Globe Here*) – that is, long before the New Radio Play (*Neues Hörspiel*) undertook such experiments. However, these early examples only began to impact on mainstream radio drama via a detour through Pierre Schaeffer's *musique concrète*, the programmes of the Club d'Essai and the development of electronic music (see Döhl 1986). In that sense, Zwetkoff's work can be said to follow a long radio-artistic as well as musical tradition in Germany. His radio play music refuses to be digested easily or to be entirely relegated to the background. Instead, it can be shown to fulfil numerous narrative functions, which I will focus on in this chapter, using audionarratology as my theoretical-analytical toolkit.

---

2   I thank the staff, notably Tanja Hofer, at the Brenner Archive in Innsbruck, which holds Zwetkoff's legacy, for giving me access to the original musical score for this radio play production. I will say more about the score below.

3   Gregor Arnold (2017: 3), in his excellent bachelor's thesis on the music used in the first 14 instalments of this radio play production, begins his typology of motifs and themes by simply distinguishing between songs and instrumental pieces. He also generally stresses the difference between motifs, i.e., fixed musical units that recur over the course of the radio play, and themes, which may entail several motifs and structurally go beyond those smaller units (ibid.). Since my focus lies more strongly on analysing the narrative functions of the music, I will not always make those musicological distinctions.

Audionarratology as a disciplinary project aims at elucidating the ways in which sounds – including voices, noises, music, silence and the various means of electro-acoustically manipulating them – intersect with narrative structures and functions in genres and media that have a strong auditory channel or are even exclusively auditory in nature (see Mildorf and Kinzel 2016, 2017; Mildorf 2019; Bernaerts and Mildorf 2021). Radio drama, as a narrative-mimetic genre in which the story unfolds only when we listen to it, is an excellent testing ground for audionarratological enquiry.

1 Functions of Music in Radio Plays

When thinking about music in radio plays, one obvious analogy is music in film, which has hitherto been given much more scholarly attention. After all, radio drama and film music have historically cross-fertilised one another in manifold ways – a fact sometimes overlooked by radio drama scholars. Thus, radio producers like Kurt Weill, Hans Flesch, Alfred Braun and others drew analogies among radio, music and film in their theoretical reflections, while Ruttmann resorted to his experience as film maker when creating *Weekend* (see Döhl 1986).

Film composers use a variety of techniques to make the music speak to the visual channel in film (see Kloppenburg 2000, 2012a, 2012b). For one thing, they can create points of synchrony between visual content and music, e.g., when the dropping down of an item onto the floor is simultaneously accompanied by an equally 'banging' musical sound. This kind of synchronous support of the visuals through music is achieved through the *technique of underscoring*. The *mood technique*, by contrast, is used to musically support the emotional or expressive content of a film scene. Music then typically underlines characters' feelings or the portrayed atmosphere more generally. Finally, the *motif technique* assigns recurring musical themes to specific characters or moments in a film.

In terms of functions, the motif technique can be said to largely assume *dramaturgical functions* in the sense that it guides viewers through the film by making them recognise visual material and their attendant musical motifs. The dramaturgical function includes characterisation as well as the building up of suspense, for example. Film music's *expressive function* intensifies our perception of and emotional response to what we are presented with in a film by underlining emotional content. The *syntactic function* is a largely structural function in that it helps segment a film's plot into scenes by offering transitions or sharp contrasts. It is also pivotal in making viewers understand changes in viewpoint, for example. In principle, these methods and functions also apply to music in radio drama. However, radio drama music is arguably different to the extent that the visual channel is entirely missing, or at least visual scenes are only created in our imagination. Music can be said to belong to the primary sensory channel in radio drama, the auditory channel. Therefore, in supporting the narrative on the sonic level, music in radio drama may play a much more central role when it comes to the various functions postulated for film music.

A typology of forms and functions specifically geared towards describing music in radio art, including radio drama and radio operas, is offered by Angela Ida De Benedictis in her study *Radiodramma e arte radiofonica* (2004). De Benedictis starts her typology by distinguishing between music that is an integral part of the radio play script and is therefore predetermined by the author and/ or radio play adapter, and music that is subsequently integrated in the radio play during production (97). Radio play music can be *pre-scripted* (and hence also prescribed) in the sense that a musical score exists. As Mechtild Hobl-Friedrich (1991: 75) points out, the music for a radio play may have been composed expressly for that purpose (original music) or some other sheet music is used.[4] The music may be *pre-recorded* and the vocal track may then be underlaid with the musical track. Music may also be *performed extempore* during the recording or the live performance of a radio play. De Benedictis distinguishes among eight different functions of radio play music (cf. 2004: 99–150):

1. Music may mark the beginning and the end of a radio play ("di apertura o di chiusura"). An example – albeit not one mentioned by De Benedictis – is the typical theme tune accompanying radio shows such as the *Suspense* series on America's Golden Age radio. Arguably, the main function of such music is to make the show easily recognisable and to alert listeners, who may be engaged in some other activity, so they can turn up the volume of their radios just on time.
2. Inside the radio play, music also assumes structuring functions: it may mark separations between or transitions across scenes ("sipario, cesura, stacco"). Thus, depending on which scene the music belongs to in a sequence of scenes, it may mark the end of a preceding scene before the new one starts (with or without music), or it may be used to signal the beginning of a new scene. It may also belong to the ending of the previous and the beginning of the subsequent scene, thus indicating a connection between these scenes. If the music stands alone between two

---

4   Needless to say, commissioning music for a radio play production is more costly. In this regard, it is remarkable that the WDR and SWR expended the money for engaging a composer, whose unique and tailor-made musical score thus gains even more in significance.

scenes, i.e., there is no overlap with the respective verbal parts, De Benedictis assigns to the music the function of a *caesura* (cf. ibid.: 106). Music may also fade into another auditory mode, e.g., sound, and this change in turn may indicate the beginning of something new (cf. ibid.: 112). De Benedictis furthermore points out that music used as a marker of a scene change can gradually assume other functions such as commenting on or amplifying the presented action (cf. ibid.: 109; see also below). This shows that the respective functions need not be discrete categories but often overlap or merge into one another.

3. When music is used as a background ("sottofondo"), De Benedictis argues, it is of such a quality that it does not distract listeners but still manages to subtly influence them as regards their perceptions of the presented action (cf. ibid.: 116). Background music may underlie the dialogue or moments of narratorial intervention, i.e., voice-over narration, and here assume signalling functions as well as the function of indicating a specific time and place (cf. ibid.: 117).

4. Music may also offer a contextual commentary, descriptive amplification or an emotional counterpoint to what is presented in the radio play's storyworld ("commento contestuale, amplificazione descrittiva, contrapunto emotivo"). By also 'interpreting' the presented content of a radio play, music operates as another expressive layer that can influence listeners (ibid.: 117). Of course, terms like 'commentary' or 'interpretation' are merely metaphorical here. Music as a sequence of tones that are brought into relationship to one another does not per se 'talk about' anything. It is essentially non-referential (cf. Wolf 2002: 78). However, listeners may still feel cued into understanding musical sequences in narrative terms (cf. ibid.: 94), and the experience of listening to music and of having emotional responses to it could be said to correlate with Fludernik's (1996) concept of experientiality, thus sharing a key narrative feature (cf. Kraemer 2015: 232). Kalinak (cf. 2010: 4) also attests for film music that it has the potential to control narrative connotations regarding characters and other storyworld elements and to thus create emotional resonance between viewers and the film's images.

5. The fifth function De Benedictis ascribes to music in radio drama is that it can be intradiegetic, thus belonging immanently to the presented action ("musica intradiegetica e/o immanente all'azione"). For example, characters may be singing or playing music or music may be part of a situational context such as a ball; at any rate, music will be emanating from a source inside the presented storyworld.

6–8. Whether intradiegetic or extradiegetic, music may evoke or help one identify characters, emotions and ideas ("identificativa di personaggi, sentimenti, idee"), levels of action and narration ("identificativa per il riconoscimento dei piani dell'azione o della narrazione"), epochs and places ("stilizzazione per il riconoscimento di luoghi o epoche").

Finally, De Benedictis briefly discusses sounds ("I rumore") as another auditory channel. As she points out, sounds can be original or artificially produced, and they can be said to assume indexical functions to the extent that listeners are forced to think about the sources from which they emanate (cf. ibid. 148). In connection to music in radio drama, it is also important to remember that music may imitate or evoke sounds (cf. Hobl-Friedrich 1991: 76), such as, for example, the movement of oceanic waves, the singing of birds, etc. – a point which is also central to programme music. In radio plays, this propensity can contribute significantly to the narrativisation of music or, conversely, to the co-creation of the audiophonic narrative through music.

Since De Benedictis discusses her eight functions side by side in one chapter (cf. 2004: 131–147), one could object that she does not sufficiently distinguish between functions that are related to the structural level of the narrative and those that are related to its contents. She also mixes functions connected to the presentation of characters' interior states or consciousness with those that are at the heart of the creation of an exteriorised storyworld. Still, in sum, these are useful functional categories to look at and to refine in an audionarratological framework.

Elke Huwiler (2005: 61), a pioneer of radio drama narratology, builds on the study by Mechtild Hobl-Friedrich (1991) and helpfully applies the terms "syntactic" and "semantic" functions in connection with the different narrative levels of *story* and *discourse*.[5] *Syntactic* functions of music encompass the segmenting and signalling functions mentioned above while *semantic* functions contribute to the meaning(s) of radio drama storyworlds. Semantic functions can have a supportive or 'accompanying' role comparable to underscoring in film (see above), or they can expand on and move beyond the meanings created through other semiotic channels (Hobl-Friedrich and Huwiler call this the "erweiternde Funktion"). Hobl-Friedrich (1991: 76) counts among the *supportive semantic functions* of music those that illustrate or characterise an aspect of the narrative[6] or that stand in as a cipher ("chiffre") for this aspect.

---

5 The *story* level roughly refers to what is presented in a narrative while the *discourse* level captures how the story is told; see Chatman (1978) for a more finely grained typology.
6 Chatman (1978: 19) distinguishes among "events" (actions and happenings) and "story existents" (characters and setting).

By contrast, the more independent subfunctions that music can assume in the category of *expansive or extended functions* include anticipation, commentary, irony, contrast, counterpoint and defamiliarisation (cf. ibid.: 78–90). We shall see that these functions play a big role in Zwetkoff's radio play music as well.

In using the terms "syntactic" and "semantic", Hobl-Friedrich and Huwiler obviously draw on an analogy between music as a sign system and that of language – an analogy which, as we saw, is also common among film studies scholars. Given the fundamental differences between music and language that I pointed out above, however, one may object to the use of these terms because it is ultimately also metaphorical. Furthermore, the boundaries between syntactic and semantic functions need not necessarily be as clear-cut in actual practice as the dichotomy suggests. For example, if different musical backgrounds are used to indicate other locations or moments in time in a radio play, the function is both syntactic (since the music marks a shift in scenes) and semantic (since the respective kinds of music are likely to correspond qualitatively to the times or locations they indicate). Like any typological categories, these terms also have their limits. Still, they are useful starting points and offer common ground for analytical discussions.

From an audionarratological perspective, it is desirable to not only distinguish between musical functions at the levels of story and discourse but, even prior to that, also between *extradiegetic* and *intradiegetic* music,[7] i.e., music which is external to the presented storyworld or which constitutes an integral part of it. Furthermore, it may be interesting to look at the question to what extent and how music may participate in a radio play's *focalisation* or perspective-taking (see Bluijs 2021).

I will now turn to the various functions that music assumes in the radio play *Der Herr der Ringe*.

2   Music in Bernd Lau's *Der Herr der Ringe*

Zwetkoff's music in the German radio play adaptation of *The Lord of the Rings* largely squares with the functions of music in radio drama identified by De Benedictis, Hobl-Friedrich and Huwiler, but it also illustrates nicely that the picture is often actually more complicated, as I will discuss in my analyses. What I refer to here as the radio play's musical 'score' is actually a conglomeration of individual sheets of music containing the various motifs, themes,

---

7 Alternatively, the terms *non-diegetic* and *diegetic* can be used here.

songs and instrumental pieces. They are contained in four boxes in the Brenner Archive at the University of Innsbruck. Zwetkoff numbered those pieces, but the score is unfortunately not in chronological order, and apart from individual clean copies, it contains many handwritten sheets of music as well as scrap notes that are barely legible because the writing has faded. An inventory of the materials also indicates that some numbers are missing.

The instrumentation is interesting as it not only envisages regular orchestral wind, string and percussion instruments but also greater variety among the percussion instruments, including, for example, sand blocks, woodblocks, temple blocks, metal sheets, marimbas, crotales, toulouhou cicadas, glockenspiel, claves, timbales, congas, bongo drums and tom-toms, as well as many darker-toned instrumental woodwind and brass instruments such as bass and contrabass clarinets, bass trombones, bass trumpets, contrabass horns, basset horns and others. This instrumentation already indicates that for Zwetkoff different sound effects were also an integral part of the musical repertoire.[8]

2.1 *Intradiegetic Music: Scenic Underscoring, Characterisation and Focalisation*

Looking at the different narrative levels at which music is employed in the radio play, one can start by distinguishing between intradiegetic and extradiegetic levels, i.e., inside or outside the presented storyworld, as I pointed out above. On the intradiegetic level music is used, for example, to realise characters' singing and revelling. Thus, we hear Gandalf sing an old song while the fellows are travelling on horseback. The song remains in the background while the narrator tells us about Pippin's feelings at that moment (CD 8, track 3, 04' 22"–4' 33"). In the subsequent dialogue, the two characters talk about which kind of song Gandalf just sang; thus, the verbal description doubles the action of singing. Gandalf explains that his song was about the Palantíri, the Seeing-stones that made it possible to look far back in time. What is evoked here is obviously the role of songs in commemorating and preserving the legendary and even mythical past, which was important in ancient and medieval musical traditions and survives to this day in folklore.

What is most striking in this scene is that a discrepancy emerges because the rhythm of the horse hoof sounds that underlie the entire scene does not

---

[8] For Zwetkoff, music always fulfilled a 'higher' function, as the dramaturge of *Der Herr der Ringe*, Oliver Sturm, told Gregor Arnold in an interview. Apparently, Zwetkoff initially did not want to accept this commission because he considered fantasy literature as 'low' entertainment. Only when he learned more about Tolkien's work did he change his mind (cf. Arnold 2017: 5).

match the pace of the dialogue nor that of the singing. The sounds strongly suggest galloping horses, and it is unimaginable that the fellows could engage in a dialogue or Gandalf sing a simple tune as calmly and easily as that without being out of breath while riding at that pace. When the Elves sing later in the radio play (CD 2, track 5, 02' 48"–03' 29"), their song also remains in the background, and the music's mysterious quality marks them as mystical creatures. This is further underlined by the sound tapestry at this point, which involves the use of high pipe tones and softly jingling percussion sounds that likewise create a 'magical' atmosphere. This example shows how intradiegetic music and song can also assume the function of characterisation.

Most of the time, intradiegetic music is recognisable because it is additionally mentioned in the dialogue or in the narratorial commentary, for example, when the narrator says that Sauron's army had the horns pipe up and they can then actually be heard, even though in a distorted sound quality (CD 10, track 9, 00' 52"–01' 01"). The music then has an illustrative function. Sometimes, however, it is not so easy to determine whether the music presented is intradiegetic or not. For example, when the fellows reach the white ladder that leads up the tree where Celeborn and Galadriel have their Elven realm, Lórien, trumpets start to play something that sounds like an alarum or fanfare (CD5, track 3, 03' 20"). However, it remains unclear whether these sounds occur inside the storyworld and are meant to invite the travellers in, or whether they signal on an extradiegetic level that the fellows are about to enter a new phase of their adventure. Possibly, they do both since the novel at this point says that "the Elf-wardens then blew a clear note on a small horn" (Tolkien 1954a/1991a: 460). This shows that music in radio drama may even cut across the two narrative levels of 'inside' and 'outside' the storyworld.

Similarly, when the fellows are at Elrond's house, where Frodo meets Bilbo again, one scene opens with an operatic-sounding song sung by an extremely high soprano voice (CD 4, track 4, 00' 00"–00' 59"). The song gradually merges with and continues alongside the narrator's voice, which tells us that Frodo observes how close Aragorn and Arwen, Elrond's daughter, are and how Frodo himself was fascinated, if not spellbound, by her glance. Closer inspection of the score reveals that this song is not separately listed as such but is in fact a slightly adapted vocal rendition of motif 58, written for flute (see Figure 11.1).[9]

The music's style is difficult to pin down. It moves across a broad vocal range, up and down, and then hovers on very high soprano notes, up to $C_6\#$

---

9 Arnold (cf. 2017: 74) overlooks this fact in his chronological list of leitmotifs (Appendix D), where he enters the song simply with a question mark, indicating that he did not identify the melody in the score.

FIGURE 11.1   Excerpt from motif 58

and even beyond – a real challenge for any soprano singer. The first sequence of an arpeggiated *a* flat major seventh chord reminds one of a similar sequence in the opening of the song "I Could Have Danced Tonight" sung by the protagonist Eliza in *My Fair Lady*. However, the melody then becomes increasingly indistinct, moving along semitone and whole-tone steps with occasional jumps to $C_6\#$ and then even D_6 and E_6 until the opening sequence is repeated again in the end. The tones produced in those lofty heights and containing so many dissonances once again give the impression of something mystical or fairylike. The music thus clearly also contributes to the overall atmosphere of the setting at that point in the radio play.

This motif is already played shortly beforehand when Frodo sees Arwen for the very first time and is quite apparently smitten with her (CD 4, track 3, 00' 37"–01' 25"), as noted before. The motif may thus be tied to Arwen as a character or to Frodo's perception of her. In the latter case, one could argue that the music assumes a focalising function, allowing us insight into Frodo's perception as well as emotional state at this point. There is no clear indication whether the song performed by the female singer merely eases the listener into the scene on an extradiegetic level or whether it represents a performance that Elrond's court and family as well as their guests are listening to at the intradiegetic level of the storyworld. The latter interpretation seems plausible, as Gandalf explained earlier that the Hall of Fire in Elrond's house was always full of music and storytelling (CD 4, track 3, 01' 47"–01' 49"). It is even possible that Arwen herself entertains the elves' guests by singing, given that the same motif was used earlier for her first appearance. Still, listeners cannot resolve this ambiguity.

2.2   *Extradiegetic Music: Sequencing, Bracketing, Cohesion*

On the extradiegetic level, the music supports the sequencing of scenes by marking the shifts between narratorial and scenic-mimetic levels. It thus assumes syntactic functions. For example, at the beginning of episode 28, dark music (motif 68 in the score) accompanies the narrator's summary of how the War of the Ring has ended and which casualties it has produced (CD 10, track 1, 00' 00"–01' 09"). By contrast, the subsequent dialogue between Merry and Pippin, who meet again after a lengthy separation, is without any music. When the narrator resumes his narrative frame text the music sets in again (ibid., 02' 25"), deep and slow tones played by a contrabass tuba that move in a very small range, first up half a tone, then back to the base tone, then up one tone and back again, then up three semitones to the minor third, and back to the base tone, returning up to the second again, where the sequence pauses before it restarts (see Figure 11.2).

The music underlines the characters' walk that was made heavy by the experience of the war. Interestingly, this music is repeated over and over again throughout the entire radio play – significantly at moments when the journey of the fellowship becomes toilsome and the fellows become weary and disheartened. Here, one can see the use of the leitmotif technique, where music functions as a cipher. Even though the music in this case does not signify the same event/action or the same character, it clearly points to a similar mood or emotional quality underlying the situations depicted.

Music can also function as a structural bracket in the sense that it signals continuity between two moments or that two scenes belong together. Thus, the transition from episode 16 to 17 is marked as a continuous one because, for just over 50 seconds, exactly the same musical sequence involving violins and flutes is played at the end of episode 16 (CD 6, track 5, 03' 50"–04' 45") as well as at the beginning of episode 17 (CD 6, track 6, 00' 00"–00' 53"). This sequence is also closely associated with Gandalf: in this case, the music marks

FIGURE 11.2   Excerpt from motif 68

the reappearance of the wizard after the other fellows have believed him to be dead. While the music accompanies the characters' dialogue during their reunion at the end of episode 16, it forms the background to the narrator's summarising commentary at the beginning of episode 17. Despite the difference in structural levels (mimetic scene vs. narratorial frame text), the continuity in music suggests that there is a linked narrative sequence that moves across episode boundaries.

Narrative continuity and cohesion are also established through the use of musical themes as leitmotifs, as mentioned above. Thus, there are distinct musical sequences when the radio play introduces women and the theme of love, employing violins and flutes – that is, essentially instruments in the higher tone ranges. An example is the moment when Éowyn, who brings in some wine, exchanges deep glances with Aragorn and their hands touch (e.g., CD 6, track 13, 00' 47"–01' 06"). By contrast, the dark riders that serve Sauron, also called Ringwraiths or Nazgûl, are accompanied by a suitably dark theme which suggests danger (motifs 21 a/b/c, 21 d/e/f). Here, four double basses play very deep tones, for example, when Frodo sees one of the dark riders for the first time (e.g., CD 2, track 4, 00' 33"–01' 49"). This shows that emotions can be evoked by means of specific instrumentation as well as distinct musical sequences. The main function of such leitmotifs is of course to ensure recognition on the listener's part, even though one may not necessarily be able to identify precisely what the music signifies. As Arnold (2017: 25) points out, the musical sequence of the Nazgûl motif is hard to make out when listening to the radio play because the tones are so deep. The impression created is that of continuous grumbling.

One of the few leitmotifs that are reserved for one thing only is the ring motif. Unlike in the film music, where Howard Shore composed four musical themes surrounding the ring – "the history of the ring", "the evil of the ring", "the seduction of the ring" and "the fate of the ring" (Adams 2002: 14–21) – the ring is denoted by only one short tune played by a glockenspiel and crotales in the radio play (motif 7a/b; e.g., CD 1, track 6, 01' 21") and often recurs only as a short sequence of chiming sounds ('ping ping').

This is interesting insofar as the metallic sound quality would suggest that the ring is clanking against another metal object or is falling onto a hard ground. However, this is of course not necessarily the case, as the ring is mostly simply in Frodo's pockets or in his hands. Arnold (2017: 18) suggests that the ring motif points to both the ring's material quality and the danger emanating from it. It can thus be said to serve an *indexing* function.[10] This indicates

---

10   Arnold does not use that term, but I think it is useful in this case.

FUNCTIONS OF MUSIC IN THE 1992 GERMAN RADIO PLAY 287

FIGURE 11.3   Excerpt from motif 7a/b

that radio play sounds and music need not be 'realistic' or 'referential' (even if only metaphorically) at all but rather have to be evocative or suggestive to alert listeners to what is going on, which may sometimes happen at a subconscious level only.[11]

2.3   *Words and Music: Complementation, Amplification and Extension*

As mentioned above, radio play music often complements narrators' verbal commentary and amplifies their descriptions; likewise, it may amplify

---

11   This is analogous to sound perception in radio drama more generally. It is, for example, well known that, before original sounds could easily be recorded and reproduced, many sounds were created by alternative means in radio studios. The best example is the creation of horse hoof sounds by clacking together coconut shells. There is obviously no 'referentiality' in the strict sense of the word here, nor even indexicality, because the thing that produces the sound is not what the sound ultimately represents. However, it is the perceived similarity and the subsequent evocation of a particular sound source that become important here.

or underline what happens or is mentioned in the characters' dialogue. For example, when Frodo talks to the Elf Gildor during the time when the Hobbits rest in the Elves' haunts, their dialogue is accompanied by the Elves' singing in the background. At one point in the dialogue, however, namely when Frodo expresses his worries about Gandalf, who has gone away, and when Gildor warns Frodo not to meddle with wizards' business, the quality of the singing changes significantly in that it becomes more piercing and siren-like (CD 2, track 8, 01' 00"–01' 47"), thus underlining Gildor's warning as well as Frodo's sense of unease. Even though the music is technically intradiegetic, it assumes an essentially extradiegetic or even authorial narrative function by supporting or amplifying another narrative channel, in this case the dialogue. Usually, this kind of amplification or extension of the spoken word is situated on the extradiegetic level of the musical channel. For example, during the War of the Ring, which is aptly accompanied by disharmonious and noisy orchestral music, the arrival of the eagles is signalled by the music even before Gandalf shouts out "Die Adler, sie kommen! Die Adler kommen!" ('The eagles are coming!') (CD 10, track 12, 00' 37"–00' 42"). The music already changes at 00' 36" with the onset of clarinets playing ascending chromatic scales. The upward movement in the music can be said to draw our 'inner eyes', to use that metaphor, up to the skies where the eagles can be 'seen'. The music – on account of its own sonic propensity to move in space – may thus also assume an indexical function in the imagined storyworld and may contribute significantly to listeners' experience of this storyworld's spatial dimensions.

That music supports the mood suggested by the narratorial commentary and thus constitutes the *mood technique* mentioned above is a very common feature in radio plays, and *Der Herr der Ringe*, too, abounds in examples of this audiophonic practice. Thus, mostly dark music underlines the dreariness and danger involved in many of the situations the fellows have to go through. I already pointed to the instrumentation across the score that involves many very deep-sounding instruments. The more interesting examples, however, are those moments when the music in fact counters the narratorial commentary, thus offering another level of communication that conveys another message to the listeners. A good example of this can be found when the Hobbits spend some time in Lórien. The narrator tells us how peaceful everything is: the sun keeps shining, and even when it rains occasionally everything emerges from it pure and fresh. The place seems like Paradise. The music, however, does not correspond to this idyllic image (CD 5, track 4, 01' 01"–01' 15"). Quite on the contrary, the unidentifiable monotonous tones played and held by the wind instruments suggest danger and thus create suspense: what is to come?

Likewise, when Elrond selects the nine fellows that are to accompany Frodo on his mission the music dramatises his speech by offering rather unnerving disharmonies that move through the brass instrument sections of the orchestra from higher-pitched to lower-pitched ones and then ending in a clamorous banging sound of the cymbals followed by the gong (CD 4, track 7, 01' 29"–01' 44"). It is almost as if the music, unlike the narratorial frame text, already anticipates a tortuous and dangerous journey. In narratological terms, we could say that the music *foreshadows* the fellowship's future. This is what Hobl-Friedrich (1991) and Huwiler (2005) capture with the term 'expansive' or 'extended function' ("erweiternde Funktion"). The music seems to be quite independent of the verbal narrative at this point and in fact contributes its own information or meaning to it. From an audionarratological perspective, one could even say that the music here assumes a role akin to that of the narrator.

3   Conclusion

This last example once again indicates that the ways in which music is employed in radio drama can in fact be quite complex. Music as one semiotic channel may independently signal what the verbal channel does not or not yet reveal to the listening audience. Since musical form can be suggestive of actions or events (think of the flying eagles) and can be affective when it is used as a mood technique, it offers listeners an additional mental scaffold whereby to create a storyworld in their minds. I used examples from different parts of the radio play production to illustrate various narrative functions, among them syntactic functions such as linking or separating scenes and sequences and establishing cohesion. Even though listeners may not necessarily remember exactly when they already heard a certain tune, the recall and echo structures of music will still make it possible for them to draw at least vague associations and to form a 'bigger picture' of the storyworld. Semantic functions such as characterising moments, places and personae in the radio play were shown to sometimes overlap with syntactic or structural functions.

At the most abstract level, I argue, the music in *Der Herr der Ringe* helps listening audiences to make sense of and gain access to an otherwise potentially unwieldy radio play and to ensure listener engagement beyond the words spoken by characters or narrator and beyond the story's actions made audible. However, one clearly has to distinguish between the experience the original radio audience had when listening to the radio play in instalments and listeners today, who can resort to the recorded version and re-listen to sequences at will. The latter form of listening makes a more analytical approach possible (cf. Mildorf 2021: 131f.).

The scores for *Der Herr der Ringe* give an impression of the diversity of Zwetkoff's musical art and of his attempt not to use music as a mere prop or background but to leave it its own artistic expression. The fact that the music often strikes one as dissonant and experimental may be a sign of Zwetkoff's own artistic predilections and clearly distinguishes his scores from those of the film trilogy. Various musical and sound art traditions in Germany, as delineated briefly in the beginning of this chapter, can be considered predecessors of this musical style. It may ultimately also be connected to the question of genre since this kind of radio drama music with its interpretative openness seems to be congenial to representing fantasy storyworlds or, for that matter, any storyworld that cannot be grasped by means of 'realistic' parameters alone. As Reinhard Döhl (1986) puts it, drawing on a term Fritz Walter Bischoff (1929: 203) used in his dramaturgy of the radio play, music in radio drama offers a 'psychological instrumentation of the dialogical action' ("psychologische Instrumentierung der Sprachhandlung"). This is certainly also true of *Der Herr der Ringe*. Its 'psychological instrumentation' works in two interrelated ways: music, because of its affective dimension, reveals the psychological states of characters or moods of situations while also evoking emotions and moods in listeners. It thus constitutes a powerful component of radio plays worthy of close attention.

References

Adams, Doug (2002). *The Music of the Lord of the Rings Films: A Comprehensive Account of Howard Shore's Scores*. Van Nuys, CA: Alfred Music Publishing.
Arnold, Gregor (2017). *Leitmotive in der Hörspielmusik von Peter Zwetkoff zum Herr-der-Ringe-Hörspiel von 1991/2*. BA Thesis. Univ. of Tübingen. Unpublished.
Bekker, Paul (1923/2014). *Gesammelte Schriften, Vol. 3: Neue Musik*. Hildesheim: Olms.
Bernaerts, Lars, Jarmila Mildorf, eds. (2021). *Audionarratology: Lessons from Radio Drama*. Columbus, OH: Ohio State University Press.
Bischoff, Fritz Walter (1929). "Die Dramaturgie des Hörspiels". *Rundfunk Jahrbuch 1929*. 202–216.
Blujis, Siebe (2021). "Earwitnessing: Focalization in Radio Drama". Lars Bernaerts, Jarmila Mildorf, eds. *Audionarratology: Lessons from Radio Drama*. Columbus, OH: Ohio State University Press. 82–100.
Blumröder, Christoph von (1981). *Der Begriff "neue Musik" im 20. Jahrhundert*. München: Musikverlag Katzbichler.

Chatman, Seymour (1978). *Story and Discourse: Narrative Structure in Fiction and Film.* Ithaca, NY: Cornell University Press.

De Benedictis, Angela Ida (2004). *Radiodramma e arte radiofonica: storia e funzioni della musica per radio in Italia.* Torino: EDT.

De Benedictis, Angela Ida (2020). "Between Art and Promotion: The Prix Italia, Its Historical Context and Aims in the First Fifty Years 1949–1998". Jarmila Mildorf, Pim Verhulst, eds. *Radio Art and Music: Culture, Aesthetics, Politics.* Lanham, MD: Lexington. 85–97.

Döhl, Reinhard (1986 online). "Musik – Radiokunst – Hörspiel". *Inventionen'86.* https://www.inventionen.de/1986/Textbeitrag-Doehl.html [25/04/2022].

Eden, Bradford Lee (2014). "Music". Stuart D. Lee, ed. *A Companion to J. R. R. Tolkien.* London: John Wiley. 501–513.

Flieger, Verlyn (2005). *Interrupted Music: The Making of Tolkien's Mythology.* Kent, OH: Kent State University Press.

Fludernik, Monika (1996). *Towards a 'Natural' Narratology.* London: Routledge.

Hobl-Friedrich, Mechtild (1991). *Die dramaturgische Funktion der Musik im Hörspiel: Grundlagen, Analysen.* Erlangen: Univ. of Erlangen.

Huwiler, Elke (2005). *Erzähl-Ströme im Hörspiel: Zur Narratologie der elektroakustischen Kunst.* Paderborn: Mentis.

Jorgensen, Estelle Ruth (2006). "Myth, Song, and Music Education: The Case of Tolkien's *The Lord of the Rings* and Swann's *The Road Goes Ever On*". *The Journal of Aesthetic Education* 40/3: 1–21.

Kalinak, Kathryn (2010). *Film Music: A Very Short Introduction.* Oxford: OUP.

Kloppenburg, Josef, ed. (2000). *Handbuch der Musik im 20. Jahrhundert, Vol. 11: Musik multimedial: Filmmusik, Videoclip, Fernsehen.* Lilienthal: Laaber.

Kloppenburg, Josef (2012a). "Verfahren: Konzepte der Verbindung von Musik und Film". Josef Kloppenburg, ed. *Das Handbuch der Filmmusik: Geschichte – Ästhetik – Funktionalität.* Lilienthal: Laaber. 125–139.

Kloppenburg, Josef (2012b). "Funktionen der Filmmusik". Josef Kloppenburg, ed. *Das Handbuch der Filmmusik: Geschichte – Ästhetik – Funktionalität.* Lilienthal: Laaber. 139–165.

Kraemer, Florian (2015). "Raum – Perspektive – Narration: Was Gustav Mahler zur intermedialen Narrationstheorie beitragen könnte". Frédéric Döhl, Daniel Martin Feige, eds. *Musik und Narration: Philosophische und musikästhetische Perspektiven.* Bielefeld: Transcript. 227–244.

Larsen, Kristine (2010). "'Behold your Music!': The Themes of Ilúvatar, the Song of Aslan, and the Real Music of the Spheres". Heidi Steimel, Friedhelm Schneidewind, eds. *Music in Middle-earth.* Zurich/Jena: Walking Tree Publishers. 11–28.

Lücke, Frank (2011). *Vom Hörspiel zum Audiobook: Die mediale Entwicklung im 20. Jahrhundert.* Hamburg: Diplomica.

Mildorf, Jarmila (2021). "'Ja, ja, so schön klingt das Schreckliche': An Audionarratological Analysis of Andreas Ammer and FM Einheit's *Lost & Found: Das Paradies*". Inge Arteel, Lars Bernaerts, Siebe Bluijs, Pim Verhulst, eds. *Tuning in to the Neo-Avant-Garde: Experimental Radio Plays in the Postwar Period*. Manchester: Manchester Univ. Press. 128–149.

Mildorf, Jarmila, ed. (2019). *Aural World-Making: Audionarratological Approaches to Sound and Narrative*. Thematic forum published in *CounterText* 5/3.

Mildorf, Jarmila, Till Kinzel, eds. (2016). *Audionarratology: Interfaces of Sound and Narrative*. Berlin: De Gruyter.

Mildorf, Jarmila, Till Kinzel, eds. (2017). *Narrating Sounds*. Thematic forum published in *Partial Answers* 15/1.

Steimel, Heidi, Friedhelm Schneidewind, eds. (2010). *Music in Middle-earth*. Zurich/Jena: Walking Tree Publishers.

Steinbach, Peter (2001). *Der Herr der Ringe*. Radio play adaptation, directed by Bernd Lau, dramaturgy by Oliver Sturm, music by Peter Zwetkoff, performed by Ernst Schröder, Manfred Steffen, Mattias Hase, Rufus Beck and many others. First broadcast by WDR/SWR January–April, 1992. 11 CDs, der Hörverlag.

Tolkien, J.R.R. (1954a/1991a). *The Lord of the Rings, Part I: The Fellowship of the Ring*. London: Harper Collins.

Tolkien, J.R.R. (1954b/1991b). *The Lord of the Rings, Part II: The Two Towers*. London: Harper Collins.

Tolkien, J.R.R. (1955/1991c). *The Lord of the Rings, Part III: The Return of the King*. London: Harper Collins.

Wolf, Werner (2002). "Das Problem der Narrativität in Literatur, Musik und bildender Kunst". Vera Nünning, Ansgar Nünning, eds. *Erzähltheorie transgenerisch, intermedial, interdisziplinär*. Trier: WVT. 23–104.

Young, Matthew (2007). *Projecting Tolkien's Musical Worlds: A Study of Musical Affect in Howard Shore's Soundtrack to* The Lord of the Rings. Saarbrücken: AV Akademikerverlag.

CHAPTER 12

The Spy (BBC Radio 4, 2012): Creating Historical Ambiance through Music in British Radio Drama

Leslie McMurtry

Abstract

Immersion into a storyworld is important for audiences, and one way to create a sense of immersion is through the use of music. Media depictions of historical periods make powerful impressions upon audiences, and historians often contest the way history is represented in media like television and radio. Nevertheless, this chapter argues that historical ambiance created through evocative music, rather than one hundred per cent period-accurate music, both fits within the production paradigm of current BBC radio practice and economically and effectively helps immerse listeners in an 'authentic' historical storyworld. *The Spy*, a BBC *Classic Serial* from 2012 based on the 1821 novel by James Fenimore Cooper, is the case study used to illustrate this claim.

1 Introduction

The sound elements of radio drama representing a historical era are carefully constructed. They contribute, at least in part, to the aesthetic that creates the idea of a historical drama. Music in historical radio drama must also fit within medium-specific codes. When these elements come together in a convincing way, immersion in a storyworld is achieved. This phenomenon is related to the undeniable power of storytelling (see Bruner 1986; Gerrig 1993), and this is specifically the case in radio drama because a lack of visual stimulation can create a bond of intimacy between the characters presented and the listener (cf. Chignell 2009: 67) as well as reaching out to listeners' emotions and feelings (cf. Crook 1999: 61), placing the listener at the centre of the process (cf. Hand and Traynor 2011: 34). To paraphrase Busselle and Bilandzic, from nothing more than a sequence of auditory symbols "we construct worlds that are cognitively and emotionally engaging" (2008: 255).

According to Hand and Traynor, music in radio drama can act as a link, as an indicator of mood, as stylised sound effect and as indexical function (cf. 2011: 50). Indicator of mood refers mainly to the emotional tenor of a scene. Stylised sound effect uses music to punctuate a scene, as a kind of grammar rather than style or content. Music used as an indexical function is music that takes place as part of the scene. All of these functions can be used to successfully immerse a listener in a radio drama world. If music in radio drama can be used to create mood, it can also therefore be used to create the mood or impression of a historical period. Therefore, I would argue that a historical mood, rather than complete historical accuracy, is created in many radio dramas, such as BBC Radio 4's *Classic Serial* adaptation (2012) of *The Spy* (1821). To make this argument, my chapter examines the genre of the musical compositions used in *The Spy* and elucidates the production process that characterises the typical BBC radio drama 'score', which is assembled rather than specially commissioned (in contrast to conventional practice in film). Furthermore, it investigates the effects this score creates with reference to the historical period *The Spy* aims to depict, analysing the way the musical compositions holistically respond to theoretical functions of music in radio drama. A particular emphasis is placed on the music of contemporary 'indie-folk' group Fleet Foxes and how their musical compositions create historical ambiance despite their lack of obvious historical congruence.

James Fenimore Cooper's *The Spy* was the first American bestseller, the first novel about the American Revolution, the first spy novel, and the first American novel to be dramatised. Media depictions of historical periods make powerful impressions on the public imagination, with Mark Glancy noting in 2005 that students were learning more about world history from movies than from school education (cf. 537). Similarly, Aurélie Godet remarked in 2012 that HBO's *John Adams* (2008) was a "an enormously influential cultural artefact", with more than 5.5 million American viewers watching the original broadcast (cf. 79). Nevertheless, professional historians are "rarely satisfied with the results of film-makers' efforts to represent the past" (Chapman 2005: 4). Previous research into history in the media has overwhelmingly focused on audio-visual depictions rather than those on radio. Therefore, while it is difficult to speculate on the influence of historical drama on British radio listeners and how it has affected their perception of history generally, as Monk (2012) was able to chart to an extent with fans of heritage film, there is evidence that BBC Radio, and Radio 4 in particular, have been influential. For example, David Hendy cites a 1972 poll of men and women listed in *Who's Who,* many of whom considered Radio 4 more influential than Parliament or the Church of England (cf. 2007: 117). Indeed, BBC authenticity, Giddings and Selby believe, "is seldom, if ever, challenged" (2001: 199). Meanwhile, the *Classic Serial* has a long history on BBC Radio, adapting its first work in 1925, and has come to serve as an indicator of quality and prestige. Adaptations from stage and print literature have long found pride of place in BBC radio drama, with the *Classic Serial* remaining a weekly fixture of the Radio 4 schedule.

2 Media Depictions of History

Stories undoubtedly influence us. In investigating how audiences understand fictional constructions in story form, Busselle and Bilandzic claim that "[i]ndividuals construct mental models of a story from pre-existing schemas and stereotypes" (2008: 258). Audiences rely in part on what they already know to construct narratives in a fictional world which they cannot, by definition, know. With such conventions in place for historical drama, audiences must similarly work to construct worlds founded on historically-based "pre-existing schemas and stereotypes" (ibid.). Ergo, a historical drama, if effective, will clearly influence our understanding of history. With media like television and radio playing "a considerable role" in such processes, the way these media "recycle" or "recreate" the past (Giddings and Selby 2001: 204) goes a long way towards contributing to what Busselle and Bilandzic refer to as the "pre-existing schemas and stereotypes" that help convincingly immerse us in storyworlds. Nevertheless, this is where a conflict between historians and programme-makers can arise, because "[a]udiences do not necessarily make a clear distinction between factual and fictional media when acquiring historical knowledge and understanding" (Williams 2008: 19). Despite the need for pre-existing schemas and stereotypes in narrative, the relationship between conceptions of history and the necessity of the plot has long been a contested one. For example, Corinna Peniston-Bird has demonstrated that the term 'Dad's Army' for the British Home Guard during the Second World War dramatically and ubiquitously inserted itself into common parlance after the tremendously popular BBC TV comedy (1968–1977) of the same name, despite the fact that there is no evidence that the Home Guard ever referred to themselves by this term (cf. 2013: 67–69). Furthermore, James Leggott highlights the "faint alarm" engendered by the fact that viewers have taken the historical comedy *Blackadder* (BBC, 1983–1989) for real history, citing a 2011 poll of Britons which concluded that one in five viewers believed the Blackadder character to have been real (cf. 2015: 63).

As noted previously, in terms of types of media, the most critical attention has been paid to the way historical films interact with their audiences, but the terms themselves are contentious. According to Chapman, a historical film is a film about the recorded past or the past that can be known, a definition that excludes costume films, period films and heritage films (as well as adaptations). Nevertheless, even Chapman concedes that defining lines are fuzzy (cf. 2005: 4). Adaptations and 'classic' literature (analogous to period films and heritage films) are less burdened with completely accurately representing the past.

3 The Classic Serial on TV and Radio

Dramatisation of 'classic' literature appeared early on European radio, with Shakespeare plays among the earliest content on British radio (cf. McMurtry 2019: 77). By the 1950s, the *Classic Serial* on British radio was a well-established genre with customary conventions and expectations, and it was only a matter of time before this migrated to early British television. Accordingly, this form was massively influential not only in British culture but, increasingly, on a global scale. Richard Butt has argued that the *Classic Serial* is inherently a stable genre, unusually so (cf. 2012: 159), as it is essentially conservative (cf. ibid.: 163) and, unlike most other areas of adaptation studies, still revolves around notions of fidelity. However, the essentially conservative and nostalgic nature of adaptations within the *Classic Serial* mould is up for debate, and specifically in terms of radio, I would contest this reading, a view echoed by Butt (cf. 2012: 160) and Monk (cf. 2012: 154; 2015: 30).

As an inevitable consequence of storyworld transportation and immersion, "fresh generations" need to be introduced to the way media tell stories "and to the vast repertory of stories which they will need to be told" (Giddings and Selby 2001: 207). Giddings and Selby argue that, more recently, *Classic Serial* has rewritten or considerably readjusted "novels to suit the perceived and expected feminist or politically correct requirements of today" (ibid.: 191). Put less patronisingly, "the past is not only dug up, it has to be restored to life in a form which is acceptable to modern consumer taste" (ibid.: 209). British television's *Classic Serial* volume of adapted drama was considerable (cf. Butt 2012: 162), but even this cannot be matched by the radio *Classic Serial*. Under the auspices of this programme, roughly twenty new serials each year are broadcast on Radio 4. For example, in 2012, the year in which *The Spy* was broadcast, authors of adapted *Classic Serials* ranged from the relatively traditional (Trollope, Hardy, P.G. Wodehouse, Dumas) to the more surprising (Harriette Wilson, John Wyndham, Thomas Mann, Ian Rankin, John Steinbeck). This shows some parallels with the 1970s *Play for the Month* on BBC TV, whose range was considered "staggeringly broad" (Monk 2015: 36).

To return to our previous definition, the *Classic Serial* in question typically deals in texts commonly held by BBC Radio 4 listeners to be 'classics'. Arguably, the cultural expectations of the radio *Classic Serial,* therefore, demand an immersive story that may be adapted to fit the codes and conventions of radio, that is, made to fit the medium of radio. For the text to fit the *Classic Serial,* it is traditionally more likely to be set in the historical past. As in all radio, the elements available to tell the story are dialogue, sound effects (SFX), music and silence (cf. Hand and Traynor 2011: 40). For example, as Alan Beck notes, radio performance differs from theatrical, television, or film performance in that costume, blocking and physical traits cannot be used to deliver essential information about a character (cf. 1997: 79). Andrew Crisell reminds us that radio requires listeners to decode information instantaneously, since, traditionally at least, there was no pause or rewind button for radio drama (cf. 1994: 4). "Visual style" in the historical film, Chapman argues, has been emblematic of "historical verisimilitude" (2005: 2); likewise, Sarah Cardwell has suggested that classic-novel television adaptations are noted for their "sumptuous, beautiful, pictorial images" strung together "smoothly" (2002: 80). Visual style and pictorial images are not available to radio. Butt argues that indicators of "classic-novel" or period pieces include "the incorporation of fine art into the program's mise-en-scène", but also "a preoccupation with authors, books, and words", and, particularly relevantly to this chapter, "a period setting and *deployment of period music*" (2012: 59; my emphasis). As has been argued, a historical drama, if effective, will influence our understanding of history, and music in fictional media like the radio drama adaptation can provide ambiance – as opposed to perfect period-accurate reproduction – in order to be effective.

4   Scoring BBC Radio Drama: *The Spy*

I will now provide a brief plot summary of *The Spy* before proceeding with the analysis of its radio drama adaptation. Set in 1780 in the neutral ground of upper New York state, the story of *The Spy* follows the tribulations of the Wharton family some five years after hostilities have broken out between Britain and its thirteen colonies, which have declared independence. Mr Wharton, a wealthy merchant, claims neutrality due to the fact that his son, Henry, is a British officer. One of his daughters, Frances, is engaged to a Virginian officer, and the other, Sarah, is courted by a British colonel. Their neighbours are the elderly Mr Birch and his son, Harvey, an itinerant peddler and suspected British spy. Harvey Birch is, in fact, an American spy who nevertheless helps Henry

Wharton escape a charge of espionage and is secretly in league with a disguised General Washington himself.

Sasha Yevtushenko was the director of *The Spy* and provided useful insights into the recording and production process. *The Spy* was recorded in BBC Broadcasting House in Portland Place on 4–6 November 2011. In broadcast BBC radio drama, in addition to being responsible for casting and writing the publicity material, the director/producer chooses the music (Yevtushenko 2019). In general terms, it takes the director/producer two days to edit one hour of broadcast material (*The Spy*, consisting of two segments of 56 minutes, required four days' editing work). Music is usually assembled from the BBC's vast music library.[1] Yevtushenko noted that there is a PPL[2] agreement with record labels which enforce certain broadcasting restrictions – for example, no more than three tracks by the same artist or from the same album can be used in a radio drama, and no more than 3 minutes from the same track.[3] Certain artists are completely off limits, such as the Beatles and the Doors, as are film music soundtracks. All music used is reported in the BBC's internal systems (Proteus), which trigger the PRS[4] payments. Yevtushenko also noted that, less commonly, music is specially composed in certain circumstances.

In terms of process, Yevtushenko noted that he spent the first day and a half of editing time on *The Spy* assembling the rough mix.[5] This determined the length of the cut. Due to the time pressure on recording, editing, producing and broadcasting so much radio drama in regular slots within the BBC radio system, Yevtushenko likened the approach to a production line, observing that he had to choose the musical score "on the fly" (ibid.). He said, "You're using the time the editors use to assemble the music", putting together a palette of audio tracks which are brought into the edit. Yevtushenko likes to have two or three options per moment where he thinks the music should go, depending on the play or the production process. Success, therefore, seems to hinge on experience (having a 'feel' for effective scoring, given the time constraints), the

---

1 According to Yevtushenko, "there is a mix of commercial music and library production music. We also use special production music resources, e.g., audionetwork.com. Of course, if one uses production music, there are not the same restrictions as apply to commercial music" (2019).

2 UK and international recorded music royalty collection. PPL collects and distributes money on behalf of performers and record companies for the use of their recorded music.

3 According to Yevtushenko, "these restrictions change year-by-year – there are new ones in place now, which differ slightly" (2019).

4 PRS collects and distributes money on behalf of songwriters, composers and music publishers for the use of their musical compositions and lyrics.

5 According to Yevtushenko, the editor usually does this without the producer present.

ability to simulate coherence from disparate sources, and an ear for attractive musical phrases: "Sometimes you happen to hit upon the right thing" (ibid.).

Production processes in BBC radio today differ considerably from those of the mid-twentieth century, although the "inevitable tyranny of the stopwatch" (Kremenliev 1949: 76) and the budget remain high priorities.[6] A producer in the current BBC radio system has generally gone through a "lengthy and complex process" (McMurtry 2019: 154) in order to bring a project to the production stage, a produced radio drama having appealed both to its producer and to the commissioning editors. Jeremy Howe, then-Commissioning Editor for Drama and Fiction, commissioned the adaptation of *The Spy*, considering it a "different" take on the American Revolution (Yevtushenko 2019). Yevtushenko admitted that he himself "struggled" with the book, finding it stylistically dense. Seeing his task as "blow[ing] some air through it", he sought to bring the exciting tale of adventure to the surface. Noting that, although the adaptation of *The Spy* predated Lin-Manuel Miranda's *Hamilton* (2015), Yevtushenko nevertheless evoked the impact of HBO's *John Adams*, which reminded international audiences that "American independence was not inevitable and did not happen overnight" (Godet 2012: 67). Seeking to give the 1821 novel a "contemporary resonance", Yevtushenko's adaptation was bookended by the music of the Fleet Foxes.

5 Functions of Music in Radio Drama

As has been established, the sound elements of radio drama representing a historical era are not haphazardly thrown together, just as a historical television programme or film does not assemble its sound elements randomly; the sound elements are at least in part contributing to the aesthetic that creates the notion of 'period' or historical drama. However, music in historical radio drama must also fit into the codes and conventions associated with the

---

6 This has clear parallels with earlier production processes for radio drama, such as with American Old Time Radio (OTR), when rapid turnaround for original music composition (around 24 hours from script to deadline) and live broadcast dictated production practices (cf. Kremenliev 1949: 76; Smith 1991: 59). It is significant that OTR drama progressed from "the stock library music cues" of the early 1930s to "tailor-made scores", while BBC-produced drama of the time period used prestige scores composed by "serious" composers such as Ralph Vaughan Williams and William Walton (cf. Kremenliev 1949: 82, 81). Even in 1949, composing music for OTR seemed like an afterthought, first considering "the difficulties of balancing the voice qualities of the cast" and the instrumentation available (ibid.: 81). Bernard Herrmann's level of genius – radio's "fastest and best composer" – was unusual (Smith 1991: 59), with Kremenliev complaining about a surfeit of "fifth-rate" composers (1949: 80).

medium. The music used in *The Spy* is, in generic terms, broadly organised into four categories: traditional folk music, orchestral 'stock' music, martial music and indie-folk. In order to develop a conceptual approach to creating historical ambiance in radio drama, it is necessary to have a more meaningful analytic tool than genre. While music specifically used in radio drama is undertheorised, two systems for analysis do suggest themselves, the first put forth by Kremenliev in 1949 and the second by Hand and Traynor in 2011 (see Figure 12.1), based on the work of Crisell (1994). Kremenliev describes four functions of music in radio drama, including "signature", "curtain", "bridge", and "background" (1949: 76). It is clear that much of this terminology is inherited from early radio drama's associations with stage theatre (cf. Krutnik 2013: 38). Many of Kremenliev's terms can be linked with similar concepts from Hand and Traynor. What Kremenliev terms "signature" is related to "mood" according to Hand and Traynor (2011: 50), in serving "essentially to create atmosphere and heighten emotion. It keeps the story moving by giving it color and by holding the attention of the listener." (Kremenliev 1949: 75) Both "curtain" and "bridge", signifying a break in structure, correspond to "music as link" as per Hand and Traynor, which "marks a boundary between one scene and the next" (2011: 50). "Background" is similar to what Hand and Traynor call "music with an indexical function" (ibid.): it gives clues as to when and where the action is happening, in order to convey meaning about the story and provide a sense of verisimilitude. Hand and Traynor define this as similar to the use of "actuality" in non-fiction radio (ibid.). In story terms, such music would be used mainly

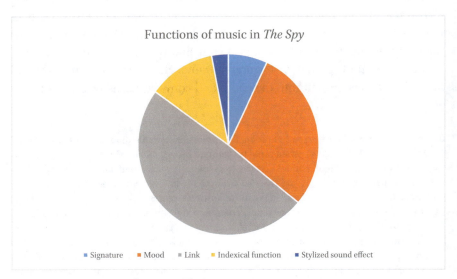

FIGURE 12.1   Functions of music in *The Spy*

diegetically, while the other functional uses of music would be used primarily non-diegetically.

The vast majority of the music (nearly 50 per cent) in *The Spy* is used as "link", helping the listener make the aural/imaginative journey between scenes. Many of the instances of "music as link" are also "music as mood". "Music as indexical function" is used much more sparingly in *The Spy*; indeed, it is represented wholly by the characters Harvey and Frances singing Isaac Watts's 1704 hymn "O God, Our Help in Ages Past" and the use of martial music during battle scenes. Likewise, the "stylised sound effect" is rare in this particular drama. To use Hand and Traynor's term, "music as indexical function" provides a sense of verisimilitude to the action and setting in *The Spy*. Eighteenth-century America would have been full of song and other diegetic music, but there is very little of this in *The Spy*. W.M. Verhoeven (see 1993) has argued that Fenimore Cooper's original novel sets a list of binaries against each other, including Americans vs. British, Washington vs. King George III, Frances vs. Sarah, and Harvey Birch vs. Mr Wharton. However, in the adaptation, Verhoeven's list of binaries does not have a musical extension. For example, we never hear European drawing room music of the period to contrast with the homespun vocals: the hymn, the martial music or the portable folk instruments (guitar, fiddle) heard in the non-diegetic mood or link music. In the novel, the Whartons' New York City home would likely have been filled with drawing room music appropriate to the period, by composers such as Haydn, Jan Vanhal, Carl Stamitz and Johann Christian Bach, perhaps played on such instruments as violins, cellos, bass, flute, oboes, bassoon, horns and keyboard (see Murray 1994). The complex and refined nature of programming as highlighted by Murray in Philadelphia taverns of the period is not reflected in *The Spy*, suggesting a greater engagement with the idea of America as 'frontier'. In keeping with a more complex and 'modern' re-envisioning of the American Revolution, this production of *The Spy* focuses on its many scenes of outdoor action rather than the interior scenes of domestic life, which dominated the original novel.

Unconsciously, perhaps, *The Spy* reflects the composite of political songs and sacred music that characterised this historical period (see Wood 2014; Crist 2003; Temperley 1997), even if the hymn chosen for Harvey and Frances to sing was less fitting than the works of William Billings (1746–1800), the preeminent early American composer whose six tunebooks contain more than 340 original compositions (cf. Crist 2003: 333). As Ferris has argued, the folk music of the rural and mountain areas in the United States is "remarkably close to that of seventeenth-century Britain" in terms of its instruments and style of singing, so the usage of the hymn is both effective and appropriate (2010: 31). Nevertheless, to pick up Verhoeven's concept of binaries, when Harvey and Frances sing this hymn together – a scene that never occurred in the book – they bring together their varying backgrounds and social classes, linking their common humanity. As Wood notes, during this period, "harmony denoted a system in which internal variety meant delightful contrast, or in more material terms, complementary and even symbiotic interests" (2014: 1087). This conception of harmony clearly reflects the relationship between Frances and Harvey in the radio drama.

The only other type of music used as indexical function in *The Spy* is martial music. As Howe notes, "[a]rmies of the eighteenth and nineteenth centuries depended on company fifers and drummers for communicating orders during battle, regulating camp formations and duties, and providing music for marching, ceremonies, and morale" (1999: 87). *The Spy* does not make use of fife and drums as its martial music, instead using bugle calls from the album *Toy Muskateer* to signal indexically that battles are taking place. While the bugle was in use during the American Revolution, it was more common for British rather than American troops (with some exceptions), the British using trumpets for "mounted troops, bugle horns or fifes and drum for dismounted dragoons serving as infantry" (Pirtle 2007). In a battle scene in episode 1, the use of echoing military drums low in the mix could be interpreted as indexical but is probably mood music, serving to intensify the action, which is then overlaid with bugle calls, which are indexically indicative of the American Light Horse troops joining the battle.

The genres associated with the different functions of the music are worth analysing. Nearly all of the musical genres used in *The Spy* can function as link, including 'stock' orchestral music like Terry Devine-King's stately French horn theme from the composition "The Search" (which is not particularly historically suitable and, given that its origins were with the Audio Music Network, likely a non-specific 'soundtrack'-like cue). By contrast, the pieces "The Miller's Boy Bridal March", "The Sailor's Wife", "Felefeber" and "Hjellane" speak to the soundworld of eighteenth-century America, bringing with them "associations of an 'authentic' Celtic folk tradition as a remnant of the 'true folk tradition' that once existed for everyday people elsewhere" (Cook 2016). This fiddle music, at least in part, originates in contemporary Scandinavia. The album *Felefeber* (which translates into "Fiddle-fever" in English), from which this track comes, was recorded in 1994 in Norway by Annbjørg Lien. "Hjellane" also originates from a Lien album, of 1989. While Scandinavian ancestral origins of Americans in the eighteenth century were so unusual as to go unrecorded on a 1790 census of New York State (over 50 per cent were of English origin) (cf. Purvis 1995: 185), very few of *The Spy*'s listeners would have objected to Lien's fiddle interpretations as they sound 'timeless'. That Lien is a renowned hardanger fiddler also contributes to the 'old-fashioned' sound.[7] "The Sailor's Wife" is a traditional folk tune (the version used in *The Spy* was played by Tim Matthiesen and Paul Lenart).

Although leitmotif is absent from *The Spy* (see Buhler 2006; Bribitzer-Stull 2015), in the sense that film composers of epic cycles like *The Lord of the Rings* (Howard Shore) and *Star Wars* (John Williams) use it, several of the 'folk' cues recur in such a way as to link events. For example, the plaintive "Hjellane" cue recurs during Mr Birch's sickness, on his deathbed, and when Harvey Birch gets revenge on the men who tormented him during the time of his father's death. Similarly, the more upbeat and homespun-sounding "The Sailor's Wife" recurs when Henry Wharton enjoys the company of his family while illicitly visiting them, and again during an intimate scene after Frances Wharton has married Peyton Dunwoodie, her Virginian fiancé. Another cue that recurs, serving as both link and mood music, is the first few seconds of "Your Protector" by the Fleet Foxes. This sad-sounding and yet tender cue on (modern) flute (played by Gwen Owen) is not period-accurate, but it well reflects the mood in scenes where characters have been captured and are awaiting death, or indeed after the tragic death of Isabella Singleton.

Although what I believe is the 'signature' music for *The Spy* recurs only four times (at the opening and closing of each of the two episodes), it is highly significant for that fact. As this music comes from the track "Heard Them Stirring" by the Fleet Foxes, it is now worth understanding why this music bears the weight of bookending, of sonically introducing us into the world of *The Spy* and then taking us out again after the episodes conclude. The Seattle-based Fleet Foxes – whose name, according to founder Robin Pecknold, was "evocative of some weird English activity like fox hunting" (qtd. in Manheim 2012) – was a "band that collided with the zeitgeist" (Poneman qtd. in Cohen and Harding 2009). Reaching international fame in 2009, their "all-ages appeal" was key to their success in the UK (Cohen and Harding 2009). Sasha Yevtushenko (2019 concurs that the band was popular the year *The Spy* was produced (2011), evoking for him a sense of American autumn, the countryside, leaves turning and folky timelessness. While the "highly literate songwriting" of its frontman is of less relevance to us here, the group's "intricate harmony singing" (Manheim 2012) "worked" for Yevtushenko (2019). He added that "the melodies weren't

---

7   This may be a consequence of the hardanger's high-profile use in Howard Shore's soundtrack to *The Lord of the Rings: The Two Towers* in 2003. Strictly speaking, the hardanger fiddle is a uniquely Norwegian instrument. Dating from the middle of the seventeenth century, it would have only been heard in the New World after the wave of Scandinavian mass immigration in the middle of the nineteenth century (see Golber 1993).

so well-known they wouldn't pull them [the listeners] out of the piece" (ibid.). In this way, as Yevtushenko points out, producers cannot use music in radio drama in the same way as for TV or cinema (ibid.). For example, knowingly or blatantly anachronistic music will give listeners pause as they do not have visual cues to clearly determine the period. Listeners who hear blatantly anachronistic music in the storyworld of *The Spy* might be confused or irritated, and it would diminish the immersive aspect. It would be difficult to achieve the cohesion of BBC TV's *Peaky Blinders* (2013–2022), which matches its musically modern signature piece – Nick Cave and the Bad Seeds' "Red Right Hand" – with a historical period setting of 1920s Birmingham.[8] Baz Luhrmann's cheerfully anachronistic musical approach in cinema to adaptations like *The Great Gatsby* (2013) and historical pastiche films like *Moulin Rouge!* (2001) make a statement of excess that is echoed and refined through the visuals. This would be comparatively hard to achieve in radio drama.

With this reasoning in mind, "Heard Them Stirring" is particularly effective because it has no lyrics but instead hinges on Fleet Foxes' soulful, folk-sounding close harmonies, and uses instrumentation that does not sound jarringly out of place (unlike, for example, other tracks on the album such as "Ragged Wood", which uses electric guitar, and "Blue Ridge Mountains", which uses piano). As previously noted, only the instrumental first few seconds of "Your Protector" are used, as the lyrics are potentially anachronistic. While the anachronistic use of modern flute in "Your Protector" contradicts the period setting, this is not obvious enough to ruin the listener's immersion into the storyworld. In the story moment, the death of Isabella Singleton followed by a few seconds' plaintive notes on flute are unlikely to jar listeners enough to stop listening, particularly as they only have time to understand unconsciously that the music reflects the mood (sad) and that a transition between scenes is taking place. Furthermore, in this particular instance, the listener – familiar with the codes and conventions of radio, even if unconsciously – understands that the flute music is not intended diegetically (a flute-playing character has not appeared out of nowhere in the story) but rather non-diegetically, as a way to indicate mood and, combined with the fading down of diegetic sounds such as SFX and dialogue, to transition between scenes.

The wordless and dramatic opening strains of "Heard Them Stirring" do raise the question of "point of audition", which can be thought of as the aural equivalent to point of view, though the term is imperfect (Chion 1994: 90). In this case, who is listening to "Heard Them Stirring"? Where are they situated? Is the music supposed to be diegetic or non-diegetic? Who is singing and to

---

8 Though, as Yevtushenko points out, this is not impossible, citing the example of contemporary music that opens each episode of *China Towns* (2019), set initially in 1879 Stoke-on-Trent.

whom? In what way does it relate to the story? Given the instrumentation – close harmony vocals with clear American folk influence as well as what sounds like a *bodhrán* (an Irish frame drum) and guitar – the clear link is to characters like Harvey Birch, who personify the 'frontier' and evoke Yevtushenko's sense of "countryside, leaves turning, and folky timelessness" (2019), which separates Birch from the more traditionally heroic military figures like Major Peyton Dunwoodie. Nevertheless, given Birch's heroic death at the end of episode 2 (which does not occur except in an epilogue in Fenimore Cooper's original novel), "Heard Them Stirring" seems to embrace a storytelling function rather like the musical equivalent of a narrator. The last scene of episode 2 includes Frances and Peyton commenting on Birch's death. This conversation is concluded with the sudden burst of the opening to "Heard Them Stirring". This involvement of "Heard Them Stirring" in the resolution can be likened to the voice of the narrator, or Fenimore Cooper himself, signifying that the story has reached its conclusion but the themes nevertheless are timeless. This is in keeping with the classification of "Heard Them Stirring" as *The Spy*'s signature piece of music.

As previously noted, it is relatively unusual in BBC radio drama for a score to be composed exclusively for a production. Instead, the job is usually allocated to the director, as with Yevtushenko and *The Spy*, to assemble musical elements to fulfil the functions as formulated by Hand and Traynor: music as link, 'mood' music, as stylised sound effect, and as indexical function, with the added category, I would argue, of "signature", from Kremenliev. He argued in 1949 that "radio music leans chiefly on the idiom of the past, on imitative rather than creative writing" (80). Given that Kremenliev was thinking primarily of American OTR network radio, whose commercial sponsors were wary of alienating its audiences, this was probably the case. When composition is not possible but instead directors rely on musical collage spun through with some of the techniques of musical composition, does Kremenliev's argument still apply? Arguably, this method is similar to the precepts of adaptation studies, where effect can be just as important as the source text. This would seem to be the case for *The Spy*, in which a variety of music that is not necessarily period-accurate has been employed to create an ambiance to fulfil the needs of the story. While not historically accurate, it nevertheless represents the emotional resonance and time period to the listeners.

6   Conclusion

We can accept that a radio dramatisation of a novel set in a historical period can tell us something both about that historical period and also the time in which that adaptation was made. Such inferences can plainly be made in the use of

Fleet Foxes, an indie-rock album, as the signature music for *The Spy*, since the music was popular at the time of its production (2011) and represented a sentiment analogous, in director Sasha Yevtushenko's mind, to the sense of timeless relevance he wanted to bring to the adaptation. In providing contemporary resonance for the American Revolution, *The Spy* presages the enormous influence of *Hamilton*, the musical, in suggesting that this conflict – which the characters themselves term a "civil war" – still offers something for modern audiences.

The dominant discourse on media and historical drama has tended to overlook radio which, given the longevity of the *Classic Serial* and the multitude of radio plays on the BBC set in the historical past (35 per cent of all new dramas on BBC Radios 3 and 4 in 2012), is unfortunate (cf. McMurtry 2019: 157). In this chapter, immersion in a storyworld has been demonstrated to be important, and one way to contribute to this state of immersion or transportation is through music, which can create historical ambiance. The music in *The Spy* does this, bringing listeners into the world of eighteenth-century America. While media depictions of historical periods make powerful impressions, the evidence from the soundtrack of *The Spy* suggests that a historical ambiance is more valuable/effective to an audience than one hundred per cent period-accurate music. This sound collage technique – rather than the composition of an entirely original score – is concomitant with the production methodology in place for BBC radio drama, given the time constraints and the role of the director. As an example of the BBC radio *Classic Serial, The Spy* fits into cultural expectations of the 'classic-novel' adaptation and within media depictions of historical drama. While *The Spy* evidences the use of many of the acknowledged functions of music in radio drama, its use of the signature cue, provided in this instance by a track by indie-folk group Fleet Foxes, is particularly noteworthy for a sense of evocation of the historical past. This is also consistent with the desire to make relevant the dominant theme of the story, i.e., that the American Revolution was ideologically complex with lasting repercussions for both combatants and non-combatants alike. The music in *The Spy*, therefore, has as much to say about the present as it does about the past.[9]

References

Beck, Alan (1997). *Radio Acting*. London: A&C Black.
Bribitzer-Stull, Matthew (2015). *Understanding the Leitmotif: From Wagner to Hollywood Film Music*. Cambridge: CUP.

---

9 With thanks to Juha Niesniemi, D.J. Britton, Maire Tracey and Sasha Yevtushenko.

Bruner, Jerome S. (1986). *Actual Minds, Possible Worlds*. Cambridge, MA: Harvard Univ. Press.

Buhler, James (2006). "Enchantments of *Lord of the Rings:* Soundtrack, Myth, Language and Modernity". Ernest Mathijs, Murray Pomerance, eds. *From Hobbits to Hollywood: Essays on Peter Jackson's* Lord of the Rings. Amsterdam: Rodopi. 231–248.

Busselle, Rick, Helena Bilandzic (2008). "Fictionality and Perceived Realism in Experiencing Stories: A Model of Narrative Comprehension and Engagement". *Communication Theory* 18: 255–280.

Butt, Richard (2012). "The Classic Novel on British Television". Deborah Cartmell, ed. *Companion to Literature, Film, and Adaptation*. Oxford: OUP. 159–176.

Cardwell, Sarah (2002). *Adaptation Revisited: Television and the Classic Novel*. Manchester: Manchester Univ. Press.

Chapman, James (2005). *Past and Present: National Identity and the British Historical Film*. London: I.B. Tauris.

Chignell, Hugh (2009). *Key Concepts in Radio Studies*. London: Sage.

Chion, Michel (1994). *Audio-Vision: Sound on Screen*. Claudia Gorbman, transl. New York, NY: Columbia Univ. Press.

Cohen, Jonathan, Cortney Harding (2009 online). "American Pastoral: Fleet Foxes Are Taking Indie Rock Back to the Country – and the Country Is Listening". *Billboard*, 7 February: 22–25.

Cook, James (2016 online). "Playing with the Past in the Imagined Middle Ages: Music and Soundscape in Video Game". *Sounding Out! The Sound Studies Blog*. https://soundstudiesblog.com/2016/10/03/playing-with-the-past-in-the-imagined-middle-ages-music-and-soundscape-in-video-game/ [05/02/19].

Crisell, Andrew (1994). *Understanding Radio*. 2nd ed. London: Routledge.

Crist, E.B. (2003). "'Ye Sons of Harmony': Politics, Masculinity, and the Music of William Billings in Revolutionary Boston". *The William and Mary Quarterly* 60/2: 333–354.

Crook, Tim (1999). *Radio Drama: Theory and Practice*. Abingdon: Routledge.

Cooper, James Fenimore (1849/2006). *The Spy*. Stroud: Nonsuch Publishing.

Ferris, Jean (2010). *America's Musical Landscape*. 6th ed. New York, NY: McGraw Hill.

Fleet Foxes (2008). *Fleet Foxes*. Music album. Subpop/Bella Union.

Gerrig, Richard J. (1993). *Experiencing Narrative Worlds: On the Psychological Activities of Reading*. New Haven, CT: Yale Univ. Press.

Giddings, Robert, Keith Selby (2001). *The Classic Serial on Television and Radio*. Basingstoke: Palgrave.

Glancy, Mark (2005). "The War of Independence in Feature Films: *The Patriot* (2000) and the 'Special Relationship' Between Hollywood and Britain". *Historical Journal of Film, Radio and Television* 25/4: 523–545.

Godet, Aurélie (2012 online). "'The West Wing with Wigs'? Politics and History in HBO's *John Adams*". *TV/Series* 1. https://journals.openedition.org/tvseries/1077 [04/06/2021].

Golber, David (1993). "What You Should Know About the Hardanger Fiddle". Guild of American Luthiers. https://luth.org/1993_0133300-golber-hardanger/ [06/07/2021].

Hand, Richard J., Mary Traynor (2011). *The Radio Drama Handbook: Audio Drama in Context and Practice.* London: Continuum.

Hendy, David (2007). *Life on Air: A History of Radio Four.* Oxford: OUP.

Howe, Warren P. (1999). "Early American Military Music". *American Music* 17/1: 87–120.

Kremenliev, Boris (1949). "Background Music for Radio Drama". *Hollywood Quarterly* 4/1: 75–83.

Krutnik, Frank (2013). "'Be Moviedom's Guest in Your Own Easy Chair!' Hollywood, Radio and the Movie Adaptation Series". *Historical Journal of Film Radio and Television* 33/1: 24–54.

Leggott, James (2015). "'It's not clever, it's not funny, and it's not period!': Costume Comedy and British Television". James Leggott, Julie Anne Taddeo, eds. *Upstairs and Downstairs: British Costume Drama Television from* The Forsyte Saga *to* Downton Abbey. Lanham, MD: Rowman & Littlefield. 58–71.

Manheim, James M. (2012 online). "Fleet Foxes". *Contemporary Musicians.* Tracie Ratiner, ed. Gale Virtual Reference Library. Vol. 73. 89–91. [05/02/19].

McMurtry, Leslie (2019). *Revolution in the Echo Chamber: Audio Drama's Past, Present, and Future.* Bristol: Intellect.

Monk, Claire (2012). *Heritage Film Audiences: Period Films and Contemporary Audiences in the* UK. Edinburgh: Edinburgh Univ. Press.

Monk, Claire (2015). "Pageantry and Populism, Democratization and Dissent". James Leggott, Julie Anne Taddeo, eds. *Upstairs and Downstairs: British Costume Drama Television from* The Forsyte Saga *to* Downton Abbey. Lanham, MD: Rowman & Littlefield. 27–44.

Murray, Sterling E. (1994). "Music and Dance in Philadelphia's City Tavern, 1773–1790". J.R. Heintz, ed. *American Musical Life in Context and Practice to 1865.* New York, NY: Routledge. 3–47.

Peniston-Bird, Corinna M. (2013). "'I Wondered Who'd be the First to Spot That': *Dad's Army* at War, in the Media and in Memory". Siân Nicholas, Tom O'Malley, Kevin Williams, eds. *Reconstructing the Past: History in the Mass Media 1890–2005.* Abingdon: Routledge. 63–82.

Pirtle, Scooter (2007 online). "Evolution of the Bugle". *The Middle Horn Leader,* http://www.middlehornleader.com/Evolution%20of%20the%20Bugle.htm [17/06/19].

Purvis, Thomas L. (1995). *Revolutionary America 1763 to 1800.* Almanacs of American Life. New York, NY: Facts on File.

Smith, Steven C. (1991). *A Heart at Fire's Center: The Life and Music of Bernard Herrmann.* Berkeley, CA: Univ. of California Press.

Temperley, N. (1997). "First Forty: The Earliest American Composition". *American Music* 15/1: 1–25.

The Spy (2012). Directed by Sasha Yevtushenko, performances by Burn Gorman, Rose Leslie, Alex Waldeman, BBC Radio 4.

Verhoeven, W.M. (1993). "Neutralizing the Land: The Myth of Authority and the Authority of Myth in Fenimore Cooper's *The Spy*". W.M. Verhoeven, ed. *James Fenimore Cooper: New Historical and Literary Contexts*. Amsterdam: Rodopi. 71–87.

Williams, Kevin (2008). "Flattened Visions from Timeless Machines: History in the Mass Media". Siân Nicholas, Tom O'Malley, Kevin Williams, eds. *Reconstructing the Past: History in the Mass Media 1890–2005*. Abingdon: Routledge. 7–28.

Wood, Kristen E. (2014). "'Join with Heart and Soul and Voice': Music, Harmony, and Politics in the Early American Republic". *The American Historical Review* 119/4: 1083–1116.

Yevtushenko, Sasha (2019). Phone interview. 5 March. Unpublished.

CHAPTER 13

Musical 'Speech Score' as Soundscape: Elfriede Jelinek's *Die Schutzbefohlenen* (2014) on the Radio

Caroline A. Kita

Abstract

Austrian author Elfriede Jelinek has openly acknowledged the influence of music on her experimental prose texts, which she has referred to as *Sprachpartituren* ('speech scores'). This essay examines how these musically-infused texts have been reworked for the radio, through a case study of the 2014 radio drama adaptation of *Die Schutzbefohlenen* (*Charges*). Focusing on the arrangement of Jelinek's text into a polyphonic dialogue between individual speakers and a chorus, and on the intra- and extradiegetic musical settings in the production, this essay reveals the unique ways that music is being used in contemporary German-language radio drama to articulate cultural critique.

Austrian author and 2004 Nobel Prize for Literature awardee Elfriede Jelinek has a long-standing relationship with the radio. Beginning with *Wien West* (*Vienna West,* NDR/WDR 1972, dir. Otto Düben), her first dramatic work written explicitly for the medium, to the recent production of *Wut* (*Rage,* BR 2017, dir. Leonhard Koppelmann), Jelinek has authored nearly forty texts that have been broadcast on all major German and Austrian radio networks. In 2004, she was awarded Germany's prestigious Hörspielpreis der Kriegsblinden (Radio Drama Prize of the War Blind) for her radio drama *Jackie* (BR 2002, dir. Karl Bruckmaier), solidifying her place in a distinguished line of authors who have influenced and shaped the genre since the mid-twentieth century.

A notable characteristic of Jelinek's writing generally, and her works for the radio in particular, is the musicality of her language. David Roesner has referred to an "aesthetics of plethora" or overfullness of sound in her works, evident in the heterogeneous interplay of voices and her attention to the sound quality of words (2014: 131, 130). Jelinek, who holds a degree in organ performance, has often asserted the significance of music for her works. In an interview with Gunna Wendt in 1996, the author claimed that she writes 'speech scores': "Ich [habe] überhaupt keine Schwierigkeiten, mich in einen

Hörraum hineinzuversetzen und eine Partitur für Sprecher zu erstellen; ich gehe da nach rein musikalischen Gesichtspunkten vor." (qtd. in Kepplinger 2007: 296)[1] While statements such as this have inspired Roesner and other scholars to examine the influence of music and musical forms on Jelinek's written language, surprisingly little attention has been paid to the adaptation of these musical texts for the purely auditory medium of the radio.[2]

This analysis of a recent radio production of Jelinek's *Die Schutzbefohlenen* (*Charges*)[3] uses this work as a case study for understanding how music and musical language can function in radio drama to encourage the listener to critically reflect on contemporary cultural discourses. It reads the musicality of Jelinek's 'speech score' and its adaptation for the radio medium in dialogue with a recent 'musical turn' in contemporary German theatre as well as the ideals of the *Neues Hörspiel* (*New Radio Drama*), a movement in German radio from the 1960s and 1970s that pushed back against traditional narrative or literary radio drama, employing the new technology of stereophonic sound in service of a "sprachkritische, experimentelle, antirationalistische Dramaturgie" (qtd. in Thiers 2016: 359; 'language-critical, experimental, antirational dramaturgy'). In this essay, I discuss how, in adapting the musical language of Jelinek's 'speech score' to the radio medium, director Leonhard Koppelmann and dramaturge Herbert Kapfer call for distinct changes in vocal colour (to indicate shifts between pathos and irony), create dramatic contrasts between voice and extra- and intradiegetic music, and emphasise the rhythmic, cacophonic sound of words. The realisation of these musical elements in the soundscape of the radio drama expands on the author's text and creates an experience in which the listener is at first drawn toward empathy with the speakers and then abruptly alienated through unexpected contrasts and dissonant outbursts. These jarring transitions provoke the listener to question the voices that they hear and to reconsider the meaning of their words, thus

---

1   'I have no difficulties whatsoever to place myself in a sound space and to construct a score for speakers; I proceed from purely musical standpoints.' This quote is excerpted from a radio essay by Gunna Wendt, "Wer nicht fühlen will, muss hören", first broadcast on Bayrischer Rundfunk (BR2) on 8 November 1996. All translations, unless otherwise stated, are my own.
2   For more on the musicality of Jelinek's language, see Janke (2003), Powell and Bethmann (2008), Pye and Donovan (2009), and Solibakke (2014). Kepplinger (2007) writes broadly of the 'resounding language' ("klingende Sprache") of Jelinek's works for the radio, but does not focus on any specific work.
3   In my examples, I refer to Jelinek's original text of *Die Schutzbefohlenen* as well as a recent English translation, entitled *Charges*, completed by Gitta Honegger in 2016. Honegger's translation of the play includes a transcript of conversations with Jelinek in which they discuss in depth the challenges that Honegger faced in relaying the musical language of this text (Jelinek 2016: 143–200). For an explanation of the translated title, see note 11.

creating a unique aural confrontation with the discourse surrounding the status of refugees and debates on integration in Austria.

1 Orchestrating a Speech Score for the Radio

Elfriede Jelinek wrote *Die Schutzbefohlenen* in 2013 in response to a protest by migrants and refugees that took place in December of 2012 at the Votive Church near the University of Vienna. A group of asylum seekers had set up camp in the church and begun a hunger strike. The protest lasted several weeks and attracted widespread media attention.[4] Theatre director Nicholas Stemann, a long-time collaborator of Jelinek, commissioned a work from her on this subject. When the text she wrote could not be immediately adapted for the stage, she published it on her website and reworked it over the course of several months.[5] It received its first public reading in Hamburg in September 2013. In 2014, this text was adapted by Koppelmann and Kapfer for a joint production by the Bayerischer Rundfunk (BR) and Österreichischer Rundfunk (ORF), and it was broadcast on 25 March.[6]

Like many of her recent works that have achieved acclaim on the radio, including *Jackie* (2004), *Sportchor* (2006), *Bambiland* (2006) and *Rechnitz* (2010), Jelinek did not compose *Die Schutzbefohlenen* as a traditional drama with explicitly defined characters, plots and settings. Instead, she utilises a form that she has developed – the "Multifunktionstext" ('multi-functional text') – which can be adapted for various purposes, performance spaces and media platforms (Kepplinger 2007: 292).[7] Jelinek refers to these works as *Textflächen* ('text planes') and Karen Jürs-Munby describes them as "montages of playfully

---

4   See Felber (2016) for further details on the origins of the protest and its outcomes. Although Jelinek does not provide the specifics of this event in her text, she includes images from the protest alongside the text on her website (see Jelinek 2013a).

5   The revisions are dated 14 June 2013, 8 November 2013, 14 November 2013, and 29 September 2015. The first stage production of *Die Schutzbefohlenen* finally took place in Mannheim in May 2014 as a co-production of the Theater of the World festival, the Holland Festival Amsterdam and the Thalia-Theater in Hamburg under the direction of Stemann.

6   This was not Jelinek's first collaboration with these artists. Previous works of Jelinek directed by Koppelmann include *Sportchor* (BR 2006), *Ulrike Maria Stuart* (BR 2007), *bukolit* (BR 2008) and *Kein Licht* (2012). More recently, he directed *Das schweigende Mädchen* (BR 2015). Kapfer and Jelinek also collaborated on the radio dramatisation of her "Privatroman" (private novel) *Neid* (BR 2011).

7   In his essay, Kepplinger in fact attributes the use of the term "Multifunktionstext" to describe Jelinek's works to Prof. Hilda Haider-Pregler.

and deconstructively manipulated quotes from a wide variety of spheres and genres, including popular culture, the media, philosophy, poetry, as well as classical dramatic literature, intermixed with what reads like the author's own 'voice'" (2009: 46). Jelinek writes that her text planes are a "Teppich des Seins und des Sprechens" ('carpet of being and speaking') which directors are invited to "sich draufstellen", "herbeizerren", "rausrollen" ('place themselves on top of', 'drag' and 'roll out') to realise their own creative vision, resulting in a wide variety of interpretations (2013b). In other words, her speech scores provide the acoustic material and it is up to the directors and dramaturges to orchestrate this material by determining how and by whom this content should be embodied on stage and voiced in the soundscape of a radio drama.

The metaphor of orchestration is fitting here, because it captures the innate musicality of Jelinek's writings. Her sensitivity to the aural properties of language shapes not only her word choice, but also the sentence permutation and syntax of her texts. In her online essay "Textflächen", she wrote that music "ist die Wiederholung, sie ist endlose Wiederholung von etwas Bodenlosem, deswegen glaubt sie ja, sie wäre einzig und tief, weil sie keinen Boden sieht, dafür aber überall herauskann [...] so ist das mit den Textflächen auch" (2013b).[8] Indeed, repetition of words and phrases is a hallmark of these texts and, like the development of a musical theme, this repetition is organic and goal-oriented. Jelinek carefully constructs her text montages so that words and phrases play off one another based on their sound, subtly shifting (a change of a vowel here, an added prefix there) or connecting one idea to another through alliterations or near rhymes.

In an interview with dramaturge Herbert Kapfer in 2011, Jelinek further elaborated on the musicality of her texts:

> Ich muss [mein Schreiben] nicht laut lesen. Ich bin ja gelernte Musikerin und schreibe, ob ich will oder nicht, sozusagen Sprachmusik. Wenn man so lange wie ich Musik gemacht hat, hat man die musikalischen Aspekte der Sprache verinnerlicht, und man arbeitet sowohl mit der Lautlichkeit der Worte, mit deren Klang man spielt, als auch eben mit dem Rhythmus. Ich verwende die Sprache quasi als musikalisches Ausgangsmaterial, und das setze ich dann zusammen, wie man halt lernt, die Themen

---

8 'is repetition, it is the endless repetition of something bottomless, for this reason it believes itself to be solitary and deep, because it sees no bottom but can emerge from everywhere [...]. It is the same with my text planes.'

von Fugen, die Seitenthemen und dann ihre Verarbeitung, Umkehrung, Spiegelung und so weiter zu organisieren. (Kapfer 2017: 226)[9]

In her discussion with Kapfer, Jelinek likens her organisation of sonorous material to composing a fugue, again intimating that her text planes straddle the borders of music and language.

In his study of musicality and theatre, David Roesner notes a key difference between the musicality of a written text and its musicality in performance. He writes: "A spoken monologue creates a definite musical shape: a melody, timbre, rhythm, duration, etc. – a *written* monologue bears the *potential* of this musical shape." (2014: 122f.) If we see Jelinek's work as making what Roesner calls an "offer toward musical realization", then it is the directors, dramaturges and actors of these works who realise the text's potential by orchestrating and acting as instruments of the words on the page. In the following, I reveal how Jelinek's musical permutations of sound remix and reshuffle the semantic meaning of words, creating a dual play of language sound and meaning. Then I analyse three ways by which Leonhard Koppelmann and Herbert Kapfer, the creative minds behind *Die Schutzbefohlenen*'s radio adaptation, realise the musical possibilities of Jelinek's speech score by emphasising vocal colour and timbre, contrasts of music with spoken word and cacophony. Throughout this essay, I reflect on how music and musicality in this radio play adaptation allow for Jelinek and her collaborators to draw attention to the voices of the marginalised and the politics of their amplification and suppression.

2   Between Supplication and Indifference: Choral Shifts in Vocal Timbre

Jelinek's text planes include no legible stage directions to indicate how the dramatic 'action' of *Die Schutzbefohlenen* should unfold. However, she does employ shifts in pronouns that imply multiple speakers and perspectives.[10] For

---

9   'I don't have to read [my writings] aloud. I am after all a trained musician and write, whether I want to or not, so to say, Speech-Music. When one has made music as long as I have, one internalises the musical aspects of language, and one works just as much with the sonorousness of words, the sounds of which one plays with as well as their rhythms. I utilise language effectively as musical raw material and I put it together, just as one learns to organise the themes of fugues, the secondary themes, and their development, inversion, mirroring and so on.'

10 For instance, *Charges* begins with the plural form of address: "We are alive. We are alive. The main thing is we live..." (Jelinek 2016: 1) ("Wir leben. Wir leben. Hauptsache, wir

this reason, nearly all productions (both for the stage and for the radio) have performed the work with an ensemble cast, dividing Jelinek's polyphonic text into a series of monologues or dialogues between individuals and groups of characters. The use of a chorus draws a direct connection to one of Jelinek's source texts for her speech score, the classical Greek drama *The Suppliants* (ca. 470 BC) by Aeschylus.[11]

The most explicit nod to the tragic chorus in the text of *Charges* can be found in the insertion of a cletic hymn into the text. The hymn has a long history in ancient Greek oral tradition and religious ritual, and it is widely accepted among scholars that the choruses found in tragedy and satyr plays descended from religious choruses (cf. Furley and Bremer 2001: 274). Cletic hymns, according to Claude Calame, are a typical prayer structure in Greek tragedy, which involve a direct appeal to three divinities (typically Athena, Artemis and Apollo), followed by a recognition of past interventions by these deities to avoid misfortune, and a plea for their continued intervention (cf. 1999: 133). It is likely that Jelinek had this form in mind when she composed the following passage:

> O droben ihr Himmlischen, wir falten fromm die Hände [...] wir beten zu euch, [...] denen die Stadt und das Land und die leuchtenden Wasser der Donau wohl und auch ihr Schwerstrafenden in den Behörden noch wohler gehört: Ihr sagt uns einmal dies, und dann sagt ihr uns das, und nichts können wir gerecht werden, doch gerecht seid ihr ja auch nicht [...]. Was sollen wir machen gegen euch?, ihr dürft alles, ihr könnt alles.[12] (2014: 4)

---

leben..." (Jelinek 2014: 3)). See Felber (2016) for more on Jelinek's use of the 'We' pronoun in *Charges*.

11 Aeschylus's drama, the first work of a planned cycle of plays referred to as the *Danaid Tetralogy*, tells the story of a group of women, the Danaids, who run away in an attempt to avoid marriage with their cousins, begging King Pelasgus and the people of Argos for protection. The German title, *Die Schutzflehenden*, captures the central conflict of the play: the Danaids plead (*flehen*) for protection (*Schutz*) from the king and are granted it. Although Jelinek's text shares with Aeschylus's drama the story of a marginalised group (here, migrant refugees) in search of *Schutz* or protection, she uses the title *Die Schutzbefohlenen* (which Honegger translates as *Charges*, i.e., those who are dependent upon or subjected to a protector), thus highlighting the lack of agency experienced by those pleading for asylum in her text.

12 "Oh, you celestial ones above, devoutly we clasp our hands, [...] we are praying to you [...] who surely own the city and the land and the Danube's glistening waters and even more surely you, the harsh punishers in the bureaucracy: you tell us this and you tell us that, and *we cannot do justice to anything, yet you are not just either* [...]. What could we

Here the 'deities' are two unidentified 'yous' (plural) to whom the city, the land and the luminous waters of the Danube river belong, and who serve as the 'harsh punishers' within the state's bureaucracy. The speakers' (identifiable here as the refugees) plea for intervention appears at this point to be fruitless, and the hymn dissolves into a reflection on the inability of the gods to be of service to those whom they claim to protect.

While these lines of supplication appear only once in Jelinek's text, Kapfer and Koppelmann's setting calls for them to be recited by a group of speakers at three different points within the first half of the radio play (*Die Schutzbefohlenen* 2014: 2' 04"–2' 40"; 12' 20"–12' 57"; 23' 07"–23' 50"). The repetition of this passage and the slow, deliberative manner of its recitation, recall the solemn, ritualistic role of the hymn in traditional Greek theatre (cf. Furley and Bremer 2001: 3). Moreover, the use of the pronoun 'you' in this refrain seems not only to be directed to the gods (or here the state), but also to the audience. If one also considers the typical role of the chorus in Greek tragedy, to relay the emotions being felt on stage to the audience and to invite them to take on the position of the chorus (cf. Calame 1999: 136f.), then we can also read this passage as building bridges of empathy between the listeners of the radio play and the speakers. The audience is invited to consider the probing questions to the 'gods' (here, the almighty bureaucracy and corporations shaping the migration debate) and to place themselves in the position of the refugees, who continue to make the same appeal to the state but receive no answer.

Yet at other moments in the text, the choral voice speaks in a distinctly different tone, heavily inflected and clearly mocking or sarcastic. In response to the plea voiced by a single speaker, "aus unseren anspruchslosen Augen werden wir sanftmütig schauen und um eine Decke und etwas zu essen bitten" ('through our unassuming eyes we will look at you softly and ask for a blanket, for food') the chorus responds:

> Ihre Augen sind ja gar nicht anspruchslos, auch wenn Sie das behaupten, sie stellen ja doch Ansprüche! Heute wollen Sie Decken, Wasser und Essen, was werden Sie morgen verlangen? Unsere Frauen, unsere Kinder, unsere Berufe, unsere Häuser, unsere Wohnungen? Was werden Sie morgen verlangen. Heute verlangen Sie vielleicht noch nichts oder nicht viel, aber morgen wird es viel sein, das wissen wir schon, deswegen sind

---

do against you?, you can do anything, there is nothing you cannot do." (Jelinek 2016: 1f.) The words in italics are my modifications to Honegger's translation, as they capture more closely the meaning of Jelinek's words.

wir die Stellvertreter von Stellvertretern von Stellvertretern. (Jelinek 2014: 6)[13]

Identifying themselves as an anonymous bureaucratic wing of the state ('the deputies of deputies of deputies'), the chorus now demands that the audience identify with the position of those who see the arrival of the migrants as a strain on their resources and threat to their livelihood. This shift in perspective is made apparent in the audio recording through a transformation in vocal colour and timbre – that is, the tonal quality of the sound. Moreover, in stark contrast to the monotonous pleading of the choral hymn, this passage varies widely in intonation and pitch, creating a dramatic build up to the final repetition of the word "Stellvertreter" (*Die Schutzbefohlenen* 2014: 9' 40"–10' 11").

In the radio play setting, both of these choral passages are accompanied by additional atmospheric music. In the repeated 'hymnal' passage, one hears the sound of bells alternating between two notes, highlighting the feeling of stasis, while in the second passage one hears a repetitive rhythmic figure that increases in tempo as the speaking voices become more and more anxious and enraged. In both cases, the musical language and musical setting of the text emphasise acoustically that which Jelinek's musical language gestures toward on the page: the sharp dichotomy between the two positions, one pleading and the other indignant. The juxtaposition of these two positions disrupts the empathetic bonds that the choral voice would traditionally evoke in the listener, provoking instead feelings of disorientation and alienation.

3 A Well-Rounded Body of Sound? Music and Musical Language in Opposition

Music can serve a variety of functions in radio drama. In the traditional literary or narrative radio drama's storyworld, extradiegetic music (in the form of introductory or closing music, or music inserted between scenes), can set the scene or create an atmosphere. Intradiegetic music, the music that the characters within the radio drama's storyworld hear, can play a more concrete role

---

13 "Your eyes are not unassuming at all, even though you say so they assume certain things – that you deserve blankets, water and food, what will you think you deserve tomorrow? Our wives, our children, our jobs, our homes? What will you ask for tomorrow? Today you might not ask for a lot, but tomorrow it will be a lot, we already know, and that is why we are the deputies of deputies of deputies." (Jelinek 2016: 8)

in the plot of the narrative, establishing specificity of place or offering clues to the kind of action taking place.

For much of *Die Schutzbefohlenen*, the use of music is primarily extradiegetic; that is, it sets the tone for the scene and marks passages of increasing tension or intensity. Music in these instances underscores the rhythmic, pulsing meter of the chorus's chanted lines and adds to the sense of urgency that the text evokes. In other sections of the radio play, however, text and music interact to serve a narrative function.[14] This mode of sound orchestration is most noticeable in the second half of the radio play production of *Die Schutzbefohlenen*, which highlights two occasions in which refugees were permitted immediate naturalisation as citizens (*Blitzeinbürgerung*) due to their special financial or social status: the Russian opera singer Ana Netrebko in 2006 and Tatjana Borissowna Yumascheva, the daughter of former Russian President Boris Yeltsin, in 2009. In discussing the case of Netrebko (who is not named in the text but referred to multiple times throughout as "this woman" ("diese Frau") or "the second daughter" ("die zweite Tochter"), Jelinek quotes from the Austrian Ministry of the Interior's statement on integration, published in 2013 under the title *Zusammenleben in Österreich. Die Werte, die uns binden* (*Living Together in Austria. The Values that Bind us Together*). The document is divided into six principles: freedom, constitutional state (or state of law), democracy, republic, federalism and separation of powers, each principle discussing the values associated with it. Under the principle of democracy, the document proclaims: "Für einen abgerundeten Klangkörper braucht es viele verschiedene Stimmen. Das Ziel einer Band ist es, die einzelnen Instrumente gemeinsam harmonisch klingen zu lassen." (Staatssekretariat 2012: 18)[15] Jelinek uses this quotation as a jumping off point for her musical wordplay. Riffing on the idea of harmonising (*Zusammenklingen*), her speaker questions whether all refugees (or only those with talents considered marketable to the state) can truly be a part of the well-rounded body of sound that composes the Austrian nation. She claims that while Netrebko can sing, the refugees "dürfen nicht klingen und nicht klagen" (Jelinek 2014: 10). The transformation of "klingen" to "klagen" (from 'to resound' to 'to complain') offers an example of the musicality of Jelinek's language and the way that it uses sound play to expand the meaning of a word or phrase.[16] Powell and Bethman describe this "musical humor"

---

14   For more on the "narrative arrangement" of music and text, see Huwiler (2010: 133).
15   For a well-rounded body of sound, many different voices are needed. The goal of this ensemble is to let the individual instruments harmonically resound together.
16   Honegger chooses a different wordplay here – from harmonise to harm: "That this woman [Netrebko] is allowed to harmonise with us, well not with us, we could get in harm's way…" (Jelinek 2016: 30).

in Jelinek's works as operating on several levels: "one semantic or metaphorical (that of the clichés of cultural conservativism that are constantly 'heard in the background' of her writing as a kind of *obligato* or *basso continuo*) and the other syntactic and metonymic" (2008: 167). Indeed, in the realisation of this passage for the radio production, the repetitive syntax of "we must not" forms a rhythmic pulse next to the vowel shifts from the short "i" to long "a" in "klingen" and "klagen". Here music highlights an association between these two phrases that is not just semantic but also acoustic. Despite the optimistic words of the state's document on integration, the participation of the refugees in the harmonious state remains elusive.

The desire for harmonic synthesis and the inability to attain it also guides the musical setting of the passage that directly precedes this monologue, and which features the recording of a soprano opera singer (*Die Schutzbefohlenen* 2014: 25' 15"–26' 29"). In contrast to the primarily atmospheric use of music that accompanied the choral passages, music in this section of the radio play hovers in between the intra- and extradiegetic (both within and outside of the narrative world). It begins as a kind of background music until it becomes clear from the speaker's monologue that this voice is the acoustic representation of Netrebko. In its intradiegetic function, this voice seems to work against the voice of the speaker; despite the speaker's hope that the refugees might be allowed to harmonise with this woman, her voice is mediated through a filter that makes it sound as though the singing is coming from far away or through a crackly speaker. The return of the chorus at the lines "na, mit uns nicht" ("well not with us") signals the fade-out of the singing voice (*Die Schutzbefohlenen* 2014: 26' 29"; Jelinek 2014: 10; Jelinek 2016: 30) and an ominous musical motif takes its place – the sound of string basses urgently playing a rising and descending scale, overlapped by the sound of an airplane (indicating how Netrebko arrived in Austria). With the words of the chorus saying "wir dürfen gar nichts, nicht einmal hier sein" ("we can't do anything, not even be here"), the bass motif disappears and we hear once again the juxtaposition of the opera-singing and the voice of a single speaker (*Die Schutzbefohlenen* 2014: 27' 12"; Jelinek 2014: 10; Jelinek 2016: 30). Thus, the setting of the music in this scene, that is, the way that the opera-singing musical motif fades in and out, resisting harmonisation with the other voices in the radio drama, is a crucial strategy for relaying the text's critique. Music highlights the speakers' fears that just as the refugees will never be able to sing with Netrebko, they will also never be truly integrated into the body of sound that is the Austrian nation. The speaker draws explicit attention to this fact a few moments later, when he remarks that all will want to hear Netrebko, but the refugees remain "ein sprechender Zug ins Nichts" (Jelinek 2014: 10). In the recording, this line, which Gitta Honegger translates as "a talking train to nothingness" (Jelinek 2016: 31), is spoken by the chorus, and once again the singing voice in the background is abruptly silenced (*Die Schutzbefohlenen* 2014: 27' 15"). In this way, the radio play soundscape uses language and music in opposition to emphasise the contrast between insiders and outsiders, those whose voices are allowed to be heard and those whose voices are silenced. In this case, music does not accompany or emphasise the words beings spoken as it might in a more traditional narrative radio drama, but is rather used to embody a specific character. The answer to the speaker's plea to partake in the body of sound is made evident through the musical setting in which the musical singing voice and the collective voice of the chorus cannot harmonise together.

4   Cacophony

If the previous episode about Netrebko employed music in opposition to musical language to plea for a 'harmonious society', then the episode on the ideal of freedom can be read as a more violent and forceful clash of sounds, a cacophonic and dissonant response to the hollow ideals surrounding the public discourse on integration. Koppelmann and Kapfer highlight the noisy nature of Jelinek's text by calling for the speakers to emphasise verbal stalls and stutters, exposing the slipperiness of the language that shapes this discourse.

Jelinek's text references once again *Zusammenleben in Österreich*, recalling a passage that pleads for Austrians to use freedom responsibly and to acknowledge, esteem and respect the freedom of others: "Freiheit bedeutet [...], dass man diese in Verantwortung für sich selbst und die Mitmenschen gebraucht und diese eigene Freiheit selbstverständlich auch bei allen anderen Menschen anerkennt, achtet und respektiert." (Staatssekretariat 2013: 10)[17] In the radio play, the speaker (whose mocking tone of voice suggests that she embodies not a refugee but rather an opposer to integration), reformulates this language in the following way:

> die Freiheit, die haben wir gebraucht, ja, genau die, wir brauchen sie, oje, nichts mehr übrig, ich wollte Ihnen noch was aufheben, aber es ist einfach nichts mehr da. [...] Ich nehme mir die Freiheit daneben, auch wenn schon ein andrer sein Handtuch draufgelegt hat, ich bin so frei, andre Menschen zu brauchen, nein, äh, zu gebrauchen, nein, falsch, die Freiheit

---

17   'Freedom means [...] that one uses it responsibly for oneself and for one's fellow human beings and that one naturally recognises, esteems and respects this distinctive freedom for all other humans.'

> gebrauche ich ja, und zwar brauchte ich sie, damit ich die Freiheit andrer ächten, äh achten kann…. (Jelinek 2014: 7)[18]

Freedom, in this passage, becomes a commodity, which the speaker tries to hoard away and keep from others. In her text, the speaker 'slips' multiple times – first she says she is free to "use" people ("brauchen") and then corrects herself, saying she means to "put them to use" ("zu gebrauchen"); then she clarifies that she means to put freedom to use so that she can "condemn" the freedom of others ("ächten"), before catching herself and correcting "condemn" to mean 'respect' ("achten"). The addition of the prefix "ge-" and the diphthong shift from "a" to "ä" reveal the precarity of freedom and respect in the face of greed and exploitation. In the radio drama, these slips of the tongue sound more like stumbles or trips. The words "äh" ("uh") and "oje" ("oh dear" or "sorry") in an exaggerated tone, and the punctuated, dissonant sounds of the speaker's shrieks, suppressed laughter and guttural noises interrupt the flow of the passage, unsettling the listener further. The cacophonous voice of the speaker in this way reveals Austria's statement on human values to be nothing but empty platitudes, easily manipulated or altogether disregarded in the face of individual self-interest (*Die Schutzbefohlenen* 2014: 15' 15"–16' 14").

The use of cacophony, like the sudden shifts in vocal colour and the opposition of voice and music, establish the soundscape of *Die Schutzbefohlenen* as an ambiguous space where listeners are confronted with a variety of perspectives that they must continuously parse out and re-evaluate. Thus, it is the sound of the words, in particular their musical quality and acoustic realisation, that prompts the listener to question the meaning of the words that they hear and to critically reflect on the moral dilemmas surrounding the refugee crisis and integration debates.

5   Conclusion

The adaptation of *Die Schutzbefohlenen* for the radio dialogues with a long tradition of experimentation with musical language in German radio drama

---

18   In Honegger's translation of this passage, she creates a different wordplay – instead of "ächten"/"achten", the speaker slips from "condemn" to "condone": "Freedom is what we need, yes, that one there, sorry, nothing's left. I wanted to save some for you and suddenly it's all gone. [...] Well then I take the freedom next to it, even though someone has already reserved it, I take the liberty to use other people, no, to put them to good use, uh, wrong, it's freedom I put to good use, I use it so I can condemn, uh condone the freedom of others, but not other people, I have no use for them..." (Jelinek 2016: 17)

as well as a more recent 'musical turn' in the contemporary German theatre scene. These connections are perhaps unsurprising if one considers, first, that acoustic experimentation in the theatrical avant-garde is deeply entangled with the development of acoustic sound art on the radio[19]; and second, that many of Jelinek's recent radio collaborators, including Koppelmann, are also influential theatre directors.

Known for its experimentation with sound and critique of language, the New Radio Drama movement in the 1960s and 70s has had a lasting impact on the role of sound and music in theatre and radio to this day. An essay by Rudolf Frisius entitled "Musik als Hörspiel – Hörspiel als Musik" ('Music as Radio Drama – Radio Drama as Music'), which appeared in a foundational text of this movement, i.e., Klaus Schöning's *Spuren des neuen Hörspiels* (*Traces of the New Radio Drama*, 1968), reveals how New Radio Drama practitioners sought to reconceptualise the relationship between language and music in the era of mass-mediated sound. He wrote that, in radio drama, the word can be 'musicalised' through 'composed language' ("komponierte Sprache") and the 'polyphonic fission' of a text ("polyphone Aufspaltung des Textes"). By composed language, Frisius means the text produced by a writer that goes beyond standard literary conventions to realise the 'acoustic pattern ("Klangbild") of language. His term, 'polyphonic fission', refers to the division of a single block of text among several voices, the removing or reworking of words, or the repetition of sections of text for emphasis (cf. Frisius 1982: 140).

Although Jelinek at one time sought to distance herself from the sound experiments of the New Radio Drama in the early 1970s, distinguishing her own language-play from their emphasis on sound effects, she shares with many writers of New Radio Drama a penchant for critiquing language by reorganising and permutating words according to their sounds.[20] And, indeed,

---

19 Mladen Ovadija has traced this history in detail, connecting the musicality of today's theatrical avant-garde back even further than the New Radio Drama, to the radiophonic experiments of the Futurists and to the *musique concrète* of Pierre Schaeffer (2013: 129–139).

20 For example, one can draw comparisons with the works of two other Austrian writers, Ernst Jandl and Friederike Mayröcker, in particular, their radio drama *Fünf Mann Menschen* (*Five Man Humanity,* SWF 1968, dir. Peter Michel Ladiges), which is considered one of the foundational works of the New Radio Drama movement, and also with Jandl's *Lautpoesie* (*Acoustic Poetry*). Yet, in her introduction to the radio drama *Wien West*, Jelinek wrote: "Meine Hörspiele sind ja sehr sprachintensiv. Das heißt, ihre Figuren entstehen aus Sprache, sprechen um ihr Leben, und sobald sie zu sprechen aufhören, verschwinden sie wieder. Ich spreche, daher bin ich. [...] Das damals neue Hörspiel mit seinen vielerlei Varianten von Schall, Geräusch, Musik, Sprachfetzen, Klang, ist von mir eigentlich immer zu einer reinen Sprachpartitur reduziert worden..." (qtd. in Janke 2014: 202) ('My radio dramas are very language-intensive. That is, their characters grow out of language, they

Koppelmann and Kapfer appear to have employed some of the techniques that Frisius identifies in adapting Jelinek's speech score for the radio, highlighting the musicality of her language and creating many voices from one text plane.

Larson Powell claims that Jelinek's text planes seek not only to exploit word sounds to question their meaning, but also to reveal the potential of other meanings and interpretations. He writes that what is analysed in Jelinek's work is "less 'language' in the 'pure' sense than the discourse [...] of which it is the vehicle" (2013: 85). Put another way, Jelinek's wordplays are more than a general critique of language and the cultural values it represents, but rather about systematically dismantling the rhetoric surrounding specific controversial cultural debates. To this end, Koppelmann and Kapfer's use of composed language and the polyphonic fission of text in the production of this radio play draw attention to Jelinek's larger project: to reduce recognisable cultural references and language ripped from the headlines of mass media outlets to sound bites, and then to re-compose them to reveal their subtle hypocrisy.

In their experiments with the musicality of sound, Jelinek's radio adaptations also speak to recent developments in the contemporary German theatre scene. David Roesner has highlighted the significance of music for the contemporary, postdramatic German theatre scene "as a rhythmical, gesticulatory, melodic, spatial and aural phenomenon *as well as* a carrier of meaning" (Roesner 2008: 48; emphasis in original).[21] For Roesner, the new uses of music in theatre have important implications for audience perception, challenging their expectations and, in particular, their beliefs about causality and coherence (cf. ibid.: 54). As demonstrated above, Koppelmann and Kapfer's adaptation of Jelinek's work draws on these same principles, using music and musical language to create ambiguity about the speakers and the meaning behind their words.

Yet, it is also important that musicality in the adaptation of Jelinek's works for the radio be considered independently of such developments in the theatre to acknowledge the unique experience of the single-channel mode of the radio. On the radio, the audience's concentration rests solely on the musical interplay of voices. This concentration on the voice is especially significant for Koppelmann and Kapfer's adaptation of *Die Schutzbefohlenen*, which stages its

---

       speak for their life and as soon as they stop speaking, they disappear. I speak, therefore I am. [...] What was once the New Radio Drama with its diverse variants of echo, noise, music, speech-scraps and sound has in my case actually always been reduced to a pure language score...')

21   Theatre scholar Hans-Thies Lehmann has identified 'postdramatic theatre' as drawing on a heterogeneity of styles, rejecting the representation of an explicit narrative or plot in favour of the innovative use of noise and music through the use of mixed- or multimedia effects (2006: 25).

critique of the public discourse on migration and asylum in Austria by turning to music – in particular the concept of harmony, which permeates the setting of Jelinek's work on all levels. Taking the rhetoric of a 'harmonious living together' that Jelinek deconstructs on the level of language in her text, they employ dramatic fluctuations of vocal tone and rhythm to realise acoustically the tensions underlying this message, forcing the listener through musical dissonances to reflect on the *cognitive* dissonance of trying to reconcile the ideal of a harmonious society with the lived experiences of refugees. In this way, their multi-layered approach to adapting Jelinek's text offers a unique opportunity to rethink how music, musical language and musical voices can be used in the radio play soundscape to voice cultural critique.

References

Calame, Claude (1999). "Performative Aspects of the Choral Voice in Greek Tragedy: Civic Identity in Performance". Robin Osborne, transl. Simon Goldhill, Robin Osborne, eds. *Performance Culture and Athenian Democracy*. Cambridge: CUP. 125–153.

Die Schutzbefohlenen (2014). Dir. Leonhard Koppelmann, script, Elfriede Jelinek, perf. Jonas Minthe, Matthias Haase, Bettina Lieder, Christoph Jöde, Janina Sachau. BR/ORF.

Felber, Silke (2016 online). "(Un)making Boundaries: Representing Elfriede Jelinek's *Charges (the Supplicants)*". *Critical Stages/Scènes Critiques* 14 (January). www.critical-stages.org/14/unmaking-boundaries-representing-elfriede-jelineks-charges-the-supplicants/ [05/05/ 2019].

Frisius, Rudolf (1982). "Musik Als Hörspiel – Hörspiel Als Musik". Klaus Schöning, ed. *Spuren Des Neuen Hörspiels*. Frankfurt am Main.: Suhrkamp. 136–166.

Furley, William D., Jan Maarten Bremer, eds. (2001). *Greek Hymns: Selected Cult Songs from the Archaic to the Hellenistic Period*. Tübingen: Mohr Siebeck.

Huwiler, Elke (2010). "Radio Drama Adaptations: An Approach toward an Analytical Methodology". *Journal of Adaptation in Film & Performance* 3/2: 129–140.

Janke, Pia (2003). "Elfriede Jelinek und die Musik: Versuch einer ersten Bestandsaufnahme". Gerhard Melzer, Paul Pechmann, eds. *Sprachmusik: Grenzgänge der Literatur*. Wien: Sonderzahl. 189–207.

Janke, Pia (2014). *Elfriede Jelinek: Werk und Rezeption*. 2 vols. Vienna: Präsens Verlag.

Jelinek, Elfriede (2013a online). *Die Schutzbefohlenen*. https://www.elfriedejelinek.com/fschutzbefohlene.htm [01/06/2021].

Jelinek, Elfriede (2013b online). *Textflächen*. http://www.elfriedejelinek.com/ftextf.htm [01/06/2021].

Jelinek, Elfriede (2014). *Die Schutzbefohlenen*. Hamburg: Rowohlt Theater Verlag.

Jelinek, Elfriede (2016). *Charges (the Supplicants)*. Gitta Honegger, transl. London: Seagull.

Jürs-Munby, Karen (2009). "The Resistant Text in Postdramatic Theatre: Performing Elfriede Jelinek's *Sprachflächen*". *Performance Research* 14/1: 46–56.

Kapfer, Herbert (2017). *Sounds like Hörspiel 1989–2017*. München: Belleville.

Kepplinger, Christoph (2007). "Partituren für den Rundfunk: Elfriede Jelineks akustische Literatur". Pia Janke et al., eds. *Elfriede Jelinek: "Ich Will Kein Theater": Mediale Überschreitungen*. Wien: Praesens Verlag. 292–304.

Lehmann, Hans-Thies (2006). *Postdramatic Theater*. Karen Jürs-Munby, transl. London: Routledge.

Ovadija, Mladen (2013). *Dramaturgy of Sound in the Avant-Garde and Postdramatic Theatre*. Kingston, ON: McGill-Queen's University Press.

Powell, Larson (2013). *The Differentiation of Modernism: Postwar German Media Arts*. Rochester, NY: Camden House.

Powell, Larson, Brenda Bethman (2008). "'One Must Have Tradition in Oneself, to Hate It Properly': Elfriede Jelinek's Musicality". *Journal of Modern Literature* 32/1: 163–183.

Pye, Gillian, Siobhan Donovan (2009). "'Schreiben und Komponieren': Elfriede Jelinek's 'Rosamunde'". *Austrian Studies* 17: 179–192.

Roesner, David (2008). "The Politics of the Polyphony of Performance: Musicalization in Contemporary German Theatre". *Contemporary Theatre Review* 8/1: 44–55.

Roesner, David (2014). *Musicality in Theatre: Music as Model, Method and Metaphor in Theatre-Making*. London and New York, NY: Routledge.

Solibakke, Karl (2014). "Geseire, Geleiere und Gehübungen: Music and Sports in Elfriede Jelinek's *Die Klavierspielerin* and *Winterreise*". *Austrian Studies* 22: 106–120.

Staatssekretariat für Integration, ed. (2013 online). *Zusammenleben in Österreich*. http://www.staatsbuergerschaft.gv.at/fileadmin/user_upload/Broschuere/RWR-Fibel.pdf [01/06/2021].

Thiers, Bettina (2016). *Experimentelle Poetik als Engagement: konkrete Poesie, visuelle Poesie, Lautdichtung und experimentelles Hörspiel im deutschsprachigen Raum von 1945 bis 1970*. Hildesheim: Georg Olms Verlag.

CHAPTER 14

Scoring the Unseen: Composing 'Film Music' for Radio Drama

Alan E. Williams

Abstract

This chapter recounts the process of commissioning, negotiating and composing an orchestral score to a BBC radio drama adaptation of John Wyndham's *The Kraken Wakes*. It explores the different types of representation used in music for audio drama, informed by film music theory. The performance and live recording of the project, viewed from a historical perspective, evokes the Golden Age of radio, while the size of the orchestra and composition methods recall the film music of the 1950s. The collaboration process resulted in a hybridised artistic product, straddling the boundaries between live event, radio drama and film score.

In 2015, I was commissioned to write the music for a radio drama to be made by Manchester-based independent production company Savvy Productions for broadcast on BBC Radio 4 the following year. The production was to be a version of the 1953 novel by John Wyndham, *The Kraken Wakes*, in a contemporary adaptation by Val McDermid. The adaptation was studded with terrifying scientifically accurate scenarios of the flooding caused by invading aliens melting the icecaps, clearly showing an unmistakably contemporary resonance with possible scenarios created by climate change. It was recorded live in front of a studio audience in the Philharmonic Studios in MediaCityUK, Salford with well-known TV actors Tamsin Greig (*Black Books, Episodes*), Paul Higgins (*Line of Duty*) and Richard Harrington (*Hinterland*) in lead roles, and the production was also notable for the performance (as herself) of Scottish First Minister Nicola Sturgeon.

But the most striking aspect to the production for the purposes of this chapter was the partnership with the BBC Philharmonic orchestra, based in Salford's MediaCityUK, and widely regarded as one of the world's finest broadcast orchestras. Orchestral Director Simon Webb was keen to ensure the orchestra was heard on BBC Radio 4, with its higher number of listeners, in order to connect with audiences which went beyond that of the UK's main classical music network, BBC Radio 3. From the outset the orchestra had made clear that they wanted to be an equal partner in the drama, which lent a somewhat elevated status to the music and the fortunate composer. The drama ran for roughly 100 minutes in two episodes, for which I composed approximately 28 minutes of music.[1]

The purpose of this chapter is to describe the creative process involved in this specific production; to compare this process, the music composition methods employed, and the aesthetic choices made with those of other radio dramas, and those of film music; and to situate the project within the field of music for media more generally. While it is true that, because certain aspects of the project make it relatively unusual, it can in no way be regarded as a 'typical' contribution of music to a radio or audio drama, I want to argue that by occupying a liminal space between live performance, concert and radio play, the project sheds light on all these forms, as well as on music for film, a heritage it draws on heavily.

1 Music in Radio Drama

Radio and audio drama, as well as closely related variants – the feature, the experimental *Hörspiel*, the dramatised reading, radio ballad, and so on – continue to attract passionate adherents, and roughly 600 hours of drama per year are broadcast on the UK's premiere speech radio station, BBC Radio 4. Boris Kremenliev, writing at the height of the US radio era in 1949, estimated that roughly a third of all radio output was drama (which would equate to 4–6 hours per day today, assuming radio stations were not broadcasting 24 hours in 1949), but lamented that "the profits of radio go into the development of a wonderful new toy [i.e., television] that may make audio broadcasting obsolete" (1949: 82). Kremenliev was not wholly correct about audio broadcasting, but he was right about the future demise of radio drama in the US. In the UK, it continued to hold an elevated status into the 1960s, with leading writers such as Louis MacNeice, Samuel Beckett and (famously) Dylan Thomas contributing important and highly regarded plays to the genre. The medium also created early opportunities for significant playwrights in the 1960s and 1970s such as Harold Pinter, Joe

---

1 A short edited video from the live performance can be accessed via the BBC website, and timings in square brackets will refer to this video: https://www.bbc.co.uk/programmes/p03vlfh3 [14/04/2021].

Orton, Tom Stoppard and Caryl Churchill (see Rodger 1982). The close relationship between British radio drama and theatre is reflected in the relative absence and at best subsidiary role of music in many radio productions – Thomas's *Under Milk Wood* (1954), for example, has only diegetic music. However, there are notable exceptions to this, particularly in dramas composed for the BBC's Third Programme (subsequently Radio 3). MacNeice collaborated prominently with leading composers Benjamin Britten (*The Dark Tower*, 1946) and William Walton (*Christopher Columbus*, 1944), while Pinter's *Voices* in 2000 represented a substantial collaboration with composer James Clarke.

By contrast, film-style composition prevailed in the golden age of radio drama on which Boris Kremenliev was commenting in 1949. Of the 'major' dramas produced when he was writing, Kremenliev believed that roughly half were recorded in Hollywood. The aesthetic of these dramas, and the way they used music, was much more like that of film – indeed his article is entitled "Background Music for Radio Drama", a title which could never have described, for example, Britten's music for *The Dark Tower*. Radio drama from Hollywood often used smaller versions of the film orchestras, with musicians numbering between fifteen and twenty. But while such mixed large chamber ensembles would seem to offer plenty of opportunity for imaginative music, what stopped radio drama music from attaining greater artistic quality in Kremenliev's view was the speed at which composers were expected to work – 1 to 2 days for 4 to 8 minutes of music, probably including part writing and orchestration given that budgets were so much smaller than for the movies. Kremenliev looked enviously across the Atlantic to England and France, noting that Ralph Vaughan Williams and Walton (he must have meant the music to MacNeice's radio play *Christopher Columbus*), as well as Arthur Honegger and Darius Milhaud were writing full orchestral scores for radio (cf. 1949: 81n4). In fact, such contributions were in the minority.

Kremenliev lists four main functions for music in radio drama: *signature* music, *curtain* music (which delineates scene changes), *bridge* music (to cover scene transitions, especially involving mood changes) and *background* music. More generally, it "serves essentially to create atmosphere and heighten emotion. It keeps the story moving by giving it color and holding the attention of the listener", attempting also to "compensate for the missing visual image" (ibid.: 76). More recent terminology is derived from film music – diegetic and non-diegetic, underscore and so on – but specific terms are also used within the industry, such as 'passage of time music' (related to Kremenliev's bridge music), and the more common 'sting' – a short section of less than 2–3 seconds derived from a more extensive music cue. Also missing from Kremenliev's list is the common use of music to indicate, along with sound effects, a time period.

Horses' hooves and carriage noises, as well as a fortepiano might well indicate a Jane Austen adaptation set in the first decade of the nineteenth century.

Richard Hand and Mary Traynor, in *The Radio Drama Handbook*, quote Andrew Crisell in giving four functions very similar to those coined by Kremenliev 50 years earlier: music as *link, mood* music, music as *stylised sound effect* (a thunderstorm indicated by a percussion instrument, etc.), music as *indexical function* (diegetic music) – although later they also add the functions of "locating the drama at a particular point in history, even in a particular place" – and drama gaining extra significance through song lyrics (2011: 57). These texts notwithstanding, by comparison with music in film, music in radio drama seems distinctly under-theorised.

2   Film Music versus Radio Drama Music

Because music's presence in film pre-dated audible speech and sound effects, it forms a part of early film theory. Gregg Redner describes the way Vsevolod Illarionovich Pudovkin responded to the new development of sound in 1929 by calling for music and sound to be independent of each other, or to be in "counterpoint" (2011: 7). Although most film music has over the history of the medium generally paralleled the action on screen, there are some notable examples of counterpoint between music and image: Ennio Morricone's quasi-diegetic use of the musical watch theme in Sergio Leone's *A Few Dollars More* (1965); or Martin Scorsese's use of the Intermezzo from Pietro Mascagni's opera *Guglielmo Ratcliff* (1895) over a brutal fight scene in his 1980 *Raging Bull*, for instance. Despite the ever-present tendency for music to be interdependent with the other elements of film (image, character, plot and so on), film theory tends to treat these elements as separate facets which comment on each other; or more precisely, the music comments on the image, since this is mostly the order in which they are produced.

In radio, commentators have tended to emphasise a much more equal collaboration between the creators. For example, composer William Alwyn said that "while working on a feature the collaboration between writer and composer was close and intimate – both script and music were carefully worked out from the inception of the subject" (qtd. in Rodger 1984: 83). This description of the production process of the radio feature – a form peculiar to radio which fuses poetic writing, soundscape, documentary and music (cf. Cleverdon 1969: 17) – applies in large measure to radio drama as well. Rodger gives details of the working process of Louis MacNeice, poet and one of the most important radio dramatists of the middle years of the twentieth century, in particular his notes to composer Mátyás Seiber for his 1947 play *Grettir the Strong*, which show the play was conceived with specific lengths of music cues, in mind (cf. Rodger 1984: 104). While in practice the difference may not appear to be significant, it can be viewed as an organisational difference, and a difference in ethos. In film, on the whole, music is added late in the process and comes as the result of a division of labour – the musician does his or her job and does not comment on the work of others. By contrast, a much more collaborative ethos prevails (or is held to prevail) in the more intimate medium of radio.

It is important to note that this difference in ethos was not necessarily one observed as a general fact, but more a question of the value ascribed by commentators to that ethos. In fact, as Kremenliev showed, conditions for composers in the Hollywood radio dramas of the 1940s were comparable in principle, though arguably worse in degree, to those found in cinema. Similarly, the idea that most of the 600 or so hours per annum of drama produced for BBC radio in the United Kingdom show this collaborative ethos between composer and writer/producer described by Rodger is unrealistic. Most radio drama generally uses stock music libraries, only involving a composer at arm's length. Ironically, this reproduces a situation described by Kremenliev as prevailing in radio drama before the war, when "radio [...] had finally discarded the stock library music cues" (1949: 76).

Equally, there are examples in cinema of film being produced with music in mind from the outset – Anthony Minghella's close collaboration with composers being a case in point, or Vaughan Williams's practice of composing the score "as, or prior to, the film being shot, rather than composing to the direct visual stimuli of the finished film" (Redner 2011: 135).

3   Commission and Production

To assess the extent to which the commissioning and composition of music for *The Kraken Wakes* corresponded to the Hollywood division of labour model, or to the more collaborative ethos of British radio drama as described above, we need to examine the process that led to its creation. *The Kraken Wakes* was commissioned as part of BBC Radio 4's substantial 'Dangerous Visions' season, which featured adaptations of science fiction, particularly those stories with a dystopian aspect. Savvy Productions, a small independent production company specialising in location-recorded drama, held an ace up its sleeve: the Radio 4 commissioner wanted more work by the 'Queen of Crime' Val McDermid, whose pacey, well-plotted novels have a huge and loyal following. McDermid had enjoyed collaborating with Savvy founder and producer

Justine Potter on a returning comedy crime drama series (initially entitled *Deadheading*), particularly her ability to create an informal working atmosphere on location while working rapidly and on schedule. Generally tending to the small-scale, Savvy had also explored territory which would more commonly be considered cinematic – e.g., their 2010 series *Amazing Grace* began with a large scale depiction of war in Sudan, employing sound design by Eloise Whitmore and music by film composer Stephen Kilpatrick.

Adapting John Wyndham's *The Kraken Wakes* also appeared to demand something on a huge scale. The plot centres around a journalist couple who, while honeymooning, observe the impact on the sea of mysterious fireballs. They become fascinated by these fireball reports, and the subsequent cover-ups by governments. The fireballs turn out to be an alien invasion, and these extraterrestrial beings – called 'xenobaths' in the novel – occupy the seabed in the deepest parts of the ocean. Unexplained technology allows them to initially destroy all shipping, then subsequently to flood the world by melting the polar icecaps. An orchestral score seemed appropriate for two reasons: one is the scale of the events described – cities destroyed, huge population shifts, ships blown up; the second is that, although we see the results of the xenobaths' attacks on humanity, and at one point witness an attack by weird automata ('seatanks'), we never actually see the xenobaths themselves. It is perhaps this unseen aspect that has made *The Kraken Wakes* one of the few novels by Wyndham not to have been televised or filmed, although it has been adapted for radio on at least four occasions.[2] The orchestra, it seemed to the composer and producer, was capable of suggesting powerfully without actually representing directly.

In several ways the production methods returned to the methods of the 1940s. It was performed in the orchestra's own studio recording space in front of a live audience, with the difference that the production team were not

---

2 Three are listed by the BBC Genome website:
   a) *Curtain Up: The Kraken Wakes*. Writ. John Keir Cross. Broadcast 28 April 1954. BBC Light Programme.
   b) *Late Night Theatre: The Kraken Wakes*. Writ. John Constable. Dir. Susan Roberts. Broadcast 21 February 1998. BBC Radio 4 (FM).
   c) Read in 16 episodes by Stephen Moore. First broadcast 23 March 2014. BBC Radio 4. (https://genome.ch.bbc.co.uk/search/0/20?filt=is_radio&q=kraken+wakes+wyndham#top [25/04/2022]).
   In addition, the website SFFAudio.com lists the following radio drama adaptation:
   d) *The Kraken Wakes*. Writ. Eric Cameron. Broadcast 1965 (exact date unknown) CBC Vancouver (https://www.sffaudio.com/archive-org-cbc-radio-vancouver-the-kraken-wakes-based-on-the-novel-by-john-wyndham/ [25/04/2022]).

able to provide sound effects in addition to the music – which would in the 'Golden Age' of radio have been produced live – as these were to be mixed in post-production. Therefore, the burden of anything 'unseen' by the live audience was to be taken by the music alone. A model for this production process preceded *The Kraken Wakes*. Composer Neil Brand had adapted Dickens's *A Christmas Carol* (1843) in December 2013 with the BBC Symphony Orchestra and the BBC Singers. This production was recorded in front of a live audience, with actors and orchestra in the same space. They chose to use standard voice microphones, and the room reverberation can clearly be heard in the voices on the clips still available on the BBC drama website.[3] But, as Laurence Raw describes, this benefited a production which "consciously drew attention to its artificiality" in a "quasi-Brechtian" manner (2015). Although the combination of live recording with actors in front of the orchestra for *The Kraken Wakes* was more or less the same as in Brand's earlier production, the team tried to make the experience more immersive and intimate for the broadcast audience: in order to minimise room noise – a problem in the relatively resonant space of the BBC Philharmonic studios – radio microphone headsets were used, allowing for some degree of the close-miked intimate vocal recording typical of studio-based radio dramas. In the event, occasionally some room resonance could be heard, particularly that of Richard Harrington's powerful baritone.

Despite these efforts, the performance/recording conditions to some degree flew in the face of received wisdom of how radio drama should be made. As Donald McWhinnie noted in 1959: "The radio composer's main concern is to avoid at all costs any feeling of the concert platform; once we associate sound patterns with rows of dinner jacketed instrumentalists we are faced with the same clash of conventions which often faces us in the theatre." (qtd. in Rodger 1984: 111) It is interesting to speculate why McWhinnie is so concerned about the perception of artificiality created by the use of the orchestra in relation to radio drama when in films the orchestra was unfailingly used for films during the same period without similar comment. Perhaps this anxiety derives from McWhinnie's view of radio as a dreamlike fusion of sound, music and language, in which neither element should draw too much attention to itself. I hoped that, by writing music which evoked the music of films – in particular scores by John Barry, Bernard Herrmann and Leonard Rosenman – it would be

---

3 See https://www.bbc.co.uk/programmes/p02dklq7/p02dkknc [14/04/2021].

the visuality of film music that predominated in both the live and the broadcast audience's reception of the play.

By writing what one might – slightly ironically – call 'film music for radio drama', we have the opportunity to compare the two forms. The process throws up questions such as: how can music relate to imagery if there are no accompanying images? Can music be in counterpoint with the narrative if there is no visual content? What does it mean to say that the music is an 'extra character' in the drama, as was required by the terms of the commission? In what follows, I want to analyse particular sections of the music and relate them to concepts which are derived either from analyses of radio drama music, analyses of film music, or both.

4 Collaborative Method

As composer William Alwyn noted, radio is a medium which encourages intimate collaboration from the outset. The small number of people involved in the creation of a radio drama allow for a much greater degree of shared artistic vision compared to the much less collaborative medium of film. We were able to ensure that the music was conceived at the outset, even to the extent that the composer and writer/adaptor agreed beforehand on which passages in the book should be adapted so that they would be suitable for a musical as well as a dramatic treatment. The initial plan was developed before the script had been written, and most of the music was composed before the script appeared, thus predating the adaptation (see Figure 14.1). The eighteen musical numbers described here eventually became twenty-three of various lengths, with some minor changes to order.

Some of these cues were what Kremenliev calls either 'bridge music' or 'curtain music', and relatively short; some underscored the dialogue (00' 15"–00' 59" in the BBC video); and some were scenes of a few minutes in length with continuous music where it was driving the action. This last category was the most technically challenging for the actors, and it depended on the musicality and exceptional coordinating abilities of conductor Clark Rundell, as well as the experience of the orchestra to keep dialogue and music together in live performance. These sections needed special attention in the rehearsal room. As time with the orchestra was limited to a 3-hour rehearsal session for the music alone, and another with the actors, we used MIDI versions of the score to rehearse timings, and those indicated in the score were adhered to as closely as possible in the live version.

TABLE 14.1   Music cues agreed with writer Val McDermid prior to composition

No.	Title	Text	Page	Length
1	Opening/ rationale	"far, far beneath in the abysmal sea, his ancient, dreamless, uninvaded sleep, the Kraken sleepeth."	10	1.30
2	Seascape with fireballs	"The sea stretched in front of us like a silken plain in the moonlight"	11	1
		"a brilliant red light as seen in a fairly thick fog, so there is a strong halation."	12	
		"a great burst of steam shot up in a great plume."	13	
3	Information	"a sudden spate of fireball observations"	20	1
4	Interlude 1	Mike and Phyllis		1
5	Descent of the bell with darker sea music	"the quiet drone of the winch"	31	3.30
		"all black and dead now…squids again… luminous fish…small shoal, there, see?"		
		"nightmare fishy horror"	32	
		"the voice cut off dead"		
6	Destruction of ships	"if ever lightning were to strike upwards from the sea" (in the novel this is reported, but we do not see it – could we?)	39	1
7	Interlude 2	Mike and Phyllis		1
8	The depth bomb	"For a long time, as it seemed, everything was intensely still…Then it came. The placid surface of the sea suddenly belched into a vast white cloud, which spread and boiled, writhing upwards."	43	30"
9	Information (reprise) – more reports of the loss of ships	"There's a rumour running wild"	90	1
10a	Escondida interlude	"Escondida's natural spirit of manana"	131	1.30

TABLE 14.1 Music cues agreed with writer Val McDermid prior to composition (*cont.*)

No.	Title	Text	Page	Length
10b	Sea tanks	"sounded like the heavy dragging of metal on stone" "the excrescence quivered but went on swelling" "seemed to split open, as if it had been burst into instantaneous bloom by a vast number of white cilia which rayed out in all directions."	137 139	2
		"they were dragged along together"	141	
11	Fear of the unknown/very dark sea (reprise of opening)	"far, far beneath in the abysmal sea"	10	1.30
12	Interlude 3 (Mahlerian)	Mike and Phyllis		1
13	The sea level rises/ construction of embankments	"machinery worked day and night...a superstructure of concrete blocks was rising the original walls...sweating thousands toiled to raise great levees and walls."	211	2
14	(Alternates with sea-tank music) until catastrophic failure of walls	A groan went up from the crowd. Suddenly there was a loud crack and a rumble of falling masonry...water poured through the gap...the wall crumbled before our eyes."	215	2
15	Mass movement of people	"a whole population was trecking southwards"	215	2
16	Inundation/ silencing of information	"towers of Manhattan standing like frozen sentinels while the glittering water lapped at their lower walls..."	228	1.30
		"the link broke off abruptly. It never worked again."	226	
17	Eerie boat journey to safety	"our progress down the river was cautious and slow"	232	2
18	The radio crackles into life/a frail hope	"I'm coming to life again, Mike"	240	1.30

5 Scoring the Unseen

Most film music theory begins with a discussion of the relationship between a narrative that is seen and an additional layer, often consisting of emotional information, that is heard.[4] This would seem initially to present a problem for the composer of 'film music for radio drama', since there are no accompanying images to which the music can respond. The response to this is threefold. Firstly, music's capacity to refer by association or convention to objects beyond itself is well known and became an important aspect of composers' technique in the form of the nineteenth-century symphonic or tone poem. While the actual objects or ideas that music was capable of representing were relatively general and restricted in number – such as the pastoral, the military, nature, national associations – these were remarkably stable and long-lasting; for example, the pastoral associations of the oboe standing in for the 'shepherd's pipe' persisted into the TV music of the 1970s – think of the theme music to the long-running British soap opera *Emmerdale Farm* (1972). Secondly, Bonnie M. Miller has recently described how creators of radio drama have viewed it as an "intensely visual experience" – with the qualification that the imagery takes place in the mind of the listener (2018: 323). Thus, if the music is responding to anything, it is a narrative which has an imagined visual content. In fact, as Miller says, in radio drama the pictures are better since the listener is invited "to participate actively in the visualisation process, to formulate mental pictures of characters, settings and scenes through the personalised act of listening" (ibid.: 322). Thirdly, film itself often communicates not through what is seen, but about what is only suggested in the mind of the viewer by the combination of imagery and sound. An obvious example would be the 'hallway' scene from Stanley Kubrick's *The Shining* (1980), in which the terrifying denouement of the scene is foreshadowed by the eerie sound world of Béla Bartók's *Music for Strings, Percussion and Celesta* (1937). Horror as a genre in particular depends on images which are suggested indirectly in the mind of the audience. In this, film functions like radio, where writers "stoke the imagination with a few visual cues and let the listeners fill in the rest" (ibid.: 326).

The diving bell scene in our production of *The Kraken Wakes* is one of the sections which needed to be carefully coordinated with the actors. In the novel

---

[4] Prendergast, for example, describes music as "auditory counterpoint to the silent film" (1992: 3); Wierzbicki describes audiences' early film experiences as linking "purely musical affect with the dynamics of the filmic imagery" (2009: 25). Morris examines German film music composer Edmund Meisel's work from the 1930s and his stated attempt at "exact conformity" between music and image (2008: 81).

it is one of the relatively few scenes in which the action is directly witnessed by the protagonists, Mike and Phyllis Watson. They are aboard a navy vessel which is sending a diving bell down to examine the deep-sea site of the impact of a series of 'fireballs' which prove to be extraterrestrial in origin. Two submariners report via an audio cable on what they can see as the bell descends – not much for most of the scene, until towards the end they glimpse something large and ominous, and the line is suddenly cut off. The steel cable of the winch to which the diving bell was attached comes to the surface minus diving bell, and it can be seen to have been fused together as if welded, which is the first concrete proof that 'something' is down there. The score uses the availability of a large string section, with cellos divided in four parts and basses in two to create a dark, opaque texture out of which material – representing half-seen 'things' – emerges. At this point, although the main 'Kraken' theme has not yet appeared, the low strings are playing in canon material which prefigures it, and out of this emerge low, dark, ominous dissonant shapes. The first time this happens is just before the first submariner reports: "There's something else out there. Right on the edge of the light." At the end of the scene, the music suddenly cuts off, in line with the submariner's line "Maybe seeing the underside would – (*Beat. Silence*)." (Williams 2016: 40)[5]

As has already been discussed, music in films does not only show what is on screen, but frequently suggests what is not seen or off screen. This passage both represents the visual obscurity through opaqueness of musical material, providing an audible analogue of the murk which obscures the submariners' view, and the glimpse of the – well, we do not know what – which emerges from the background. This process of representation is facilitated by the clever way McDermid uses the audio feed from the diving bell as a device to embed narration. So, temporarily, we have a narration – which is still within the diegesis – and its musical interpretation. Events within the narration are sometimes preceded by their analogue in the music and sometimes followed by it, depending on whether the function of the music is a representative or an emotionally reactive one. When the submariner glimpses the kraken, the music precedes the observation because the function is a representative one; when the submariner's audio feed is cut off, this is the action, so the music reverts to emotional reaction.

---

5 This scene was in fact the first to be written, in August 2015, when I had been offered the opportunity to have it ready to contribute to the BBC Philharmonic's Proms concert with Jarvis Cocker's *Wireless Nights* programme, which also had an undersea theme – ironically, it followed an extract by John Williams's score to *Jaws* (1975). Once the script arrived in November 2015, I recomposed it so that it better fit the dialogue written by McDermid.

6   Music as Action

Rodger states that radio drama music "often had to participate in the dramatic action" (1982: 64). This comment seems to refer back to the 1940s methods related to the Hollywood studio structure for radio drama described by Kremenliev, where it "compensates for the missing visual image" (1949: 76). When music participates in dramatic action, be it accompanying actual visual images in film, or imagined ones in radio drama, it responds to 'sync points' – moments of action in a film, for example, where precise synchronisation between music and narrative is called for. In fact, as film composer Hummie Mann points out, there may be a small degree of tolerance in the synchronisation between the musical change accompanying the visual action and the seen action – he gives 0.2 seconds as the maximum tolerance for a musical cue to be perceived as in sync with an action, although it may require greater precision to synchronise to sound effects or repeated predictable action (cf. 2015: 236). Habitually, close synchronisation between visual action and music is known as 'mickey-mousing' because of its prominence in animated cartoons, so it remains a point of aesthetic judgement as to how much of the action should be scored using sync points (ibid.: 52).

Bernard Herrmann's famous high string motive for the shower scene in *Psycho* (1960) is often described as if it alone represents the action; for example, Sullivan says "the slashing glissandos seem to stand in for the stabbing knife", which is never actually seen by the audience (2006: 255). What confirms for the viewer that the stabbing occurs are the sound effects created by a melon being stabbed. The music precedes the stab – creating a halo of terror around the scene – but the stabs are not synchronised with visual hits, since these shots are not present.

In *The Kraken Wakes*, the production team planned to add in some sound effects in post-production – after the 'as-live' recording had been made. In one crucial scene of the drama, the music would have to inform the live audience that an action of some kind was taking place. This is the scene where protagonists Phyllis and Mike are on a fictional Carribbean island, Escondida,[6] hoping to report on the landings of the xenobaths' 'seatanks', weird metallic vehicles which emerge from the depths and capture living creatures using sticky tentacles or 'cilia' which drag their unfortunate prey back down to the depths of the sea. This is one of the few cinematically 'visual' scenes in the novel. The

---

6   It is worth pointing out that 'Escondida' means 'hidden' in Spanish.

absence of 'live SFX', unlike 1940s production methods, meant that music alone had to convey the actuality of the action.

The conceit of the scene is that Mike and Phyllis are there to record a news report, and therefore we have a real-time narration in Mike's voice as he 'records' his responses – providing both a pragmatic solution to the problem of the lack of visuals alongside a deepening of the 'horror' effect. This is created by the orchestral music 'being the scene', which is interpreted a few seconds later by the real-time narrator, Mike. As the 'seatanks' have never been witnessed, the character Mike struggles to articulate the weirdness and horror of what he is witnessing, and is forced to grasp at unconvincing similes, all the while as the orchestral music is telling the audience that something horrific is happening using the film music language of 1950s B-movies. The musical reference point was Bernard Herrmann's score to *The Day the Earth Stood Still* (1951), particularly with its incorporation of then unusual electronic effects. Thus, in keeping with the principle of horror, the power of the scene is derived from suggestion – the audience's minds race to fill in the information gap created by the slow-arriving explanatory narration. Unlike in *Psycho*, the music *is* the action – the sync points with the imagined visuals occur in the music, even though we have not yet been fully informed what it is that is happening.

A specific example of a sync point where the music is the action occurs as Mike is describing the expansion of a balloon-like structure emerging from the top of one of the 'seatanks'. This 'expansion' is shown (after the narration in this case) by ten-part divisi strings gradually glissando-ing from a mid-range cluster to a widely spaced chord. It should be clear to the audience what is happening here at the moment the 'event' occurs in the score: at the end of this process there is a short pause, then a 'bursting' sound, using a combination of pizzicato glissando clusters in the strings and descending glissando scales on a Hammond organ (02' 30"–02' 40" in the BBC video). The narration follows the action, but the audience (one hopes) infers from the 'bursting' moment in the score that something has burst 'like a balloon', since what else do balloons do? The absence of the visual stimulus here is an advantage for the composer; the music can represent the action without risk of 'mickey-mousing', since this can only occur when there is a real – i.e., not the imagined – visual image.

7   Music as Narrative Commentary

If music is capable of representing the actuality of action, of 'being' the action, it is equally possible for it to step out of the diegesis and comment on the story like a Greek chorus. This is a feature that has been disputed in relation to film music. Nick Davis denies the possibility of music's being able to narrate, "since it lacks one of the minimal constituents of a narrating act: it does not produce perception of deictically shifted action, taking place in a space-time different from that of communication" (2012: 1). Yet this is exactly what happens in much classical song – e.g., Robert Schumann's *Dichterliebe* (1840) continually undercuts the statements made by the poet with ominous foreshadowing of pain and death – a comparison also made by Redner (cf. 2011: 19). This is music with a choric function of commenting on the drama, a key aspect of opera as well as lied, in fact any classical work with text. Wagnerian *leitmotiv*, much discussed in narratology and semiotics, is a technique allowing dramatic irony to occur on stage; characters and subjects have an associated musical motive which can be referred to even when the character or subject is not visible (see Tarasti 1979). In its basic form, music can inform the audience that what the characters believe is not the case – in the BBC video of the recording of *The Kraken Wakes*, Dr Becker, played by Richard Harrington, says "that's what we want you to get across to your audience: it's exciting, but it's not threatening". This is immediately followed by a musical symbol of ill omen – low strings playing a gathering chromatic line (Williams 2016: 5). Here there can be no doubt that the "it's not threatening" statement is incorrect, or that the music's role is to inform the audience that this is indeed the case.

8 Music, Anachronism and Intertextuality

I have previously referred to one of radio drama music's main functions – i.e., that of informing listeners of period. For example, Savvy Productions' *Queens of the Coal Age* (BBC Radio 4, 2013) was set in 1993 and begins with Annie Lennox's 1992 hit "Little Bird", initially as title music, then transferring in a favourite radio drama move to the diegesis via a car radio. But both radio drama and film can also use music anachronistically, often to add a layer of intertextual meaning. *Star Wars* (1977, now subtitled *A New Hope*) has a scene in which the protagonists walk into a bar on the planet Tatooine, where a band plays John Williams's version of 1930s jazz (which some may say sounds more like 1920s jazz). Forrest Wickman has discussed the references this scene makes to the scene in Rick's Bar in *Casablanca* (1942), although the music might better link it to the opening speakeasy scene in *Some Like it Hot* (1959). Either way, the music provides a non-narrative link to another cultural context.

In *The Kraken Wakes* a decision was made early on that although the production was to be updated to the contemporary or near future, the sound world of the score would reference film music of the 1950s, the period of the novel (1953). This proved too much for some audience members – one tweet in response read: "Great production, tho messing w my head – 1950s music, but set in present #DangerousVisions" (Moonmoggy). This decision – what Mann calls the "policy" of the film music (2015) – was made for several reasons. Firstly, it is hard to imagine what genre of music style could have been invoked that would unequivocally have said 'contemporary' and yet still be performable by a symphony orchestra. Most media music is now composed using Digital Audio Workstations, which allow simultaneous use of audio recordings manipulated digitally and midi-controlled samples – which are in effect another layer of digital sound. Timbre tends to take a main role rather than melodic theme or harmony. While some music, such as that of 'spectralist'[7] composers Gérard Grisey and Tristan Murail, has since the 1980s privileged timbre over other aspects of music using purely acoustic sources, I felt that making such a score would prevent the production from communicating directly with the audience because of the unfamiliarity of the musical style. Secondly, orchestral film music since the late 1980s has been dominated by non-thematic construction, predominantly driven by multiple percussion tracks, single lines of material, rhythmic ostinato and an absence of recognisable themes, with the addition of 'ethnic' instruments and vocals projecting sincerity (for example, most scores by Hans Zimmer). This vocabulary radically reduces the semantic possibilities of film music, and in a production where the music had to do more than just track the adrenaline levels of the main characters, contemporary film scoring would have limited the effectiveness of the project. In addition, much contemporary film music relies on overdubbing to achieve a supercharged orchestral sound – and virtual orchestral libraries reflect this. My music was to be performed live, and I had access to the standard four horns, not the ten of contemporary Hollywood sound.[8] Lastly, I also wanted to pay homage to the great era of film score, to celebrate the skill and craft of Bernard Herrmann, Jerry Goldsmith and John Barry, amongst others.

Whatever the justification, the reference to anachronistic film music styles enabled a level of intertextual reference to take place. I modelled the 'seatanks' noise on the sound of the robot exiting the flying saucer in *The Day the Earth Stood Still*, albeit constructed from the harmony I had used throughout the score, as well as some timbral shifts which rooted it more to the avant-garde than just to Herrmann's sound world. Secondly, as the couple are en route to

---

7   The term 'spectralism', while rather disputed, generally refers to composers who explored material derived from the harmonic spectrum.
8   Note that this reliance on massed horns (as an example) for expressive or heroic effect is derived ultimately from late Romanticism, and hence is also in a real sense anachronistic.

FIGURE 14.1   Part of 'La Habana', the original lead sheet with the Kraken Wakes theme

Escondida – a 'tropical paradise' – I referenced Barry's lush scores to the James Bond movies, which are often set in desirable locations. Although the adaptation is set in the present day, it is more or less impossible to capture the sense of glamour and pleasure that such a trip would have suggested in the 1950s; this was one of the main sources of appeal of the Bond movies as the UK moved out of 1950s austerity and conformity, so it seemed irresistible not to include this Latin jazz version of the main theme (see Figure 14.1).[9]

The theme reappears several times throughout the score, including in the final scene. This is an emotional manifesto by Phyllis bringing in themes of rebuilding, hope and family, and as such it strikes a slightly incongruous tone. Wyndham's novel has two endings – a shorter version of the novel was published in the same year in the US. McDermid has combined elements of the two versions, but in both there is an element of *deus ex machina* in the sudden revelation of an ultrasonic device that defeats the xenobaths. The whole of the final speech has a valedictory quality to it and suggested the clipped RP-delivery of 1950s British films. The underscore here was really a homage to Mahler – it was modelled on the adagietto from his Symphony No. 5 (1904) – but using the main 'Kraken' theme. The feel of the Romantic string-based orchestration under the dialogue is similar to the use of Rachmaninoff's Piano Concerto in *Brief Encounter* (1945). These are just two examples which show how the anachronism of the music style allows intertextual references to other stories, and to the world of film itself.

---

9   I had, in fact, written this theme itself in 2014 on a flight travelling from Cuba to Grand Cayman (a suitably Bond-ish itinerary) and performed it several times as a jazz musician, prior to including it in the score.

9 Musical Structure as Driving Force

Redner uses the cinematic, and more generally the aesthetic, philosophy of Gilles Deleuze to demonstrate that music can have a structuring purpose in some film, instead of simply paralleling the image (see 2011). One of his examples is highly relevant to the score for *The Kraken Wakes*: Leonard Rosenman's score for *East of Eden* (1955). From a composer's point of view, Redner's notion that the musical structure could in some way drive the film's narrative (2011: 23) seems uncontroversial, since this is how a great deal of opera works. Opera plots are frequently poorly constructed, and music's role is often to fill in the structural gaps, as well as drive the emotional narrative. Redner's analysis is, to some extent, driven by a need to say something more than the simple observation that the music informs the plot structure. For example, he states in relation to *East of Eden* that the obvious musical structuring device is the existence of two different and separate harmonic worlds, one tonal, representing the "goodness of Cal's brother Aron, while the atonal content represents the internal psychological torment of Cal. Unfortunately, once one has established this, there is little that can be read into the complex structure of the score." (ibid.: 172) However, although the observation that the musical structure drives the narrative may seem simplistic from the point of view of the analyst, for the composer the means of making musical structure drive the plot is not so easily achieved.

On the local level in *The Kraken Wakes*, montage technique was used to suggest the cutting of one shot to another in order to drive the narrative in the 'seatanks' scene on Escondida. This would have been less effective had there been visual imagery, since the quick following of the changes of viewpoint might have been seen as 'mickey mousing'. In film montage sequences, the music's function, as Larsen says, is the "musical simplification of the mosaic of film images" (2007: 191). Louis Andriessen claimed that Stravinsky learned montage technique in his own scores from early cinema, and the Stravinskyan flavour of this scene's music is certainly not far removed from *The Rite of Spring* (1913) in its construction or sound world (cf. 2006: 160–164). But for Redner this narrative drive comes from music at a deeper structural level. In *East of Eden*, composer Leonard Rosenman, a pupil of Arnold Schoenberg, was symbolically opposing dissonant material with more tonal material, and it is the working out of that opposition that drives the narrative forward on some level. Redner (2011: 54) sees in the atonal aspect of Rosenman's score a reflection of Deleuze's "nomad science" and in the more traditional material a "state science" – almost as if Rosenman were recomposing Wagner's *Die Meistersinger von Nürnberg*

(1868). While the way in which Redner maps the two aspects of Rosenman's score onto opposing characters in the Cain and Abel story of *East of Eden* may appear simplistic, there can be no doubt that the reconciliation of tonal and atonal material is and often has been a concern of composers, whether in the concert hall or in the cinema.

In *The Kraken Wakes*, there are two broad processes taking place across the music. The first is that the main theme, heard in its entirety first in the Barryesque passage underscoring the flight to Escondida, is presented in fragments (sometimes quite obscure) prior to its full occurrence, meaning that much of the thematic material of the score is interrelated. The second is that the theme's atonal – or extended tonal – nature is presented first as jazz in a tonal (more or less) setting, then as truly atonal music in the 'seatanks' scene, and then, finally, the last movement presents the theme in a setting which attempts to reconcile these two aspects, also bringing together all of the themes used in the piece to suggest a resolution. Do these structuring devices, one harmonic, the other thematic, succeed in driving forward the narrative? As the composer, I can only say I hoped they would.

10 Conclusion

The process of writing and reflecting on overtly cinematic music for a radio drama reveals some differences between the medium of film, where images are provided for the audience, and radio, where listeners are required to supply their own. However, the two media are not so far apart as initially one might think, partly because of cinema's use of visual suggestion or simply non-visual storytelling, and partly because of what Bonnie M. Miller has called radio drama's "intensely visual experience". What differences do exist are related to the music's role in responding and representing the actuality of events – in radio, it can do a great deal to present objects and processes referred to in the narrative and drive the narrative forward; in film, it often takes the role of revealing the emotional level of the narrative, rather than reflecting every moment of action on screen. Audience responses to the live performance, and to the radio broadcast on the whole, showed that the anachronistic aspect of the score was not a problem for most, and that in this way the great era of orchestral film scores established a vocabulary of reference which has not yet lost currency. Perhaps this common heritage is not surprising. After all, as Bernard Herrmann once said: "I learned to become a film composer doing two or three thousand radio dramas." (qtd. in Larsen 2007: 126)

References

Andriessen, Louis, Elmer Schönberger (2006). *The Apollonian Clockwork*. Amsterdam: Amsterdam Univ. Press.

Cleverdon, Douglas (1969). *The Growth of Milk Wood*. New York, NY: New Directions.

Davis, Nick (2012). "Inside/Outside the Klein Bottle: Music in Narrative Film, Intrusive and Integral". *Music, Sound and the Moving Image* 6/1: 9–19.

Hand, Richard J., Mary Traynor (2011). *The Radio Drama Handbook: Audio Drama in Context and Practice*. London: Continuum.

Kremenliev, Boris (1949). "Background Music for Radio Drama". *Hollywood Quarterly* 4/1: 75–83.

Larsen, Peter. (2007). *Film Music*. London: Reaktion.

Mann, Hummie (2015 online). *The Temporal and Rhythmic Effect on Musical Composition and Form When Scoring Dramatic Moving Picture*. PhD Thesis. Univ. of Salford. http://usir.salford.ac.uk/id/eprint/36893/ [14/04/2021]. Unpublished.

Miller, Bonnie M. (2018). "'The Pictures Are Better on Radio': A Visual Analysis of American Radio Drama from the 1920s to the 1950s". *Historical Journal of Film, Radio and Television* 38/2: 322–342.

Moonmoggy [@moon_moggy]. "Great production, tho messing w my head – 1950s music, but set in present #DangerousVisions #TheKrakenWakes Part 1". Twitter, 28 May 2016. https://twitter.com/moon_moggy/status/736561397719531520.

Morris, Christopher. (2008). "From Revolution to Mystic Mountains: Edmund Meisel and the Politics of Modernism". Robynn J Stilwell, Phil Powrie, eds. *Composing for the Screen in Germany and the USSR*. Bloomington and Indianapolis, IN: Indiana University Press. 75–92.

Prendergast, Roy M. (1992) *Film Music: A Neglected Art*. London and New York, NY: Norton.

Raw, Laurence (2015 online). "*A Christmas Carol* by Charles Dickens, BBC Radio 4, 20 December 2014". https://www.academia.edu/10161050/A_Christmas_Carol_by_Charles_Dickens_BBC_Radio_4_20_December_2014 [14/04/2021].

Redner, Gregg (2011). *Deleuze and Film Music: Building a Methodological Bridge between Film Theory and Music*. Bristol: Intellect.

Rodger, Ian (1982). *Radio Drama*. London: Macmillan.

Rosenman, Leonard (1968). "Notes from a Sub-Culture". *Perspectives of New Music* 7/1: 122–135.

Sullivan, Jack (2006). "'Psycho': The Music of Terror (Alfred Hitchcock, Composer Bernard Herrmann)". *Cineaste* 32/1: 20.

Tarasti, Eero (1979). *Myth and Music: A Semiotic Approach to the Aesthetics of Myth in Music*. Paris: Moton.

The Kraken Wakes (2016). Writ. Val McDermid. Dir. Justine Potter. BBC Radio 4. Ep. 1 broadcast 28 May. Ep. 2 broadcast 4 June.

Wickman, Forrest (2015 online). "*Star Wars* is a Postmodern Masterpiece". *Slate*. http://www.slate.com/articles/arts/cover_story/2015/12/star_wars_is_a_pastiche_how_george_lucas_combined_flash_gordon_westerns.html?via=gdpr-consent [14/04/2021].

Wierzbicki, James (2009). *Film Music – A History*. London and New York, NY: Routledge.

Williams, Alan E. (2016 online). Full musical score of *The Kraken Wakes*. https://figshare.com/articles/dataset/The_Kraken_Wakes_full_score/7347392?backTo=/collections/The_Kraken_Wakes/4300817 [25/04/2022].

Wyndham, John (2008) *The Kraken Wakes*. London: Penguin.

Index

abstract sound/music 22, 33, 106, 170, 188, 216, 218
accelerando 252
acousmatic music 9, 33, 45, 47, 70, 71
acoustic scenery 20, 28, 29
action 4, 6, 19, 20, 26, 29, 32, 36, 45, 55, 57, 66, 67, 72, 82, 108, 115, 140, 183, 191, 202–204, 206, 210, 227, 233, 239, 244, 251, 279, 280, 282, 285, 290, 300–302, 314, 318, 329, 333, 337–339, 344
Adamov, Arthur 119
Adams, James Truslow 169
adaptation 10, 11, 23, 27, 29, 34–36, 41, 51, 58, 80–82, 86–89, 93, 95, 96, 98, 103, 124, 134, 138, 139, 146, 153, 154, 173, 175, 209, 244, 275, 276, 281, 283, 292, 294, 296, 297, 299, 301, 305, 306, 310–312, 314, 321, 323, 326, 329, 331–333, 342
Aeschylus 315
affective dimension 290
Ahern, David 155
akousticons 89
akustische Kulisse 20
Albinoni, Tomaso 264
Alfano, Franco 111
Algemene Vereniging Radio Omroep (AVRO) 78, 79, 82, 86, 89
Allietti, Carlo 110
Alwyn, William 329, 333
American Broadcasting Company (ABC) 236
Ammer, Andreas 76, 100, 292
amplification 115, 279, 287, 288
Andersen, Hans Christian 82
Andriessen, Jurriaan 85, 95, 343
Angioletti, Gian Battista 118
Antill, John 142–145, 148
Antoine, Jean 50–52, 65, 72
Apollinaire 60
Arnheim, Rudolf 3, 12, 22, 25, 27, 28, 31–33, 37, 39, 41, 108, 109, 147, 160, 226, 230, 241, 244, 254, 258, 272
Arrieu, Claude 71
Ars Acustica 2

Art et Action theatre group 45, 46, 60, 66, 67
Astruc, Alexandre 150
Atelier de Création Radiophonique 145
Atkinson, Brooks 171, 188
atmosphere 5, 28, 53, 57, 84, 140, 192, 220, 223, 224, 227, 228, 239, 258, 276, 277, 283, 284, 300, 317, 319, 328, 331
atonality 39, 241, 343, 344
Attali, Jacques 263–265, 272
attention 1, 7, 27, 28, 54, 57, 70, 91, 94, 140, 146, 196, 214, 228, 234, 235, 241, 263, 268, 270, 275, 290, 295, 300, 310, 312, 314, 319, 323, 328, 332, 333
audionarratology 6, 10, 12, 14, 15, 99, 259, 272, 273, 275–277, 280, 281, 289, 290, 292
augmentation 226, 242, 249
aurality 1, 20, 59, 68, 102, 215, 220, 221, 226, 259, 301, 304, 312, 313, 323
Australian Broadcasting Company (ABC) 9, 130–133, 135–145, 147–163
Autant, Édouard 45, 47, 58, 59, 60–62, 66, 67, 69, 70, 71
avant-garde 26, 45, 66, 67, 70, 89, 92, 93, 97, 112, 115, 150, 154, 155, 212, 226, 241, 322, 341

Bachelard, Gaston 144, 145, 160
Bach, Johann Sebastian 95, 173, 263, 264, 301
Bacilek, Jeanne 80, 98
background 1, 4, 10, 20, 28, 39, 40, 54, 56, 58, 103, 107, 110, 116, 122, 141, 182, 192, 197, 221, 228, 233, 237–241, 243, 245, 246, 251, 253, 260, 267, 276, 279, 281–283, 286, 288, 290, 300, 302, 319, 328, 337
Badings, Henk 86, 89
Bain, Leslie Balogh 177, 179, 183
Balázs, Béla 233, 254
ballet 87, 94, 111, 170, 184
Bal, Mieke 3, 12
Band, Lothar 37, 38
Barber, Samuel 87
Barrie, J.M. 119
Barry, John 332, 341, 342, 344

Barthes, Roland   269, 270, 272
Bartók, Béla   336
Barzizza, Pippo   110
Barzun, Henri-Martin   60
Basco, Sancia   119
bass   28, 54, 155, 198, 286, 319, 337
bassoon   122, 198, 199, 301
Bataille, Georges   152
Baudelaire, Charles   62
Bayerischer Rundfunk (BR)   310, 312, 324
BBC Drama Department   133
BBC Radio 3   306, 327, 328
BBC Radio 4   11, 293, 294–297, 306, 309, 326, 327, 330, 331, 340, 345, 346
BBC Radiophonic workshop   2
Becker, Alexandra   89
Becker, Rolf   89
Beckett, Samuel   12, 15, 74, 146, 149, 150, 327
Beethoven, Ludwig van   14, 170, 176, 178, 185, 189, 215–219, 264
Belgische Radio- en Televisieomroep (BRT)   90, 260
Bemporad, Giovanna   119
Benedetto, Umberto   119
Benjamin, Walter   2
Bergson, Henri   45, 60, 72
Berio, Luciano   93, 94, 99, 102, 107, 112–121, 124, 127, 128
Berlioz, Hector   169, 171, 179
Bernaerts, Lars   1, 6, 12, 13, 15, 76, 79, 91, 98–100, 257, 259, 272–274, 277, 290, 292
Berna, Marie   174
Bernhardt, Sarah   51, 52
Beuger, Antoine   266, 267, 269–272
Beversluis, Martien   81, 99, 101
Bex, Maurice   51, 52
Bijma, Greetje   95
Billings, William   301, 307
Billy Rose Theater Division (NYPL)   167, 169, 172, 177
Bischoff, Fritz Walter   21–23, 29, 30, 34, 37, 276, 290
Bizet, Georges   34, 173
Black, Frank   246, 249
Blanc, Giuseppe   104
Blay, John   152
Blitzstein, Marc   186, 189, 190
Blok, Jan   88

Böcklin, Arnold   174
Bodenstedt, Hans   26, 48
Bodini, Vittorio   120
Boekel, Meindert   89
Bolchi, Sandro   117
Bolter, Jay David   257, 272
Bonaparte, Napoleon   177
Bosch, Hieronymus   265
Brahms, Johannes   171, 177, 181, 182, 185, 193, 262
Brand, Neil   332
Brandon, Arie   86, 232
brass instruments   28, 54, 62, 198, 282, 289
Braun, Alfred   27–29, 127, 277
Brecht, Bertolt   2, 29, 33, 34, 38, 332
Breil, Joseph Carl   238
bridge   4, 5, 10, 85, 86, 134, 233, 235, 237–240, 243–246, 249, 251, 253, 316
Bridson, D.G.   143–145, 147, 148, 160
Bringolf, Ernst   38
Brissoni, Alessandro   117–120
British Broadcasting Company (BBC)   2, 11, 13, 14, 80, 82, 109, 130–140, 142–149, 151, 155, 160, 161, 234, 259, 293–299, 304–306, 309, 326–328, 330–332, 337, 339, 340, 345, 346
Britten, Benjamin   133, 139, 146, 163, 258, 328
Brookes, Herbert   132, 133, 136
Brooks, Geraldine   156
Broome, Richard   156
Brothers Grimm   82
Bruckmaier, Karl   310
bruitistes   48, 56
Brusse, M.C.   82
Büchner, Georg   29
Buhrman, Bert   237, 252, 254
Bulte, Ineke   78–80, 83, 84, 91, 94, 98
Bulwer-Lytton, Edward   86
Butor, Michel   93
Butting, Max   105
Buzzati, Dino   117

cacophony   218, 264, 270, 311, 314, 320, 321
caesura   109, 279
Cage, John   93, 157, 267, 272
Calder, Alexander   170
Cameron, Eric   331
Camille, Paul   53, 59
Campo, Cristina   118

INDEX

Canadian Broadcasting Corporation (CBC) 331
canon 126, 337
cantata 33
Cardew, Cornelius 155
Carsana, Ermanno 119
Casella, Alfredo 106
Cavalcanti, Alberto 115
Cave, Nick 304
Ceccanti, Mauro 123
cello 62, 96, 159, 198, 237, 301, 337
Cendrars, Blaise 60
Cernecca, Domenico 119
Cézanne, Paul 60
character 3, 4, 10, 11, 20, 28, 31, 33–37, 39, 53, 56, 63, 80–82, 84, 85, 88, 90, 95, 115, 122, 123, 125, 126, 134, 136, 145, 151, 192, 195, 200, 202–204, 207, 210, 239, 257–261, 272, 275, 277, 279, 280, 282, 284–286, 288–290, 293, 295, 297, 301, 303–306, 312, 315, 317, 320, 322, 329, 333, 336, 339–341, 344
characterisation 4, 5, 7, 29, 218, 258, 259, 261, 277, 280, 283
Chignell, Hugh 1, 12, 76, 98, 293, 307
Chilton, Charles 87
Chion, Michel 231, 304, 307
choir 40, 80, 90, 94, 169, 197, 270
Chopin, Frédéric 55, 84, 215–219, 224, 229, 262, 263, 265
choral music/voices 59, 91, 224, 276, 316, 317, 319
chord 196, 213, 242, 249, 252, 284, 339
chorus 6, 11, 25, 29, 46, 58, 63, 138, 146, 183, 252, 310, 315–319, 339
chromaticism 82, 241, 242, 245, 251, 252, 288, 340
Churchill, Caryl 328
cinema/film music 9, 54, 56, 76, 77, 80, 115, 134, 135, 139, 141, 149, 304, 330, 343, 344
cipher 280, 285
clarinet 8, 29, 198, 199, 237, 282, 288
Clarke, James 328
classical music 7, 8, 10, 49, 58, 82, 85, 89, 90, 94, 96, 98, 110, 167, 169, 172, 195, 196, 207, 238, 240, 245, 259–263, 265, 313, 315, 327, 340
Classic Serial 11, 293–297, 306, 307

Claudel, Paul 56
cletic hymns 315
Cleverdon, Douglas 2, 12, 146–149, 160, 329, 345
Clewlow, Frank 132, 135–137, 140, 143, 160–162
closing 4, 6, 20, 83, 126, 244, 251, 261, 303, 317
Club d'Essai 46, 47, 51, 70, 145, 276
Coates, Albert 180
Cocker, Jarvis 337
Cœuroy, André 47, 49–54, 72
collage 2, 48, 59, 81, 92, 93, 213, 264, 265, 267, 269, 305, 306
colour, tone/vocal 7, 267, 311, 314, 317, 321
Columbia Broadcasting System (CBS) 136–139, 143, 153, 162, 172, 214, 231, 234, 236
Columbia Workshop 136–139, 214, 224, 255
commentary, music as 4, 6, 7, 29, 67, 116, 203, 233, 251, 261, 279, 281, 340
commission/commissioning 4, 11, 25, 33, 34, 38, 49, 53, 79, 85, 93, 97, 110–112, 135, 137, 141, 148, 154, 155, 167, 171, 174, 193, 196, 217, 278, 282, 294, 299, 312, 326, 330, 333
composer 4, 9, 10, 11, 25, 29, 30, 31, 33–35, 37, 40, 45, 49, 50–57, 69, 70, 71, 76–79, 81–83, 85, 86, 89–93, 97, 102, 106, 107, 110–113, 116, 123, 126, 127, 130–138, 140–144, 146–148, 150, 151, 153–155, 158, 159, 170, 171, 173, 181, 183, 186, 191, 193, 194, 196, 207, 212, 213, 220, 233–237, 239, 241, 243, 249, 251, 252, 260–264, 266, 267, 277, 278, 298, 299, 301, 303, 327–331, 333, 336, 338, 339, 341, 343, 344
composition 5, 29, 50, 51, 55, 56, 59, 69, 70, 91, 124, 130, 139, 140, 145, 150, 151, 158, 159, 192, 195, 196, 198, 202, 210, 212, 215, 218–220, 258, 266, 267, 269–272, 299, 302, 305, 306, 326–328, 330, 334
concerto 10, 128, 180, 188, 261, 263, 342
conductor 10, 31, 46, 51, 60, 80–82, 85, 89, 93, 96, 106, 134, 138, 191, 192, 194, 195, 215, 235, 333
Congrès international de l'art radiophonique 48, 50, 57
Connolly, Richard 149, 150, 161, 162

Constable, John 331
Convalli, Enzo 117
Cook, James 155
Cooper, James Fenimore 11, 293, 294, 301, 305, 307, 309
Cordell, Kathryn 239
Cordell, William 239, 244, 245, 251
Corwin, Norman 10, 137–139, 142, 143, 162, 163, 212–218, 221–224, 226–231, 237, 239, 254
Coulander, Harold 171
counterpoint 4, 6, 7, 63, 146, 279, 281, 288, 329, 333, 336
Crawford, Jesse 236, 242, 254
crescendo 176, 224, 249, 252, 267
Crews, Albert 234, 237–239, 240, 241, 244, 254
Crisell, Andrew 12, 297, 300, 307, 329
Crook, Tim 1, 3, 12, 140, 161, 293, 307
Croyston, John 149, 161
Crumpton, Charles 176
Csokor, Theodor 30, 31
Cubism 60
curtain 4, 10, 108, 109, 124, 233, 237, 239, 244, 251–253, 258, 300, 328, 333
Cusy, Pierre 53, 59, 63, 73, 74, 108, 127

Dadaism 70
Dallapiccola, Luigi 106, 107, 113, 128
Dampier, William 156
Damrosch, Walter 172, 173, 189
Danish National Radio (DR) 10, 191, 192, 193, 199, 209
Danish Radio 191, 196, 197, 208, 210
Darstellung 4
Daudet, Alphonse 173
da Venezia, Gastone 119
Davico, Vincenzo 110
Davis, Georges 237, 238
Davis, Judy 154
de Backere, Florian 96
De Benedictis, Angela Ida 1, 3, 4, 9, 102, 103, 105, 108, 111–113, 115, 116, 121, 122, 124, 127, 128, 276, 278–281, 291
de Bergerac, Cyrano 119, 173
Debussy, Claude 179–181, 184, 241
de Chirico, Giorgio 102
Deckers, Jeannine 155
de Cler, Jan 88
decrescendo 249

de Dood, C. 80
Defoe, Daniel 156
de Groot, Boudewijn 265
de Groot, Hugo 80–82, 84, 85, 88, 99
Deharme, Paul 47, 56, 63, 69, 72, 73
de Jong, Sarah 151
de la Motte Fouqué, Friedrich 35
Delaunays, Robert 60
del Corona, Rodolfo 110
de Leath, Vaughn 250, 255
de Leeuw, Ton 85, 101
de Leur, Joop 80
Deleuze, Gilles 343, 345
DeLys, Sherre 157, 158, 159
de Marez Oyens, Tera 89–92, 94
de Maupassant, Guy 39
Dermée, Paul 47, 51–53, 66, 69, 71, 73
de Rotrou, Jean 119
Descaves, Pierre 50, 55, 64, 67, 73
Devine-King, Terry 302
Diaghilev, Sergei 184
dialogue 1, 7, 11, 27–29, 32, 36, 37, 39, 63, 130, 132, 138, 146–148, 152, 176, 182, 202–204, 206, 208, 216, 234, 235, 238, 239, 241, 244, 251, 279, 282, 283, 285, 286, 288, 297, 304, 310, 311, 315, 321, 333, 337, 342
Dickens, Charles 332, 345
diegesis. *See* narration
Diemoz, Luigi 120
Digital Audio Workstation 341
director 9, 27–31, 39, 50, 51, 53, 65, 70, 76–78, 82, 84, 87, 89, 95, 97, 108, 110, 112, 114, 121, 132–134, 137, 139, 141, 153, 162, 174–176, 195, 219, 234–238, 240, 241, 243–246, 252, 263, 298, 305, 306, 311–314, 322, 326
dissonance 27, 82, 218, 239, 264, 284, 290, 311, 320, 321, 324, 337, 343
docudrama 77, 82, 90
docugraphies 90, 95
documentary 22, 77, 84, 90, 93, 103, 112–116, 130, 137, 141, 142, 146, 148, 153, 155, 156, 258, 329
Donnelly, James 141, 142
Downes, Edward Ray 178, 183
Drakakis, John 103, 108, 109, 128, 146, 161, 258, 273
Dramatic Control Panel 2, 133

INDEX 351

dramatisation   176, 181
dramaturgical function   277
Dryden, John   173
dubbing   113, 341
Düben, Otto   310
du Bois, André   87
Dumas, Alexandre   173, 296
Duncan, Alastair   148
Dunlevy, Maurice   152, 161
Durbridge, Francis   82
Dylan, Bob   265

echo   62, 121, 212, 289, 323
Eco, Umberto   6, 12, 118
Eisler, Hanns   33
electroacoustic music   2, 48, 51, 70, 113, 116, 127, 212, 220, 221, 223, 229, 259, 272
electronic music   8, 9, 40, 86, 113–120, 127, 134, 137, 147, 152, 155, 276, 339
Elektronisches Studio   3
Elgar, Edward   178, 180, 185
Ellis, Vivian   84
emotion   4, 8, 24, 29, 36, 37, 81, 82, 84, 85, 88, 91, 115, 134, 139, 142, 215, 233, 239, 243–245, 251, 277, 279, 280, 284–286, 290, 293, 294, 300, 305, 316, 328, 336, 337, 342–344
Enders, Richard   34
English, George Selwyn   148
Ente Italiano Audizioni Radiofoniche (EIAR)   104, 111
entertainment   1, 49, 66, 77, 82, 89, 282
entr'acte music   81, 82, 95
ephemerality   46, 49, 69, 134, 202, 233, 235
Erslev, Anne   198, 210
erweiternde Funktion   280, 289
euphony   216, 220–222
event   20, 24, 30, 34, 35, 39, 40, 82, 107, 110, 121, 123, 146, 173, 181, 192, 221, 239, 251, 268, 280, 289, 303, 331, 344
Everyman   173
Évian Conference   186
experientiality   279
Experimental Hour   137
experimentation   2, 5, 8, 9, 11, 19–23, 26, 30, 32, 40, 45–49, 60, 63–67, 69–71, 73, 76, 77, 79, 86, 90–94, 97, 99, 102, 103, 105–108, 110–114, 116, 121, 130–135, 137, 138, 142, 143, 145–149, 150–153, 158–160,
176, 194, 215, 224, 228, 275, 276, 290, 310, 311, 321–323, 327
Experiments in Symphonic Drama   169, 170, 175, 177, 178, 180, 188
Exploring the Arts   169, 172
Expressionism   241
expressive function   277
extradiegetic music   6, 258, 280–284, 288, 310, 311, 317, 318, 319
Eyk, Tonny   90

fading   40, 87, 121, 131, 133, 134, 176, 181, 182, 207, 217, 219, 222–224, 228, 244, 249–251, 253, 279, 282, 304, 319
Falco, Louis   94
Fanfani, Ottavio   115
Farrell, William B.   178, 179, 184
fascism   104, 110, 111, 168, 212–214, 264
feature   2, 53, 103, 130–150, 152, 153, 155, 156, 158, 159, 160, 327, 329
Features Department, BBC   133, 140, 141, 143, 145, 147
Federal One   167, 168
Federal Theatre of the Air   168, 169, 171, 174, 175, 188
Federal Theatre Project   9, 167–172, 174, 176–178, 180, 185, 186, 188, 189, 190
Felton, Felix   234, 237, 240, 241, 254
Ferguson, Marijke   89
fermata   203, 209, 249, 253
Ferrero, Mario   119, 120
Ferrieri, Enzo   117
film   3
film music   1, 2, 4, 5, 10, 11, 40, 41, 52, 55, 81, 83, 85, 137, 141, 147, 233, 234, 240, 241, 245, 258, 261, 276–281, 286, 290, 294, 298, 303, 326–331, 333, 336, 338–341, 343, 344
film musical   171
Finch, Peter   143, 144
Fischer, E. Kurt   19, 40, 42, 258, 273
Flanagan, Hallie   168, 169, 171, 175, 188, 189
Fleet Foxes   294, 299, 303, 304, 306–308
Fleischman, Théo   56
Flesch, Hans   20, 21, 277
flute   8, 53, 62, 122, 198, 237, 238, 283, 285, 286, 301, 303, 304
focalisation   3, 4, 281, 284
Fokin, Mikhail   198
folk music   89, 93, 155, 239, 275, 294, 300–306

foreshadowing 239, 251, 268, 289, 340
fortissimo (ff) 53, 182, 217, 236
Foster, David 151
Foster, Lynn 138
Frampton, Roger 152
Franck, César 262
Fraser, Cecil 137, 140, 142
Free, Colin 149
French New Wave (Nouvelle vague) 150, 161
Freud, Sigmund 60
Frisius, Rudolf 322–324
Fuchs, Viktor Heinz 29
fugue 126, 314
Funkoper 9, 19, 36, 104
Funkrevue 33, 34
Futurism 26, 70, 105, 106, 128, 212, 213, 232, 322

Gart, John 237, 243, 252, 255
Gavazzeni, Gianandrea 106
Gazzolo, Nando 115
Geeraerts, Jef 10, 257, 260, 263, 264, 266, 272, 273
Genette, Gérard 257, 273
genre 2, 3, 7, 9, 19, 21, 23–25, 32–34, 36, 38, 41, 50, 57, 59, 65, 67–69, 76–79, 82, 84, 85, 87, 89, 90, 95, 96, 97, 102–104, 109, 115, 126, 130–132, 134, 137, 141, 146, 148, 152–154, 156, 169, 171, 191, 193, 194, 210, 240, 257, 258, 277, 290, 294, 296, 300, 302, 310, 313, 327, 336, 341
Géo-Charles (Charles Louis Prosper Guyot) 55, 56
Germinet, Gabriel 47, 53, 55, 59, 61, 63, 68, 73–75, 108, 127
Gervasio, Raffaele 110
Gesamtkunstwerk 23, 24, 31
gesture, musical 30, 221, 223, 226
Ghedini, Giorgio Federico 111
Ghil, René 62
Giagni Giandomenico 119
Giannini, Ettore 110
Gilbert, W.S. 168, 173
Gilliam, Laurence 42, 137, 140, 147, 161
Giuntini, Aldo 212, 213, 231
glissando 203, 206, 245, 338, 339
Glocken 19, 39, 40
Goebbels, Heinrich 5

Goehr, Walter 19, 36–39
Golden Age radio 139, 143, 149, 151, 231, 278, 326, 332
Goldoni, Carlo 173
Goldsmith, Jerry 341
Goll, Claire 55
Goll, Yvan 55
Gorbman, Claudia 231, 233, 255, 307
Gorli, Sandro 123
Gozzi, Carlo 118
Grabbe, Christian Dietrich 29
Green, Paul 171, 185, 188–190
Gregorian chant 94, 275
Greig, Tamsin 326
Grieg, Edvard 172, 173
Griffi, Giuseppe Patroni 112
Grisey, Gérard 341
Grofé, Ferde 178, 183
Gronostay, Walter 19, 25, 30, 33, 38, 39, 40
Groupe de recherche de musique concrète 51
Grusin, Richard 257, 272
Guala, Filiberto 114
Guerrieri, Gherardo 119
guitar 237, 301, 304, 305
Gunold, Rolf 27
Guthrie, Tyrone 81, 133, 161

Hagemann, Carl 23, 27, 28
Halffter, Rodolfo 264
Hammerstein, Oscar 171
Hand, Richard 1, 13, 234, 255, 258, 273, 293, 294, 297, 300, 301, 304, 305, 308, 329, 345
Hardy, Thomas 296
harmony 7, 23, 53, 196, 197, 199, 212, 220, 239, 241–243, 246, 252, 263–265, 270, 271, 302, 303, 305, 319, 324, 341–344
Harrington, Richard 326, 332, 340
Hartogensis, Harold 179, 180, 188
Harty, Hamilton 178
Haydn, Joseph 55, 301
HBO 294, 299, 307
Heinitz, Wilhelm 32
Henderson, Moya 154, 155, 161, 162
Hendrix, Hanneke 266, 271
Hendrix, Jimi 128, 265, 274
Hendy, David 294, 308
Henri, Pierre 141

INDEX

Hermann, Gerhart 35
Herrmann, Bernard 137–139, 229, 234, 237, 243, 255, 261, 299, 308, 332, 338, 339, 341, 344, 345
Hertz, Alfred 179
Heylbut, Rose 235, 239, 240, 255
Higgins, Paul 326
Hindemith, Paul 29, 33, 34, 37, 51, 52, 105, 196
Hitchcock, Alfred 137, 261, 345
Hobl-Friedrich, Mechtild 1, 5, 7, 278, 280, 281, 289, 291
Hogan, John V.L. 172
Hollander, John 229, 232
Holm, Emil 193
Honegger, Arthur 45–47, 56, 58–60, 66–71, 328
Honegger, Gitta 311, 315, 316, 318, 319, 321, 325
hoorspel 76–78, 84, 98–100
Hörbilder 22, 48
Hörfolge 9, 19, 22, 33, 34, 38, 39, 104
horn 8, 56, 62, 198–200, 282, 283, 301, 302, 341
horror 39, 334, 336, 339
Hörspiel 5, 9, 19, 23, 25, 31–33, 36–38, 40, 76, 92, 99, 100, 103, 121, 128, 129, 134, 153, 154, 258, 273, 274, 290, 291, 322, 324, 325, 327
Hörspielpreis der Kriegsblinden 276, 310
Hörspielsinfonie 22, 23
Hörsymphonie 276
Hugo, Victor 59
humour 50, 88, 318
Huwiler, Elke 1, 2, 4, 6, 13, 76, 79, 99, 234, 255, 259, 273, 280, 281, 289, 291, 318, 324
hymn 92, 104, 171, 208, 301, 315–317

Ibo, Wim 87
Ibsen, Henrik 172, 173
Idzerda, Hanso 79
Iken, Karl 170
illustrative function 80, 154, 283
Impressionism 148, 212
incidental music 7, 55, 83, 108, 112, 139, 144, 173, 234, 240
indexical function 269, 280, 286, 288, 294, 300–302, 305, 329

indie music 294, 300, 306
instrument 7, 8, 26–28, 39, 40, 46, 50, 53, 54, 63, 65, 89, 102, 104, 107, 112, 122, 154, 155, 192, 195, 196, 198, 199, 203, 220, 237, 241, 262, 272, 282, 286, 288, 289, 301, 303, 314, 318, 329, 341
instrumental music 5–7, 10, 28, 31, 40, 46, 58, 62, 63, 110, 116, 154, 215, 216, 229, 240, 241, 252, 260, 272, 276, 282, 304
instrumentation 107, 121, 196, 198, 209, 222, 224, 236, 282, 286, 288, 290, 299, 304, 305
interlude 56, 109, 197, 221, 227, 229, 244, 334
intermediality 15, 69, 258, 259, 261, 273, 274, 292
intonation 4, 317
intradiegetic music 4, 6, 7, 10, 55, 258, 279–284, 288, 310, 311, 319
Ionesco, Eugène 149
irony 7, 144, 281, 311, 340
Italian radio 104–112, 115
Ives, Charles 138

Jacobs, Ruud 89
Jacoby, Elliott 250, 255
Jandl, Ernst 322
Jarry, Alfred 150
jazz 7, 33, 37, 55, 56, 59, 89, 90, 92, 196, 241, 340, 342, 344
Jelinek, Elfriede 11, 310–325
jeux radiophoniques 56
John Adams 294, 299, 307
John, Alfred 30
Jones, David 146
Joplin, Janis 265
Joyce, James 107, 118, 157
Jürs-Munby, Karen 312, 325

Kagel, Mauricio 5, 92–94, 99, 101, 153, 154, 161, 163
Kahn, Douglas 226, 232, 274
Kapfer, Herbert 311–314, 316, 320, 323, 325
Karelsen, Dolf 82, 83, 99
Kästner, Erich 34, 104
Katholieke Radio Omroep (KRO) 78, 79, 82, 85–89, 92–96, 260, 273
Katzman, Louis 237, 249, 255

Kempinski, Leo A.   236, 239, 255
Kern, Jerome   171
Kerouac, Jack   89
Kesser, Hermann   28
Keuls, Yvonne   90
KFAC   173, 174
Kilpatrick, Stephen   331
Kim, Jane   176
Kinzel, Till   6, 14, 99, 259, 273, 277, 292
klankbeeld   77, 90
Kleijn, Kommer   82
Klepper, Jochen   30, 33
Kneal, Nigel   117
Kodály, Zoltán   177, 183
Kogelheide, Ralph   40
Kommerij, Bert   97
Kooij, Maarten   89
Koopman, Wim   90
Koppelmann, Leonhard   310–312, 314, 316, 320, 322–324
Koussevitzky, Serge   178
KQV   174
Kramer, Lawrence   229, 232
Kremenliev, Boris   237–239, 241, 246, 251, 255, 299, 300, 305, 308, 327–330, 333, 338, 345
Kremer, Ray   215
Krieg, Hans   82, 100
Krulwich, Robert   158, 162
Kubrick, Stanley   336
Kühn, Oswald   35
Kunst, Jos   90
Kutschke, Beate   3, 13

Labelle, Brandon   229, 232
Labiche, Eugène   117
Ladiges, Peter Michel   322
Ladler, Karl   7, 8, 14
Lajos, Kovacs   82
Lambert, Constant   134
Landi, Giovanni   117
Landowski, W.-L. (Alice-Wanda)   55, 56, 73
Landy, Leigh   220, 223, 226, 232
Langgaard, Siegfried   195
Lara, Louise   45–47, 58–62, 66, 67, 69, 70, 71
La Rosa Parodi, Armando   110
Larronde, Carlos   45–47, 56, 58–71, 74, 75
l'art radiophonique   12, 48, 72, 73
Lau, Bernd   276, 281, 292

Lebrancón, José Iges   2
Lehmann, Hans-Thies   323, 325
Leibniz, Gottfried Wilhelm   263
Leimer, Kurt   262
leitmotif   7, 29, 31, 239, 283, 285, 286, 303, 340
Lelieveldt, Philomeen   9, 76–78, 80, 85, 86, 89–92, 95, 100
Lemaire, Cor   82, 88, 100
Lenart, Paul   303
Lennox, Annie   340
Leone, Sergio   329
Leonhard, Rudolf   26
Leoni, Franco   110
Léry, Maxime   52
Lewis, Sinclair   168, 174, 185
Lewis, William   214
Lewton, Sherman Paxton   238, 244, 255
Leydi, Roberto   114, 115, 117
Liberatore, Ugo   119
Lien, Annbjørg   302
Light Programme   331
linking   6, 109, 289, 302, 336
listener   1, 6–8, 11, 20, 24, 28, 33, 37, 45, 46, 53, 54, 59, 64–68, 81, 87, 90, 93–95, 108, 109, 124, 126, 130, 134, 136–138, 141, 142, 145, 149, 172, 174–176, 192, 213, 215, 220, 228, 230, 237, 249, 251, 257, 278–280, 284, 287–290, 293, 294, 297, 302, 304–306, 316, 321, 326, 336, 340, 344
listening   54, 58, 70, 76, 95, 112, 121, 138, 144, 146, 147, 151, 153, 157, 158, 188, 215, 216, 220, 223, 224, 226, 227, 229, 258, 269, 270, 272, 279, 284, 286, 289, 304, 336
Liszt, Franz   179, 185, 195
literarisches Hörspiel   20
live broadcast   9, 10, 21, 24, 40, 46, 48, 49, 50, 51, 58, 61, 76, 78, 79, 87, 90, 94, 96, 97, 103, 104, 109, 110, 134, 138, 141, 142, 153, 167, 172–174, 176, 179, 180, 185, 191, 192, 209, 212, 215, 217, 234, 244, 253, 258, 260, 278, 299, 314, 326, 327, 331, 332, 333, 338, 339, 341, 344
Lo Gatto, Ettore   118
Longfellow, Henry   183
Lopez, Emile   88
Lorca, Federico García   120, 122
Lorentz, Pare   137
Lortzing, Albert   34

Luhrmann, Baz   304
luisterspel   76
Lully, Jean-Baptiste   173

MacCallum, Mungo   147, 161
Mackey, David   233, 237–239, 244, 251, 255
MacLeish, Archibald   137, 214, 232
MacNeice, Louis   146, 161, 162, 258, 274, 327–329
Maderna, Bruno   102, 112–128
Madsen, Virginia   9, 130, 131, 135, 140, 149, 150, 152, 153, 155, 157–159, 161, 162
Maeterlinck, Maurice   118
Magnetophon   142
Mahler, Gustav   14, 291, 342
Maigret, Julien   56
major scale/chord   170, 174, 176, 178, 203, 206, 217, 251, 252, 263, 264, 284
Malatini, Franco   150
Malipiero, Gian Francesco   106, 111
Malko, Nicolai   148
Mallarmé, Stéphane   184
Mamorsky, Morris   234, 235, 237, 239, 240, 244, 255
manipulation, electronic/digital   27, 40, 89, 90, 91, 94–96, 124, 159, 258, 259, 272, 313, 321, 341
Mann, Chris   156, 157
Mann, Hummie   338, 341
Mann, Thomas   296
Marinetti, Filippo Tommaso   41, 105, 128, 212, 213, 230–232
Marinkovic, Ranko   119
Marrow, Macklin   183, 189
Martin, Ysobel (Isobel)   15, 174
Mascagni, Pietro   329
Masefield, John   132, 133, 135, 136, 162
Mase, Owen   81, 100
Masetti, Enzo   110
Masnata, Pino   105, 128
Mason, Arthur   139, 162
Massine, Léonide   170
Mattfeld, Julius   234, 255
Matthiesen, Tim   303
Mattolini, Marco   117
Matulay, Laszlo   215, 225, 226
Maurri, Enzo   119
Mayröcker, Friederike   322
McDermid, Val   326, 330, 334, 337, 342, 346

McLennan, Andrew   148–151, 153–157, 161, 162
McWhinnie, Donald   146, 332
Meano, Cesare   110
media studies   2, 11
Meisel, Edmund   336, 345
melody   29, 40, 197, 200, 224, 228, 230, 239, 241–243, 258, 270, 271, 283, 284, 314
Meloni, Nino   117, 119
Mendelssohn, Felix   81, 84, 173
Mendelssohn, M. Friedrich   36
Merlin, Angelo   117, 119
metaphor   6, 22, 23, 31, 60, 147, 152, 212, 259, 268
Metropolitan Opera   172
metteur en ondes   50, 70
Meyrink, Gustav   39
mickey-mousing   338, 339, 343
Mignon, Paul-Louis   70
Mildorf, Jarmila   1, 3, 6, 12, 14, 15, 76, 99, 100, 127, 259, 272, 273, 275, 277, 290–292
Milhaud, Darius   53, 56, 328
Miller, Bonnie M.   336, 344
Mills, Felix   238
Minghella, Anthony   330
minimal/minimalistic music   81, 106
minor scale/chord   170, 171, 177, 179, 180, 181, 186, 188, 199, 200, 202, 203, 206–208, 251, 263, 264, 285
Miranda, Lin-Manuel   299
Misch, Ludwig   32, 34, 36, 38
mise en abyme   259
Miserendino, Aurelio   117
Modernism   10, 70, 134, 135, 145, 167, 170, 188, 241
Modigliani, Gino   110, 128
Moffitt, John C.   168, 185
Molière (Jean-Baptiste Poquelin)   120, 124
Mon, Franz   92, 94, 100
monologue   32, 59, 206, 314, 315, 319
montage   9, 19, 21, 22, 30, 33, 34, 41, 86, 90, 94, 142, 223, 237, 239, 240, 258, 259, 312, 313, 343
Monteux, Pierre   179
Monteverdi, Claudio   95
mood   4, 6, 8, 11, 139, 152, 176, 181, 199, 207, 217, 230, 233, 236, 239–245, 251, 275, 277, 285, 288–290, 294, 300–305, 328, 329

Moore, Stephen   331
Morandi, Guglielmo   117
Morley, Christopher   119
Morricone, Ennio   329
Morson, Gary Saul   268, 269, 271, 273
Morteo, Gian Renzo   119
Mortley, Kaye   152
mosaic   133, 221, 343
Moses, Charles   132, 143, 162
motif/motive   27, 31, 32, 40, 56, 81, 109, 134, 138, 203, 220, 239, 261, 276, 277, 281, 283–287, 319
movement   3, 5, 7, 50, 55, 60, 66, 83, 90, 135, 141, 154, 170, 176, 181–183, 202, 206, 215–217, 223, 239, 263, 280, 288, 311, 322, 335, 344
Moyer, Lewis W.   174
Mozart, Wolfgang Amadeus   174, 181
Multifunktionstext   312
Murail, Tristan   341
musical genre   7
musical instrument   2, 96
musicalisation   10, 27, 28, 215, 226, 227, 229
musicality   9, 10, 133, 151, 215, 219, 220, 221, 229, 310, 311, 313, 314, 318, 322, 323, 333
musical notation   29, 30, 69, 200
music and language   3, 4, 8, 10, 25–28, 41, 58, 91, 110, 233–235, 241, 245, 252, 253, 257, 259, 260, 263, 281, 310, 311, 313, 314, 317, 318, 320–324, 332, 339
music as metaphor   3, 22, 23, 60, 61, 130, 269, 271, 288, 313
music cue   176, 216, 217, 219, 220, 234–236, 241, 245, 251–253, 299, 302, 303, 306, 328, 330, 333, 334
musicians   8, 9, 24, 50, 51, 54, 58, 76–80, 82, 84, 89, 90, 92, 94, 96, 97, 105, 106, 110, 121, 127, 131, 132, 135, 138, 140, 143, 159, 161, 193, 194, 237, 328
music in radio plays   5, 55, 103, 277
music theatre   21, 22, 24, 29, 32, 35, 36, 38, 41
musique concrète   47, 51, 70, 113, 137, 141, 147, 159, 276, 322
musique radiogénique   50
Mussolini, Benito   104, 212, 213, 232
Mussolini, Vittorio   213, 216, 230, 232
Mutual Broadcasting System (MBS)   172, 236

narration   4, 19, 20, 24, 25, 32, 34–38, 105, 107, 110, 142, 148, 183, 221–224, 229, 238, 239, 244, 258, 261, 279, 280, 337, 339

narrative   2–4, 11, 19, 22, 30, 34, 40, 46, 58, 60, 78, 85, 90, 96, 132–134, 147, 153, 157, 170, 176, 187, 188, 220, 223, 224, 233, 235, 239, 243–245, 258–260, 262, 268, 269, 271, 272, 275–280, 282, 283, 285, 286, 288, 289, 295, 311, 317–319, 323, 333, 336, 338, 340, 343, 344
narrativisation   4, 6, 280
narrativity and music   3, 8
narrator   6, 32, 35, 87, 96, 115, 144, 148, 151, 257–260, 261, 272, 282, 283, 285, 286, 288, 289, 305, 339
National Archive and Records Administration (NARA)   167, 169
National Archives of Australia (NAA)   132, 137, 160–162
National Broadcasting Company (NBC)   12, 172, 189, 235, 236, 238, 239, 246, 254, 255
Nattiez, Jean-Jacques   4, 14, 219, 229, 232
Nawler, S. I.   177, 181, 182
Nederlandse Christelijke Radio Vereniging (NCRV)   78, 79, 84, 89, 90–92, 94, 96, 99–101
Nederlandse Radio Unie (NRU)   77, 84, 87, 93
Netrebko, Ana   318, 319, 320
Neues Hörspiel   2, 76, 77, 92, 128, 154, 276, 311, 322
new music   2, 48, 212, 276
New Objectivity   29, 33, 37
New Radio Drama. See Neues Hörspiel
Nick, Edmund   34, 37, 104
Nielsen, Ludolf   14, 193, 194, 210
noise   25, 26, 47, 56, 59, 71, 103, 106, 108, 113, 124, 182, 199, 213, 215, 224, 227–229, 263, 269, 323, 332, 341
noises   1, 2, 23, 25, 28, 103, 106–108, 112, 115, 124, 181, 215, 216, 220, 223, 266, 267, 269, 270, 277, 321, 329
non-referentiality   279
Noordijk, Eddy   82
Norddeutscher Rundfunk (NDR)   310
Nowra, Louis   150, 151, 161
Nugent, Frank S.   171, 189

Obey, André   118
objet sonore   47, 71
oboe   8, 198, 301, 336
Oboler, Arch   139, 234–236, 240, 244, 251, 255
Oedipus Rex   38, 43, 44, 173, 184, 261
Ojetti, Paola   117

INDEX 357

Old Time Radio (OTR) 299, 305
opening 4, 6, 20, 40, 47, 63, 70, 80, 84, 85, 87, 88, 115, 124, 145, 152, 183, 222, 237, 239, 244, 251, 283, 284, 303, 304, 335, 340
opera 9, 21, 23–25, 29, 32–38, 56, 57, 76, 80, 86, 134, 140, 168, 170, 173, 177, 183, 192, 197, 203, 229, 253, 318, 329, 340, 343
operatic singing 37, 319
operetta 32, 38, 80, 82, 171
Opernquerschnitt 25, 34, 36, 39
oratorio 32–39, 56, 59, 64, 66, 67, 110
orchestral music 10, 11, 46, 50–53, 58, 64, 66–68, 83, 89, 148, 167, 173, 176, 194, 195, 215, 236, 241, 245, 264, 282, 288, 300, 302, 326, 328, 331, 339, 341, 344
orchestration 50, 52, 58, 62, 226, 240, 241, 243, 313, 318, 328, 342
original music 5, 40, 56, 78, 81, 83, 85, 87, 95, 131, 135, 137, 138, 140, 153, 154, 178, 196, 201, 217, 234, 238, 239, 254, 258, 278, 280, 299, 301, 306, 342
original sound 96, 287
Ormandy, Eugene 177, 180
Orton, Joe 328
Österreichischer Rundfunk (ORF) 312, 324
ostinato 249, 253, 341
Ostrovskij, Aleksandr Nikolaevic 118
O-Ton-Hörspiel (original sound radio play) 104
Owen, Gwen 303
Oxilia, Nino 104

Paap, Wouter (F. Luisteraar) 84, 85, 100
Pascal, Victor 15, 51
Pasolini, Pier Paolo 113, 128
pastoral 8, 40, 336
Paul, Charles 245, 246, 248–250, 255
pause 5, 7, 217, 222, 228, 249, 285, 297, 304, 339
Pecknold, Robin 303
Percher, Annie 155
percussion 30, 40, 46, 53, 59, 152, 282, 283, 329, 341
performance 1, 9, 24, 39, 40, 45, 46, 49, 54, 58, 60, 62, 63, 68–70, 78, 80, 87, 93, 96, 97, 114, 130, 131, 136, 143, 146, 147, 153, 156, 157, 171, 172, 181, 192–194, 197, 209, 214–216, 262, 266, 267, 270, 278, 284, 297, 310, 312, 314, 326, 327, 332, 333, 344
performer 40, 41, 76, 93, 130, 131, 133, 147, 153, 168, 175, 215, 219, 243, 260, 298

Petrassi, Goffredo 106
Pettman, Dominic 270, 273
Philadelphia Symphony Orchestra 177, 179–181
pianissimo (pp) 199
piano 46, 55, 58, 81, 88, 95, 173, 213, 215–219, 222, 223, 228, 234, 236, 265, 304
Pinter, Harold 149, 327, 328
Piovesan, Alessandro 112
pitch 7, 63, 91, 133, 220, 222, 224, 228, 241, 258, 317
Pizzetti, Ildebrando 106, 111, 112
Plato 169
Pleiter, Gerrit 91, 92, 100
plot 3, 7, 11, 24, 29, 31–33, 35, 36, 39, 110, 145, 154, 198, 203, 224, 275, 277, 295, 297, 312, 318, 323, 329, 331, 343
Plotkin, Leah 169
Plush, Vincent 141
Poe, Edgar Allan 39
poetry 27, 30, 59, 61, 65, 68, 80, 89, 110, 144, 148, 152, 156, 159, 168, 214, 215, 217, 218, 228, 313
Pola, Alexander 88
Polet, Sybren 95
political dimension of music 10, 21, 64, 78, 79, 82, 109, 168, 170, 185, 186, 188, 218, 257, 260, 261, 263–266, 271, 301
Pollock, Muriel 242, 255
polyphony 11, 63, 65, 91, 310, 315, 322, 323
Pongs, Hermann 33, 34, 43
Poort, Coen 90
popular music 7, 8, 34, 37, 49, 58, 82, 88, 89, 138, 196, 252, 260, 265, 306
Porrino, Ennio 110
Porter, Jeff 138, 139, 163, 234, 255
Poste colonial 45, 49
Poste national 49
Poste parisien 49
Potter, Justine 331, 346
Pousseur, Henri 93, 98, 101
Povel, Léon 86, 87
Pownall, David 1, 3, 14
Pratella, Ballila 48
pre-recorded music 19, 278
pre-scripted music 278
presentation. See Darstellung
Pressburger, Giorgio 120
Prix Italia (Italia Prize) 12, 84, 86, 91, 94, 95, 112, 121, 124, 127, 128, 145, 148, 154, 155, 276, 291

producer 1–3, 5, 8, 26, 34, 45, 46, 51, 53, 59, 64, 67, 70, 77, 88, 90–92, 97, 127, 130, 131, 133, 135, 137–140, 142, 144–146, 148–150, 152–154, 156–158, 213, 219, 234, 235, 241, 244, 277, 298, 299, 304, 330, 331
programmatic music 29, 126, 188, 213, 216, 280
Prokofiev, Sergei 180, 184, 264
Propp, Vladimir 3
prosodic features of music 7
Pucci, Fiorenza 119
Puccini, Giacomo 24
Pudovkin, Vsevolod Illarionovich 329
Puecher, Virginio 119

Quasimodo, Salvatore 120

Rachmaninoff, Sergei 174, 175, 180, 188, 342
Radio Audizioni Italia (RAI) 3, 9, 103, 104, 111–120, 122, 126, 128, 150
Radio Bremen 90
Radio-Cité 49
radio composer 37, 229, 234, 241, 242, 332
radio drama music 8, 10, 76, 80, 84, 85, 97, 278, 290, 328, 333, 338, 340
radiodramma 103, 111
Radio Eye 131
Radiokapellmeister 10, 191, 192, 194, 209
Radiola 49
Radiolab 158
Radio-L.L. 49
radio opera 2, 9, 19, 21, 24, 32, 35–38, 71, 76, 93, 103, 111, 112, 116, 124, 126, 130, 278
Radio-Paris 49, 50, 53, 66, 67
radiophonic music 9, 45, 48, 50, 55, 57, 59, 94
radiophonic techniques/means 4, 9, 45, 49, 71, 76
radio play, definition of 2
radio play music 5, 278
Radio PTT 49
radio revue 33
Radiotelevisione Italiana (RAI) 104
Radio Tour Eiffel 49
Radio Vitus 49
Ramuz, Charles-Ferdinand 35
range of voice 28, 159, 168, 187, 194, 220, 222, 224, 227, 229, 241, 263, 271, 283, 285, 296, 339

Rankin, Ian 296
Realism 80, 268
Record Group 69 167
recording 21, 24, 27, 40, 58, 78, 86, 87, 94, 95, 106, 123, 124, 137, 138, 140, 141, 167, 169, 172, 173, 176, 177, 193, 215, 220, 262, 341
Redner, Gregg 329, 330, 340, 343–345
Reesen, Emil 10, 191, 194, 195, 197–202, 204, 208, 209, 210
referenced music 258, 260, 264, 272, 342
reference, music as 22, 47, 55, 91, 93, 113, 167, 185, 197, 199, 202, 208, 261, 275, 294, 339–341, 344
referentiality 3, 6, 287
Reith, John 133
remediation 257, 258
repetition 7, 56, 62, 94, 169, 175, 200, 214, 221–224, 243, 284, 285, 313, 316, 317, 322, 338
Rettenberg, Milton 237, 249, 255
Reumert, Poul 192
reverberation. *See* echo
revue 9, 33, 34, 76, 77, 82, 195
rhapsody 133, 144, 145, 148
rhythm 4, 25, 27, 30, 40, 63, 65, 67, 83, 91, 106, 110, 126, 133, 137, 151, 196, 197, 199, 220, 223, 227, 237, 239, 241, 242, 249, 253, 258, 282, 311, 314, 317–319, 324, 341
Ricono, Connie 119
Riisager, Knudåge 193, 211
Rijkschradio Nederlandse Omroep (RNO) 82, 83
Rimbaud, Arthur 62
Rimsky-Korsakov, Nikolai 83, 174, 175
Rinke, Günter 1, 7, 14
ritardando 249, 252
Roberts, Leslie Evan 175
Roberts, Susan 331
Robson, William 137, 214
Rocca, Enrico 109, 128
rock music 89, 152, 272, 306, 307
Rodger, Ian 328–330, 332, 338, 345
Roesner, David 310, 311, 314, 323, 325
Roland Holst, A. 86
Romanticism 8, 192, 196, 237, 239, 241, 260, 341, 342
Roosevelt, Franklin Delano 9, 167, 171, 185, 186
Rosenman, Leonard 332, 343–345

Rossican, Isja 82
Rossini, Gioachino 238, 249
Rossi, Vittorio Giovanni 119
Rostand, Edmond 173, 174
Roussel, Albert 55
Rousselot, Jean-Pierre 62
Rühm, Gerhard 154
Rundell, Clark 333
Russolo, Luigi 26, 42, 48, 213
Ruttmann, Walter 22, 23, 30, 40, 48, 63, 115, 276, 277

Saba, Nanni 118
Sacher, Paul 116, 122
Sachs, Andrew 259
Sackville-West, Edward 146, 163
Safka, Melanie (Melanie) 91
Saint-Exupéry, Antoine de 86
Saint-Saëns, Camille 55
Sala, Oskar 137
Salter, Harry 248, 255
Sanden, Aline 197
Sandor, Ralph (Alexander Semmler) 243, 246, 247, 255, 256
Sanger, Elliott 172
Sanguineti, Edoardo 93
Saroyan, William 230, 232
Satie, Erik 169
Savini, Alberto 118
Savinio, Alberto 102, 103, 129
scenario 70, 96, 110, 112, 167, 182, 240, 266–268, 272, 326
scene 1, 4, 6, 7, 9, 15, 19–22, 25, 28–30, 33–35, 37, 39, 40, 45, 56, 63, 81, 85, 108, 109, 112, 115, 122, 134, 139, 148, 159, 176, 195, 197, 202, 206, 208, 217, 221–224, 233, 236, 239, 240, 241, 243–246, 251, 253, 258, 261, 266, 277–279, 281–285, 289, 294, 300–305, 317–319, 322, 323, 328, 329, 333, 336–340, 342–344
Schaeffer, Pierre 9, 45–49, 51, 63, 70–72, 74, 75, 220, 276, 322
Schiller, Friedrich 55, 117
Schindler, Anton 170, 189
Schmidt, Annie M.G. 88, 101
Schmidt, Louis 82, 83
Schmitt, Florent 50–53, 71, 72
Schnog, Karl 33
Schoenberg, Arnold 39, 138, 343

Schoen, Ernst 21, 32, 38
Schöning, Klaus 91, 92, 94, 100, 104, 121, 129, 141, 153, 154, 163, 322, 324
Schonmann, Evelyn 176
Schoonderwalt, Herman 89, 90
Schubert, Franz 44, 55
Schulhoff, Erwin 33, 38
Schumann, Robert 340
Schütz, Heinrich 95
Schwitters, Kurt 27
score 4, 10, 11, 24, 25, 29, 30, 31, 34, 40, 46, 48, 51, 52, 58, 68, 77, 79–82, 84, 85, 89, 91, 92, 94, 97, 112, 123, 134, 137–139, 148, 154, 191, 193–195, 201, 202, 209, 215, 234, 235, 237, 258, 276, 278, 281, 283, 285, 288, 290, 294, 298, 299, 305, 306, 310, 311, 313, 314, 315, 323, 326, 328, 330–333, 337, 339–344, 346
scoring 209, 235, 237, 240, 241, 253, 298, 341
Scorsese, Martin 329
Scott, Robert Falcon 137
Scribe, Eugène 118, 120
script 30, 31, 77, 85, 96, 109, 127, 137, 139, 162, 169, 172–174, 176, 177, 181, 219, 236, 255, 260
Sczuka, Karl 112
See, Cees 89
Seiber, Mátyás 330
Seitz, Robert 29, 36, 38
semantic function 6, 10, 103, 114, 159, 212, 215, 216, 221, 226, 229, 230, 280, 281, 314, 319, 341
semiotic channel 3, 5, 6, 280
semiotic system 10, 258
Semmler, Alexander (Ralph Sandor) 243, 245, 247, 255, 256
Sendespiel 44, 103
separating 6, 124, 289
sequence 4, 172, 174, 176, 240, 268, 278, 279, 284–286, 289, 293, 343
Sereni, Vittorio 119
series 9, 21, 34, 39, 71, 82, 83, 86, 87, 89, 92, 93, 95, 96, 133, 134, 140–142, 167–169, 171–176, 181, 185, 186, 188, 217, 218, 224, 238, 239, 245, 265, 268, 278, 315, 331, 337
Sermonti, Vittorio 117, 118, 120
Service de la recherche de la radiodiffusion-télévision-française 51

INDEX

setting   4, 11, 29, 32, 36, 37, 40, 71, 92, 113, 122, 124, 169, 196, 199, 202, 207, 208, 210, 220, 224, 233, 238, 239, 244, 245, 251, 275, 280, 284, 297, 301, 304, 310, 312, 316, 317, 319, 324, 336, 344
Shakespeare, William   120, 124, 154, 172, 173, 179, 181, 296
Shaw, George Bernard   117
Sherwood, Robert E.   117
Shield, Roy   236, 249, 250, 256
Shore, Howard   286, 290, 292, 303
Shumer, S.J.   177, 183
Sibelius, Jean   15, 174, 181
sideshadowing   268, 271
Sieveking, Lance   133–135, 142, 163
signal   8, 278, 283, 289, 302
signalling function   279, 280
signature, music as   82–84, 89, 104, 300, 303–306, 328
silence   1, 54–56, 96, 103, 106, 115, 215, 224, 227–230, 244, 259, 267, 277, 297, 337
silent film   21, 26, 233, 235, 236, 240
Simonson, Lee   184
simultaneity   7, 60, 61, 91, 106, 122, 124, 212, 227, 257, 259, 264, 277, 341
singing   28, 29, 88, 94, 183, 187, 197, 220, 222, 279, 280, 282–284, 288, 301–304, 318, 319
Sitwell, Edith   134
Skouboe, Else   192
Smalley, Dennis   220–223, 232
Smith, Carleton Sprague   169
Smith, Ivan   148, 149
Socrates   169
song   28, 29, 34, 37, 40, 55, 56, 80–82, 88, 93, 106, 183, 185, 192, 197, 212, 217, 229, 230, 238, 244, 253, 264, 265, 275, 276, 282–284, 301, 329, 340
sonic dramaturgy   20–23, 25–28, 30–32, 34–36, 38, 39, 41
sonic montage   21, 22, 30
sonographies   90
Sophocles   173
soprano   28, 58, 152, 283, 319
sound   1, 2, 5, 6, 10, 19, 20, 22, 23, 25–28, 30, 31, 39, 40, 48, 62, 63, 89, 90, 91, 95, 96, 103, 106, 107, 110, 114, 115, 116, 121, 126, 134, 139, 141, 142, 144, 146, 151, 154, 195, 199, 212, 215, 216, 219, 220–223, 226, 227, 259, 260, 261, 263, 265–267, 270, 272, 276, 277, 280, 282, 283, 286, 287, 304, 305, 314, 320–323, 340
sound cue   215, 223, 228, 230
sound effects (SFX)   20–23, 25–29, 31, 37–39, 41, 46, 52, 56, 59, 80, 86, 87, 90, 96, 103, 107–109, 112, 134, 150–152, 154, 175, 197, 199, 215, 219, 220, 224, 226, 235–237, 239, 241, 244, 282, 294, 297, 301, 304, 305, 322, 328, 329, 332, 338, 339
sound film   9, 19, 22, 30, 56, 80, 233, 257
sound theatre   1
sous-jacente   63
space   2, 3, 32, 39, 60, 61, 71, 80, 81, 105, 121, 122, 124, 131, 132, 135, 144–146, 149, 152–154, 156, 157, 159, 217, 223, 228, 236, 244, 270, 271, 288, 311, 312, 321, 323, 327, 331, 340
spectromorphology   220
speech   3, 10, 11, 28, 31, 91, 158, 209, 224, 229, 238, 239, 266, 289, 310, 311, 313–315, 323, 327, 329, 342
Sprachpartitur   11, 310
stage theatre   2, 4, 9, 19–25, 29, 32–38, 40, 41, 65, 66, 76, 77, 82, 92, 93, 96, 97, 107, 108, 136, 175, 203, 239, 244, 251, 295, 300, 312–316, 340
Stamitz, Carl Philip   301
Starink, Jan   93
Steinbach, Peter   275, 292
Steinbeck, John   296
Stein, Richard   32
Stemann, Nicholas   312
stereophony   2, 63, 86, 90, 121–124, 149, 259, 272, 311
Stevenson, Cecil   176, 178, 185
Stevenson, Robert Louis   119
Stewart, Douglas   136, 137
Stiemer, Felix   39, 40
Stockhausen, Karlheinz   92, 155
Stoeckart, Jan   88
Stokowski, Leopold   177, 179–181, 184
Stoppard, Tom   328
Storaci, Egidio   110
story and discourse   3, 4, 280, 281
story existents   4, 280
storytelling   77, 93, 95, 284, 293, 305, 344
storyworld   1, 3, 6, 11, 257–259, 275, 279–284, 288–290, 293, 296, 304, 306, 317
Straesser, Joep   90

Strategier, Herman 85
Strauss, Richard 192, 197, 198, 241
Stravinsky, Igor 33, 35, 38, 170, 264, 343
Strawbridge, Edwin 184
strings 50, 54, 196, 198, 199, 202, 217, 236, 237, 282, 319, 337–340, 342
Studio Akustischer Kunst Cologne 141, 153
Studio d'Essai 46, 51
Studio di Fonologia 3, 9, 113, 114, 116–120, 122, 126–128
Sturgeon, Nicola 326
Sturm, Oliver 282, 292
Südwestdeutscher Rundfunk (SWR) 275, 278, 292
Sullivan, Arthur 168
Supervielle, Jules 118
Surface Tension 131, 151, 156, 157, 161
Surrealism 70, 93
suspense 11, 82, 206, 258, 275, 277, 288
Swift, Jonathan 156
symphonic drama 9, 167, 169, 171, 172, 174, 175, 182, 186
symphonic poem 57, 58, 174, 185
symphony 2, 9, 10, 22, 23, 27, 31, 46, 47, 50, 55, 57, 58, 60–62, 64, 115, 133, 139, 141, 143, 167, 169–172, 174–176, 181, 182, 185, 186, 191, 192, 194, 197, 198, 215, 216, 239, 240, 276, 336, 341
synaesthesia 61, 62
syncopation 82, 223
sync points 338, 339
syncretic sonic dimension 126
syntactic function 6, 91, 277, 280, 281, 285, 289, 319

Tarasti, Eero 3, 15, 340, 345
Tardieu, Jean 46, 69–71, 74, 75
Tchaikovsky, Pyotr Ilyich 170, 173, 174, 177, 178, 180, 181, 183, 186, 262–264
technicians, sound/radio 9, 26, 30, 31, 46, 50, 51, 76, 87, 127, 175, 193, 215, 265
tempo 27, 28, 83, 105, 133, 221–224, 236, 317
te Nuyl, Peter 95, 96
ter Braak, Krijn 95
text 7, 20–23, 25–27, 31, 34, 35, 37–40, 46, 53, 57, 58, 62, 68, 69, 70, 76, 77, 80, 82, 88, 91, 94, 96, 103, 108–111, 113, 115, 121–124, 154, 156, 173, 176, 191, 197, 201–203, 207, 210, 217, 226, 228, 230, 233, 268, 275, 285, 286, 289, 297, 305, 310–324, 340
texture of music 5, 63, 221, 222, 226, 228, 337
théâtre radiophoné 103
The Beatles 298
The Doors 298
The Listening Room (*TLR*) 131, 150, 151, 153, 155, 157, 159, 162
theme 4, 7, 10, 88, 126, 170, 202, 207, 210, 214, 233, 237–240, 245, 246, 250, 262, 276, 277, 281, 286, 305, 314, 341, 342, 344
theme music 173, 237, 336
The Symphonic Drama Hour 169, 172
Third Programme 145, 328
Thomas, Dylan 12, 146, 327, 328
Thorp, George 180, 186
timbre 5, 7, 28, 50, 53, 62, 63, 110, 115, 220, 221, 223, 228, 236, 241, 314, 317, 341
title music 80, 95, 340
Toch, Ernst 33
Tolkien, John Ronald Reuel (J.R.R.) 10, 275, 282, 283, 291, 292
Tomasi, Henri x, 46, 51, 53, 56–58, 75
tonality 202, 203, 206–208, 210, 252, 317, 343, 344
Toop, Richard 153, 154, 163
transition 4, 40, 55, 63, 81, 123, 217, 220, 244–246, 251, 258, 277, 278, 285, 304, 311, 328
transmediality 45, 68, 69, 70, 274, 275
transmedial narratology 259
Traynor, Mary 1, 13, 258, 273, 293, 294, 297, 300, 301, 305, 308, 329, 345
Treep, Nico 82
Treloar, Phil 152
tremolo 56, 206, 236, 263
Trollope, Anthony 296
trombone 81, 198, 237, 282
Truman, Edward 236, 249, 250, 256
trumpet 81, 90, 198, 217, 237, 282, 283, 302
Tsai-Yen 118
Tucholsky, Kurt 34
Turchi, Guido 110
Turnbull, Robert 236, 238, 249, 251, 256
Turner, Alexander 137
typology of musical functions 4, 276, 278, 280

Ulman, Jane 150, 151, 153, 163

underscoring   29, 39, 169, 176, 234, 239, 240,
    277, 280, 344
Unione Radiofonica Italiana (URI)
    104, 108
Urban, Herbert   23, 72

vamp section   246, 253
van Bergeijk, Floris   96
van Cappellen, Willem   80, 81
van de Griend, Koos   83–85, 100, 101
van der Linden, Dolf   89
van Doesburg, Cor   94
van Epen-de Groot, Else   85, 88
van Eyk, Ab   77, 89, 90, 92, 94, 95, 97, 101
Vanhal, Jan (Johann Baptist Wanhal)   301
van Hemel, Oscar   85
van Loggem, E.   82
van Rossum, Frans   92, 93, 97
van Woerkom, Theo   89
vaudeville   9, 76, 77, 168, 236
Vaughan Williams, Ralph   299, 328, 330
verbosonic radio play   90–92
Verdi, Giuseppe   173, 240
Vereniging van Arbeiders Radio Amateurs
    (VARA)   78–82, 87, 89, 101
Verma, Neil   1, 15, 234, 256
Verne, Jules   59
Vers in het gehoor   89, 90
Vertov, Dziga   115
Viala, Akakia   46
Vico Lodovici, Cesare   120
Vinot, Maurice   53
viola   53, 81, 198, 237
violin   53, 62, 155, 195, 198, 237, 261, 263, 285,
    286, 301
vocal music   7, 10, 276
vocal shadowing. *See* sous-jacente
Vogt, Willem   79
voice   1, 25, 27–29, 31, 33, 35, 37, 39, 40,
    46, 56, 58, 59, 61–67, 71, 87, 91,
    93–96, 107, 113, 115, 122, 134, 137,
    138, 141, 143, 144, 146–148, 151, 153,
    169, 170, 183, 187, 196, 197, 199,
    201, 203, 214, 215, 217, 220–224, 227,
    228, 236, 239, 240, 241, 252, 259, 261,
    266, 267, 269, 270–272, 277, 279, 283,
    299, 305, 310, 311, 313, 314, 316–324, 332,
    334, 339

voice-over   25, 279
volume   1, 7, 26, 28, 37, 60, 199, 217, 222, 224,
    249, 251, 258, 278
von Heister, Hans Siebert   22, 23, 27, 31
von Hofmannsthal, Hugo   119
Voskuil, J.J.   95
vox mundi   270
Vriend, Jan   90
Vriezen, Samuel   10, 257, 260, 266, 268,
    270–272, 274
Vrijzinnig Protestantse Radio Omroep
    (VPRO)   79, 84, 96, 99, 274
Vugliano, Mario   108, 129

WABC   172
Wagner, Richard   23, 24, 31, 61, 170, 173, 178,
    181, 241, 265, 306, 340, 343
Walton, William   134, 299, 328
Wantzin, Sigurd   199, 211
Watts, Isaac   301
WEAF   172
Webb, Simon   326
Weege, Robert   27
Weill, Kurt   23, 24, 27, 29, 33–35, 37–39, 105,
    171, 185, 196, 234, 277
Welles, Orson   59, 137, 139, 151
Werner, Max   90
Westdeutscher Rundfunk (WDR)   3, 90, 91,
    94, 141, 153, 275, 278, 292, 310
Whipple, James   240, 246, 253, 256
Whitehead, Gregory   269, 274
White, Lew   252, 253, 256
Whiteman, Paul   178
Whitmore, Eloise   331
Wien West   322
Wijfjes, Huub   80, 87, 88, 100, 101
Wilde, Oscar   10, 173, 191, 192, 197, 198, 203,
    204, 208, 209
Williams, John   303, 337, 340
Wilson, Harriette   296
WIP   174, 178
WJZ   172
WMEX   174
WNYC   158, 173, 174, 177, 181, 189
Wodehouse, Sir Pelham Grenville (P.G.)   296
Wolf, Werner   4, 15, 259, 274, 279, 292
woodwinds   28, 50, 54, 198, 282
WOR   172

word, spoken   5, 7, 61, 85, 91, 111, 132, 259, 288, 314
Worthörspiel   20, 30
Wortspiel   20
WQXR   172, 214
Wylie, Max   231, 234, 240, 241, 244, 256
Wyndham, John   11, 296, 326, 331, 342, 346

Yeats, W.B.   86, 133

Yeltsin, Boris   318
Yevtushenko, Sasha   298, 299, 303–306, 309
Yumascheva, Tatjana Borissowna   318

Zappa, Frank   91
Zeitoper   36
Zimmer, Hans   341
Zwetkoff, Peter   10, 275, 276, 281, 282, 290, 292

Word and Music Studies

21. *Word, Sound and Music in Radio Drama.* Pim Verhulst and Jarmila Mildorf, eds. 2024.
20. *Music in the Apocalyptic Mode.* Lorenzo DiTommaso and Colin McAllister, eds. 2023.
19. *'Make It Old': Retro Forms and Styles in Literature and Music.* Werner Wolf and Walter Bernhart, eds. 2022.
18. *Arts of Incompletion: Fragments in Words and Music.* Walter Bernhart and Axel Englund, eds. 2021.
17. *Music, Narrative and the Moving Image: Varieties of Plurimedial Interrelations.* Walter Bernhart and David Francis Urrows, eds. 2019.
16. *Song Acts. Writings on Words and Music.* Lawrence Kramer. 2017.
15. *Silence and Absence in Literature and Music.* Werner Wolf and Walter Bernhart, eds. 2016.
14. *Essays on Literature and Music (1985 – 2013) by Walter Bernhart.* Werner Wolf, ed. 2015.
13. *On Voice.* Walter Bernhart and Lawrence Kramer, eds. 2014.
12. *Word and Music Studies: Essays on Performativity and on Surveying the Field.* Walter Bernhart, ed. in collaboration with Michael Halliwell. 2011.
11. *Self-Reference in Literature and Music.* Walter Bernhart and Werner Wolf, eds. 2010.
10. *The Gaze of the Listener: English Representations of Domestic Music-Making.* Regula Hohl Trillini. 2008.
9. *Essays on Word/Music Adaptation and on Surveying the Field.* David Francis Urrows, ed. 2008.
8. *Selected Essays on Opera by Ulrich Weisstein.* Walter Bernhart, ed. 2006.
7. *Word and Music Studies: Essays on Music and the Spoken Word and on Surveying the Field.* Suzanne M. Lodato and David Francis Urrows, eds. 2005.
6. *Opera and the Novel: The Case of Henry James.* Michael Halliwell. 2005.
5. *Essays on Literature and Music (1967–2004) by Steven Paul Scher.* Walter Bernhart and Werner Wolf, eds. 2004.
4. *Word and Music Studies: Essays in Honor of Steven Paul Scher and on Cultural Identity and the Musical Stage.* Suzanne M. Lodato, Suzanne Aspden, and Walter Bernhart, eds. 2002.
3. *Essays on the Song Cycle and on Defining the Field: Proceedings of the Second International Conference on Word and Music Studies at Ann Arbor, MI, 1999.* Walter Bernhart and Werner Wolf, eds. 2001.

2. *Musico-Poetics in Perspective: Calvin S. Brown in Memoriam.* Jean-Louis Cupers and Ulrich Weisstein, eds. 2000.
1. *Word and Music Studies: Defining the Field. Proceedings of the First International Conference on Word and Music Studies at Graz, 1997.* Walter Bernhart, Steven Paul Scher, and Werner Wolf, eds. 1999.

Printed in the United States
by Baker & Taylor Publisher Services